GALVANIZING NOSTALGIA?

GALVANIZING NOSTALGIA?

Indigeneity and Sovereignty in Siberia

Marjorie Mandelstam Balzer

CORNELL UNIVERSITY PRESS   ITHACA AND LONDON

First published 2021 by Cornell University Press

Library of Congress Cataloging-in-Publication Data

Names: Balzer, Marjorie Mandelstam, author.
Title: Galvanizing nostalgia? : indigeneity and sovereignty in Siberia / Marjorie Mandelstam Balzer.
Description: Ithaca, [New York] : Cornell University Press, 2021. | Includes bibliographical references and index.
Identifiers: LCCN 2021032693 (print) | LCCN 2021032694 (ebook) | ISBN 9781501759772 (hardcover) | ISBN 9781501761317 (paperback) | ISBN 9781501759789 (epub) | ISBN 9781501759796 (pdf)
Subjects: LCSH: Indigenous peoples—Russia (Federation)—Siberia—Ethnic identity. | Yakut (Turkic people)—Russia (Federation)—Siberia. | Buriats—Russia (Federation)—Siberia. | Tuvinian (Turkic people)—Russia (Federation)—Siberia. | Sovereignty. | Siberia (Russia)—Social conditions. | Siberia (Russia)—Politics and government.
Classification: LCC DK758 .B35 2021 (print) | LCC DK758 (ebook) | DDC 957—dc23
LC record available at https://lccn.loc.gov/2021032693
LC ebook record available at https://lccn.loc.gov/2021032694

For all who hold the interests of Indigenous peoples in their hearts and minds, and for those Indigenous activists who have passed on

"What happens in Siberia matters to the rest of the world."

—*Financial Times* editorial, June 27, 2020

Contents

Preface: Credits, Claims, and Confessions

If you were a Native Siberian whose village had been burned by arsonists to make way for coal mining, how would you react? If you were an Indigenous Turkic-language speaker who was told by Moscow authorities to cut all ties with your distant cultural kin in Turkey, would you protest? If you were a Buryat living on Russia's border with Mongolia, would you assert your right to increase economic and religious exchanges with your Mongolian cousins? If you were an impoverished Tyvan living in the magnificent Altai Mountains, would you welcome the first railway line to come to your remote republic, bringing economic development?

These are some of the hot issues that brought me to write this book about Siberia, land of the cold, affected more intensively by extremes of climate change than many other places. Frustrated by the lack of knowledge of Siberia, especially its vast Far East, on the part of most people I meet, including my students at Georgetown University, I decided to combine an eclectic personal history of fieldwork and scholarship into a book with broader appeal and scope than those I usually write or edit. Based on field and historical research in three strategically chosen republics of Russia—Sakha (Yakutia), Buryatia, and Tyva (Tuva)—this book highlights the viewpoints of Indigenous individuals and groups.

While becoming increasingly common in social, cultural, and political anthropology, multi-sited fieldwork projects are by definition unwieldy. My approach is unabashedly and of necessity ad hoc. As I was taught in my anthropology graduate training (at Bryn Mawr long ago), anthropologists need to be sensitive to eclectic and unexpected narratives and opportunities wherever they are found. The bit of insight that one may glean from something that occurs out of the corner of a photograph, video, or festival may turn out to be central to the picture one later draws in a writing process that by definition becomes selective and subjective. Since it breaks ground in multi-sited comparative and collaborative fieldwork, this book, while not written to stress methodology, is an exemplar of opportunity anthropology without opportunism.

Inspired by United Nations definitions, I accept as Indigenous more groups than are usually included in Russian conceptions, ranging from legal categories of "small-numbered peoples of the North, Siberia, and the Far East" to Native peoples with their own nominally "titular republics." My narratives and profiles of Siberians include additional interlocutors, wherever appropriate. Thus, the book encompasses "old-settlers" calling themselves Siberiaki, Moscow bureaucrats, Russian energy barons, and newcomers of all ethnic backgrounds who regularly arrive in Russia's Far East, whether by chance, force, or hope.

Russia is entering a new period of profound and dangerous instability, made worse by the coronavirus pandemic. Sadly, we all understand better what nostalgia means as we long for times in the past when we perceived more agency and control over our lives. How people choose what to hope for, and how to use that longing productively, is a key to various culturally shaped futures. Studying discourses and dynamics of nostalgia is not a luxury but a necessity for basic learning and insights into possibilities of creative recoveries. As elsewhere, Indigenous peoples in Russia have been particularly vulnerable when health care deteriorates in the wider context of political and social unrest. I position myself as an analyst of what I hope will be empathy-stimulating cameos of Siberian survival in a new sense of that term. I am neither an advocate for increased Indigenous independence in our interconnected world nor an apologist for greater political and social assimilation within Russia. The book explores what possibilities Indigenous peoples and Russians have for relative degrees of cooperation and self-determination.

Since 2016, a new stage of interaction for me with Siberians has been the creation in Cabin John, MD, of a "Siberian compound," where my neighbors and friends in the house next to mine are the Solovyevs, a Sakha-Buryat family who founded the diaspora group Sakha Open World, and who regularly help guests from the Sakha Republic and elsewhere in Russia with their US itineraries. Together we have hosted many visitors, shared many fires, and discussed many issues of the day and night. I owe a profound debt of gratitude to Vera and Zhargal Solovyev for the worlds and networks they have opened to me.

Mega-credit is due to my long-term collaborator and sometime coauthor, the Sakha sociologist and former parliamentarian Uliana Vinokurova, whose brilliance and kindness up to the last minute of editing helped inform my text. Extra-mile readers of the manuscript for insights and corrections include Zoya Anaiban, Alexander Bapa, Yeshen-Khorlo Dugarova-Montgomery, Robert Montgomery, and Vera Solovyeva.

On a single morning in 2020, I was humbled to find five stunning emails from Sakha and Tyvan friends answering questions about loose ends as I completed the book. I am deeply thankful to those who have hosted me in the republics of Sakha, Buryatia, and Tyva, or have befriended me while traveling or living in the Indigenous Siberian diaspora. These include (but are not limited to) Liubov Abaeva, Angelika Akimova, the late Eduard Alekseev, Zoya Alekseeva, Ivan Alekseev (Khomus Ujbaan), Ivan Argounov, Tatiana Argounova-Low, Alexander Artemenov, Rigoletta Artemonova, Aidyn Byrtan-ool, Roza

Bravina, Natalia Budaeva, Daria Burnasheva, Andrei Borisov, Stepanida Bor-
isova, Alexandra Chirkova, Nachyn Choreve, Albina Diachkova, Valentina
Dmitrieva, Asia Gabysheva, Chimita Garmayeva, Antonina Gavrilyeva, Anatoly
Gogolev, Elena Gorokhova, Wanda Ignat'eva, Zinaida Ivanova-Unarova, Mon-
gush Kenin-Lopsan, German and Klavdia Khatylaev, Maria Koryakina, Yuliana
Krivoshapkina, Zoya Kyrgyz, Nikolai and Natalia Mestnikov, Zoja Morokho-
eva, Liudmilla Nikanorova, Afanasy Nikolaev, Darima Nikolaeva, the late
Kongar-ool Ondar, Anuta Pavlova, Ekaterina Pavlova, Alexei Romanov, Ekat-
erina Romanova, Aldynai Seden-Khuurak, Budazhap Shiretorov, Ivan Shamayev,
Platon Shamayev, Lydia Shamayeva, Sergei Shapkhaev, Olga Shoglanova, Oleg
Sidorov, Lena Sidorova, Liubov Starostina, Viktor Struchkov, Valentina Süzükei,
Alexander Sveshnikov, Alena Shveshnikova, Kyunney Takasaeva, Inna Tarbas-
taeva, Alexei Tomtosov, Liuba Tomtosova, Olga Ulturgasheva, Mir Umchanov,
Irina Urbanaeva, the late Vasily Yakovlev, Villiam Yakovlev, Marina Yakovleva,
and Yury Zhegusov.

Russian/*rossiiane* colleagues to whom I owe debts, and sometimes provocative
learning, include Sergei Arutiunov, Olga Balalaeva, the late Leokadia Drobizheva,
Dmitri Funk, Andrei Golovnev, Elsa-Bair Guchinova, Valentina Kharitonova,
Oleg Kharkhordin, Olga Murashko, Natalia Novikova, Irina Olimpieva, Emil
Pain, Nikolay Petrov, the late Alexander Pika, Victor Shnirelman, the late Galina
Starovoitova, Valery Tishkov, Nikolai Vakhtin, Galya and Igor Zevelev, Natalia
Zhukovskaia, and Natalia Zubarevich.

I am blessed by the rapport I have found with my partner at Georgetown
in Indigenous Studies, the team teacher for "Indigenous Peoples, Conflict and
Resilience" Bette Jacobs. Special thanks are due early readers Alexander Etkind,
Elise Giuliano, Paul Nadasdy, and Piers Vitebsky. US, Canadian, British, European, and Japanese colleagues who have encouraged or productively challenged
me include Mikhail Alexeev, Anders Åslund, Mark Beissinger, Anya Bernstein,
Alexia Bloch, Michael Brown, Timothy Colton, Melissa Chakars, Edith Clowes,
Julie Cruikshank, Georgi Derlugian, Brian Donohoe, Jenanne Ferguson, the late
Murray Feshbach, Michael M. J. Fischer, Gail Fondahl, Paul Goble, Daniel Gold-
berg, Katherine Graber, Bruce Grant, Patty Gray, Lenore Grenoble, Robin Har-
ris, Donald Horowitz, Mihály Hoppál, Caroline Humphrey, Eric Kasten, Laurel
Kendall, Anna Kerttula, Alexander King, Charles King, Marlène Laruelle, Alaina
Lemon, Gail Osherenko, Robert Orttung, Margaret Paxson, Eleanor Peers, Wil-
liam Pomerantz, Alfred J. Rieber, Diana Riboli, Nancy Ries, Douglas Rogers,
Jeanmarie Rouhier-Willoughby, Blair Ruble, Nazif Shahrani, Gulnaz Sharafutdi-
nova, Ippei Shimamura, Peter Solomon, Peter Schweitzer, Ronald Suny, the late
Barbara Tedlock, Judyth Twigg, Aimar Ventsel, Katherine Verdery, David Wolf,
Sufian Zhemukhov, and Andrei Znamenski.

I am grateful to Leslie English for life-long editorial lessons. At Cornell University Press, I am beholden to the talents of Roger Malcolm Hayden, Jim Lance, Jennifer Dana Savran Kelly, Carolyn Pouncy, and Bethany Wasik for pushing the book through delays, virus, and more.

My institutional credits begin with the University of Washington for inviting me to give their annual lecture honoring the late historian of Russia Donald Treadgold. This lecture in 2009 was the initial spark leading me to decide to compare the three republics. I am indebted to Georgetown University, the International Research and Exchanges Board (IREX), the MacArthur Foundation, the Social Science Research Council (SSRC), the National Endowment for the Humanities (NEH), the American Museum of Natural History, the Kennan Institute of the Smithsonian's Woodrow Wilson Center, the Ammosov Northeast Federal University (formerly Yakutsk State University), the Academy of Sciences Humanities Institute (formerly Institute of Languages, Literature, and History), and the Arctic Institute of Culture and Art for fieldwork and/or research support.

My life partner, Harley David Balzer, has sustained and inspired me with intellectual and emotional life support beyond anything I can express in words.

Note on Transliteration

I follow Library of Congress transliteration style, unless a name has become entrenched in the literature in another form (Yakutia rather than Iakutia), or an individual prefers another spelling for a name. For Sakha words, I use é instead of a backward e (Э) since they are nearly the same sound. For the sound that approximates "gh" I use ҕ. For Turkic terms that have slipped into Russian usage with an "s," I use the more accurate "h." Where appropriate, I use ü for the Turkic sound that approximates "eu." Special terms provided here are mostly from the Turkic Sakha and Tyvan languages or the Mongolic Buryat language. Where other language terms are relevant, for example from Russian, I indicate their provenance. A few online links use the Cyrillic alphabet if the source is not available in transliteration.

FIGURE 1. Map of the Federation of Russia.

THE BEGINNING OF NOSTALGIA

FIGURE 2. Cartoon "The Beginning of Nostalgia" by Liana Fincke 2015.
© Liana Fincke, Courtesy of the *New Yorker*.

CONTESTED ECOLOGICAL, CULTURAL, AND POLITICAL SOVEREIGNTY IN RUSSIA

New degrees of instability in Russia require asking new questions and revisiting old ones. Could Russia fall apart along the lines of its internal republics, as did the Soviet Union? What are the orientations of non-Russian peoples of Turkic and Mongolian backgrounds, far from Moscow? What does self-determination mean in the Russian context? How has Moscow-based recentralization influenced various groups, including Russians, in the republics? How can we define "center," "periphery," and "federal" when these concepts shift with various levels of political administration? Is ecology activism viable in the republics, given new threats to the environment and climate, as well as sharpening curtailment of civic society in Vladimir Putin's Russia?

To probe these critical issues, I suggest that a fragile and disorganized dynamic of differential, nested sovereignties has developed within Russia, centered on its frequently overlooked "ethnic republics." This dynamic provides significant lessons for conceptualizing the fluidity of nationalism, ethnonationalism, indigeneity, situational identities, spirituality, and cultural revitalization. For an anthropologist, these key concepts are best understood through the arguments and emotions of people whose stories are poorly known and rarely analyzed. Counter to stereotypes about Siberia, many of my Siberian interlocutors are nostalgic for imagined better times prior to periods of outsider repression. How they have galvanized that nostalgia opens paths to unfamiliar, often dramatic and cathartic narratives of human suffering, courage, and resilience.

How is collective trauma processed and transcended? I build on anthropological and comparative literature concerning the multiplicity and synergies of nostalgia and memory. In the process, I explain debates in anthropology and history concerning cultural authenticity, tradition, and cultural change. My understanding of indigeneity derives from United Nations and international human rights perspectives, from participation in Indigenous peoples' protest movements as an ally, and from creating an Indigenous Studies network at Georgetown University. My initial encompassing definition is that Indigenous individuals are those who self-identify as Indigenous. Further and crucially, they are members of groups without their own nation-state whose struggles for some degree of self-determination are bound with their sense of rootedness to particular lands, their homelands.

As the Sakha (Yakut) activist Antonina Gavrilyeva explained to my friend and colleague Vera Solovyeva (2018, 139): "It is a people's right to live on their ancestral land, and it is their duty to protect and preserve that land. Indigenous Peoples must have a prerogative in [the] decision-making process about developing their territories and using natural resources." Antonina brought this basic "nothing about us without us" assertion to the United Nations Indigenous Peoples' Forum, where peoples with republics within a larger state such as Russia [*Rossiia*] are considered Indigenous, as are smaller groups of Indigenous peoples without republics, pushed historically to fringes of their homelands with shrinking populations and minimal territorial administrative protection. The UN approach contrasts with official policy in Russia that proclaims only "Small-numbered Peoples" [*malochislennykh narody*, infelicitously nicknamed *maly narody*, small peoples] with populations arbitrarily defined as under fifty thousand can be legally recognized as Indigenous (compare Balzer 2017; Donohoe et al. 2008). In this context, as elsewhere, sovereignty definitions and claims become matters of degree and negotiation, a painful process as Indigenous peoples with developing ethnonational identities and self-awareness of historical injustice emerge from colonialism and varieties of neocolonialism.

Most Siberians are not secessionist, and outsiders should not declare separatist sentiments until people themselves do so. Yet tensions over land, resources, authority, and cultural rights have created processes of polarization as well as ethnonational consolidation. Separatist sentiments may coalesce quickly when people perceive dangers as serious as those of a sinking ship, as happened in nearly all the republics of the Soviet Union after the failed putsch of August 1991. In contrast, a dominant trend in the past thirty years has been Siberian people's intertwined striving for self-determination, cultural revitalization, and spiritual vitality. These good-faith efforts and dreams are threatened by political, social, and ecological change at multiple levels of multiethnic Russia. People are struggling for cultural dignity.

Based on field and historical research in the republics of Sakha (Yakutia), Buryatia, and Tyva (Tuva), this book highlights the implications of Indigenous groups' concerns.[1] I began long-term fieldwork in Yakutia in 1986 while on the official US-USSR cultural exchange and worked in the other republics after the Soviet Union fell apart, with frequent returns and renewed contacts with friends and interlocutors from each republic. Focus on three strategically chosen republics enables comparing and contrasting interethnic relations, language politics, and the salience of demography, resource competition, environmental degradation, increased religiosity, and contingent histories of federalism. (See Figure 1.)

Since I began writing this book, the urgency of Indigenous grievances has accelerated. I analyze causes of 2019 protest demonstrations in the Buryat and Sakha republics, ramifications of monster forest fires linked to arson, intensified river pollution from diamond-mining accidents, and village resettlements due to flooding. As risks associated with civic protest have increased, so have sporadic demonstrations in Russia due to local ecological disasters, rigged elections, and corruption exposés. What makes people brave enough to protest publicly? What are the sinews of civil and civic society in the republics?

The republics of Far Eastern Siberia derived from a preemptive Leninist recognition of the resistance potential of Turkic and Mongolic Indigenous peoples (compare Sablin 2018). In the 1920s, Yakutia and Buryatia were granted "autonomous" status within the Soviet system, in part to keep their influential leaders, intelligentsias, and numerically significant populations from secession. Tyva (Tuva), having come into the Soviet Union in 1944, has a more radical legacy of relative independence and secessionism than the other two republics.

An important claim in this book is that cultural and political revitalization has been relatively more viable, although still difficult and diverse, in areas where Siberians have their own republics. Despite the increasingly symbolic nature of republic status, Indigenous groups without such "titular" homeland bases are in a much less advantageous position (compare Osipov 2015). Smaller groups without republics have had only loose umbrella organizations to rely on for mobilization, such as the embattled federal-level RAIPON (Russian Association of Indigenous Peoples of the North, Siberia, and the Far East) or local-level group associations (Balzer 2017).

My political anthropology comparison of these three fascinating but understudied republics makes this project unique. Conclusions emphasize variations in their histories of relationships to central authorities in Moscow and in the conditions that stimulate ethnonationalism. Some general patterns compared to other groups inside the dubiously named "Russian Federation" may be discerned. Named ethnic republics, called "autonomous" in the Soviet period, have facilitated ethnonational mobilization, providing sociopolitical structures within which non-Russians have mobilized their "imagined communities" to seek social, cultural, and ecological rights (Anderson 1991; Baiburin et al. 2012; Vinokurova 2018).

Language rights and conditions for land-based spirituality are sensitive barometers of republic-level Indigenous-Moscow government relationships throughout Russia. Cultural revitalization has become increasingly politicized, undermined by central government policies and constitutional changes that are contested by non-Russians. A tragic example that resonated throughout many non-Russian communities was the 2019 self-immolation of the Udmurt historian Albert Razin over renewed Russification language policies. While Razin was from the Udmurt Republic of central Russia, people in the republics of Siberia's Far East perceived his powerful sacrifice as significant for them too. Many argue that the positive synergism of spiritual and language revitalization is threatened when young people are not able to thrive in Indigenous language education programs.

Development programs in the republics reflect degrees of ecological sensitivity and at best uneven track records in providing legal protections for Indigenous communities. Local activism in turn has been based on varying political receptivity, uneven federal-level attention, and differential resource wealth. As elsewhere in the global North and Arctic, activism in Siberia has occurred in a context of energy exploration and mining interests that have increasingly intruded into many Indigenous communities in the past two decades.[2] In general, Tyva has been the least developed of the three republics, and Sakha the most. However, some local districts and political administrations within the republics have established more specific economic development agendas. Post-Soviet amalgamations of territories in Russia, including the disbandment of the Buryat satellite regions of Ust-Orda and Aga, have been particularly disastrous for non-Russians' abilities to maintain their cultural identities and any shred of self-determination.

Self-determination for Indigenous groups in Russia's republics is problematic when many of the republics have majority or plurality Russian populations. However, being a minority is far from the key to Indigenous status or identity, especially in Siberia, with its historically shifting and varied legacies of uneven colonial settlement in different remote regions. Many Indigenous Siberians prefer not to think of themselves as minorities, given that some were majorities in their homelands until relatively recently. The Republic of Tyva continues in the post-Soviet period to have a substantial majority of Tyvans, and demographers predict it may within the next decade become nearly monoethnic.

A contrasting dynamic is evident for those who claim to be Siberiaki, a locally emergent mixed ethnic Slavic-Native identity. The terms "Siberiaki" and "Siberia" are each controversial. Many of my Russian and non-Russian interlocutors confirm the appropriateness of calling all the territory east of the Urals "Siberia," as is the conventional political-geographic Western approach. However, some Russians insist that a special Far East ésprit de corps makes them uncomfortable being called "Siberians" or "Siberiaki." They look down on the moniker "Siberiaki," associating it with those who had peasant and Cossack ancestors who settled Siberia in the seventeenth and eighteenth centuries and intermarried with Indigenous women. Some are horrified that it has become a census category. Others, often from Russian Orthodox Old Believer communities, embrace their Siberiaki identities. They have created their own movements inside the republics of Sakha, Buryatia, and Tyva for recognition as "Indigenous."[3]

This book explores possibilities that Indigenous peoples and local Russians have had for cooperation and self-determination in Siberia's Far East. My approach is to analyze ethnonationalism as a valid expression of the nexus of cultural and political identity (Balzer 1999, 2012, 2017; Connor 1994). Ethnonationalism is conceptually different from chauvinist hate-mongering, also known as racism. Dangerous polarization based on advocacy of "pure-bloodism" may be increasing in Russia, surfacing in the interaction of Russian toughs called "skinheads" and perceived threatening Asian-looking migrants. Yet violent incidents have been sporadic, localized, and falsely attributed to non-Russian nationalist-extremists.[4] I see room for a middle way, for negotiated civic society to grow. The recent histories of ecology movements in the republics may provide a positive example of incremental change based on interethnic cooperation, despite frequent repression. Societal awareness of the importance of environmental protection was highlighted by President Vladimir Putin himself naming 2017 the "Year of Ecology," a gesture that could be seen either as propaganda or a symbolic step in the right direction.[5]

The intermediating concept of "ethnonationalism," in tension with ethnicity and nationalism, can potentially enable productive paths toward a liberal nationalism that ideally would stimulate creative forces within a well-functioning federal system (compare Tamir 1993). Ethnicity can be considered as a mildly politicized construction of cultural difference, and nationalism as a striving for some level of self-determination (Balzer 1999, 6; compare Eriksen and Jakoubek 2019). Dangers resulting from economic and political use and abuse of ethnic "brands" should be acknowledged (Comaroff and Comaroff 2009; Brown 2003) but not exaggerated for cases within Russia. More serious is the alarming potential for political violence when sovereignty bids are repressed harshly (Horowitz 2000; Protsyk and Harzl 2013; Roeder 2018). In Russia, we see a depressing pattern familiar from other cases, that federalism is often invoked in its breach, as President Putin's speeches frequently demonstrate.[6] I argue that a nested sovereignty, or matrioshka sovereignty, has developed in the post-Soviet period.

A preponderance of negatively synergistic conditions is necessary for national secession campaigns to be successful, as the political scientist Philip Roeder (2018) has argued using cases that feature the former Soviet Union. Independence movements require more than "expressing identities, grabbing riches, releasing emotions, or righting wrongs," and none achieves internationally recognized statehood through strategic violence alone (Roeder 2018, 171). Nationalist charismatic leaders must use persuasion on a massive level, generating sustained coordination of intense campaigns to mobilize their peoples so that they are willing to risk danger to resolve serious grievances. The larger goal of separatism must be combined with brilliant programmatic objectives, accumulated tit-for-tat violence, breakdowns of protracted negotiations with an intractable state, and effective use of resonating myths for peoples to eventually become unable to imagine viable alternatives. These conditions are not present in most of contemporary Russia, with the possible exceptions of forcibly incorporated Crimea and parts of the North Caucasus. Nonetheless, possibilities for legitimate expressions of moderate sovereignty and indigeneity within a federal state have been shrinking in the past two decades.

This book is inspired by two influential friends, the late Russian sociologist-presidential advisor Leokadia Drobizheva (2005; Emelianenko interview 2017) and the late, assassinated politician-scholar Galina Starovoitova (1997). Each fought in her own way for the principle that the best way to prevent interethnic strife in multiethnic Rossiia is to empower non-Russians within a negotiated federal system.[7] Since post-Soviet Russia has inherited a federal system that is unwieldy, asymmetrical, and notoriously unfair in its distribution of resources, negotiated federalism has become a crucial and particularly difficult dimension for its survival. Far from a luxury to be discarded when Russia's economy experiences turbulence, federalism is key to its multiethnic compositional framework.[8]

My fieldwork-based analyses include comparisons to relevant theoretical literature, building on those who have studied the breakup of the Soviet Union (Beissinger 2002; Martin 2001; Roeder 2018) and those who have examined various center-periphery dynamics within Russia (Giuliano 2011; Kolstø and Blakkisrud 2004; Kolstø and Blakkisrud 2016; Osipov 2015). Their political science approaches and sociological surveys provide key background for my long-term engaged anthropology. My goal is an intertwined methodology and analysis that is intrinsic to productive comparisons. The methodology is qualitative and collaborative, as well as flexible in seizing opportunities.

Identity Crystallization and Nostalgia

In the summer of 2000, sitting in the Yakutsk office of a deputy to the Sakha parliament, charmingly named Il Tumen or "meeting for agreement," I witnessed an extraordinary parade of the Sakha professional elite streaming into the deputy's office to pour out complaints against the central government in Moscow. Their language constituted the most polarized nationalist, including separatist, outbursts I had heard since beginning fieldwork in the republic in 1986. I have come to see that moment as nationalist crystallization, provoked by the officially announced abrogation of Sakha Republic's (Yakutia's) hard-negotiated 1995 bilateral treaty that had endorsed a multileveled sharing of the republic's considerable resources. It was the beginning of Vladimir Putin's consolidating rule over Russia, part of his initial campaign of recentralization after the post-Soviet flourishing of a sarcastically named "parade of sovereignties" during President Boris Yeltsin's two terms in the 1990s.[9] Within a few days, many of these same professionals, some of whom were parliament deputies and lawyers, moderated their rhetoric and consoled themselves that the treaty had been temporary in any case, with a statute of limitations that would have to be renegotiated.

Such highly emotional moments, and the zigzags of politicized resentment and concern that they reveal, rarely are analyzed adequately from multiple levels in a social science literature focused on enumerating dry "factors" that generate "interethnic conflict." However, many have appropriately pointed out that the rhetoric of nationalism, rather than cultural identity itself, often fuels such conflicts and shapes their parameters.[10] I privilege context-oriented theories, rather than searching for prioritized general explanations or a single underlying cause for ethnonational-associated tensions. Political, economic, and social dynamics of post-Soviet changes in each republic are far too interconnected, synergistic, and contingent for designating dependent or independent variables in neat grid-bound systems of analysis.

Ideas of national identity crystallization related to late Soviet and early post-Soviet histories have been circulating since at least 1990. My early version was buried in a defunct journal, but similar concepts have been discussed by others.[11] In Mark Beissinger's political science analysis, focus is on "thickened history and the mobilization of identity," as well as tides of nationalism, and the failures of certain anomalous cases, including Tuva/Tyva (Beissinger 2002, 147, 231). Perhaps due to an emphasis on the "bandwagon" effect of escalating horizontal ties within the former Soviet Union, Beissinger uses a starting date for his quantitative study of nationalist mobilizations that omits relevant Yakutsk protests in the spring of 1986. These Yakutsk student demonstrations, occurring while

I was living in a university dormitory during my first fieldwork in the republic, preceded the more famous Kazakh (Almaty) protests later that year.[12] Beissinger thus missed a chance to delve into the tantalizing Tuva/Tyva and Yakut/Sakha cases.

My modest theorizing in this book focuses on key crystallizing events, as well as questions of leadership and its resonance. Leaders, exploiting emotional fluidity, may turn events born in times of chaos into societal, organizational change. The process enables the transformation of what Anthony Wallace (1956), a pioneer in the study of "revitalization movements," long ago termed "goal culture." While I admire the American anthropology "revitalization movement" literature, I refrain from reifying culture as something holistic and reject identifying expected "stages" or types of revolution. Inspired by the process-oriented "becoming national" literature that our best historians and anthropologists have produced (Eley and Suny 1996; Duara 2004; Roshwald 2006; Suny 1994; Nadasdy 2017), I find that cultural revitalization sometimes comes "in the nick of time" for Indigenous peoples but often is "too little, too late." Revitalization is rarely empowering by itself but, like leadership, may be sustained only under appropriate conditions.

The anthropologist Caroline Humphrey (2008), featuring "troubled times" cases from China's Inner Mongolia, theorizes that particularly dramatic junctures in history, characterized by revolutions and new religious movements, may create conditions for charismatic personalities who make astonishing leaps of imagination. Her "perspectival" argument may be distilled to suggest that nationalistic leaders tend to rise to the occasion during key events, although Humphrey warns that Mongol concepts of destiny and reincarnation may alter "decision-events" in ways that may seem irrational to outsiders.[13]

I use the concept "galvanizing nostalgia" in active and passive senses. Nostalgia can be a widespread condition that many in a society or community feel as an amorphous longing when a way of life has been lost. The condition itself may galvanize members of a society into greater reflection about their lives, beyond the source of their next meal. To understand nostalgia in this way, one must respect the potential intelligence and value of all members of a society, rural and urban, formally educated or not.

In a more direct and active usage, it takes a leader to galvanize nostalgia toward social and political change. Who that leader is, whether from a formally educated intelligentsia or not, and what aspects of a historical period are longed for, whether Soviet or earlier, become key to whether the process is productive or destructive. Who judges productivity or cultural benefit becomes an "eye of the beholder" hermeneutic. A creative approach for a budding charismatic leader may be galvanizing nostalgia, defined as the conscious search for a usable past that can help unite an ethnonational group and enable its members to focus on cultural change and social reform.

Nostalgia, including collective nostalgia stimulated by ethnonational intelligentsias, may take diverse, sometimes overlapping forms. The term's original use was psychological and medical, as coined by the Swiss physician Johannes Hofer in a 1688 dissertation combining the Greek *nostos*, or homecoming, with *algos*, meaning pain (Beck 2013). The longing or melancholy that was seen as an illness or mania for a soldier's lost homeland was eventually transferred in popular conceptions to a more metaphoric condition, susceptible to personal or political manipulation. (See Figure 2.)

The term has been associated with East European studies, including study of postsocialist citizens of the Baltics looking back to their pre-Soviet early to mid-twentieth-century nation-states before they were occupied and repressed (compare Todorova and Gille 2012; Etkind 2013). The concept in anthropology has been explored to "contribute to a better understanding of how individuals and groups remember, commemorate and revitalize their pasts, and the crucial role played by nostalgia in the process of remembering" (Angé and Berliner 2016, 2). This monograph contributes to that effort, revealing a range of reactions to post-Soviet modernity and its discontents.

The late Harvard professor and comparatist Svetlana Boym (2001) eloquently expounded on nostalgia as retrospective and reflective, with potentially prospective and restorative aspects. Reflective nostalgia, often personal and capable of stimulating empathy, involves an incomplete and inaccurate "process of remembrance" tinged with longing and loss. In contrast, retrospective nostalgia is more likely to be used and abused by conservative nationalists, since it "proposes to rebuild the lost home and patch up memory gaps" with false certainty (Boym 2001, 41). Boym warns that retrospective nostalgia is common after revolutions or other violent social upheavals and poses threats by promising to accomplish the impossible, while sometimes trafficking in conspiracy theories. Retrospective nostalgia's subversive hallmarks are antimodern or "off-modern" mythmaking, and the exploitation of national symbols (Boym 2001, xvi). Notorious Russian nationalists such as Alexander Dugin, Dmitri Rogozin, and Boris Gryzlov, encouraged by Vladimir Putin when he finds it convenient, provide ample illustrations.[14] However, post-Soviet extremist nationalists need not be the main exemplars of collective nostalgia.

In my adaptation, groups combining reflection and retrospection may be inclined to a romantic nostalgia—longing for aspects of a "golden age" represented by selective pasts when the given group had more power over its own destiny. Indigenous groups recovering from colonialism and various forms of neocolonialism may be especially attracted to leaders using compelling and specific idioms of romantic nostalgia. Considering the cases featured here, this is exemplified by harmless Sakha romanticizing of their epic *olonkho* tradition and their Turkic Uriankhai Sakha ancestors. Some Tyvans express nostalgia for a sovereignty that was not really so independent in their pre-Soviet Tannu-Touva period overlapping in time with Baltic nations' statehood. Buryats occasionally valorize Chingis (Genghis) Khan as "moral" and "defensive" in his territorial expansion, unifying Mongol peoples. These examples reveal different levels of identity reflection, and different temporalities.

Ecology movements among all three groups featured here have aspects of the more productive, nonchauvinist, nationalist, and transnationalist nostalgia (compare Dawson 1996). People look back to when lakes, forests, and pastures were maintained by sustainable disciplines of Indigenous traditional knowledge, and forward to preventing pipeline spills or negotiating carbon exchanges due, for example, to methane-gas-prone tundra ravages and reliance on coal.

Golden ages are viewed through often-distorting rear-view mirrors, with their selected objects of adoration, including folk heroes, either closer or farther away than outsider historians' versions of reality might suggest (Hobsbawm and Ranger 1983). Ideals include a range of societies and sovereignties (Nadasdy 2017, 310–11). The experiences of the Soviet era, viewed in sharply divergent interpretations in the post-Soviet period, provide little basis to imagine a golden age for most former Soviet citizens, Russians and non-Russians alike. Nearly every family I have met in Russia and from Russia since 1975 was affected somehow, mostly tragically, by Stalinist repressions. My extended family (on my father's Mandelstam side) is included. Soviet-period poverty is often recalled without nostalgia, especially in villages in the Far North Sakha Republic, where I was told by one grandmother that when she was a girl she was often so cold even in early summer that she would put her bare feet in warm cow dung to stay warm. Generational variations are huge, and some rosy recollections may involve romanticizing one's vigorous youth.[15] More accurately, much of the Soviet period is remembered for its (minimal) social safety nets, public egalitarianism, and nominal support for ethnonationalist identities that "gelled" within particular designated, named territories.

Caroline Humphrey (2002, 29) reminds us about mythmaking just after the Soviet collapse: "Many people nevertheless wanted out of the suffocating mesh of benevolence and cruelty." Her research focused on 1990s dispossessed migrants, refugees and youth gangs, especially in Buryatia. Critiquing "shattered worlds," they juxtaposed stability in the Soviet era with "discourses of discontent" (compare Oushakine 2009; Ries 1997; Yurchak 2006). Many were territorially unmoored, although the youth gangs had carved out new subdivided urban territorialities. My contrasting focus is on mythmaking and memory as they relate to larger, significant territories that have become saturated with meaning as homelands to be regained and maintained. While the rear-view mirror may include distortions of the Soviet period, recalled imperfectly as a period of stability when some did not know they were poor, it mostly reflects earlier pre-Soviet times of perceived wealth and confidence. For the groups featured here, this often means valorizing times when kinship reciprocity was oriented to one's extended family and larger clan groups, celebrated with seasonal rituals and respect for ancestors.

Invention of Tradition, First Nations, Agency, and Anthropologists

Envision a conference in Alaska on Indigenous communities, development, and historical legacies that occurred in the past decade. Away from the formal sessions, a Russian-American established anthropologist and a young Sakha scholar had a debate during which they seemed to talk past each other on the subjects of cultural revitalization, public rituals in the Sakha Republic, and the "invention of tradition" (compare Hobsbawm and Ranger 1983; Otto and Pedersen 2005). The anthropologist, knowing well the legacy of Soviet repression in Siberia, was skeptical that any deeply spiritual shamanic tradition could be resurrected in the post-Soviet period, much less in the form of mass seasonal rituals honoring the summer solstice, called in Sakha the *Yhyakh* ceremony. The Sakha scholar—for whom that ceremony is sacred for personal, spiritual, and community-building reasons—was offended, although privately concerned about the scale and spending at some recent republic-sponsored stadium-sized rituals. Not knowing the specific literature on the invention of tradition, and its nuances concerning different degrees of authenticity and nation-building validity, the Sakha interlocutor understandably bristled at the phrase. People do not invent tradition out of thin air. Rather, they may select and adapt heartfelt and meaningful ancestral traditions to fit the times. Furthermore, this sincere Sakha ritual participant correctly sensed that the anthropologist's skepticism may have been influenced by his respect for Russian Orthodoxy and its long-term legacy in Alaska and Siberia.[16]

This delicate encounter reminded me how frequently Sakha interlocutors during the June summer solstice celebrations had warned me not to use the word "festival" for the elaborate multiday events, but rather to think of them as composite revitalized rituals, games, dances, and horse races honoring, through opening fire spirit offerings, the pre-Christian pantheon of Sky Gods (Tengri) and the life-giving forces of the Sun at its peak, so precious in Siberia (Figure 3). As a foreign anthropologist, my opinion occasionally has been sought regarding the authenticity of ethnographic details. I have demurred. However, in public, including on Sakha TV, I happily have praised revival of the eloquent white shaman's opening prayers, sunrise offerings of fermented mare's milk (*kumys*), and trance-like marathon circle dancing (*okhuohai*) accompanied by improvisational poetry. I regularly have surprised people by adding that "every generation remakes its own traditions." I have been less interested in differentiating what aspects of the cultural revival were authentic than in discovering and recording diverse controversies surrounding the multiple meanings and new-found exuberance that the Yhyakh generates. Who am I to decide whether holding hands to the sun palm out or palm in during prayer is authentic?

The famous scholarship stream that was launched by Eric Hobsbawm and Terence Ranger, and refined by Richard Handler along with many others, has been most coherent in depicting European or French-Canadian Québécois consolidation of national identities through "a process of formalization and ritualization" in modern times of rapid societal transformation (Hobsbawm and Ranger 1983, 4; Handler 1988). For me as well as my Sakha colleague, "invention of tradition"

FIGURE 3.   Us Khatyn [Three Birches] circle dance at summer solstice Yhyakh ceremony, with *sérgé* in background. 2013. By author.

has a ring of conscious artificiality that is manipulative and elite-driven, as in the extreme cases of Nazi Germany's Hitler, Serbia's chauvinist nationalist leader Slobodan Milosevič, or the Bosnian Serb war criminal Radovan Karadžić, who was arrested while cannily disguised as a folk healer. Authenticity is a claim often coopted by nationalist fundamentalists who resist cultural change in each generation. The Marxist historian Hobsbawm (Hobsbawm and Ranger 1983, 7) ironically observed: "plenty of political institutions, ideological movements and groups—not least nationalism—were so unprecedented that even historic continuity had to be invented."[17]

An update and partial way out of the notorious traps that shaped colonial encounters is provided by those Indigenous scholars who recognize the pitfalls of "colonized minds" beholden to the indignities of living with European categories of citizenship, nationhood, territoriality, and sovereignty (compare Simpson 2014; Simpson and Smith 2014; LaDuke 2015; Nadasdy 2017). Through this recognition comes understanding of colonial and neocolonial legacies. Such reflection enables newly adaptive ways to construct multileveled and situationally sensitive Indigenous identities, in order to cultivate creative sovereignties better suited to values and legal frameworks that support Indigenous rights and worldviews. This in turn may stimulate the respect for Indigenous agency that has been missing in some outsider anthropologist accounts. Its dynamics provide the reason why we have no right to judge rituals like Yhyakh using loaded terms like neotraditional or inauthentic.

Paul Nadasdy (2017, 4), in an insightful Indigenous perspectives monograph on the Yukon First Nations of Canada, explains that culturally specific assumptions "about space, time, and sociality" are the heart of sovereignty politics. His front-lines participatory account recognizes that First Nation state formation in Canada has been a hard-won process requiring new ways of thinking about territoriality, citizenship, and history. Similar but not the same as the Siberian republic formation cases within Russia, statehood within Canada, constructed through Western, semidemocratic, and often constraining "entailments," has meant painful tradeoffs as hunters have had to become bureaucrats (Nadasdy 2013; 2017). When an Indigenous group, such as the Kluane, needs to define and divide hunting territories that it never thought of as owned, its members become at risk of losing ways of knowing and understanding time, space, and reciprocity among humans and animals.

Reconstructed history becomes key to processes of nation building, as Prasenjit Duara (2004) has suggested for Manchuria and Nadasdy (2017, 249) has elaborated for Yukon: "the emergence of First Nation nationalism, then, requires not the replacement of a kin-focused sense of history with a nation-focused one, but the imposition of a notion of linear progressive history as *the* principal means for relating to the past (and, thus, to the present and future as well). Once this has been accomplished, then 'pre-national' modes of relating to the past can be appropriated, transformed and subsumed into national history." Nadasdy's gist, with lessons for historians and anthropologists, is that it is arrogant to assume that Euro-American approaches should have a monopoly on how to define time or the value and use of tradition (compare Fabian 1983; Ssorin-Chaikov 2017). Anthropologists—when we are sensitive to comparative, multiple, overlapping, and alternative perceptions of time—are in logical positions to analyze and respect variations of cyclical, nonprogressive, and nonevolutionary time without falling into an alternative trap of romanticizing or privileging some ur-primitive era of exotic Noble Savage enlightenment or traditional knowledge purity (Nadasdy 2017, 258–60, 307). This has implications for how and why Indigenous groups in Siberia are using large- and small-scale rituals, recovered spirituality, and reevaluated history to regain senses of self-worth in newly adaptive, nation-building ways that transcend what have become "invention of tradition" clichés.

The Eurocentricity of the original provocative invention of tradition perspective forces anthropologists to think harder about how and why we choose our comparative cases. Looking to our own traditions, we can adapt the "method of controlled comparison" of Fred Eggan (1954) privileging close commonalities comparisons over more generalized compare and contrast theories (compare Kapferer and Theodossopoulos 2016; Kendall 2021). For example, the relatively recent twentieth-century quasi-state formations of Canada's First Nations, especially the territory of Nunavut, may correlate in approximate timing, protracted negotiation processes, legal status, and economic dependencies with Russia's quasi-sovereign republic formations—making their comparison logical. Settler colonialism as a popular umbrella concept has been too varied in space and time across continents to enable nuanced comparisons without considering many additional criteria and contingent contexts. In brief, British colonial Africa and India are less useful for modeling debates about Indigenous traditions, cultural change, and agency than Canada, Australia, and New Zealand.

A twentieth-anniversary successor volume to *Invention of Tradition*, edited by Ton Otto and Poul Pedersen (2005), called *Tradition and Agency: Tracing Cultural Continuity and Invention*, with a useful postscript by Terence Ranger, demonstrates these comparative logics by highlighting a range of cases richer than the original volume. Each chapter examines "questions of cultural continuity and discontinuity, agency, and the use of cultural resources" (2005, 7). For purposes of comparisons with Siberia, the final chapter on Australia and New Zealand by Erich Kolig (2005, 293–326) is particularly compelling.

Kolig sympathetically focuses on controversies surrounding the "indigenous cultural renaissance," recognizing a range of positions and reasons for Māori and Aboriginal authenticity claims and public (non-Native) misunderstandings of them. The implicit "interestedness" of knowledge (á la Habermas) and cultural revival in the context of a relatively tolerant and liberal political climate do not make Māori and Aborigines cynical manipulators of current realities, but rather rational appraisers of possible political and legal opportunities. They are not naively nostalgic for the whole of "'good old pre-European days,' exciting a wave of emotional longing for a past long since repressed by European domination . . . [or] a wish to return to a pre-European 'golden era' . . . [Instead] even the most extreme expression of nostalgia is ultimately an engagement with Modernity (or post-Modernity) and a creative attempt to shape the future, rather than return to the past" (Kolig 2005, 296). This has led to a complex continuum of "revitalizing existing traditions, resurrecting abandoned ones, or inventing new ones" (Kolig 2005, 296). Cultural revitalization and its discourses have reinforced specific, Indigenous purposes in the real world of twenty-first-century energy politics, land grabs, and tourism. Court cases over what lands were traditionally sacred and which rituals were secret yet crucial to a tribe's (*iwi*, Māori) existence become matters of contestation won or lost on the grounds of Indigenous and non-Indigenous, anthropologist and ecologist, definitions of authenticity. In this context, the Māori author Hirimi Matunga (1994, 220) has understandably defined *Waahi Tapu* (sacred site) in as broad terms as possible: "not only burial places, mythical sites, historical and archaeological sites, but also traditional resource sites . . . and confiscated lands."

In sum, the content of what is sacred itself may shift with circumstances, opportunities, and generations, causing some Indigenous leaders to be in direct lines of backfiring White backlash. Using historic victimization arguments in court cases is particularly tricky, "entailing the entitlement to special legal and moral consideration, on which much of the weight of the revival movement rests" (Kolig 2005, 301). Whether or not we agree with Kolig's weighting or his terming victimization "ideological transfer," it is clear that the stakes for anthropological expertise and reputation become high when disputes go to court and the fluidity, multivocality, and internal contestability of cultural traditions are denied.

Unlike one of my PhD thesis advisors, the Aborigine expert Jane Goodale, I have never been asked to testify in an Indigenous land compensation claim or sacred site case, nor would I be permitted to in Russia as a foreigner. Such cases occasionally are contested in Siberia and hinge on much narrower definitions of sacred land than Matunga's. Like other aspects of Indigenous rights already discussed, they are more likely to be settled in favor of an Indigenous community if that community is within a republic, rather than a Russian region (compare Varfolomeeva 2019; Balzer 2017). The weight of selective, postmodern, post-Soviet cultural revitalization has rested not on highly publicized court cases but on glimpses of empowerment derived from savvy local political leadership, multipronged economic integration transcending colonial-style resource extraction, community ritual celebration, private and public spiritual recovery, social reciprocity, and ecological awareness.

Engaged and Collaborative Fieldwork in Villages, Towns, and My Backyard

In 2010, several days before I was to leave the Sakha Republic after a productive stint of summer fieldwork, I was horrified to discover that my most current notebook was missing. It went missing just after an extensive interview in a private apartment-office with one of the Sakha activists of the ecology group Save [the] Lena [River]! My fears were compounded with worry for the activist, for the friend who had picked me up after the interview, for the friends with whom I lived, and for what the disappearance might signify as a return to Soviet-style surveillance. Sadly, it reminded me of the blatant and latent ways I had been watched back in 1986, in the Soviet period, when I first did a half-year of fieldwork in the republic, then called Yakutia. I was still seared by those bad old days, when I had been falsely accused of being an outside agitator during and after the pro-glasnost youth demonstrations in Yakutsk that were somewhat simplistically condemned as nationalist.[18] Could we really be returning to the days when I was accused of being an American spy, rather than a legitimate anthropologist? Could another bout of testing be in my future, as in 1986 when the driver of a turquoise taxi that had been following me for days threw a glass bottle at my feet to see how I would react when it shattered? (Answer: angrily.) I desperately wanted the missing notebook to turn up, and its return to be proof that my fears were unfounded, even paranoid.

As I write these words, I am smiling at the recovered notebook, its contents safely transposed into my computer. But before the sympathetic reader imagines a happy ending, you must understand that it turned up only after six months, in the car of my trusted driver-friend, after he had searched all its crevices repeatedly in the days after it went missing. Someone such as an FSB (new version of KGB) intelligence officer had plenty of time to have palmed the notebook from the unlocked car and copied it before returning it. Daily life in Russia, especially but not only for foreign anthropologists, is ambiguous—filled with suspicions, surprises, and emotional extremes. Several Sakha friends and colleagues to whom I confessed the story were convinced that the notebook had been temporarily stolen after I had foolishly left it in the car, to give me a warning: interviewing ecology activists whose group was under pressure to stop publicizing oil leaks into the Lena River was risky. Of course I knew this, but degrees of surveillance were vague. I had spent much of my summer attending solstice ceremonies and working with healers and shamans. I intentionally waited until the end to interview some of the more controversial political and ecology-oriented activists. The glorious days of 1990s go-anywhere, see-anyone freedom, when I returned to the republic nearly every year after spring semesters at Georgetown University, were over.

Since 1986, my wide-ranging research and interviews have been puzzling to authorities, as well as to friends and fellow cultural anthropologists, sometimes overlapping categories. Rather than a narrow ethnographic focus, such as weddings, which had fascinated me in 1986, I seemed to want to know too much about everything. Even in 1986, weddings led to gender relations, interethnic relations, rural-urban differences, "traditional" vs. "modern" approaches to family values, semi-public programs of ethnic-based affirmative action, nonsanctioned ethnic-based urban enclaves, politicized sponsorship of elaborate alcohol-soaked events, youth anger, and Communist Party corruption.[19] The interrelated linkages of multiple themes that seemed logical to me appeared threatening and propagandistic to those not used to broad-sweeping, open-ended interviews. I loved having conversations that went to unexpected places, and thus I began some of my best, long-term friendships and collaborations with people who later became officials in the post-Soviet government of the Sakha Republic. This included the mayor of Yakutsk and the ministers of education and of culture. "Studying up" evolved with friends' careers rather than as a planned enactment of Laura Nader's famous strategy (1972).

Studying impoverished villages as well as ghetto-like barracks with outhouses on the outskirts of Yakutsk was also a process that evolved. In 1986, in the 1990s, and into the 2000s, friends I had made at the university and the Ministry of Culture took me home to their extended families. What began as delightful yet haphazard acceptance of invitations became a conscious, successful pattern. By 2013, I had managed to visit many of the thirty-four internal regions (called *ulus* in Sakha) of the republic, the largest in Russia with a population just over a million. I visited a remote Far North hunting camp near Verkhoyansk (famed as one of the coldest inhabited places on earth, although admittedly I went in summer); lived in several villages in the notorious-for-its-gulags Srednaia Kolyma region; saw ice floes the size of New York apartment buildings during its breakup on the Lena River in late May; danced all night at solstice ceremonies in Suntar; and worked with a Sakha parliament deputy in her home region of Mirny after floods had ravaged this famous diamond-mining area in the south of the republic.

Several sites of periodic living arrangements in the central part of the Sakha Republic were especially significant. They were public enough to render any attempt at pseudonyms, whether of villages or of people, somewhat artificial.[20] The first was my long-term relationship with the village of Katchagatsa (Megino-Kangalas *ulus*), where I first worked in 1986 with a group led by ethnographer-archeologist Anatoly Ignatevich Gogolev, and returned several times to stay with a revered local schoolteacher. The second was my stay in the village of Tiuktiur (Kangalas *ulus*) in 1995, to live with a wonderful multigenerational family of cattle raisers who promised to speak to me only in Sakha, not Russian. (The promises often were broken.) The third was enabled by my long-term friendship with the family of the art historians Zina and Vladimir Ivanov, who welcomed me in their gorgeous Yakutsk apartment, filled with avant-guard art and oriental rugs, over many years of comfortable and comforting rapport.

My fourth and most consistent long-term home (in various permutations, including at the dacha) has been with the family of the sociologist and public persona Uliana Vinokurova, my co-author on several joint projects, a former republic parliament deputy, and the person to whom I owe some of my most synergistic thinking. Uliana is known as a champion of Indigenous non-Russian peoples of the North, not only of Sakha ethnonational rights. When the Soviet Union collapsed, she articulately mitigated notoriety in Moscow as a "Sakha nationalist" by proclaiming: "There are places for all those in the republic who wish to see her as a mother, not a stepmother" (Vinokurova 1992, 4).

Repeat visits and long-term fieldwork were less feasible in Buryatia and Tyva than in Sakha. However, I have worked in Buryatia and Tyva during several trips. In both republics, I was able to augment close relationships formed with Buryat and Tyvan Fulbright scholars who had worked with me at Georgetown, visiting them or their families. I used conferences as initial entrées or liminal spaces in 2005, 2010, 2015, and 2016. I took advantage of invitations to travel beyond the capitals of Ulan-Ude in Buryatia, and Kyzyl in Tyva. In Buryatia and the Irkutsk region, this included a memorable stay on the sacred Olkhon Island in Lake Baikal. Travel to the Tunka Valley, where I participated in a *tailagan* ceremony honoring a mountain God, gave me access to near-legendary ecology activists who had helped divert a pipeline.

In Tyva, I was able to visit a nomadic camp in the mountains and to explore the controversial Scythian archeological site "Valley of the Kings" in the Western Sayan Mountains. Most of my formal interviews in Tyva were in Kyzyl, with religious and political leaders. I was openheartedly received in monasteries, institutes, schools, museums, the local parliament, and in several (competing) shamanic healing centers.[21] Since working in Tyva, I have befriended Tyvan musicians and scholars working abroad on numerous occasions for updates and insights. One artist has shared valuable narratives of his youth that included the tragically unstable period of 1990, when the republic erupted in poorly known and inadequately understood violence. His critical reading of my Tyva chapter has improved it considerably.

Since I edit the translation journal *Anthropology and Archeology of Eurasia* that publishes the work of scholars from the former Soviet Union, some of my colleagues in the three republics are authors I have helped in their careers. Connections with these ethnographers and sociologists in the three republics have been enormously helpful during my stays in the republics, at conferences, and once I have returned home.

In our world of complex interconnections, the networks of Native diasporas formed by Sakha, Buryat, and Tyvan leaders in the United States and Europe have been easy to find, work with, and help support. I have created a "Siberian compound" with my neighbors—a Sakha-Buryat family, the Solovyevs, who founded the group Sakha Open World. I have helped to host many friends and colleagues from the Far East in my home, at Georgetown University, at jaw harp (*khomus*) and throat-singing concerts, and at conferences or workshops in various venues around the world. I was privileged, for example, to help organize a series of MacArthur-Foundation-funded meetings between Native Siberians and Native Americans during the 1990s, and I have maintained many of these contacts. In 2014, I helped organize a day-long international round table at Fort Ross, California, celebrating Sakha (Yakut)-Pomo Indian interconnections. The day unexpectedly concluded in a Pomo sacred lodge. In 2020–2021, our compound held a house concert of Sakha and Tyvan musicians and many "socially distanced" fire-pit rituals and discussions with Siberian friends from Sakha and Tyva.

Collaboration where I can find it has been the key to my ability to think beyond data collection and "participant observation" in specific field sites. This has sparked my understanding of the interrelatedness of seemingly disparate themes, people, and places. Interaction in multiple contexts is what brings comparative fieldwork to the level of what my Latin Americanist anthropology colleague Joanne Rappaport calls "co-theorizing" (2005).[22] In a felicitous twist, my close Sakha friend and co-author Uliana Vinokurova has become fascinated by comparisons among Sakha, Buryatia, and Tyva (Vinokurova 2017). She has worked in Buryatia several times, overlapped with me once in the Tunka Valley, and shared field data, interviews, and insights that have been enormously stimulating. In 2019, we together served as advisors of the Sakha sociologist Daria Burnasheva for her doctoral thesis on Arctic identity at the University of Warsaw.

As with most anthropologists, my interconnections belie any dualism implicit in the term "glocal." Friendships, fieldwork, formal interviews, and sustained conversations over many years have created a mesh of mutual understandings that defy and transcend categories of interlocutors. This is evident in my growing rapport with my friend and neighbor Vera Solovyeva, who has influenced the manuscript with a culturally fluent insider's insights, a colleague's scientific breadth, and an ecology activist's heart.

Rapport does not happen with everyone and may blossom and then disappear. I have rarely felt in the field that I was being manipulated or lied to outright, although officials in awkward positions have occasionally needed to wink when their assistants walked in. During the protracted period of writing this book, I have learned harsh lessons in the process of asking English-fluent people from the three republics featured here to read drafts of my profiles for accuracy and deeper perspective. I understand that what I write may have unexpected emotional impact and bring back unwanted memories. What seems like intriguing history to me may be a political minefield with unexpected consequences for them. Misunderstandings, usually cleared up, have occurred with several Buryats in Mongolia, Britain, and the United States. They have caused me to reflect on unseen wounds inflicted when a homeland is truncated, poverty creates long-distance dependencies, and religious feelings are suppressed. Such lessons have stimulated me to act as a pro bono expert in several US religious asylum cases for non-Russians from Russia.

While primary data for anthropologists is derived from diverse personal communications and interactions, I have supplemented these through access to several private archives, on Sakha ecology activism, Buryat history, and Tyvan interethnic relations, as well as by participating in the coronavirus-stimulated communities of online conferences, meetings, and memorials.

Collaboration through "engaged anthropology" and what I term "opportunity anthropology," focused on critical issues with long-term resonance, is what I hope enables me to explore numerous dimensions of indigeneity and sovereignty without presuming to speak for any particular Native person or group. My close relationships have given me access and perspective without making me beholden to multiethnic colleague-friends, including Russians, for analyses. My reticence to make judgments about authenticity, constructed identities, and what some have termed "neo-traditionalism" (Pika and Prokhorov 1994; Grant 1999) stems from a sense that we are living in times of too much turmoil to fully assess legacies, including understanding whether a new religious movement will become a lasting religion or fizzle. Views of my interlocutors are too diverse, and their debates too interesting, to overgeneralize about current processes of cultural and political change. One person's galvanizing cultural revival is another's invention of tradition. Anthropologists need to maintain open minds concerning authenticity, honesty, and reflexive comparative learning.

Organization and Goals: Beyond Parades

This monograph is organized to present profiles of the three featured republics in an order that enables a sequential unfolding of their salience for the survival of multiethnic Russia. The republic cases are presented as cameos of emblematic themes. The Sakha Republic is "rich and pivotal," reflecting its diamonds and other key resources. The Republic of Buryatia is "gerrymandered and struggling," due to its historical legacies of regional divisions imposed from above. The Republic of Tyva is "a borderline state with demographic advantages," due to its geography, history, and the overwhelming majority of its titular nation.

The profiles of Sakha, Buryatia, and Tyva, given diverse historical legacies, cannot be perfectly parallel, but I explore national identity and civic-society-building processes along multiple salient lines. These are: crystallizing moments that stand out in specific historical contexts of interethnic relations; language politics; demographic and economic background; ecological protests; and cultural-spiritual revitalization. For each case, internal complexities and debates are acknowledged, including differentiating elite, intellectual urban-based nationalism from less vocal village-based ethnonational and local identities and tensions. The resulting study is a contribution to legal anthropology and to community-oriented analyses situated in various levels of social and political contexts. I argue that leaders, while often emerging from intellectual or professional elites, may not necessarily do so.

Chapter 4, "Crossover Trends," describes multiple ways Turkic, Mongolian, Russian, and other citizens in the three republics have interacted with each other, neighboring peoples, and Moscow authorities. The chapter describes multileveled horizontal and vertical ties that are crucial to any federal system, and to the health of a struggling civic society. Key themes and trends are discussed by analyzing economic contexts, legacies of Eurasianism, Turkic-Mongolic language politics (including Russian-Slavic backlash), youth camps and festivals, and the rise of the spiritual movement Tengrianstvo in the context of Buddhist and Russian Orthodox revivals.

Historical, linguistic, and religious ties expressly reformulated for new post-Soviet times enable us to think more deeply about the interrelationship between transnational cultural identities and economic-political activities. Cultural connections include joint film and sports projects, as well as conferences and debates concerning mutual cultural heritage of languages, epics, and shamanic perspectives. Economic connections include new markets on old borders, complex negotiations concerning energy and ecology issues, as well as unsavory business deals. Cross-republic political communications, entailing public and private interactions, have been difficult but not impossible to trace. Informal contacts have led to discussions of cross-republic strategies regarding the federal center and legal issues. Debates abound concerning the appropriateness or effectiveness of elections at various levels, Moscow-imposed "jubilee-ization of history," and the effectiveness of street protests.

Featured in chapter 4, and tying my book themes together, is the dramatic appearance in 2018–2019 of a new "rabble-rousing" Sakha leader-shaman named Alexander Gabyshev. Alexander, a suffering widower and former plumber, began walking from Yakutsk, the capital of Sakha Republic, on a protest journey to Moscow that went through Buryatia. Bragging that he wants to oust President Putin from the Kremlin by 2021 in an exorcism ritual planned for Red Square, he became a sensation in the Russian media, especially on the internet. He reached page 4 of the *New York Times* on October 10, 2019, in part because he was arrested by Russian authorities in Buryatia and sent back to Yakutsk. His arrest was the proximate but not sole cause for demonstrations in Buryatia and the Sakha Republic. Alexander managed to garner increasing numbers of multiethnic followers, alarming authorities in Buryatia and Moscow. His "long walk," and the discourse around his mixed shamanic-holy fool rural-urban background, has been as much about the process of mobilizing broad-based opposition to Putin, "that demon in the Kremlin," as about actually reaching Red Square. He was charged with political extremism, and an official inquest into his psychological health was launched. A return to the Soviet practice of punishing dissidents, including shamans, with psychiatric clinic-prisons and debilitating drugs at first was narrowly averted by his excellent pro bono lawyers. However, he was condemned to an indefinite stay in a psychiatric hospital in 2020, and a criminal case was brought against him in 2021. His actions and shamanic self-identity are controversial with every Siberian I know. They raise precisely the questions and debates that I explore in this book about leadership in times of trouble, dangers of political polarization, and difficulties of claiming authenticity. Alexander also exemplifies conundrums of writing about changing and situational identities (compare Derluguian 2006).

Conclusions return to larger issues of redefining federalism, self-determination, and leadership in Russia. They incorporate analysis of 2020 changes in the Russian Constitution toward a more unified, authoritarian Russian state. My chosen themes are inevitably moving targets in times of change, but I have tried to capture snapshots that may endure. Given the contingent nature of indigeneity and sovereignty, I am reticent to espouse general lessons.

Interrelated themes that depict Indigenous interrelations with each other and the state in Siberia are outlined in a way that can be compared to Indigenous movements elsewhere.

This book is part of a growing understanding of multiple interconnected levels of global and local responses to "emerging ecological and social crises" (Canty 2019; Raygorodetsky 2017). Ramifications of nostalgia are discussed in the context of conversations surrounding historical monuments, politicized cultural-spiritual revitalization, ecology activism, and striving for Indigenous homelands. Under what conditions is it possible for ecology movements to be transformed into wider civic society activism? What do crises of climate change and health, exemplified by the coronavirus, expose about underlying societal weaknesses and resilience? What do crossover trends such as Turkic-Mongolic versions of Eurasianism, the new religious movement Tengrianstvo, and the growing significance of Buddhism mean for diverse people within the three featured republics? I grapple with what it means to Indigenous groups and individuals to taste degrees of sovereignty and then have homeland hopes thwarted. Rather than a "parade of sovereignties," that simplistic and inaccurate description of the results of President Yeltsin's nationality policies, this book illustrates the perils of squandering opportunities for self-determination.

SAKHA REPUBLIC (YAKUTIA)
Resource Rich and Pivotal

Authorities in the republic do not control and have not controlled the situation in the large energy worker compounds, whether for Transneft, Rosneft, Gazprom, or Surgutneftegaz. These are closed enclaves, where Yakutsk officials are allowed only for ceremonial purposes to cut ribbons.

—Sakha commentator on COVID-19 and more, spring 2020

We started the Save Lena! ecology campaign in 2008, with the threat of the oil pipeline going under and along the river. People were worried that pipes would break. We got signatures against poor technology [not all development]. But people have become passive. They don't want to go to unsanctioned protests.

—Yury Zhegusov, sociologist, Institute of the Humanities and the Indigenous Peoples of the North, June 4, 2015

Some places like Kiŋylyakh in the Verkhoyansk Mountains are just too sacred for most Sakha or outsiders to go. People shouldn't climb to the top where the stone figures are—it is a portal to the Sky and the Sky deities. But some are making it into a tourist zone. They are trespassing and violating Sakha traditions, at their peril.

—Sakha man, summer 2017

Our Sakha language is like cream, easy on the throat.

—Traditional saying

Sakha ethnonational solidarity and concerns about losing control of the vast Sakha Republic (Yakutia) homeland and its famously rich resources have been leitmotifs in many of my conversations since I began fieldwork in the republic. Major themes that repeatedly emerge in republic relations with Moscow officials include language politics, ecology activism, sacred land, and defining sovereignty. This chapter explores these issues and their demographic and economic background by considering the ebbs and flows of permissible Sakha activism within the context of a social and political landscape that has changed radically during the post-Soviet period. It concludes by assessing the interrelationship of social and spiritual values and political change.

Since 2015, Sakha language rights have brought crowds to the streets of the capital Yakutsk, especially since many thought cultural sovereignty was already won. That spring, parents of children in Sakha-language entry-level schools bravely rallied at Friendship Square to protest "cost-cutting" education policies emanating from Moscow designed to consolidate Sakha-language schools into Russian-language ones and curtail the number of teaching hours permitted for the Sakha language.[1] While this has affected only a few schools in Yakutsk, it has had more effect in predominantly Sakha rural regions where teaching in the Sakha language is the norm. Official celebrations of Russian-language authors in the republic, and constitutional changes enacted in 2020, have further under-scored Russian-civilization-privileging messages.[2]

Sakha-language proficiency and Sakha identity are correlated in the republic, often in highly emotional terms. Statistics are problematic and debated. Fear and hope seem to vie with each other in claims concerning language recovery. In 2015, the Sakha linguist Ivan Alekseyev called Russification of the Sakha a crisis. Many Sakha lament a decline in the number of Sakha who know their Native language well and rue the paucity of Russians who learn the Sakha language. In the republic the term "Sakha" is the ethnonym Sakha use when speaking among themselves, juxtaposed to "Yakut," the nonpejorative Russian term for the people and language. In Russia, Yakut is more commonly used. Many Sakha have given up trying to get Russians to call them Sakha. The ethnically mixed Sakha-Russian journalist Vitaly Obedin reminisces that "When I was young, I did not even know the word *Yakuty*, only *Sakhalar* [Sakha], because we spoke only Sakhaly in the village."[3]

Mixed signals abound. In the 2010 census, Sakha (Yakut) claimed knowledge of their native tongue at an impressive rate of over 90 percent, despite years of Russification and unequal bilingualism favoring Russian in the Soviet and post-Soviet periods. Only 5.3 percent of Sakha stated that Russian was their native language in 2010, although in Yakutsk alone, the share of predominantly Russian speakers is high among Sakha. Since the 2010 and 2021 censuses are flawed (for different reasons), attention should be paid to local researchers.[4] In 2017, a Sakha interlocutor insisted new generations of Sakha are learning Sakhaly and that once again, as they did before the 1917 revolution, "some Russians are making the effort to learn Sakha."

Since 1986, I have observed in many Yakutsk families that the children know the Sakha language poorly but are embarrassed to admit it and adamantly claim Sakha as their ethnonational identity. Alternatively, some have learned the Sakha language late, as teenagers or adults, in a self-aware language recovery process that has been personally painful for many. Other Indigenous groups throughout the republic—especially Éveny, Évenki, and Yukaghir—have become "Yakutized," as well as "Russified," causing various degrees of resentment. By 2010, these groups helped augment the number of people claiming knowledge of the Sakha language. Since self-identification on ethnonational affiliation and self-assessment on the "mother tongue" indicator were key principles guiding census takers, more Sakha claimed the Sakha language as their mother tongue than probably was warranted. This has become all the more likely in the subsequent years of increased urbanization throughout the republic.

Beyond language recovery politics, a limited sovereignty has been celebrated. The Sakha Republic's first post-Soviet 1992 Constitution, ratified before Russia adopted its own in 1993, and the bilateral treaty signed by Sakha President Mikhail Nikolaev and Russia's President Boris Yeltsin in 1995, provided Sakha leaders with hopes that they were on the threshold of unprecedented control over what they perceived as their own rich resources. This short but heady period of negotiated federalism was soon squelched in the first presidential term of the recentralizing Vladimir Putin, beginning in 2000. In response, street protests and more organized mass demonstrations have sometimes erupted over specific grievances.

In 2012, along with many other concerned citizens in Russia, protesters in Yakutsk demonstrated against perceived Duma election fraud and against President Putin's decision to run for a third term. In 2015, a multiethnic crowd of thousands filled a main Yakutsk square to protest a "planned from above" chemical processing plant. My Sakha interlocutors were concerned that the plant represented a threat to their crucial artery, the Lena River, as well as their ability to make key development decisions. In 2017, Sakha and Russians in Yakutsk were among the many in cities throughout Russia publicly protesting officials' endemic corruption. By illegally demonstrating, they were risking arrest. Turnout was estimated at over one thousand demonstrators in Friendship Square in freezing weather. In 2019, Sakha and Russians in much fewer numbers braved sleet in Yakutsk to legally demonstrate concerns about agricultural policy and illegally express alarm over the house arrest and pending trial of the Putin oppositionist "shaman Alexander [Gabyshev]." By 2020, residents of the republic had become terrified that energy worker compounds administered from Moscow, such as the Power of Siberia pipeline to China at Chianda and militarized transport hubs like Tiksi in the Arctic on the Northern Sea Route, were becoming breeding zones for the coronavirus. No longer demonstrating, they were looking for legal ways to respond to political and economic decisions made in Moscow without their participation and consent. In 2021, protesters in sub-freezing Yakutsk, including young people, joined the wave of unsanctioned demonstrations held across the country to support the jailed activist Alexei Naval'ny.

How did "center-periphery" relations become so dysfunctional? Understanding key historical legacies of differentially perceived interethnic and center-periphery relations provides a framework for understanding societal change and the crystallization of Sakha (Yakut) identity.

Crystallization of Identity in Conditions of Unstable Federalism

The radicalization of ethnic-based Sakha rhetoric in 2000 against President Putin's bilateral treaty abrogation became a turning point in galvanizing Sakha ethnonational identity. It can be matched with another, earlier crystallizing moment that dominated my 1986 field experience and, more importantly, remains seared in the memories of participants (Figure 4). Indeed, events of the spring of 1986 have become legendary, already magnified as historically significant. Some Sakha provocatively claim that they were the first non-Russian group to protest openly against Soviet rule, before the Kazakhs erupted over the installation of a non-Kazakh Communist Party leader, and before Armenians demonstrated for the territory of Nagornyi-Karabagh (Artsakh) against Azerbaijan (compare Beissinger 2002).

The Yakutsk 1986 incident began with an alleged beating of some Sakha university students, including young women, by Russian toughs, some of whom were rumored to be wearing Soviet army uniforms. Several days later, hundreds of Sakha students marched down Lenin Prospect to Lenin Square, demanding to see the chief of police. They were incensed that no Russians had been arrested, and that several students had landed in the hospital. They also explained that they wanted the benefits of Gorbachev's perestroika and glasnost to reach their republic. Eventually, student leaders were expelled, and some activists had their lives changed forever by the confrontation.

I was nearly expelled from the republic as an "outside agitator," until cooler heads prevailed and I was permitted to do fieldwork in villages, as I had requested before I arrived, away from the overheated politics of the capital.[5]

The 1986 event, described as scandalous by some who tried to cover it up, was hardly the first "ethnic brawl" that had occurred in Yakutsk in the Soviet period. However, the demonstration was the first to receive federal-level, extremely negative publicity as "nationalist" (see also Argounova-Low 1994; Argounova-Low 2012). While local Communist officials denied they had an ethnic tension problem, putting the blame squarely on ill-brought- up youth, many privately

FIGURE 4. Yakutsk State University ice skating at site of interethnic fight, 1986. By author.

considered that these altercations revealed simmering ethnic-based animosities. They explained that Sakha had become "second-class citizens" in their own homeland, and that Russian "newcomers" frequently got preferential treatment such as better housing and better jobs. Few, however, were as "radical" and bold as the students. Most schools and places of work were relatively well integrated. By the 1990s, local residents attributed street fights in Yakutsk and in provincial towns to an incendiary mix of interethnic tensions, widespread alcoholism, and criminal gang competition.

After 1990, more hopeful political developments were gelling. A group called Sakha Omuk (The Sakha People) sponsored cultural, ecological, political, and economic rights campaigns. Led by Andrei S. Borisov, a theater director who became the longest-running minister of culture in the history of the republic, Sakha Omuk functioned like a popular front, bringing together diverse groups. Members were active in electing reformist deputies to legislatures at various levels, in passing sovereignty legislation, and in drafting the Sakha Constitution, passed in 1992 by the reformist republic legislature after a professionally diverse committee had read the constitutions of most countries in the United Nations. My colleague and sometime-co-author Uliana Vinokurova was a member of this committee, appointed by the republic president. She recalls with bittersweet joy the intense process of creating the first draft of the Sakha Constitution, proud that they passed it before the Russian Federation had ratified its own constitution.[6]

The moderate and popular (as well as populist) Sakha President Mikhail E. Nikolaev was elected in a fair and transparent election and served until President Vladimir Putin came to power. Reformist Sakha leaders emphasized unifying, not polarizing, the republic's multiethnic population. Andrei Borisov explained to me in 1991: "Sakha Omuk was formed in response to Gorbachev's call for new ideas. It is not a [chauvinist nationalist] Party." By the mid-1990s, many Sakha Omuk members had channeled their political energies into official capacities, becoming deputies in the new parliament and ministers in the government. With a taste of power, they became less "radical" and more prospective.

Another, more fully interethnic group called My Yakutiane (We Yakutians) formed in 1996 and continued to gain adherents into the Putin period, over-lapping in membership with a fledgling opposition party called Novaia Yaku-tiia (New Yakutia), led by the businessman Fedot Tumusov, who later joined the federation-based party For a Just Russia. In the parliament, optimisti-cally termed Il Tumen or "Meeting for Agreement," deputies of Sakha back-ground dominated beyond their share of the republic population. A fascinating dynamic of strategic opposition to the republic president evolved, until this structural "balance of powers" was nipped in the bud in the early 2000s. In the same transitional period, pressure mounted from Moscow to "correct" the republic Constitution. It went through several iterations before it was deemed congruent with the Russian Federation's 1993 Constitution. Sakha continue to express nostalgia for the 1992 original version, celebrated each year on Repub-lic Day (April 27).

Historical memory recovery was stimulated by revising Soviet propaganda emphasizing the peaceful incorporation of Yakutia into the Russian Empire in the seventeenth century and belittling the degree of economic efficiency and literacy among prerevolutionary Sakha (compare Cruikshank and Argounova 2000). However, in 2007, with encouragement from Moscow officials, the repub-lic turned its annual summer solstice ceremony into an extravagant celebration of "375 years of Yakutia's entry into Russia," using the implicitly voluntary *vkhozh-denie* for the word "entry" and downplaying any violence that occurred when the first Cossacks conquered the region and placed a fort with lookout towers at the settlement of Yakutsk. Witnessed by Moscow dignitaries, a commemorative statue of the Cossack leader Petr Beketev was placed overlooking the Lena River near Yakutsk's revitalizing old town, accompanied by strong Russian Orthodox iconography signaling Christianization of the Sakha "pagans." The fuss over Beketov, touted as being the founder of Yakutsk in 1632 when it was already a Sakha settlement, and over the anniversary was a stunning example of what I term the "jubilee-ization" of history. It was highly controversial among the Sakha intelligentsia.[7]

Many Sakha envision a prerevolutionary time counter to Soviet propaganda when multigenerational families lived together in cattle and horse-raising homesteads of considerable wealth, as depicted by the nineteenth-century Polish exile-turned-ethnographer Wacław Sieroszewski, whose monograph, reprinted in Russian as *Yakuty*, became a post-Soviet bestseller (1896; Takasaeva 2017). As we sat in a spacious *balagan* (log home) overlooking fields, forests, and a lake, one pony-tailed Verkhoyansk homesteader, hunter, and prayer leader (*algys-chit*) recalled that on the maternal side of his family, he could trace his ancestry on that land back twelve generations. "At the peak of our wealth [before the revolution reached the North]," he recounted, "we had a deer herd of about five hundred kept elsewhere [with local Éveny], and over five hundred horses and three hundred cattle kept here." They also had around seventy work horses. His wise and wealthy ancestor was Mitrofan, known for tact and kindness with his workers:

> One worker gambled away a whole herd of deer, plus his sleigh and sled deer. The sleigh had been filled with furs, for trade farther south. But instead, he'd been waylaid, and drank and gambled. In his shame, he stayed away nearly a whole year. But he missed his wife and kids and decided to risk coming back. He struggled back home and when he arrived, he had just the reins of the sled deer in his hands. When Mitrofan's wife caught sight of him, she ran out and started to berate him, telling him he was good for nothing, had stolen from them. But then Mitrofan came out and said "No, dear wife, be quiet. This man is smart—he's saved himself. That is what is most important, his life. And he has brought home sleigh reins that are of great value because of their craftsmanship, hard to replace. Give him food. Let's send him back to his family with a cow and a calf. His children are hungry and need milk." Thus Mitrofan gained a very loyal and very sheepish worker.[8]

The most passionate post-Soviet historical revisions have focused on twentieth-century figures such as Platon Sleptsov, pseudonym Oiunskii, from the term *oiuun* (shaman), revolutionary, folklorist, and founder of the Institute of Languages, Literature, and History, today's Humanities Institute, who died in Stalin's jails in 1939. Other revered Sakha intelligentsia of the period spanning the revolution into the Stalin era include the writer and ethnographer A. E. Kulakovskii, the dramatist and reformist A. I. Safronov, the writer N. D. Neustroev, the jurist-dramatist-politician V. V. Nikiforov, and the activist P. V. Ksenofontov—all of whom were punished for nationalism in the Stalin era (compare

Argounova-Low 2012). These "best and brightest" of the republic are mourned today by Sakha who say that they, like other Indigenous peoples, can ill afford to lose their educated elite, and that losses are magnified when groups are small.

Associates of the entire well-educated and wealthy Ksenofontov family were arrested in a mass purge today termed the Ksenofontovshchina, which Sakha historians estimate may have jailed over 260 people. Its Lena River estate-owning patriarch was Vasilii, whose iconographic sons included Pavel, a revolutionary who broke ranks when the Bolsheviks refused confederal status for Yakutia; Gavril, an ethnographer; Nikolai, a lawyer; Arkhadii, an engineer—dreamer; and Konstantin, who escaped to America via China. Many of those arrested were sent to the notorious Solovetsky camps in northern Russia, where most perished, although three made a dramatic escape to Finland. A special delegation of Sakha went to the territory to place a memorial cross and plaque there in 2010.[9]

At the Sakha language theatre in 2010, I attended an astonishing, cathartic premiere of a play called *Kuemel* (Ice Break Up), by Kharuskhal (Vasilii Vasil'ev's pseudonym meaning "Protection, Defense"), directed by Andrei Borisov, about the late 1920s repression of Sakha caught in the Ksenofontov purge. As the curtain fell, the mostly Sakha audience rose to its feet with a spontaneous surge of clapping, sobbing, and shouting unlike anything I have ever seen in the theater. The Sakha sociologist Uliana Vinokurova called it an "egregor" moment, using the Greek term for intense community solidarity. Indeed, its group therapy value seemed to rival any of the many conferences and rituals I have attended in the post-Soviet years memorializing the lives of Oiunskii, Kulakovskii, and the Ksenofontovs. *Ice Break Up* has continued in the repertoire for a decade, becoming a symbol of Sakha revisionist history with a morale-building purpose. A 2019 debut of the play *Fate* by the director Ruslan Tarakhovski, roughly based on a novel by Nikolai Zolotorov, whose pen name was Yakutskii, has added to the current sense of nostalgia for romanticized pre-Soviet times, as have several Sakha-language epic films.

Ravaging of the small Sakha national elite festered among the intelligentsia during the Soviet period. One particularly bitter repression occurred after Stalin died, in the 1950s. Its target was a small revisionist group around the historian Georgii Basharin, and among those repressed was the sociologist Ivan Argounov (for whom a yearly seminar was later named). Esteemed senior professors and academicians active today were caught in some of these repressions and easily recall who defended Basharin. In the post-Soviet period, some have openly termed all the repressions "Sakha elitocide," and have claimed that destruction of the wealthy and the intellectuals influenced the Sakha *genofond* (gene pool) for the worse. I have argued with interlocutors in villages and towns against this unscientific interpretation of genetic history, but I understand their pain. Demographic and economic contexts are critical for understanding the bitterness, as well as widespread hope for better federal relations.

Demography, Diamonds, Rust, and Energy Companies

While mournful claims of Sakha elitocide may be hard to prove with genetics, shifting demographic proportions have been politically and socially significant. In 1926, the Sakha, in a territory almost the size of India, comprised about 82 percent of the population. By 1989, they were only 33 percent, numbering 381,922, while Russians constituted about 50 percent. In the 2010 census, Sakha resident in the republic were listed at 466,492 or an eerie 49.9 percent of the population, with Russians listed as 353,649 or 37.8 percent of the population. Given this denial of the predicted Sakha majority, as if 50 percent was some sort of psychological threshold, these numbers seem suspicious, as do other figures from the 2010 census.[10] By 2020, the total republic population was just under a million. Sakha interlocutors express concern over the manipulation of the 2010 and 2020–2021 censuses. The republic remains multiethnic, with other Northern Indigenous groups (Éveny, Évenki, Yukaghir, Chukchi) composing a small but recognized 7 percent of the population. A recent influx of Central Asian and Caucasus migrants, as well as refugees from the East Ukraine conflict that began with the 2014 invasion of Crimea, adds to the mix.

In 2014, a planeload of refugees from the Ukraine conflict learned only after they had taken off from Moscow that they were headed to Yakutsk. Their astonishment was matched by local resentment over the influx of refugees from Ukraine without adequate provision for them. These issues are polarizing but thus far manageable. By 2021, the republic's 55 percent Sakha majority was widely acknowledged, and local leaders were trying to accommodate unhappy refugees. Openly chauvinist rhetoric continues to be ineffective in a republic with greater-than-federation average interethnic marriage rates, although these rates have declined since the Soviet period ended. Many leaders, including heads of the Sakha government, regularly stress unifying, not polarizing, the republic's peoples.

In 2010, the republic officially was 64.1 percent urban, concentrated in the main towns of Yakutsk, Mirny, Lensk, and Neriungri. The figure was probably higher. By 2015–2020, estimates of urban residency had soared to over 70 percent, including people who were still registered in villages but had actually moved to urban centers.[11] Yakutsk bears the brunt of several generations of rural residents pouring into this main city. The overstuffed and underserviced capital struggles to keep up with demands from migrants from within the republic and from the former Soviet Union. Shanty towns and *khrushchevki*, Khrushchev-era wooden dorm-like structures with outside plumbing, are being replaced by a proliferation of gleaming, stilted high-rises built on fragile, unstable permafrost. A charming wooden "old town" with a sparkling trade center for tourists includes a rebuilt Russian Orthodox church and one early tower built by Cossacks for their first fort in the seventeenth century. The tower is a replica, since youths rumored to be Sakha angry at a symbol of Russian colonialism, but possibly just tossing cigarettes while drunk, burned an original remnant tower that had survived the Soviet period. The reproduction has burned several times, confirming political intent.

Republic demographic increases were projected at 5.7 percent in a pre-pandemic 2020–2024 prognosis but should be revised sharply downward.[12] Yakutsk residents numbered 269,601 by 2010, or nearly a third of the republic's population, and reached over 310,000 by 2020. Migrants include vegetable traders from Central Asia, especially Tajikistan, and construction workers from the North Caucasus. Muslim groups have established the first mosque in the capital, receiving some city funds. An oil company engineer from Dagestan explained to me that he had brought his extended family to the Northeast to escape the instability of his homeland and find a "peaceful, ordinary way of life" in Yakutsk, despite its harsh climate.[13] Sadly, the housing registration and fines office revealed a different story, as I learned the hard way twice by finding myself in the midst of long lines of angry, edgy people who sometimes broke into scuffles. Waiting in line in 2013, I was told I had just missed by one day an outbreak of violence between Russian and Central Asian supplicants that had temporarily closed the office. By 2019, unemployment in the Sakha Republic officially reached 6.9 percent and probably was much higher, confirming demographic strains on social safety net resources.[14]

Temporary traders set up seasonal markets on tracts of land on the outskirts of town in zones that are informally labeled "the Chinese market," and "the Gypsy market." Over many years of periodic residence in the capital, I have heard both appreciative and resentful comments about these markets, their safety, their (high) prices, and their rough bargaining rules of the game. Sakha friends, including some in the political and cultural elite, have made enough disparaging, ethnically discriminatory comments about "Gypsies" (*tsygane*, never Roma) and Chinese to make me realize that, as elsewhere, such "outsiders" are perceived as a threat to Sakha safety and a solidarity mobilizer. Some Sakha have confessed that they are relieved when winter comes and the "Gypsies and Chinese go South," since the crime rate is perceived to go down. In 2017, a Sakha friend who had worked in the main Sakha craft factory Sardana complained that every year the "industrious Chinese steal our fur boot, mitten, and coat designs," mass produce them, and sell them at the Chinese market and internationally for much less than the hand-sewn Sardana wares.

Far from the capital, Sakha buzz about under-reported large-scale labor projects that involve temporary workers perceived as invaders. The temporary nature of individual stays tends to undercut traditional Sakha values of rooted-ness and commitment to particular lands. The workers include low-paid Central Asians in energy industry shift assignments, lumbering by North Korean worker-contractors, and an unusual agricultural experiment run by Chinese entrepreneurs. I learned of this unexpected Chinese project in the Northern *ulus* of Verkhoyansk, while traveling to a village on an isolated bumpy dirt road. "Look there," my Sakha host said, pointing to a stretch of verdant valley, green in summer. "That is where a group of Chinese tried for four years to set up large-scale hot-house vegetable farming, unprecedented this far north. He added: "At first we were skeptical and nervous about a Chinese invasion, but the cabbages and other vegetables were welcome, and prices in our markets went down. They stayed to themselves, worked hard, and brought in more people. But then," he said, laughing, "the rabbits got to them; there were too many rabbits to shoot. They were defeated not by our cold winters or our inhospitable reception but by our indigenous rabbits."[15]

The Sakha republic is huge (3,083,523 square kilometers), with over 40 percent located above the Arctic Circle. Its historical borders as Yakutia Gubernia were more extensive, reaching to the Okhotsk Sea and part of the Irkutsk region (Nizhnaia Tunguska) until 1922. Most Sakha leaders, except a few in the early Yeltsin period, wisely refrained from raising territorial expansion claims. Rather, they focused on wresting from Moscow authorities a share of the republic's considerable resources, boasted in many official speeches to contain "the entire Mendeleev table." Although the republic is officially listed has having relatively high per capita incomes compared to other regions of Russia, its Indigenous peoples are among the poorest. The Sakha Republic requires "northern subsidies," especially for its rural population, but it has vast and underexploited mineral (diamonds, gold, tin, and copper) and energy (oil, gas, and coal) wealth. Old, literally rusting infrastructure from Soviet-period urbanization and industrialization has been a hindrance in the republic's mixed and struggling economy, especially in its relatively southern diamond industry towns of Mirny and Lensk, its main coal town Neriungri, and its Lena River Arctic hub port, Tiksi.[16]

Some federal-level support of the Arctic has led successive heads of the republic to emphasize its Arctic identity and goals, including international networking (Burnasheva 2019). Arctic significance, centered on Tiksi, has increased significantly under Putin, with haphazard development of the Northern Sea Route. Lip service concerning Indigenous communities continues into the 2020s, as energy exploitation and militarization of the Northern Sea Route proceed. In the Far North beyond Verkhoyansk, some pre-Russian Revolution Sakha families adapted to reindeer breeding and intermarried with Éveny and Dolgan, a mixed ethnic group of Russian, Éveny, and Sakha background. Some have continued reindeer breeding, hunting, and fishing livelihoods into the post-Soviet period, as have the legally recognized "small-numbered Indigenous peoples"—Éveny, Évenki, Yukaghir, and Chukchi. A 2015 statement by the republic head Egor Borisov on development of the Arctic epitomizes familiar tensions concerning the need for "legal reinforcement of social protections for residents of the indigenous small-numbered peoples of the North from large-scale resource companies."[17]

In the bulk of republic territory, in the thirty-four local regions called in the Sakha language *ulus*, Sakha traditional-style homesteads are focused on cattle and horse breeding, with intensive haying in the summer and a few greenhouses for supplementary tomatoes and cucumbers. City dwellers, including some who have lived in Yakutsk for multiple generations, try to make it back to their villages and "small homelands" to help with the haying season in the short summer (Figure 5). In 2021, I was told that the rural parents of a young Sakha family emigrating abroad poignantly had cried to them, "Who will do the haying?"

The taiga landscape in much of the republic is replete with lakes. Sakha jokingly say their ideal meadow-filled farm (*alaas*) has "one lake per household" and a herd of cattle and horses. Cattle have been in precipitous decline in the post-Soviet period, as the unstable economy and breakup of collectives meant that in some cases former sovkhoz members received only "half a cow" (personal communication, Viliui *ulus*, 1991).

Many who have had to leave their homesteads have been forced to become "reluctant entrepreneurs," small-scale traders of goods and services.[18] A 2009 Sakha activist report stated that the republic had lost nearly half of its animals from 1990 to 2008, primarily reindeer but also about 40 percent of its horses. By 2014, the numbers of cattle were estimated to be down to 194,000 from 409,000 in 1990, cut by close to 50 percent due to various intertwined economic, political, and ecological causes.[19]

A devastating "open letter" signed by a group of farmers and rural civic leaders in 2015 blamed Egor Borisov for these losses and for "the collapse of agriculture in the republic, corruption, and the destruction of the Sakha people."[20] Appealing to Borisov as born in a village himself, the letter's authors—from

FIGURE 5. Haying in Oiusaardakh village, mayor of Srednyi Kolymsk helping his mother, 1994. By author.

central regions of Ust-Aldan, Amma, Tatta, and Churabcha—lamented that 70 percent of rural areas required subsidies, that youth unemployment was at an all-time high, that unprecedented sums were spent on public relations, and that "if your pension is 100,000 rubles, a villager's is only 10,000." Citing "insulting" statements by Borisov concerning unproductivity of agricultural credit, they sorrowfully asked: "Could it be that you are no longer interested in the problems and life of the local population?" Noting that Borisov and his family "live on our taxes," they noted: "We in the villages work without days off, holidays, paid vacations, or sick leave and cannot even dream of paid travel." The letter writers bitterly asked how Borisov could have abandoned his compatriots and his people—for example, by "giving out 120 hectares of land to Chinese and Koreans . . . as well as hundreds to newcomers in Viliui, Kéntike, and Nam [regions]." They returned to the issue of lost animals by stating that "billions" budgeted for their shelters were wasted.

Despite widespread discontent, Egor Borisov was reelected for a new five-year term as "head of the republic" in 2014, with only a 51 percent voter turnout. However, the Putin administration pressured him to resign in 2018, and his successor, Aisen Nikolaev, the young, dynamic Sakha former mayor of Yakutsk, was first appointed and then elected head of the republic, in part on the hopes that the wealth of the republic would be better managed.

By 2019, numbers of cattle and deer had declined from the previous year, with a 3.4 percent decline for cattle and a 1.6 percent decline for reindeer. Horses, however, were making an unexpected comeback.[21] Horses have long been especially prestigious in the republic, including adapted-to-the-North fat furry horses prized for their nutritious meat by Sakha and by Japanese scientists and businessmen. An example of the reverse urbanization minitrend was a Sakha businessman based in Yakutsk who, having profited from a flourishing jewelry business, found his business in decline due to fewer luxury-market customers. He decided to return to raising horses on a thousand hectares of newly bought land, off a road in the direction of his original family homeland. His project represents activating productive nostalgia based on traditional Sakha values (husbandry of homestead land and horses) that could become an inspiring example to others. The land was bought under privatization conditions that permit more than long-term leasing but continue to reserve for the federal government any underground resources—such as diamonds, coal, gold, or uranium—that might be discovered on that land.

Diamond wealth has been by far the most successful of the republic's industries and exports, starting in the Soviet period, when the world's second largest open-pit diamond mine (Figure 6) was developed in the south of the republic near Mirny (compare Tichotsky 2000; Argounova-Low 2004).

Since the mine violated on a colossal scale Sakha norms of not digging unnecessary holes in the earth, early rumors abounded of diamond-mine discoverers and engineers (Russians and non-Russians alike) being supernaturally punished

FIGURE 6.   The Mirny mine (a former open-pit diamond mine) in Sakha (Yakutia), Eastern Siberia, Russia. Source: Wikimedia Commons, used by way of Creative Commons Attribution-Share Alike 3.0 Unported license.

for their mining activities. One Sakha family I know continues to attribute its multigenerational misfortunes to ill-gotten wealth from working as diamond executives. Although some diamond wealth has been discovered in the Russian North near Arkhangelsk, the Sakha Republic continues to produce over 95 percent of Russia's diamonds, despite the decline of the main mine at Mirny. Some republic residents critique their leaders for becoming too complacent about this, "putting too many eggs in the diamond basket." A colleague recalled that in the 1990s, leaders mistakenly thought "the negotiated treaty with the Center would last forever, and the diamond resources would too" (personal communication, June 2015).

At the peak of negotiated federalism in the 1990s, republic authorities under President Mikhail E. Nikolaev were able to wrest about 33 percent of diamond-industry profits away from Moscow bureaucrats and to buy diamond-finishing equipment from Belgium.[22] A jewel-grade diamond sizing and polishing factory was established outside Yakutsk. The republic-run closed joint-stock diamond company ALROSA guaranteed that designated percentages of considerable shared profits would be distributed in the republic subregions. Republic authorities also negotiated direct trade agreements with companies like famed South Africa-based De Beers for diamond sales (Balzer and Vinokurova 1996).

Diamond dynamism was the basis for the comet-like career of ALROSA's Russian director Viacheslav Shtyrov, who became the second republic president in a 2000 election filled with "dirty tricks." He was later confirmed as a President Putin appointee (compare Orttung et al. 2000). Claiming birth in the republic, he promised that the diamond industry would benefit not only his family and business associates but also republic residents at all levels. However, diamond profit "trickle down" was among the first financial arrangements to be curtailed after President Putin came to power. Sakha dominance within ALROSA was quashed in a series of nontransparent moves that included a suspicious street attack in Moscow against an ethnically Sakha diamond magnate, whose two hands were broken after he refused to sign documents ceding Sakha control. He was hospitalized for months, and someone else was found to sign the documents. By the time the international Valdai Discussion Club visited the Sakha Republic in 2009, visitors were told that only diamonds-in-the-rough were being exported, and that the republic had no diamond processing of its own, although a firm under ALROSA called ÉPL continues to process and sell finished diamonds.

Authorities seemed to be downplaying and downgrading a stunning experiment that had enabled the republic to transcend its colonial-like status as merely a raw materials source by becoming a processor of jewel-grade diamonds. Economic competition with South Africa, Israel, and India, as well as a general downturn in luxury sales, has made the diamond industry less profitable than Sakha businessmen had hoped. By 2017, a serious flood in the tunnel mine Mir controlled by ALROSA resulted in deaths, dramatic rescues, and protests. It accelerated attempts to open yet another mine in Niurba *ulus* in a protected ecological zone. These events have made the rocky record of ALROSA in the republic increasingly suspect.[23]

A 2019 narrative of a Mirny-based Sakha family member recalling the accident is worth highlighting to understand the way it changed workers' feelings about their security, their safety, and their interethnic relations. "My [uncle] is an engineer with ALROSA—he has a big job that still requires being underground. The really important above-ground jobs go to Russians. For Sakha, it is hard to get ahead there. Before and during the accident, water was coming in and Sakha and other workers recommended that the mine be evacuated and repaired. But a higher-level boss, the main engineer said, no, keep working. Many died there, about eighty workers." My interlocutor explained that this relative had maintained Sakha traditions while working in the mine, "always going into the taiga, hunting, and praying, knowing appropriate *algys* [blessings, prayers]." He attributes his survival to this connectedness with his surroundings. "He says *algys* when he goes underground, into the mine. But he keeps working there, even though he hates it and hates that it is not safe. He says if he did not work there, someone else would take his place. He helps his whole extended family financially." During the accident, he was saved because someone else had taken his place during his regular shift. "He felt terribly guilty about it—lost a lot of weight, got ill from the pressures of so many funerals and so much grief. He has been doing rituals constantly in honor of the dead." The accident had a crystallizing effect on how some Sakha, especially the younger generation, think about the diamond industry. One Sakha friend confirmed: "My daughter and her friends used to wear their diamonds with pride—and now they don't wear them, on principle. They say, 'What are diamonds worth, if they kill people?'" (compare Solovyeva 2019).

Other major extractive industries in the republic include gold and uranium. While these are mostly associated with Sakha and Russian business magnates who have government connections, an Évenki community collective was given a license to participate in a gold-mining conglomerate in the Neriungri region, beginning in 2014. Sixty percent of the start-up capital came from a republic fund to enhance Évenki well-being in compensation for losing lands to the planned and unpopular Kankun Hydroelectric Dam, and 40 percent came from an existing gold company inexplicably called Amber, based in the Évenki Iengra district.[24]

A significant economic drive in several regions involves the growth of the energy industry, transcending years of specialist wisdom warning that the costs of extractions and pipelines in the Far East were prohibitive. In 2020, electricity costs in Sakha were reportedly ten times more than in Moscow. The long-entrenched coal industry, developed in the post-Soviet period with the participation of the South Korean firm Khende for both domestic use and export, is a major source of pollution. More farsighted and scientifically creative are bold new advances in solar energy: for example, large-scale experimental panels in Batagai. This is particularly crucial given that the Batagai Crater, a rapidly collapsing "permafrost" breach 3.5 times larger than similar craters in the Canadian North, confirms Siberia as a hot spot of intensifying climate change. In 2010, a Sakha cultural activist in Verkhoyansk, several hours drive from Batagai through a stunning mountain range, correlated cratering with climate change:

> Near Uetaakh is a place where the land has collapsed into a chasm as deep as a mountain going down. It happened in the last ten years . . . Everyone knows that such dangerous places are rife in the mountains. Near there is where they found that ancient horse—such things are reemerging as the land shifts. Permafrost changes don't begin to describe it. There are more fires, more craters in bigger territories. The land has collapsed in a huge territory. It is as if a lens of ice has been broken through. People are working on layers that are being revealed. It might be good for the archeologists—but it is very unsettling for the rest of us. Sure, I think that global warming exists.[25]

Solar energy has been supported by the innovative company SakhaEnergo, under the former army general, military engineer, and Évenki leader Anatoly Chomchoev. He also has founded a nonprofit called Test Ground of Cold, in part to address dramatic climate change evidence in the republic.[26] Widely admired in the republic as a passionate leader who cares about the environment, he contrasts sharply with other nonlocal energy executives.

Among the first in the 1990s to delve into Eastern Siberian gas and oil extraction was the ill-fated company Yukos, chaired by the subsequently jailed tycoon and former deputy energy minister Mikhail Khodorkovsky. In Sakha, his company interests were mostly (hostilely) taken over by government controlled Rosneft. Gazprom and Rosenergo also have been increasingly active in the region in the past decade. Focus has been on buying or leasing lands for extraction and pipeline transit. The communities most affected are not only Sakha horse and cattle breeders but also Évenki and Éveny reindeer herders. An activist told me in 2012, "Gazprom is buying up all the land that Éveny and Évenki reindeer breeders use, that they need." Local perception is that outsiders with megabucks can come in and transform rural Sakha, Éveny, and Évenki communities, bypassing or bribing local authorities. As a Sakha colleague explained in 2015: "There is more corruption than I ever remember. Sakha Republic was not like that before . . . This is not economic progress—it is feathering the nest of a privileged few at the expense of others . . . It is especially bad in the Far North where people are not paying enough attention."

At least four oil refineries operate in the republic, some with financing from China. A typical agreement for one in Aldan *ulus* was signed between the Chinese investor Huaqing Housing Holdings and the Yakutsk-based Tuimaada-Neft [Tuimaada Oil] led by the Sakha businessman Ivan Makarov, who also chairs Sakhatransneftegaz, a gas pipeline operator majority-owned by the republic government. Combining economics, politics, and immunity, Makarov became a United Russia party deputy in the republic parliament, Il Tumen.[27]

A well-publicized pipeline agreement with China was signed in Yakutsk in 2014, ESPO—East Siberia-Pacific Ocean Oil Pipeline. This was a "phase 2" expansion of a line built by Transneft that was originally supposed to skirt Lake Baikal, but protests there, and other political considerations, caused President Putin to suggest a more northerly route, with phase 1 beginning in 2009. Publicity for the line touts its "high-pressure sealing." However, numerous violations have occurred in its building and contracting, especially at pump stations and oil tank facilities near the Lena River and at population centers at Lensk and Aldan. Specialists are particularly concerned about insufficient wrap-around tunneling where it crosses the Lena River at Olekminsk. The line also links a new oil and gas Tass-Yuriak field with a separate spur, financed in part with British Petroleum and Chinese investment. The controversial five-thousand-kilometer pipeline is projected to supply a special high grade of Siberian oil to China, Japan, and Korea.[28] By 2019, local villagers in the Sakha Republic had become sarcastic about this Power of Siberia pipeline and its newsworthy name. Today, they are furious that they were not consulted regarding its route, and that they have reaped no energy benefits. Far from empowering them in any way, in many places they are still reliant on polluting coal energy. Local residents complain that Siberia's valuable resources were sold at low prices to the Chinese.

Since the annexation of Crimea in 2014, the United States and the European Union have imposed sanctions on Russia, widely affecting its citizens, including in the Sakha Republic. President Putin repeatedly proclaims that these sanctions have made Russia stronger, despite steep declines in the ruble's value and in energy prices. His reasoning is that Russia's domestic industries can be supported, and will grow and flourish, without Western imports. In the Sakha Republic, this has been felt through intensified pressures to develop more industries, including several oil refineries and a highly controversial gas-processing chemical plant near the Lena River at Nizhnii Bestiak, opposite Yakutsk. This is also near the site of a planned first railway bridge over the Lena River, but its funding reputedly was diverted to Crimea. An additional ripple effect has been that a World Bank program to refurbish and further develop a system of kindergartens was canceled. Not only the ruble and basic infrastructure but also social programs have been affected by Russia's foreign policy, resulting Western sanctions, and Putin's counter-sanctions. By 2020, "Crimea Is Ours" exuberance had worn off for many citizens of Russia.

Ecology Activism

Intensified development has brought increased concerns for the ecological health of the republic. Some Sakha activists, such as the educator and Congress of Sakha People deputy Ivan Shamayev, have made direct correlations between the despoliation of Sakha lands by outsiders and the need to take control of sustained development for the benefit of the Sakha people. While some of the rhetoric has been nationalist, it has resonated directly with people who have long integrated their sense of well-being with their close-to-the-land livelihoods. Horse and cattle breeders stress values that enable harmony with a fertile but fragile permafrost oecumene, where sacred groves punctuate the landscape. Long ago, spirit-enforced prohibitions forbade the puncturing of land with any sharp objects. The open-pit diamond mine at Mirny has become a symbol of the horrors of overdevelopment for Sakha ecology activists. The value of the precious and precarious Mother Lena—one of Siberia's huge northern-flowing river arteries that has been a Sakha lifeline for centuries—has become another rallying cry.

By 2009, the republic's Save [the] Lena! campaign, founded in 2007–2008, took on special power and poignancy when new and faulty construction on the East Siberia-Pacific Ocean Oil Pipeline was said to have caused at least three breaches into the river. This was at first a multiethnic and semiofficial movement, since the republic's own, aptly named Ministry for Nature Protection produced reports, public and secret, condemning Lena River despoliation. In the Sakha language, the ministry name includes the word "Nature," *Aiyylgha*, containing the core word for "spirit," and some ministry officials have tried to maintain that spirit.[29]

Calling the ESPO underwater crossing of the Lena "nothing but an oil bomb," the Save Lena! website explained dangers and activist countermeasures in detail: "With the aim to protect this mighty river, we organized the first stage of the social action Save Lena! . . . We urged the company and government to minimize the ecological risks by using the tunnel method of crossing. The action went with big public involvement—we managed to unite our forces and gathered more than twenty thousand voices for Lena's protection."[30] However, despite the alarm sent to all levels of government, by the spring of 2009 Transneft had quickly built a "trench crossing" of the Lena at Solyanka village near Olekminsk.

The original organizer of Save Lena! was Ekaterina Evseyeva, founder of the Эйгэ (Eyge [Éigé], "Surroundings," Sakha) environmental education center, with colleagues Valentina Dmitrieva, of Eyge and the civic society coalition Our Homeland Yakutia; Arsen Tomsky of the company Sakha Internet; Maria Ivanova, editor of the major newspaper *Yakutsk vechernyi*; the sociologist Yury Zhegusov; and the technical specialist Terentii Ermolaev. They were supported by the professional Coalition of Ecologists of Siberia and the Far East, as well as by the Russian branch of the World Wildlife Federation and the London Zoological Society. By 2010, when I visited their cramped offices in a small private apartment, they were under threat, pressured to drop their international funding or be branded "foreign agents," and warned to cease their highly successful publicity and judicial campaigns. While Save Lena! became inactive online, Eyge has continued as a community-organized "center for ecological enlightenment."

In interviews over the past decade with interlocutors who need to remain anonymous, I learned that the pipeline had been touted in the republic as the "construction project of the century," even though local geologists and specialists in the Yakutsk-based Permafrost Institute had recommended a different route. "Our republic authorities were too weak," explained one interlocutor, and so Save Lena! members decided to introduce a "collective court case" on the municipal level, together with the Évenki Indigenous Association, and with extensive open testimony of experts against the pipeline. "We won, even though we did not have fancy paid lawyers," but there was a predictable appeal, and the next two times the republic courts rejected further claims. "It was our first win that was surprising," explained the activists, "and so we gave up on that [legal] direction." A prominent lawyer working with them was Viacheslav Sobelev, and V. Varlamova has won cases subsequently. The local Sakha Permafrost Institute continues to voice complaints, especially concerning lack of appropriate linings in pipeline canals.

One activist with the penname of Sanaia [Sorrow] is connected with the Community Ecology Center and its local offshoots, begun by scientists for the health of the republic. They monitor "fast track" projects that obfuscate full environmental impact by dividing each mining, logging, and energy project into multiple components "to confuse people." The activists catch "huge violations" and are particularly irked by Moscow scientists' rubber stamping or ignorance, since they "do not know local conditions."

While acknowledging some partnership with the Ministry for Nature Protection, activists explain that their collaboration became strained after the court cases, and that mutual understanding between republic and federal (Moscow-level) authorities has deteriorated. My sense of increased monitoring of the monitors coincided with my suspicion that I was followed after interviewing activists.[31] Five years later, some of the leaders of the original group Save Lena! had been cowed, but younger activists stepped forward with a similarly named We Defend the Lena! movement. In the past decade, local level enthusiasm at various ecology centers has centered on monitoring water quality, especially in Olekminsk and Lensk. Given unchecked industrial waste runoff and open dumps in northern high-density population centers such as Tiksi, Batagai, Verkhoyansk, Viliuisk, Mirny, and Yakutsk itself, ongoing plans include water monitoring throughout the republic, working with local teachers. Évenki and Éveny coordinators are included, such as the Éveny representative Svetlana Egoreva, who has critiqued gold industry processing in Aldan. On a field trip in Aldan, local reindeer routes were studied for how they have been adversely influenced by gas pipelines and influxes of workers.

Sakha Republic was early to adopt a Law on Nature Conservation, in 1991 before Russia's Duma passed a similar law (Burnasheva 2019, 135). Expert testimony for energy projects has been built into republic law, but experts are sometimes ignored or discredited. One confided in frustration in 2015: "The energy workers are constantly violating ecological standards, promising much but they are only promises. [We] know how to speak well, but what is happening on the ground is horrible, and [we] are powerless to stop it."

Existing pipelines and planned mines infringe on some lands that are nature preserves (*zapovedniki*, Russian) or parks (*parki*). Residents are especially concerned about these precious, supposedly protected sacred lands. By 2017, some lands that were designated Special Ecological Zones in Niurba were being undermined by development interests with deep pockets and the ability to bribe local officials to support development in court cases. The unbribable, popular *ulus* head Boris Popov was fired and placed under house arrest for trying to defend the ecological zones. His case represents an example of thwarted leadership and repressed attempts to create civilian-official synergies that could form the basis of local civic society building.

Activists are increasingly worried about the polluting gold and coal industries in Southern Sakha, including inside republic and federal level preserves. Sakha consumers in towns and villages complain they are forced to use the most polluting kinds of brown coal, perhaps a symptom of the decline of the increasingly desperate industry. Coal mining management has been notorious throughout Siberia for ruthless displacement of communities standing in the way of development. Outside the republic, in the Yenisei River area, a mixed ethnic village was burned in a suspected case of arson to make way for coal extraction. The victims were too terrified to bring a court case, although they reported the tragedy to RAIPON leaders in Moscow, enabling Indigenous ecological activists to spread warnings about it (Balzer 2017, 12).

Illegal forestry devastation has especially insidious effects, sometimes hidden deep within difficult-to-access regions. In 2015, a colleague from Oymyakon explained: "The implications of ecological destruction in the fragile Far North are particularly serious. In the preserve, hunters are constantly seeing how the forests are being illegally cut down. First it seemed like it was just a little bit at a time, but it builds up—the hectares just get eaten away." An ecologist later explained more precisely that Oymyakon is known for illegal cutting for basic housing for the locals, but that the illegal forestry in the south of the republic has been far worse. This Indigenous expert suggested a scale of relatively serious levels of illegal logging by outsiders at one end, in contrast with logging by local hunters and fishers whose needs are modest and sustainable yet remain technically illegal.

Illegal logging, including possibly by Chinese workers, was said to be the initial spark for forest fires that ranged out of control in the Far East in the summer of 2019, devastating an area as large as that of the simultaneous and far more widely publicized fires in the Amazon. Huge resentment and unhelpful rumors accompanied news of the fires, which were hard to cover up. Fires began in the Far East region of Primorye before those in the Sakha Republic, and some flyover videos seemed to implicate arson to hide illegal Chinese logging. Without specifying ethnicity-based blame, an ecology activist wrote to me in August 2019: "Siberia is burning, and in Yakutia [Sakha Republic] there are many fires. On WhatsApp helicopter videos are circulating. Local people also have written that they observed outsiders in the fire zone before the fires. People suggest that in spring a vast forest was cut down and that loggers did not want the evidence of their crime exposed." Another interpretation of the fires is that they could help clear land that can then be tested for underground resource exploitation. However, a Sakha colleague based in Yakutsk warned: "In Yakutia, the result will be different. Permafrost under exposed forest melts and crawls, creating bog as in the Batagai area of Verkhoyansk. And it makes it harder for anyone to access resources."[32]

In 2020–2021, forest fires proved worse than previous years and were widely attributed to climate change as well as arson. Some, including rural informants of the ecologist Vera Solovyeva, also viewed their underlying causes as due to lack of understanding of the benefits of traditionally sanctioned controlled burns based on Indigenous ecological knowledge (Solovyeva 2021; compare Whyte 2018).

Official efforts to monitor and organize ecological concern have been worthy of notice but not enough to keep up with the problems. In 2014, Aisen

Nikolaev, then-mayor of Yakutsk before becoming republic head, together with the Ministry for Nature Protection, Russia's Foreign Ministry, the Ministry of Youth and Family, and the Ministry of Education, hosted the Tenth International Youth Ecological Forum.[33] An Ecology Fund and a parliamentary advisory committee were instituted in 2015, along with local ecological councils in the regions. For example, in Amga *ulus* an "ecology council under the Amga inspectorate of nature" was created by drawing in grassroots civic society leaders such as the head of a fathers' group called BAAT, a women's group activist, a leader of local youth naturalists, a kindergarten teacher, a schoolteacher, two librarians, and a local youth representative of the Sakha network named for O. P. Ivanov-Sidorkevich.[34] They organized an ecology bulletin, an ecology training program in the schools, and regular volunteer trash pickups. Such local volunteerism is rooted in ancestral ecological values, yet the style harkens back to Soviet-period *subbotniki*, Saturday labor that was rarely fully optional. By the 1990s, enthusiastic youth brigades had mobilized in several regions specifically to clean sacred sites. Another harnessing of ecological activist energy was the proclamation of a republic-wide Day of the Lena River, complete with a literary contest for the best essay on ecological awareness. Since 2015, this new tradition has continued on July 2 with official propaganda.[35] Many of these efforts resemble activities by organizations sarcastically nicknamed GONGOs—governmentally organized nongovernmental organizations. In this context, President Putin's naming of 2017 as the Year of Ecology can be seen as an attempt to coopt the issue.

The more independent Congress of Sakha People, created in 1992 to "unite the Sakha people," met in Yakutsk in 2019 with a focus on ecology. Some of the organizers and participants, including republic Il Tumen deputies, were pressured to pull out, but the congress proceeded with sessions that included "land, ecology, and control." Meeting only for the third time, most of their presentations were in the Sakha language. All too familiar exposés on energy industry disasters on the Viliui River and diamond industry accidents were enumerated, with emphasis on the deteriorating health of locals and need for further scientific documentation.[36] Fedot Tumusov, the For a Just Russia oppositionist deputy from Sakha Republic to Russia's Duma, warned of the ripple effects of unchecked development and road building in the North, where "we must not separate state funding from community needs. We have heavily burdened life conditions in the North and must not be made to pay for our roads." Earlier, after a small community protest over undrinkable water on the banks of the Viliui River, he demanded the resignation of the republic's ecology minister, Sakhamin Afanasev, and the firing of ALROSA diamond industry executives for culpability in river contamination at Viliui and elsewhere.[37]

Confirmation of ecological fears has come in the form of extensive flooding in the republic. Among the worst was the 1998 flood at Lensk, now fully rebuilt in record time with emergency federal funds, but many floods have occurred since. The 2003 Yana River flood was particularly painful, as was one on the Yana in 2009, a year before I visited the region. In the village of Elges, a local cattle herder explained: "Villages where the flooding was worst were Sartang and Barylaas. Sartang warned Barylaas that the flooding was heading their way. But they did not believe it—this had never happened before. And so even the second village was wiped out when it didn't have to be—tragically."

Although some Sakha residents persist in not linking these floods with climate change or industrialization, that has begun to change. An official survey sponsored by the Humanities Institute acknowledged yet downplayed problems, concluding "public perception is dominated by skeptics, considering climate change as a factor complicating sustainability of the urban environment."[38] Sakha President Egor Borisov in 2013, when he was still allowed to be called "president," similarly recognized environmental instabilities but stopped short of blaming increased industrialization for climate change: "As many as twelve municipal regions suffered from spring and summer floods. But while one part of the republic was suffering from floods, another experienced lack of water . . . serious difficulties with the supply of goods to Northern Russia during the navigation period occurred."[39]

In the past decade, flooding has meant numerous village evacuations, creating the ripple effects of a psychology of uncertainty exacerbated by economic fears. By 2020, approximately ninety-six villages were said to have been relocated or in need of relocation. An acquaintance rather cynically claimed that some Sakha families along the Lena were benefiting from repeated compensations for annual flooding of their riverbank homes, when they had already moved to higher ground.[40] Fraud, if it has occurred, is probably exceptional; clarifying journalism would help. Many villages have had to be moved in the Verkhoyansk region alone, with minimal assistance, insurance, or news coverage.

Additional ecological disasters include eroded islands off the Arctic coastline and further ramifications of extensive permafrost melting. Increasing amounts of swampland in the spring, followed by intense heat later in the summer, render animal-based homestead and village lifestyles difficult to maintain. In addition, swampland has developed from melting permafrost at other times of year, and some summers have been cold and rainy. These variations mean that the capriciousness of climate change wreaks havoc on planning and strains values of long-inculcated ecological flexibility and adaptation (Solovyeva 2021).

In the vast Sakha Republic, communities have experienced different kinds of ecological problems and responded to them in diverse ways. As the sociologist

Yury Zhegusov pointed out in 2015: "Industrialization is not so serious in many areas of Sakha, for example [my homeland] Tatta *ulus*. But people do worry about ecological change—last year there was a flooding of the hayfields and people were worried about how they would feed their cows." He refined the urbanization trend: "Everywhere people have had to give up their cattle and move to more urbanized places . . . It is the elders over fifty who are trying to hold on to their cattle, but the young people don't necessarily want to farm—although some of the younger ones are going into horse breeding on a larger scale, rather than cattle raising" (personal communication June 4, 2015).

This variation on the "can't keep 'em down on the farm" phenomenon has specific implications for Sakha ecological awareness. Since many urbanites keep up with their root communities by going home for haying, holidays, and family events, they also have developed a strong sense of "small-homeland" loyalty that enables networks and homeland community solidarity (*zemliachestvo*, Russian) to be maintained in the city. This is especially crucial in precarious economic conditions when, as one friend put it in 2015, "people are pouring into Yakutsk, creating an overflow with not much industry to sustain workers." News of local oil spills and other disasters travels fast, whether or not it makes official channels or newspapers. Examples of this include oil spills from tankers on the Lena and on the Indigirka during the always chaotic and breathtaking ice breakup in the spring of 2015. The first spill occurred in May near Olekminsk, and the second in June, in the North in Abyi *ulus*. After word of mouth had magnified the disasters, details were posted officially. The ships were evacuated, and the spills contained under difficult conditions.[41]

By 2015, a new well-publicized threat loomed, the possible introduction of a gas-processing chemical plant in Megino-Kangalas *ulus* near the Lena's riverbank at Nizhnii Bestiak, opposite Yakutsk. The politics behind the gas-chemical-plant project are murky, but the reaction to it became a microcosm of an impressively fast-responding civic society mobilization that some thought no longer likely. Regional officials themselves balked at the project, and two thousand to seven thousand citizens (depending on whose estimates are used) from both sides of the Lena River responded with petitions and a major rally in Yakutsk.[42] With other leaders, Rudolf K. Mikhailov spearheaded a community coalition called We Are Against the Gas-Chemical Plant. The movement began under the moniker "We Defend the Lena!" and by midsummer that group had been made semiofficial. During the rally, tapping into Sakha nationalism, an anonymous interviewee on a local news broadcast explicitly fretted about the danger of nonlocal workers flooding into the region and disturbing "our Sakha culture." A more universal banner at the rally (in Russian) reminded: "Health and Ecology Are Not Renewable Once Spoiled."

Citizens from Megino-Kangalas, the region most at risk, were particularly active in opposing the fledgling project, concerned about the quality of their increasingly brackish water and further deterioration of their rural lifestyles. The demographics of the rally ranged widely, with university students collecting signatures. A young friend involved in the movement explained that she is heartened that "middle aged people in their forties and fifties are protesting; in other words, people with some experience and knowledge are waking up that they need to act on ecology issues." A Sakha economist privately assessed the protests and the economics of the project, predicting that eventually a "technological solution to address ecological concerns" could be found: the site would have to be changed to somewhere "far from any main rivers," and "adequate oversight" would need to be guaranteed.[43] In 2015, a republic delegation including the ministers for nature protection and of development was sent to explore an already-running prototype in the Urals for feasibility in permafrost conditions. People wondered whether their contradictory portfolios would hinder their effectivity, and whether it was a brilliant propaganda ploy. Officials in person and on TV calmed the protesters with assurances that it was premature to complain before any final decision had been made on the plant or its environmental impact report. Protesters specifically condemned documented subsidies for Surgutneftegaz projects, including a road that is used by their workers and not the public.[44]

The result of all this protest, and perhaps cool-headed republic leadership using expert testimony prevailing behind the scenes, is that the chemical plant was first postponed and then diverted to a less visible site farther south in the Irkutsk region, not in a republic but within an area Buryats consider part of their traditional homeland. While one lesson may be that protesters can win occasional successes if they rally enough people, sadly the case is not so simple. The new plant is close to the source of the Lena River, harming Buryats living nearby and affecting communities in the Sakha Republic downstream.

Additional community-based ecology battles demonstrate the importance of multileveled appeals and interethnic cooperation. In 2011–2012, plans for basalt mining and a factory were blocked by villagers of Sinsk, Khangalas *ulus*, with local Sakha and Évenki pressure led by the schoolteacher and local council deputy Maria Golokova. They lobbied Yakutsk officials and submitted documents to the UN. Legal and moral arguments about ecological risk, local population health, biodiversity and cultural legacy prevailed at least temporarily over economic development, with a new protection zone planned. However, currently a basalt factory in nearby Pokrovsk has been polluting the Lena River. In 2021, in the already extensively damaged Viliui River region, villagers of Chinéké won their Sakha supreme court case against a solid waste landfill that would have ruined a local park. To win, pensioners and many others donated rubles toward the legal proceedings that were supported by the republic-wide ecology activist group Eyge. Another fight led by Eyge began in 2021 against a signed agreement with the Chinese metallurgical company Jinyan to build a coke factory in the southern town of Neriungri, just when such dirty technology is being phased out in much of the world.

A disaster was averted in 2020–2021 with the deferral of logging tenders along the scenic Amga River, after local and republic-wide protests called attention to the lack of Indigenous consultation and the inadvisability of importing loggers (including Chinese) during the coronavirus pandemic. The proposed logging also violated Évenki claims of contractual "territory of traditional land use" rights. Some perceived as symbolic that later in the spring, triplets were born to a cow in that same Amga *ulus*. Sakha celebrated by touting this "good luck omen" as a reinforcement of the traditional value of the human-animal connection (*kihi-kueuhu*) during spring fertility renewal. In the past decade, some have felt a pull back toward fulfillments of a rural life, with a renewed respect for animal husbandry and agriculture.

Sacred Parks, Protected Lands

As we have seen, some of the most significant environmental protection has come, and indeed needs to come, from within the republic government, with the cooperation of a nonradicalized civic society. This is a pragmatic approach repeatedly emphasized by the Sakha sociologist and former parliament deputy Uliana Vinokurova, who has served as an advisor to the Ministry for Nature Protection. A particularly important manifestation, where ecological and cultural interests converge, is the multitiered system of nature preserves, even if their restricted access is not always respected or enforced. Social considerations complicate policy: overly protected lands can have debilitating ramifications for Indigenous reindeer breeders, hunters, and fishers if they lose access to lands they consider traditional by usufruct (compare Fondahl 2003; Fondahl and Lazebnik 2001; Fondahl et al. 2014). Thus, delicate handling of local multiethnic relations becomes a factor in ecology politics, so that Indigenous groups such as the Éveny and the Évenki do not become perceived or accused poachers on their own lands.

By the end of the 1990s, under President Mikhail Nikolaev, the protected lands system impressively had expanded from Soviet times to encompass over 14 percent of the republic's territory, with two federal-level reserves (*zapovedniki*, Russian), forty-four republic-level "resource reserves (*zakazniki*, Russian)," four national nature parks (*parki*, Russian), twenty-six *ulus*-level protected landscapes, forty-one reserve lands, and numerous "nature monuments."[45] By 2017, according to the official website of the republic, under the law "On Special Preserved Nature Territories," approximately three million hectares came under protected categories, called in Sakha *Ytyk kéré sirdér* (sacred places preservation), nearly a quarter of the whole republic. This includes 2 federal-level reserves; 1 botanical garden under the jurisdiction of Russia's Academy of Sciences; 6 federal-level National nature parks (*Natsional'nye prirodnye parki*, Russian, including Lena Pillars); the state-protected "Ian Mammoth" Pleistocene-era protected site (*zakaznik*, Russian); 113 republic-level resource reserves (*rezervaty*, Russian); 26 unique lakes; 2 special landshaft protected sites (*okhraniaemye landshafty*, Russian); 17 natural monuments (*pamiatniki prirody*, Russian); and 16 protected zones (*zony pokoi*, Russian).[46]

A vivid example of a protected zone is the Kytalyk (Crane, in Sakha) Wetland Resource Reserve, 24,911 square kilometers within the Arctic Circle that achieved republic-level status in 1996, with some funding from World Wildlife Foundation (Germany). Founded by the Évenki scientist Nikolai Germogenov, local Sakha and Évenki community leaders supported the project. For example, Ivan Diachkovski, a Sakha activist with a shamanic family legacy, became a self-designated manager-defender of this home to Siberian cranes, sacred for many Sakha, as well as wild reindeer, bears, sables, ermines, foxes, and rare musk oxen. For many years, he lived in the reserve. While his enthusiasm occasionally outpaced his knowledge, as when he tried to cradle cranes for schoolchildren or transport wounded cranes, he exemplifies the commitment of some rural leaders to literally revitalizing symbols of Sakha tradition in new ways. Jewelry, art, and dance groups named Kytalyk depict and valorize the Siberian crane. In Sakha lore, it is said that if a person sees a pair of cranes dancing at sunrise, the viewer will be blessed for life. Ivan's father showed him dancing cranes while he was a sickly child, and he attributes his recovery to the cranes.

In a 2007 interview with me, Ivan emphasized the alarming interconnectedness of Sakha's ecology with China: "Look at where the migrating cranes from the South are starting from. Their home turf in China was right in the area of the disastrous Three Gorges Dam. [Their migration has been influenced by] horrible effects of industrialization, creation of artificial swamps, and worse."[47] Subsequently, these ramifications may have influenced Chinese authorities to support recovery projects for the famed Siberian cranes, provide money for crane reserves, and sponsor scientific research on the cranes. Ironically, Siberian crane seasonal migrations have given the Chinese a slim basis for claiming a stake in the Arctic and membership in the Arctic Council, along with other hot issues such as energy development (with Gasprom) in Yamal, Northern Sea Route shipping, and trade.[48]

The magnificent Lena Pillars Park is a special case of multipronged mobilization. It was ratified in 1995 as a republic-level natural protection site, with 485,000 hectares. Many Sakha had for centuries revered it as a pilgrimage destination, best accessed from the Lena River. By 2012, its local administrators had achieved their dream of its recognition as a United Nations World Heritage Site, "one of the unique places on the planet with a relatively untouched by humans ecosystem." Some exulted: "After many years of efforts to have the Lena Pillars Nature Park included in the list of world heritage, it has finally happened!"[49] Others were concerned that the upgrade to a federal-level park lessened local and republic control over incursions. Indeed, violations in the extensive rocky, forested area have been less easy to monitor and prosecute.

My experiences at the Lena Pillars (Cliffs) have always been numinous (Figure 7). In 1986, I went with a colleague's family via a tourist boat. As we were descending from the peak, we heard the unmistakable chant of a spontaneous *okhuohai*, improvisational poetry chanting accompanied by a circle dance, emanating from the clearing we had just left. We raced back and joined a circle of about twenty gracefully swaying people from another boat. In 1992, I returned with friends, including then newly appointed Minister of Culture Andrei Borisov, and we created our own dance circle of talented singers, who took turns leading mesmerizing chants for hours near the precipice overlooking the sea-like Lena. Several other times I was with musician friends, and each hiking, campfire, and dancing encounter in the park, recently renovated with a reception pavilion and sacred post (*sérgé*), renewed our sense of powerful joy to be alive in such an exhilarating, seemingly miraculous place. This helps explain why my Sakha friends say they are at once proud that the Pillars have been recognized as one of the world's wonders, and yet are also leery of the impact too much tourism may bring.

Many Sakha feel the same way about another astonishing sacred place, called Kiḥylyakh, high in the Verkhoyansk mountain range in the Far North, where enormous rock formations form fantasy-provoking natural sculptures. Some have seen warriors, lovers embracing, and a woman with arms raised in prayer to the sky. Some resonate with a wise elder seated at a stone table or a musician playing a jaw harp. Others recall the Sakha horse deity D'öhögöi Ayii and an Évenki woman who turned into a bear, according to local legends. Many are awed by rays of phosphorescence coming off the peak, said to have deterred frightened Soviet miners. Until recently, when the peak, one of its precipitous access paths, and a nearby base came under the jurisdiction of the republic's Ministry of Tourism and Business, Kiḥylyakh was considered to be off-bounds to most mortals, forbidden to everyone except shamans and those willing to seek spiritual enlightenment in self-punishing humility. The ascent takes five to eight hours.

FIGURE 7. Lena Cliffs. By author.

FIGURE 8. Kiḧylyakh stone figures on sacred mountain top, 2010. Used with permission by the healer Mikhail Mikhailovich Postnikov.

When I did fieldwork at Kiḫylyakh in 2010, one local elder called it a "blessing place" and recalled it as a site of legendary shamanic competitions. "In the old days," before the tourism boom, women were prohibited if they were not female shamans (*udagan*, Sakha), precisely because it was considered to be a dangerous, spirit-filled portal to the sky (Figure 8). Currently, its main guide, Rigoletta Artemonova, born around 1969 in a nearby village, is an impressive Sakha woman, known for her athleticism and spiritual power, learned from one of the underground local male shamans (*oiuun*, Sakha) of the Soviet period. He was secretly called "*Iubaan-oiuun*, keeper of Kiḫylyakh," and Riga shyly admitted after some coaxing, "Iubaan showed me *aptaa*—how magical the mountains are and how healing."[50]

Spiritual and Cultural Ramifications

At the heart of all Sakha ecological concerns are philosophical issues that reach well beyond any one preserve violation, tourist site, diamond mine, chemical plant, or oil pipeline to various contested definitions of sacred land and homeland development. At one level, the whole of Sakha territory, in its current political boundaries, is sacred. In this sense, the Sakha phrase *ytyk sir* (sacred land) is comparable to the Māori concept *Waahi Tapu*. At a more specific level, special places of extraordinary beauty tied to historical heritage, sacred ceremonies, and ancient trees, mountains, cliffs, and river valleys are to be especially cherished and sustained. It may seem ironic or hypocritical that a Sakha energy company executive can call one of his companies Tuimaada Oil, using the Sakha name of the Lena River Valley that is home to the republic capital and is considered the very center of Sakha sacred territory. But he may well not see irony or contradiction, given his effusive public statement in honor of the summer solstice in 2015: "The solstice ceremony Yhyakh is the most important festival in Yakutia, symbolizing the awakening of nature. Without a doubt, Yhyakh is the spiritual fundament of the Sakha people, which is inextricably connected to nature. Yhyakh each year gets increasingly elaborate."[51] Ivan Makarov seems to have mastered the art of disconnecting his Sakha spiritual identity from his master-of-industry job.

A substantial list of sacred sites has been documented by the Ministry of Culture, and the sites have various kinds of protection at *ulus*, republic, and federal levels. Some sites overlap with the local natural protection zones (for example Lena Pillars/Cliffs), but emphasis is on places with specific cultural footprints. In 2013, Oksana Tagytovna Mikhailova, a dedicated self-identifying "Yakutianka" of mixed-ethnic Tatar-Russian heritage, responsible for compiling this list for the federal government, explained to me that they had submitted cases for "158 beautifully documented archeological sites—and about 20 are sacred places." She added, "We are in a new process with this register, and so we don't know how our suggestions will be verified. We are pretty sure that 100 percent will not be accepted. We turned in forty kilograms of documents. The ratification of our suggestions will mean money will be needed to protect them."[52] Indeed, as money has become short for cultural projects, and as a new minister, more associated with sport than culture, has taken the theater director Andrei Borisov's place, some of these protection applications have been rejected. Yet the principle remains that it is crucial to keep places of extraordinary cultural patrimony secure. Among the main places are burial sites; farmsteads with *sérgé* (decorative horse posts) older than forty years; sacred groves with towering trees festooned with offerings and accompanied by *sérgé*; as well as many summer solstice ceremony sites on the outskirts of villages and towns.

One key to Sakha definitions of a sacred site is that it epitomizes the connection of Sakha individuals with their homeland, with the spirituality of what is termed in the Sakha epics as "the middle world," *ortu doidu*, the basis in the natural-social world of *sier tuom*, ritualized respect within the Sakha belief system (*itégél*) (Fedorov 2011). Spiritual revitalization in the republic since the late Soviet period has taken many forms, some competitive with each other, often involving a complex mix of Russian Orthodoxy, Turkic cosmology, animism, and shamanism. An early cultural revival advocacy group took the name Kut-Siur, glossed as Heart-Soul-Mind-Body. Among its leaders was the late Sakha linguist Lazar Afanas'ev, who promulgated *aiyy yeurekhe* (benevolent spirit teaching) in newspapers, speeches, seasonal rituals, and community center cosmology displays. Especially popular in the 1990s, his followers were able to integrate their "return to traditional values" ecology advocacy and language revitalization into a republic-wide *aiyy yeurekhe* school program (Afanas'ev 2002). This was subsequently curtailed as the republic Ministry of Education was brought into greater compliance with Moscow-directed federal standards. But some teachers and village leaders continue to be loyal to the ideas, if not the specific program.

One famed and popular Sakha healer, Ed'ii (Older Sister) Dora, has combined curing individuals with increasingly advocating attention to healing the ecology of the whole region, especially along the sacred Lena River and its tributaries. Dora explained after one devastating flood: "Nature has eyes, a bellybutton, and roots, veins. The spirit of our great earth has east, west, north, and south sides, with a strong foundation. We, the Uriankhai Sakha, created strong, were born on that very place that the spirit of Nature built his hearth. We are designated to live in harmony with Nature . . . yet we, despite considering ourselves a wise people in preserving our language and history, have violated the behests of Nature and for that sin are being punished. Nature, insulted, has responded with the bitter tears of a flood" (Protopopova 1999, 177–78).

A healer with whom I worked closely, the late Klavdia Maksimova, who took the pseudonym Saiyyna (Summer), has had groups of followers chant during her rituals: "I am well. I am Sakha. I am here, in and with this land" (Balzer 2012, 125, 150–53). In a philosophy she termed the "Triad of Cosmos-Person-Land," she made the connection for Sakha followers that their well-being was integrally connected with the health of their homeland, conceived as their whole republic and smaller local birthplaces. Her teachings live on, with followers active in a healing center on the outskirts of Yakutsk, and in purification rituals at the entrance to the annual summer solstice ceremonial grounds at Us Khatyn (Three Birches), near Yakutsk.

Two additional rival spiritual centers have been established in Yakutsk, one an impressive temple-like structure called Archie Dieté, or House of Purification, and the other a more modest traditional-style *balagan* (log house) on the edge of town, called Aiyy Dieté, or House of Spirits. Both sponsor ceremonies and literary evenings. They have outposts in various towns and villages and have been active in Sakha language and literature recovery as well as the rekindling of ecology-oriented Sakha rituals, especially the summer solstice celebration Yhyakh, which many consider the Sakha New Year.[53] Since 1992, it has been an official republic holiday, with local *ulus* taking turns sponsoring the main annual festival. Each Yhyakh has a particular theme (approved by the Ministry of Culture), including epic (*olonkho*) valorization, interethnic harmony, and anniversaries of the Great Fatherland War (World War II).

To elaborate on the book's introduction, the widely celebrated Yhyakh has come to symbolize the resurgence of Sakha pride, but it too has many debated manifestations. In 2015, the official republic-level ceremony, designated a special *Olonkho Yhyakh*, was held for three days in Churabcha *ulus*, with an unprecedented budget and such an extravaganza opening that some in attendance considered it to have become "too much show and too little heartfelt ceremony."[54] Central on the ceremonial grounds was a newly built giant sculpture, an artificial "sacred tree" (*al lukh maas*), rising from a Sakha *balagan*. Art critics and traditionalists warned that the symbol of a tree growing out of a house evoked abandoned homesteads, precisely the reminder of lost ways of life and values that haunts Sakha striving for cultural renewal and greater attention to family-oriented morality. Was this nostalgia inspiring or discouraging? Friends saw irony in an Yhyakh far from the capital, presumably "more authentic," becoming "more artificial" and gossiped that money designated for the event was used to build a local road and to line bureaucrats' pockets.

Judging from my observations of many Yhyakh at many levels over nearly thirty years, the annual festival at Us Khatyn, honoring the sacred Tuimaada Valley, has successfully weathered the complex balances of modernity, ritual, celebration, and prayer that mark the ever-evolving "living tradition" of Yhyakh. (See Figure 3.)

A friend who has helped organize the Tuimaada Yhyakh, commented: "what is important is neither money nor weather but the sustainability of traditional rituals and sacred games that we have rekindled with tenderness, as we evolved in the socialization of our people over the past twenty years. We had a special solidarity this year the likes of which I had not seen before."[55] In 2020, fearful of losing spiritual communion at summer solstice precisely when it was needed during the coronavirus pandemic, organizers managed to sustain some ceremonies, keeping fire offerings, prayer, and ritual drinking of fermented mare's milk. A few socially distanced cultural and political leaders participated, partially broadcast online. Former Minister of Culture Andrei Borisov explained several days later that he had prayed and made fire offerings of *kumys* with his epos theater team in the large *urasa* (birch tent amphitheater) at Us Khatyn: "I said the prayer and something came over me, it was extremely powerful to be there. As in the times of Ellei, our ancestor who founded the ceremony, the *urasa* became our temple, our sacred space, and we ourselves became sacred in a dimension I had not been before."[56]

The keeper of the Us Khatyn sacred site, the Sakha ethnographer Villiam Yakovlev, is also president of the nongovernmental association Ytyk Sirdérgé (Sacred Places). In 2014, he confessed to me that he was weary of arguments surrounding the symbolism of various recently built pavilions in the extensive ceremonial grounds, especially concerning the huge copper-clad *altan sérgé* that has become a major ritual focus, and a planned spiral calendar marking its hilltop. He explained: "The ancient Sakha spiral calendar is the most important, most resonant [of our projects]. We want to have sunrise ceremonies honoring the solstice right at *altan sérgé*, as we have begun to do in these last years, exactly at the right time, so that the sun and the shadows come just right to the multiple *sérgé* that are set up there [in a line down a hill]." For Villiam and other spiritual revitalization leaders, the past decade has been a critical time to attract the loyalty and fascination of the next generation of Sakha before it is too late: "We want to appeal to Sakha youth—and to Sakha parents who had children after the Soviet Union collapsed. Many Sakha at the end of the Soviet period were not believing in things Sakha so much as they were looking for something more international to believe in . . . This goes deeper than merely rekindling Sakha cosmology—it addresses a general spiritual yearning."[57] In 2017, Villiam proudly hosted a summer solstice celebration of "international shamans" from Australia, Mexico, and the Altai in his home *ulus* of Suntar.

Rich, Pivotal, and Misdirected?

At a 2013 Yhyakh held in a vast meadow outside the village of Maia in Megino-Kangalas *ulus*, where I lived in villages in 1986 and 1995, I was privileged to attend a celebratory feast, complete with horse-meat shashlik, fish soup, stuffed entrails, and many other delicacies, set up for dignitaries and guests in a gigantic summer tepee-like *urasa*. Hoisting a wooden chalice of *kumys*, the Vladimir Putin-appointed republic head Egor Borisov decided to deliver an elaborate introductory toast that touched on the sacred meaning of the solstice, as well as on pressing issues of the republic. Borisov proudly proclaimed:

> We have just a few thousand short of a million in the population in our huge republic. Each year our children are more in number, and more talented at winning prizes in culture and science . . . We will soon have the twentieth-year anniversary of our declaration of sovereignty. I am sure our future is bright, that our children will live better. Our territory is huge, one-fifth of the Russian Federation . . . We have everything with which to grow. We have under our feet all the resources that are possible for living well, living with dignity. This is what we will pass on to our children. The people of Yakutia, Yakutiany—composed of over one hundred different ethnic groups—are very talented. This is our real wealth, our base, our best achievement. Let us toast to that—so that our people will always live in optimism.[58]

Borisov's speech seemed to distill a politician's sense of when to seize a public, ritualized moment with understanding that his people, broadly defined, need optimism. The economic and political context was that he had just negotiated a new, relatively beneficial arrangement of Moscow subsidies to the republic based on anticipated energy resource profits. Borisov obfuscated the degree to which the "under our feet resources" were those of the republic (compare Rogers 2015). His well-honed tone addressed both Sakha solidarity and multiethnic harmony, using the formula "Yakutiany," meaning all citizens of Yakutia. By 2015, he was reconfirmed as republic head in what many perceived as a rigged election, since, as elsewhere in Russia, no viable opponents were permitted to run. Many hoped that Borisov's ethnically Sakha successor Aisen Nikolaev, known for ecology sensitivity, could do better. However, by 2020 Nikolaev too was widely recognized as trapped and beholden to Moscow authorities.[59]

Optimism about negotiated sovereignty has steadily declined in the post-Soviet years. Many who call the Sakha Republic their homeland—whether Sakha, Éveny, Évenki, Yukaghir, Tatar, Russian, Ukrainian, or others—experienced a surge of hope for greater control of their enormous resources in the early 1990s, only to have those hopes dashed. Some in the Sakha leadership have channeled their sovereignty aspirations into ecologically savvy development plans, outreach for direct trade and foreign investment, and especially into a nonchauvinist cultural revival that they feel they can and should guide without federal-level (Moscow) interference. But they are often thwarted. Raised expectations can produce a dangerous dynamic of hardened interethnic relations, as theorists such as the historian of China Prasenjit Duara warn (Duara 1996, 150–77). Many Sakha resent what they view as Russian Orthodox and foreign missionary presumptions that they have a "spiritual vacuum" in their republic that requires filling. They are astonished that educating their children in the Sakha language could be considered an affront to Russian civilization (compare Ferguson 2019).

Beyond the enormous wealth of mineral and energy resources, some Sakha are renewing "back to the land" rural values that celebrate human-animal connections. They are proud of a tradition that enabled many homesteaders, including in Far North regions such as Verkhoyansk, the ability to thrive in compounds supported by horse and cattle herds that could sustain extended multigenerational families.

Nostalgia comes in many forms and may reference various time periods. A darker side of nostalgia and cultural activism emerged in 2019–2020, exemplified by the Sakha men's group Us Tumsuu [Gathering], led by Innokenti Makarov—a warrior in the epic film *Tygyn Darkhan* and current self-appointed defender of the Sakha people against illegal migrants, whether from Kyrgyzstan or the North Caucasus, perceived to be dangerous to traditional Sakha ways of life.[60]

Some of my interlocutors are worried that the extravagant cultural revival represented by the summer solstice ceremonies and sacred lands recovery will become unsustainable or rendered into a superficial show. Some fear that focus on entering the *Guinness World Records* for numbers of people playing the traditional instrument *khomus* or for dancing *okhuokhai* in "traditional costumes" diverts attention from important self-determination priorities. A Sakha friend commented in 2019 with sorrow, "There's a saying going around: 'All that our youth are into is "songs and dances," since it seems we are doing "cultural revitalization" without real land and legal claims to back it up.'"

Cultural revitalization itself is an achievement led and enjoyed by many Sakha of numerous backgrounds. Open celebration of solstice and other ceremonies at the regional and village level has become an accepted part of post-Soviet Sakha life, far deeper than sponsored Ministry of Culture projects of Sakha elites. Long-ing for perceived simpler times of implementing locally sensitive Indigenous knowledge through prayer and spiritual awareness is manifest in such diverse place-oriented forms as homesteading, animal husbandry, controlled fire burn advocacy, sacred site protection, and toponyms recovery. Key indexes of cul-tural pride include Sakha-language schools, a folkloric art revival movement elegantly displayed in the Sakha National Art Museum, sounds-of-nature music experimentation exemplified by the disc "The Call of the Ancestors," and a roots-seeking group of pilgrims who call their project "On the Path of the Ancestors," discussed in chapter 4.

REPUBLIC OF BURYATIA
Gerrymandered and Struggling

> The movement to make Sagaalgan [Buddhist New Year, spring harbinger] a national holiday in 1992 was a big deal. In the 1990s, people would wear national dress, [attend] theatrical performances in the Buryat Drama Theater . . . It was an uplifting and exciting experience to see this happening. It was seen as an important sign of cultural revival and "Buryatness" . . . [It is] still a big deal.
>
> —Yeshen-Khorlo Dugarova-Montgomery, June 6, 2020

> Buryats have multiple, overlapping identities, pan-Mongolic, Russian, Buddhist, and proper Buryat . . . due to Buryatia being on the border of multiple worlds.
>
> —Irina Garri, Buryat scholar, Association for the Study of Nationalities, Columbia University, April 25, 2015

> A global and local balance deterring polarization [is needed], rendering ludicrous all *ulus-almak* [kin-based] ambitions or any pretensions toward full independence of Buryatia.
>
> —Nikolai Abaev (2014, 129–30)

> Shamans and lamas must unite, to be useful to society and our people . . . We must revive and not just survive. We are a great people with great culture and religion . . . Ecology is in our genes. We are children of Tengeri.
>
> —Dasha Lama Danzan-Khaibzun Samaev, before his death, 2005

The splintering of Buryat identities has occurred on numerous fronts, beginning with difficulties of maintaining the Buryat language in a multiethnic and demographically divided homeland. In 2014, the symbol-conscious then-head of the Republic of Buryatia Viacheslav V. Nagovitsyn briefly greeted a crowd in Buryat, a Mongolic language, on the Day of the Buryat Language, proclaiming: "In the modern world a huge place in society is occupied by the mass media. This fully pertains to the problem of the preservation of the Buryat language." He then quickly switched to Russian, his native tongue, to provide data on Buryat language programs and scholarship. He stressed the significance of the leading role of the Buryat television company Buryatia, and its channel Mir-Buryatia (World of Buryatia, Russian), as well as Arig Us (Pure Water, Buryat). He praised the Buryat language publishing house Buryad ünén and bragged that "many regional newspapers are published in the Buryat language."[1] Like Buryat identity itself, the issues surrounding his performance were multifold and coded. Later deposed, the unpopular Nagovitsyn, a nonlocal Russian, had far poorer knowledge of the Buryat language than his predecessor, Leonid Potapov, Buryatia's first post-Soviet president from 1991 to 2007, a local Russian who grew up in a predominantly Buryat village.

In 2017, the ethnically mixed Buryat-Russian Alexei Sambuevich Tsydenov was first appointed and then elected head of the republic. Political insiders considered him a perfect compromise, with a Buryat father yet politically and culturally Russified. While some view him as Buryat, others feel that he is not "really Buryat," and that any head of the republic should express an active Buryat cultural identity through language and religion. Many republic citizens were not surprised when President Putin replaced Nagovitsyn under circumstances that included allegations of corruption. Tsydenov, a publicity-savvy youthful railway executive born in Chita, was elected by 87 percent of the vote in September 2017 with only 41.7 percent of the electorate turning out. He epitomizes Moscow-approved leadership. More interested in economic development than language or identity politics, he is said to be "caught between" local Buryat movements and Moscow demands. A labor leader in his youth, with an Order of Friendship medal for internationality cooperation, his political campaign included singing with a Turkish choir to celebrate Days of Moscow in Buryatia.[2]

Buryat colleagues with roots in villages have admitted they see themselves as weaker in their cultural revival than the Sakha, because they feel they were historically targeted as a border people with strong Buddhist-Mongolic ties, to be brainwashed with education that supported Russification. One interlocutor explained, "Buryats have long placed an emphasis on education. People in the villages would even sell a cow to make sure a promising child could go on for higher education."[3] A simmering, deep resentment of Russification has caused some Buryats to compare themselves unfavorably to other non-Russians living in constitutionally recognized republics. Programs privileging the Buryat language have been under siege at least since 2015. Pressure from the federal-level Ministry of Education to increase Russian language teaching in villages placed demographically dispersed Buryat communities in peril of losing favorable conditions for passing the Buryat language to the next generations.

Throughout the republic, urban language politics have served as proxies for identity politics. Street protests erupted in 2015 over a non-Buryat-speaking republic appointee as rector of the main local university. This and other out-sider appointments stimulated resentment, since some Buryats perceived them as symptoms of a larger problem with neocolonialism. Activists admit that they are frustrated by a repression malaise that only rarely has led to protests. There-fore, the surprise of substantial popular protests in 2019 made them all the more significant.

In 2019, large protests were staged in the capital after local authorities arrested the Sakha opposition leader "shaman Alexander" on the outskirts of Buryatia's capital, Ulan-Ude. Busloads of detentions received extensive media coverage. While many were later released, organizers were detained for future trials, and some of Alexander's mixed-ethnic supporters were specifically targeted. Fur-ther arrests occurred in 2020. The unstable political context was as important as Alexander's arrest, since reasons for protests had been accumulating. For example, election fraud was alleged when the mayor of Ulan-Ude, Igor Shuten-kov, won in 2019 on possibly falsified vote tallies. Many believed the real winner was the Buryat Communist Party candidate, Viacheslav Markhaev, not the Rus-sian Shutenkov, officially backed by the United Russia party.[4] While few openly express interest in secession, some intellectuals, such as the historian Nikolai Abaev cited in the epigraph, periodically warn of independence perils.

As in other republics, protests from below over cultural, ecological, and eco-nomic issues have been sporadic yet significant in Buryatia in the past decade. It has been particularly difficult to mobilize civic society in Buryatia, due to its his-tory of divided territory, demographic imbalances, and impoverishment. Many Buryats prefer to be discreet and quietly rekindle various versions of religious practice, emphasizing complex and at times idiosyncratic variations on Bud-dhism, shamanism, and Orthodoxy. This was the message from Dasha Lama Samaev quoted above, whose Buryat orientation represents one of several, some-times openly competing, religious revitalization strands.

Certain trigger or crystallizing issues have put strains on the famed Buryat tendency toward restraint and seeming resignation to fate. One example of public resentment was generated when a Moscow propaganda video valorized Buryat soldiers fighting in Ukraine as "Putin's Militant Buryats." As the Buryat journalist Aleksandra Garmazhapova cogently explained in 2016 after the video went viral, many Buryats worried that their unemployed sons had been lured into war by promises of lucrative salaries, few had wanted to play imperialist proxy roles, and most serious of all, "no one is allowed to speak for the whole people."[5]

Keeping Garmazhapova's wise warning in mind, this chapter explores why interethnic relations involving Buryats and others have been described with dia-metrically opposite conclusions, why identity politics are particularly complex in Buryatia, and how the boundaries of the republic have become threatened. A geopolitical discrepancy between Buryats' concept of their homeland as Greater

Buryatia and internal republic boundaries within Russia is revealed. Multiethnic ecological activism is highlighted, including its interconnections with Buddhist, shamanist, and Russian Orthodox revival projects. We turn first to historical boundaries, demographic legacies, and the geopolitics of Buryatia's location on the border with Mongolia.

Historical and Demographic Contexts for Identity Crystallization and Shattering

South of the Sakha Republic along the Lena River lie the famed Lake Baikal and the Republic of Buryatia. In the early Soviet period, its republic predecessor was much larger. Founded in 1923, the Buryat-Mongol Autonomous Republic covered most of the territory that Western (Cis-Baikal) and Eastern (Trans-Baikal) Buryat pastoralists—herding horses, cattle, sheep, and camels—inhabited before the Russian Revolution. Historically, two major cultural-influence zones developed in Greater Buryatia: the Western zone experienced greater Russification, urbanization, and Russian Orthodox influence, while the Eastern area retained more "traditionalist" pastoralism, with impoverished villages and a Buddhist-shamanist cultural mix. Exceptions to these well-known patterns developed, making neat generalizations difficult. Today, some Buryats claim that their rightful territories were split into five pieces, since the 1923 republic boundaries omitted two parcels used by the pastoralists, and two more beyond the republic were lost more recently.

Radicalization of many Buryat intellectuals and political leaders occurred when Buryatia was gerrymandered in 1937, split into an arc of land surrounding Lake Baikal, on the Mongolian border, jutting west. Two satellite regions were embedded into Irkutsk oblast (Ust-Orda okrug) and Chita oblast (Aga okrug). Perceived oppositional Buddhist and Native Communist leaders were repressed throughout the early Soviet period, especially in the 1930s. Survivors learned a "weapons of the weak" strategy of cooperation with the predominantly outsider authorities appointed to Communist Party posts in the republic (compare Scott 1987; Humphrey 1998). Officials never fully managed to coopt the local communities nominally under their control. At least in some cases, they themselves became complicit within a compelling Buryat politics that absorbed multiple influences and made them their own.

The Soviet Union's nominally autonomous Buryat-Mongol republic became simply the Buryat ASSR in 1958, symbolically and literally discouraging Mongol connections.[6] As a Buryat friend who prefers anonymity explained in 2016: "In the Soviet period, the authorities were most threatened by the Mongol ties—and the

Buryat-Mongol solidarity that had been an historical part of our identity. Today many people go there [to Mongolia] and are impressed. They go on vacations, to shop, to learn." Stressing civilizational differences related to the settlement of Buryat nomads on the Russian side, as well as kinship commonalities related to disputed attribution of ancestry to Chingis Khan, s/he added, "Now Mongolia is a model, but it was not like that in the past. Rather, we Soviet Buryats were supposed to be their models, or it was more of a competition. But it is not a big brother relationship either way." For people of mixed ethnic Buryat-Russian backgrounds, sometimes romanticized Mongolian connections were only one part of their crucial yet amorphous roots seeking on both sides of the divided Mongolia-Russian border. By 2019, the celebrated 750th anniversary of the Golden Horde, some Buryats made renewed calls for their republic to be named Buryad-Mongol, substituting a "d" for "t" for more accurate pronunciation and resonance with Mongolia.[7]

Within Russia, the emotionally fraught legacy of Buryat association with the satellite Ust-Orda and Aga okrugs lasted until the mid-2000s, when the Putin administration conducted two referenda (in 2006 and 2008) to abolish these recognized nationality-based districts and merge them into their surrounding Russian regions. Using economy of size rationales, Moscow bureaucrats and some local officials pushed consolidation through. The process, in Russian called *ukrupnenie*, had been tested in the precedent-setting abolition of the Komi-Permiak okrug. The anthropologist Anya Bernstein (2013) appropriately emphasizes that Buryats themselves term this process "dismemberment," playing on a "body politic" metaphor that is a major theme in her monograph.

For many local Buryats, the twin blows of phased okrug elimination were far more than an ethnically neutral economic and administrative restructuring, but rather a process that denied them special influence or leadership in their satellite territories. I came to understand this intertwined political and economic dynamic as a key crystallizing event when talking in 2007 to one of the Ust-Orda cultural leaders, who must remain anonymous. S/he bitterly explained that the 2006 referendum in Ust-Orda had been falsified, and that massive propaganda concerning the economic benefits and special subsidies amounted only to unfulfilled promises. S/he knew no Buryats who had voted for the abolition. Some family members, colleagues, and friends had moved to Ulan-Ude rather than stay in a territory that had become uncomfortable for many in the local Buryat intelligentsia. My interlocutor insisted that it was not just the local Buryat elites who were feeling disenfranchised. Increasingly impoverished, many Buryats of the okrug had lost their jobs, their sense of security, and their cultural pride, despite a few token remnants of funding for a local museum.

In the Aga region, merged into Chita in 2008 using another contested referendum that created Zabaikal krai, Buryats were similarly concerned that they were becoming increasingly small minorities in lands that they once considered their own. In addition, they worried about growing corruption. This was the district from which the well-known mixed-ethnic singer Iosif Kobzon went on to become an elected (and later US-sanctioned) Duma deputy. He was nicknamed "Sinatra" because of links to a Russian mafia group. By 2013, Liubov Bairova, a Buryat ethnographer, had staged a one-woman protest on the steps of the Ulan-Ude government administration building, advocating "Return Ust-Orda and Aga to the Buryats!" Explaining that it was too complex and dangerous to organize a major demonstration, but that many Buryats were behind her, she claimed that the living standards of Buryats had fallen in these districts since the mergers, and that promised schools, hospitals and stores had never materialized.[8] In 2014, the issue was raised again by a university economist, Margarita Namkhanova, who suggested that a new "production district" merging Buryatia and Zabaikal could help the region overcome its economic crisis.[9] In 2015, a teacher's strike erupted in Zabaikalsk, and a scandal publicized well beyond the republic involved official local approval for Chinese leasing extensive lands in Zabaikal krai.[10] In 2017, protests extended to demonstrations against wealthy Chinese buying land for luxury summer homes on the famed and sacred Olkhon Island, discussed ahead. By 2019, protests in at least fifty cities in Russia opposed Chinese use of Baikal's water and forests.

Nationalist protests and discourses have been under-reported in Greater Buryatia, in part due to the Russian version of "divide and rule" gerrymandering. Tsarist and early Soviet nationality politics were inconsistent and varied in their ramifications, depending on where they were applied and by whom. In the case of the Buryat homeland, their purposes and results were less to manipulate specific elections, as the original use of the word "gerrymandering" implies, than to dilute potential Buryat demographic strength and political influence in a major strategic border zone. Buryat demographic proportions juxtaposed to colonial and Soviet Russian newcomers increasingly have been to Buryats' disadvantage, at least since the advent of the Trans-Siberian and Baikal-Amur rail lines in the region (Marks 1991; Khamutaev 2008). In the 1926 census, Buryat were 237,501 or about 48 percent of their republic's population; by 1989, they numbered 421,380, constituting only 24 percent of the republic's population. In Russia's 2010 census, they numbered 461,389 within Russia, but were 282,839 in their republic, or about 30 percent. Buryats have maintained about 50 percent representation in their parliament, called the People's Khural, a proportion some Russians consider unfair (Popkov and Tyugashev 2014). Census data for 2020–2021 have been delayed. A slight rise in the overall population of 986,109 is possible, but no ethnic proportions have been published.[11]

As in the Sakha Republic, open membership in parties identified with chauvinist nationalism has been unpopular, perceived to be unproductive in the post-Soviet period. The first elected president of the republic, the Russian Leonid Potapov, tried to steer a pragmatic course away from perceived Russian or Buryat favoritism, as have his successors. Nonetheless, when President Yeltsin visited the republic in 1992, a few protesters from a fringe and fledgling Buryat-Mongol People's Party headed by Professor Mikhail N. Ochirov waved placards with the slogans: "We Demand the Reunification of the Buryat-Mongol Lands," and "No Russia in Buryatia—Buryatia Alone." This early post-Soviet experimentation was a crystallization period that included a few exuberant congresses with Mongolian delegates, but it quickly dissipated. By 1995, according to Buryat interlocutors, People's Party membership had dwindled, due to intimidation against their leaders and a pragmatic sense that then-impoverished and self-preoccupied Mongolia was not likely to subsidize an expensive and politically risky independence movement.

In the past decade, selective interest in Mongolia as a model, if not a benefactor, has increased as Mongolia's economic improvement has accelerated. Mongolian tourists and trade goods have flooded the region. The Moscow-based Russian historian Aleksandr Morozov has warned that "the example of a successful, ethnically close, independent state [on Buryatia's border] inevitably will be perceived by part of the Buryat elite as an inspiring example to emulate."[12] By 2020, joint Buryatia-Mongolia-China economic projects and exchanges had been launched, partially stimulated by a 2018 state visit by Alexei Tsydenov to Mongolia. What was earlier perceived as a dangerous cultural-political affiliation had become coopted as official United Russia party policy (compare Nowiska and Zhanaev 2016).

In the 1990s, moderate, Buryat-oriented parties or organizations included the All-Buryat Association for Cultural Development; Negedel (Solidarity, in Buryat), an organization for promoting Buryat culture and language; the People's Patriotic Party; and the Democratic Buryatia Movement. In addition to cultural revitalization, focus was on enabling negotiated conditions for greater local-level political participation, as well as greater economic empowerment. A decade later, the All-Buryat Association for Cultural Development was still viable, as was the Congress of Buryat People, with a return to emphasis on cultural rights rather than political activism. Since President Putin came to power, local parties have floundered as Buryat leaders have recognized their dependence on Russian subsidies. Buryatia, like the Sakha Republic and Tyva, has one of the lowest per capita incomes in Russia. Credit worthiness, bank reserves, and other indicators are also low. Buryatia ranks with Tyva and the Altai Republic as among the greatest recipients of federal funding.[13]

Since 2012, space for loyal opposition and political mobilization has shrunk considerably. In 2012, Nadezhda Nizovkina, a leader of Buryatia's Solidarity movement, was detained and placed in a psychiatric hospital.[14] In 2013, the historian Vladimir Khamutaev, one of the founders of the All-Buryat Association for Cultural Development and a leader of the Congress of Buryat People, was hounded from his post as a respected senior researcher at the Academy of Sciences Institute for Mongolian, Buddhist, and Tibetan Studies. In 2011, he had publicly refuted celebrations of the 350th anniversary of Buryatia's "voluntary integration" into Russia and then republished his popular book, based on archival materials, on Buryatia's forced incorporation (Khamutaev 2012).[15] By 2015, Vladimir Khamutaev had been granted political asylum in the United States. That same year Evgenii Khamaganov, chief editor of the opposition website Asia-Russia Today, had his neck broken in a beating by unknown attackers in Ulan-Ude, as publicized by members of the Buryat National Movement for Democracy and Freedom. In 2017, he died in a hospital under suspicious circumstances. Dorzho Dugarov, who later fled to Lithuania, considered the death and 2015 attack to be politically motivated after numerous threats.[16] Dugarov, according to Buryat friends, considered himself a loyal and patriotic citizen of Russia, a member of the liberal Russian Yabloko Party and the movement Oborona (Defense). He was also a "founder of our national movement" who was "hounded out . . . under terrible pressure, and threats to his family of four children." With Radzhana Dugarova, he established the group Erkhe (Justice, Buryat), discussed ahead. The exile of leaders like Khamutaev and the Dugarovs is mourned by members of the Buryat intelligentsia, one of whom in 2016 explained with a sigh that "many of the most talented are leaving."

Perceived provocations include the already mentioned appointment "from above" of a Russian rector at Buryat State University in 2015. Knowing the risks, protesters nonetheless mobilized in the main square of Ulan-Ude in another identity-crystallizing moment. They protested the appointment of a rector with little knowledge of Buryat culture or language and called for the ouster of then-republic head Viacheslav Nagovitsyn, a specialist on the composer Dmitri Shostakovich who had been their unlikely leader since 2007. While Buryatia's nationality policy proclaimed balance in preserving ethnic parity for Russians and Buryats in government posts, the brave protesters differed. Some accused Nagovitsyn of making interethnic relations worse by perpetuating a "Russian yoke" over Buryats that had lasted too long. One of the most articulate of the protesters was Viacheslav Markhaev, a Buryat deputy in Russia's Duma, who accused the leadership of circulating power among an exclusive Putin-approved elite, including some "outsiders" such as Nagovitsyn, born in Magnitogorsk.[17]

In 2017, Bair Tsyrenov, a dynamic Khural duma deputy and member of the Communist Party, representing a younger Buryat generation yearning for a reputedly more secure life under the Soviets, managed to get himself in trouble with police. He staged a one-person protest in front of the parliament, captured on TV, against election candidate vetting, by holding a sign decrying political election "filters." Later, railing against Moscow-level and Chinese corruption, he warned that Buryatia cannot develop without refined, well-targeted, and locally supported subsidies from the federal center. "Without serious government programs, the problems won't be resolved . . . Siberia and the Far East are special regions, where development in tsarist Russia and especially in the Soviet period required stimuli so that people would continue to live there . . . [Instead], Moscow spends enormous sums on [corrupt] mega-projects."[18] His outburst was meant to be patriotic, the opposite of Buryat nationalism, but political authorities did not see it that way.

Beyond Neocolonial Discourse: Usable Pasts?

Can we see any collective inspiration for ethnonational identity building in sporadic, diverse and often symbolic protests? Given how much Russification has occurred in the region's history, and how debated its salience is, answers depend on one's interlocutors in these sensitive matters. In 2020 republic head Alexei Tysdenov, emphasizing the republic's multi-nationality heritage, celebrated the anniversary of Buryatia's first post-Soviet Constitution (ratified in 1994) by proclaiming that it "guarantees preservation and growth of historical, national and spiritual traditions, and also the cultures and languages of all the peoples residing in the republic."[19]

To deepen perspective, Buryatia was one of the republics where the capital Ulan-Ude was left with just one Buryat-language school by the end of the Soviet period. While Buryat-language programs helped somewhat in the post-Soviet years, many of my interlocutors resent ongoing linguistic Russification in public venues. A People's Khural law passed in 1999 encouraged use of Buryat first and family names, but it has not taken hold as well as Buryat cultural revivalists had hoped. A school program introduced in 2014 was meant to stimulate Buryat-language recovery, but its study was made "voluntary." In time for the school year of 2017, a language survey indicated decline of Buryat-language teaching in secondary education, to the point where only 3.7 percent of the teachers in the school system were offering the Buryat language to 67,287 Buryats, out of 132,475 pupils.[20] In the past decade, Buryat-language use has become more token than typical for urban Buryats (compare Graber 2020).

Bright spots referencing different times crucial in shaping Buryat identity and values have been the revivals of the Buddhist New Year Sagaalgan, and the Buryat heroic epic *Gésér*. By the late 1980s, Sagaalgan, glossed as White Month or Clear

Moon, was celebrated increasingly openly as a Mongolic tradition with roots going back at least eight hundred years.[21] The highlight of the lunar calendar, marked in early February, it was made a national holiday in 1992. At once domestic and community oriented, pre-Buddhist and Buddhist, it has joyous annual-renewal significance for many Buryats, as indicated in the opening epigraph of this chapter. Along with newly emerging lamas, the talented poet Bair Dugarov was among those who led the movement to make this earlier banned celebration officially recognized.

In the 1990s, riding a wave of cultural-revival exuberance, Dugarov also founded the Gésér Society, named for the main hero of the Buryats' signature epic. *Gésér* had been suppressed in the 1940s and reevaluated after Stalin's death in the 1950s. In the post-Soviet period, intellectuals embraced the epic as a source of inspiration, poetry, and heritage. The Gésér Society has sponsored conferences and festivals. It represents a poignant, nostalgic view of Buryat village life. Celebration of the Buryat language and epics is encapsulated in Dugarov's touching poem "Sayan Elders":

> I remember my Sayan elders
> Nameless to the world, connoisseurs
> Of trips on horseback, lighting of campfires
> and the unrestrained round-up of wild boar.
>
> In isolated winter huts, by summer haystacks
> I listened to the stories of their forefathers
> And the land would fill with the breath of their legends
> Like the smoke from old men's pipes.
>
> And the Gésér legends would blossom
> Into nine branches, embracing the taiga, in the blueness . . .
> And the tips of my family tree/Extend into the mute depths of the
>   Mongolian steppe.
>
> I could have listened to them day and night.
> I remember all that they have told me.
> And I am proud that the youth of my village
> Consider me an elder.[22]

The results of efforts to revive the *Gésér* epic have been mixed: it may have had less enduring mass appeal than the more diverse Sakha *olonkho* genre. While many newspapers, TV and radio programs (*Arig Us*; *Buriad-FM*), and online discussions are held in Buryat, some have questioned whether the Buryat language needs to be a "marker" of Buryat identity at all.[23]

A compelling complement to *Gésér* is represented by the Buryat folkloric art revival best exemplified by the charming work of Zorikto Dorzhiev. His stylized mastery of warriors, nomads, monks, maidens, falcons, horses, and the south wind bring the past alive in new ways, with humor, detail, and drama. An exquisite catalogue of his work begins with an epigraph that captures a paradoxical theme of my book:

> If memory is only imagination,
> Then sink in it, and you will find something
> Nobody has ever seen.[24]

Debates among Buryat intellectuals concerning when and how the Buryats became "a people" reveal widely divergent positions. Some point to a prominent bronze eagle sculpture, erected in 2013 at a gorgeous overlook near Elantsy above the Tazheran steppe, as representing the mythical progenitor of the Buryat nation, or at least its Trans-Baikal Olkhon branch. This romantically situates Buryat origins in a distant golden past.[25] In contrast, my friend and colleague the Buryat ethnographer Zoja Morokhoeva considers major ethnonational crystallization processes to have been stimulated by the Russian Empire's "reforms of 1822," including the important role of Buryats in the steppe duma, plus several "rebellions" that Buryats organized as they chafed in "us vs. them" terms against outsider rule before the Soviet period.[26] In contrast, Cambridge University-trained Marina Saidukova has stressed that most Buryats were far too nomadic and splintered into clans to have had a national consciousness in the nineteenth century, much less in an earlier folkloric past. She considers more recent Soviet and post-Soviet interethnic relations to be salient.[27]

Elena, a Buryat grandmother and matriarch in a village on the sacred Olkhon Island, pulled me aside somewhat conspiratorially in 2005 and literally sang a paean from her youth to the early Soviet Buryat-Mongol Republic with the following refrain (in Russian): "Buryats are Mongols; Buryat culture is Mongolic; the Buryat-Mongol Peoples' Republic lives in people's hearts." However, the dynamic philosopher turned Buddhist nun Irina Urbanaeva insisted, in contradiction to Elena's song, that Buryats were delighted when the word "Mongol" was dropped in 1958, because they needed to see themselves as going it alone, shaping their own special Buryat-ness within the framework of later Soviet, as well as Mongolic Buddhist and shamanist traditions.[28] In sum, generational, personal, and class variations make a difference in what one is nostalgic for, and to what time period one relates when pinning sometimes ephemeral hopes on one's people's solidarity.

Debates continue today regarding tribal affiliations. The Mongolic-speaking Buryat—whose ancestors spanned the borders of present-day Russia, Mongolia, and China—are usually divided into five major tribal groups whose relative salience has varied over time: Bulagat, Khori, Ekhirit, Khongodor, and Tabunut. Their significance had diminished by the twentieth century but remains an aspect of complex self-identities for a people known for memorizing genealogies of multiple generations. In 1990, just before the Soviet Union collapsed, a genealogy contest was held at a spirited glasnost-celebrating festival, won by a young woman who remembered seventeen generations. Tuiana Dugarova optimistically considers historical clan line recollection back seven generations to be the norm. However, increasingly common have been the urbanized Buryats ashamed to admit to shamans and outsider ethnographers that they do not know their clan affiliations.[29] This self-consciousness, contributing to galvanizing nostalgia, in turn has stimulated a resurgence of urbanized *tailagan* (kin-based ceremonies, with animal sacrifices) and a roots-searching drive to return to "mini-homelands" when they are known, sometimes accompanied by rituals to appease long-neglected ancestral spirits.[30]

Some young urban Buryats have helped to bring the *tailagan* back to their villages and clans, returning to their homelands. Since their wealth has put them in a position to give back to impoverished relatives, they are able to sponsor transport, housing, and food for summer ceremonies and reunions, usually held in July. Research into family trees becomes crucial, with a goal to uncover more than seven generations. These are private ceremonies, involving sacrificed sheep and prayer-blessings from a hired *böö* (shaman-elder), preferably but not necessarily a kinsperson. The tradition has been recovered with degrees of success, sometimes after a hiatus of twenty or more years.

Unlike "inventing tradition," this adaptive, contextual, and emotional process is rekindling its embers. Perhaps at the very moment specific kinship connections to ancestral lands seem to be slipping away, people respond with determination to recapture some sense of home and ecological consciousness on a substantial yet manageable scale before it is too late. Who is leading this eclectic and ramifying process? While its leaders may be predominantly educated elites with resources, its impulses and resonance derive from a range of urban and rural communities, from known respected extended families (e.g., the Dugarovs) and from rekindled kin groups including Bulagat, Khori, Ekhirit, Khongodor, Sartul, Songol, and others. They advocate responsibilities and rights to ancestral lands, using the concept "law of ancestors," *ëho zanshal*.[31]

Ecological Activism and Economic Contexts

A particularly strong set of national identity triggers can be seen in how Buryats and Russians have rallied, together and separately, in ecological activism against the despoliation of the world's largest, deepest, and most magnificent freshwater lake, Lake Baikal, protected by Russian law in 1992 and made a World Heritage Site in 1996.[32] The once-quaint coastline of Baikal, dotted with fishing villages, is filling up with gaudy elite dachas and tourist hotels, especially on the Irkutsk road side of the lake. Industrial waste has threatened its clear water and its famed unique freshwater seals. Federal-level protections were weakened in 2020. Baikal itself, called in Buryat "Baigal dalai," is far from the only gem of the region, broadly defined. Due to their interconnected waterways, some feel that the pure, smaller Khubsugul dalai (Blue Pearl Lake) in Mongolia is part of Greater Buryatia, as are Lake Gusinoe, the foothills of the Eastern Sayan Mountains and the Tunka Valley, with surrounding mountain peaks called the Tunka Alps. Buryats anthropomorphically explain that its northern and southern peaks symbolize the "male and female" (in'-ian) origins of the Sayan system, and that in the foothills of the Sayan peak Altan Mondarga [also Mundarga] is the birthplace of the great Chingis Khan. Nearby is the homeland of the Buryat epic hero Gésér Khan.

The peak of Buryatia's ecology protests revolved around threats to Lake Baikal, 20 percent of the world's fresh water reserves, caused by energy-industry sponsorship of pipelines and by the notorious Baikalsk pulp and paper factory, including its shifting management's continued attempts to reconstitute in various forms. Current anger has centered on destruction of forests for fancy dachas—some owned by "foreigners," variously defined—on the sacred island of Olkhon. More subtle ecology orientation can also be seen in the revival of interest in Tibetan medicine and the traditional, Buddhist-based, deeply ecological knowledge that it represents. Traditional shamanic world views and protection of sacred sites also influence Indigenous views of where development is appropriate. Alarming estimates cite more than one hundred ecologically threated areas throughout Russia's Far East.[33]

The region's special beauty has been celebrated by propagandizing the hundredth anniversary of Russia's first nature preserve, the Barguzin Reserve, and by creation of the Kodar Protected Ecology Zone in Trans-Baikalsk, under the aegis of the 2017 Year of Ecology. The range of ecologically valued places in Greater Buryatia, beyond the prized Lake Baikal, is considerable, as described in reference volumes such as that by A. B. Imetkhenov and D. G. Chimitov (2016). As of 2020, using data from its official site, the republic had fewer preserves and less territory devoted to ecological protection than the Sakha Republic. This included two biospheres and one federal level preserve, as well as two national parks and three protected zones "of federal level significance." At the regional level, thirteen reserves, one nature park, six recreational centers, and sixty-two protected sites (pamiatniki, Russian) of various sizes and cultural meaning are designated, including four within the general ecological zone of the crucial Lake Baikal hub.[34]

Republic ecology is administered unevenly by a prosaically named service, Bur-prirodnadzor (nature use oversight).

Officially protected areas, important as they are, do not compensate for general development trends that undermine the intent behind the preserves. The previous chapter outlined a 2017 decision to locate a processing plant producing methanol, ceramide, and other chemicals near the source of the Lena River in the Irkutsk region, after protests in the Sakha Republic had rendered it problematic. The plant creates ripple effects in a widespread area without adequate oversight. Authorities may have perceived remote rural residents to be less likely to mobilize against development than those in the Sakha Republic, despite previous ecology activism in Buryatia.

The ramifications of arson are notorious. In 2020, two regional officials, including an assistant mayor, were arrested for grassland and forest arson in the Ust-Kut region on the Irkutsk side of the border with Sakha Republic. The incident shocked even hardened locals and activists. While they may have been trying to gain money from Russia's Ministry of Emergency Response for a controlled burn that went wrong, local reporting indicates the fires exposed political rivalry between mayors over territory and economic development.[35]

Ecology activist groups in Greater Buryatia range from the local to the international and span all definitions of nongovernmental organizations (NGOs), government-organized nongovernmental Organizations (GONGOs), and permutations in between. Republic-level groups began with the Soviet-period Ecological World of Baikal—chaired by the Buryat scientist, parliament deputy, and professor Sergei Shapkhaev, who later created the Buryat Regional Organization on Lake Baikal (BRO-Baikal). Shapkhaev, whose diplomatic skills were legendary, was a role model and beacon for activists until his death in 2018.[36] Mongolia-sponsored hydroelectric stations influencing the Baikal-Selenge river delta were among the projects he warned against in public appearances, under the rubric "SaveBaikal." Somewhat ironically, given cultural solidarities, their popular slogan became "Save Baikal from Mongolia." An affiliated set of activists have formed the Baikal Movement, or the Movement to Protect Baikal (compare Agarkova 2010).

Founded in 1995, the youth activist group Rebirth of Siberian Lands by 2020 was endorsed by the Irkutsk region as a charitable fund, led by Elena A. Tvorogova. The group created the first online course to teach about Lake Baikal. It balances diverse goals, exposing election fraud, protesting forced settlement removals, and promoting sustainable business.[37] ARIGUN, an ecology educational center, is led by Svetlana Khernetkina-Buentueva. A looser set of local organizations was formed to defend the Tunka Valley and its sacred sites against pipelines, including Zov Arshana—Call of Arshan (Mountain Springs), and

Sayany, named for the Sayan mountain range. In the village of Bolshoe Galoust-noe in Baikal National Park, the Buryat schoolteacher Faina Mangaskina has mobilized her networks to monitor pollution and promote cultural revival.

The famous group Baikal Environmental Wave, led by the Russian activist-scientist Marina Rikhvanova, constitutes a special case of environmental activist bravery.[38] Born as a club in the late Soviet period and converted to a registered nongovernmental organization by 1992, it has monitored Lake Baikal pollu-tion, especially illegally dumped effluents such as lignin-based slurry from the enormous Baikalsk cellulose mill. By the mid-2000s, Baikal Wave grew to an organization of twenty-one multiethnic employees and many volunteers, sup-ported with local and international funding, especially Pacific Environment and the Ford Foundation. In 2008, Rikhvanova won the prestigious Goldman Envi-ronmental Prize. Pacific Environment nominated her for activism and research on the ripple effects of chemical pollutants on humans and the milk of Baikal's freshwater seals, the earless *nerpa*. She used part of the prize money to stimulate the local economy with ecotourism, arts, crafts, and small business support. After 2000, her group, and her British partner Jennis Sutton, experienced offi-cial monitoring and harassment, including periodic office raids and computer confiscation. Particularly dramatic was a night raid in 2007 by fifteen masked men wielding iron bars and shouting Russian nationalist slogans. They invaded and wrecked an environmentalist camp that Marina Rikhvanova had helped to organize. One person was killed, and five seriously injured. Arrests were made of environmentalists and some perpetrators, in this murky incident possibly meant to put a chill on all environmental monitoring. Among those arrested was Rikhvanova's son, who allegedly was framed as one of the brawlers, and released only after a year. By 2013, Baikal Environmental Wave was fighting designation as a "foreign agent." In 2016, its organization, based in Irkutsk, was classified as a foreign agent and liquidated. However, their efforts live on in a scientific research program to study why the peerless earless seals, adorable "charismatic animal" exemplars for global ecology activists, experienced mys-terious die-offs in 2017.[39]

In contrast, some less independent organizations enjoy official endorsement. These include the Baikal Ecological Network and an animal rescue group called Zoogallery. In addition, the Bol'shaia baikal'skaia tropa (Great Baikal Trail), led by Andrei Sukhnev, is an Irkutsk ecotourism organization affiliated with Buryatia's Ministry of Natural Resources. The ministry in theory is under the purview of the republic's environmental oversight program, although it focuses on development projects in an arrangement rife with conflicts of interest. It is notorious for its corruption, and in 2017 its assistant director Alexandr Lbov was arrested.

At the international level, World Wildlife Fund, Greenpeace, Global Response, Green Cross, Taiga Rescue Network, the Tahoe-Baikal Institute, and Pacific Environment have worked with local partners at various levels, as has UNESCO. Their initial successes have slowed, given the difficulties of registration under the Russian Duma's 2007 and 2012 nongovernmental organizations laws. In a quirky charm offensive, since 2007 the German beer company Heineken has sponsored an ecology-education project called Clean Shores of Baikal promoting trash pickup and ecological awareness.

This plethora of multileveled and multipurpose ecology groups, their shifting affiliations, and their various newsletter and online manifestations show that ecological protection has been a hot, emotional issue that will not go away. President Putin has declared himself an ecology protector on numerous occasions, despite his stances on energy development and the positions that lower-level bureaucrats have taken. As in the Sakha Republic, Baikal-region ecology groups have morphed, using different names and coalitions when officials have tried to stop them. Some continue to have ethnic-based Buryat leadership, while others are more self-consciously multiethnic. Concerns are usually locally targeted and Baikal oriented, rather than reflecting more general worries about the effects of industrialization on climate change. However, some scientists understand that avalanches in the Sayan Mountains and lowered Baikal water levels probably have systemic climate-change causes. As elsewhere, the ambiguity of causality makes it easier for opponents to launch arguments against activists.

Starting in the Soviet period, with its prevailing Communist Party planning psychology of Man over Nature, Lake Baikal has been under threat from explosions to widen the Angara River, from the 1959 hydroelectric dam on the Angara near Irkutsk, from subsequent hydroelectric station projects, from the pulp and paper factories of Baikalsk (founded 1966) and Selenginsk (founded 1974), and from other industrial dumping including mercury, antinomy, sulphates, chlorides, and municipal waste. The Baikalsk cellulose mill for decades produced vapors of dangerous methyl mercaptan that could be smelled miles away.

By 2008, country-wide protests managed to halt the Baikalsk pulp and paper plant, but it was reopened by decree in 2010. Its phaseout by 2013 was announced, despite some fourteen thousand workers depending on the plant for their livelihoods. When I was in Irkutsk in 2005, a small group of environmental activists were maintaining a constant picket that continued for years. A memorable placard during a later demonstration in Irkutsk against the mill featured one of the unique freshwater seals saying "Mr. Putin, don't kill me." At this writing, the plant, owned by the industrialist Oleg Deripaska through the firm Continental Management, has been declared financially and technologically unviable, after a failed attempt to make it a closed-system mill. Unemployed workers (mostly non-Buryat families) seek alternative jobs, and the mayor of Baikalsk has been working with the Baikal Environmental Wave for a greener city. Natural purifiers in the lake, including the freshwater plankton *Epischura baicalensis*, have partially regenerated the ecosystem.[40]

Uranium production and various pipeline proposals have generated particularly dire concerns. Starting in 2007, protests were launched against the newly constructed Angarsk nuclear power pilot program (an International Uranium Enrichment Center), a hundred kilometers from Baikal. Most alarming, by 2015 Russia's Ministry of Finance produced a budget that zeroed subsidies for the country's Clean Water Fund and decreased by 25 percent funding for the "protection of Lake Baikal and socioeconomic growth of the Baikal Nature Territory."[41] Two pipeline proposals of the past decade have been derailed, although the oil pipeline that was supposed to go through the Tunka Valley was shifted northward across treacherous terrain and caused spills in the Lena River, as we have seen (Figure 9).

The Tunka Valley drama is particularly instructive, since a range of interpretations have been advanced for why the anti-pipeline protest was successful. Primary credit usually is given to a combination of Irkutsk, Ulan-Ude, and local activists, professionals, and enthusiasts, joined in their concern about the decimation of local pastoralist livelihoods in territory that is predominantly a national forested preserve (Tunka National Park) and integrated ecologically

FIGURE 9.   Baikal pipeline protest. By author, 2005.

with Lake Baikal. Local dependence, including by some Russians, on hunting, fishing, foraging, and tourism spurred opposition. By 2003, a survey conducted by the Buryat Regional Organization on Lake Baikal revealed that two-thirds of the Tunka area population was against the pipeline (Hengesback and Shapkhaev 2003, 18–20). The politics of oligarchs and cronies around President Putin played a considerable role, including the well-known arrest of Mikhail Khodorkovsky, whose Yukos company was the sponsor of the oil line.[42]

In the Tunka Valley in 2010, I relished an alternative, spiritual interpretation of his arrest given by the Russian anthropologist Natalia Zhukovskaia, an expert adviser with long-term field experience in the region. Addressing a mixed group of ethnographers and shamanic practitioners with the presentation "How a Coalition of Shamans and Lamas defeated Yukos," she explained that locals believe their own gods and spirits united to defend their lands, livelihoods, and sacred places from despoliation.[43] Shamans, Lamas, and mountain spirit priests who had rarely gotten along prayed together at sacred sites in 2002 "for the first time in 400 years," against the pipeline and the hubris of progress-promising Yukos representatives. Especially prominent were worshippers of the local mountain spirits, *khadasha* [glossed as "one who honors the spirits of the mountains"], sometimes linked to ancestral spirits.

Five major sacred sites were threatened, and many smaller *arshan* (springs). Members from four Tunka villages went to every meeting they could, whether local or in towns, to agitate for a referendum against the pipeline. Some leaders, educators and doctors, were not allowed on buses and resorted to horses to arrive at meetings on time. Natalia received a protest petition, to be distributed in Moscow, signed by people of diverse religious traditions, including a few local Dukhobors, but no Russian Orthodox. It said, in paraphrase, "We from three valuable traditions, for reasons of our suffering, are writing to save our sacred pure Baikal. Together with our magnificent Gods of the Great Sayan Mountains, with our clan ancestors and our shamanic ancestors, we cannot give agreement to the oil company. We are for the purity of our sacred Baikal, of all Nature and its Forested Valley."

The folklore that has developed around this now-legendary spiritual coalition reveals something that also happened in secret with shamanists of diverse places in the Soviet period: they were able to convince themselves that their spiritual power and the power of their deeply conservationist ancestral values were stronger than current temporal authorities.[44] The Buryats' campaign, in other words, helped to renew their faith in themselves.

In sum, protests, rallies, and arrests around the broadly defined ecology movement have centered in Irkutsk and Ulan-Ude but spread throughout Buryatia where they are needed. They have included Buryats and Russians in leadership positions, with enough of a broad base to enable many activists and new leaders to emerge. They constitute a loose movement with shifting priorities and specific politics in many manifestations. Baikal and the Tunka Valley have become national symbols for Russians, exemplified by the leadership of the village writer Valentin Rasputin (1989) and by the limnologist Marina Rikhvanova, and for Buryats, exemplified by the writer Ardan Angarkhaev, who helped create the Tunka National Park, and by the late Sergei Shapkhaev, head of the Buryat Regional Organization on Lake Baikal.

In 2014, right after the summer solstice, the village of Arshan in the Tunka Valley, at the foothills of the Eastern Sayan Mountains, experienced an extreme ecological disaster in the form of an avalanche that wiped out nineteen homes and took much else with it.[45] Many saw meaning in the sparing of local Buddhist temple-datsans and the Russian Orthodox church. Villagers fear a repetition, since the mountain peaks that in living memory had always been filled with snow are now barren of it by midsummer. Environmental instability, recognized by some as related to climate change, seems to mirror and perhaps exacerbate increasing instability in interethnic relations.

Interethnic Relations

Contested claims to the complex national significance of Lake Baikal usually have not led to interethnic tensions. However, such tensions have been under the surface for many years, occasionally erupting in street-level drunken brawls, in neo-Nazi raids on ecology activists, in Buryat demands that elected deputies or education leaders speak the Indigenous language, and in familial discouragement of interethnic marriages, which are common nonetheless.

One of the most revealing places to study interethnic relations in Buryatia is the Akha (Buryat; Oka or Okinskii, Russian) region, famed for its jade and other mineral resources, where Akha Buryats with the Soyot Indigenous group form the majority population, and relative newcomer Russians constitute a minority within the district. While the Turkic language- speaking Soyots traditionally practiced hunting, reindeer and yak breeding (fishing was considered sinful), the Buryats were more focused on cattle and horse breeding, and Russian colonists were border guards, administrators, horsemen, and fishers. Historically, this loose ethnic-based division of labor was maintained, but it was scrambled in the Soviet and post-Soviet periods, especially with the onslaught of a polluting gold industry since the 1930s and jade discoveries since the 1980s.

The Soyots gained formal recognition as an Indigenous people in 2000, although some Buryats and Russians dispute their legitimacy as a separate ethnic group, given historical assimilation processes, mostly with Buryats. Russians of mixed ethnic backgrounds sometimes claim Soyot or Buryat identities, and situational identities are tolerated, if not the norm. Part of the district has been designated a "Territory of Traditional Subsistence Use" under 2007 Russian law, but much of Akha is federal-level forest land, subject to legal and illegal incursions, especially by outsider loggers and geologists. The Buryats' word for these mostly Russian geologists and other outsiders is *mangad*, a derogatory term for Russians possibly derived from *mangadkhai*, a monster or "dangerous other" in Buryat epics.

As elsewhere in Buryatia, Akha Buryats consider their land sacred, expressed as *toonto*, one's birthplace and its ancestral kinship connections (compare Dugarova 2014, 148; Varfolomeeva 2019, 228). Further sacred space indicators are the *oboo*, loosely piled stone stacks used as altars for offerings by any traveler expressing respect for local spirits while moving across the landscape. Stone in multiple forms thus has value, with native jade found in Akha doubly precious symbolically and commercially, due to its marketability in Russia and China. Claims to gemstones in Buryatia are contested in moral and legal terms, leading to messy entanglements, semilegal and illegal mining, as well as bloodshed, for example at the nearby Dylacha mine owned by Évenki but wrested from their tradition-based trade by Russians affiliated with intelligence services (compare Balzer 2017, 12–13; Varfolomeeva 2019, 62).

With moral justification as background, young Buryat men in Akha have been making risky raids on jade mines by night, getting shot at by guards, and treating their adventures as high-stakes hunting, embarked on only after prayers to ancestors and personal understanding that one must not be greedy when taking natural resources (Varfolomeeva 2019, 253–54). These youth, socialized in traditional values with relatively little formal education, are not staging open protests against local Russians. Rather, their exploits are oppositional and subversive in James Scott's sense (1987). They represent an Indigenous variation of working the system, in Alena Ledeneva's sense (1998). Their activities are controversial in Akha, with some admitting "jade is our pain," while others declare "jade is our life."[46] Resulting tensions, with ramifications for ethnic polarization, could be exacerbated with further bloodshed in the name of mine security.

At its most polarizing, Buryats resent Russian racism that has led to unpunished violence against Buryats inside and outside the republic. The human rights youth group Érkhé (Justice) was formed by the ethnologist Radzhana Dugarova and Dorzho Dugarov to monitor such incidents and protest diminished Buryat sovereignty. The banner of its now archived website reads "Buryat historical-political portal," and proclaims "We are against the destruction of the Buryat autonomies and the Buryat republic."[47] More current are the less politicized

Buryat culture and arts site http://soyol.ru/ (*soyol*, culture, civilization); and the Buryat Facebook network Etnicheskaia Buriatiia (Ethnic Buryatia), exploring Buddhist and nature-based traditions. Both are open to anyone.

The Buryat youth-oriented website Site of the Buryat People, www.buryatia. org, active since 2001, labels anti-Buryat prejudice "Buryatophobia." In 2007, after five Buryats were killed in separate Moscow incidents, a Buryat graduate student and a co-founder of the site explained, "Non-Russians are called 'slit eyes' by [Russian nationalist] skinheads. One Buryat girl was attacked in Moscow and it was deemed a robbery—yet the robbers happened to leave gold and diamond earrings on her! Often such incidents are just called 'hooliganism' rather than crimes of ethnic hatred."[48]

Surveys have indicated Buryat preferences for monoethnic dormitories and concern about increased tensions in rural and urban areas. While a Khural-sponsored survey in 1995 recorded that only 3 percent saw interethnic relations as conflictual, by 2010 a more substantial stratified sample indicated 35 percent had experienced interethnic tension, with more Russians perceiving instability (43 percent) than Buryats. Sociologists administering the survey to 401 people in rural regions blamed increased poverty, alcoholism, and suicides. At the 2011 Congress of Ethnographers and Anthropologists of Russia, one team member stressed that tensions have increased because "economically there is nothing to divide." She conceded that their multidisciplinary team was surprised at the alarming results.[49] By 2014, a report on suicides in Russia indicated that rates were particularly high in Buryatia; perusal of the Buryat press reveals this trend continues.[50] In 2015, a high federal-level official at a seminar in Novosibirsk attributed increased interethnic tension and protest in Buryatia to outsider spies, diplomats, and agitators, using well-worn tropes to divert attention from internal social problems and highlighting the importance of Buryatia as a republic with foreign borders. Concerns about penetration of foreign bodies has increased since then, especially with fears of COVID spread from China and Mongolia.

An intriguing survey in 2002 at Buryat State University, featuring interviews with 186 students, found that 36 percent of Buryats favored "positive discrimination" for Buryats while only 4.5 percent of Russians favored this. Revealingly, 7.6 percent of the Buryat students favored independence for the Buryat Republic, and 3.5 percent favored annexation of Greater Buryatia by Mongolia. Their findings imply that in 2002, a full 11.1 percent of elite students favored secession. According to interlocutors and news stories, this number may have increased.[51] This context helps to explain why the head of a "geopolitical civilization laboratory," the Buryat historian Nikolai Abaev (2014, 129–30, and chapter epigraph) felt the need to publicly reject perceived dangerous independence aspirations. A sensational advocate of secession was the Buryat émigré to the United States

Mergensana Amar, who, fearing repatriation, committed suicide while in US Immigration and Customs Enforcement (ICE) custody in 2018.[52]

In sum, most acknowledge that political secession is highly impractical and ecology activism increasingly risky. Rather, many Buryats have been turning inward or to religious communities for renewal and hope.

Multidirectional Religious and Spiritual Revival

The reputation of Greater Buryatia as an oasis of multiethnic harmony has been based partly on long-term legacies of pragmatic cooperation in the tsarist and Soviet periods, and partly on nonconfrontation teachings within Buddhist and shamanist traditions. I view this harmonious reputation as valid but not rock-solid. Reputations change, as do conditions of interethnic relations, especially where local-level, micro-interethnic experiences are far more salient than generalizations about the entire historical Buryat homeland. Exemplary models of peaceful coexistence include the multiple generations of local Russians, sometimes calling themselves Siberiaki, who absorbed some Buryat shamanic values and rituals. On a rocking fishing boat, I observed Russians and other non-Buryat fishermen giving offerings to Lake Baikal spirits for better fishing and auspicious weather.[53] However, such charming and gentle accommodations may be swamped by more recent religious competition and by exposé accounts and multigenerational memories of colonial history. Fragility is indicated in close study of religious diversity and regional history, specifically related to religious practices and memories of repression.

By 2012, official registration of religious groups in the republic had reached nearly two hundred, including sixty-seven Russian Orthodox, fifty-seven Buddhist, and three shamanist (Shaglakhaev 2014, 7). The numbers reflected the majority Slavic population, including long-term Old Believer communities that had taken refuge in Buryatia. This religious census did not include the traditional (mostly Polish) Catholic community, centered in Irkutsk since their ancestors' exile in the nineteenth century, nor the Protestant missionaries who arrived in the region in the post-Soviet period. Activities of the Chinese proselytizing group Falun gong in Buryatia were not acknowledged. In the past decade, official religious group registration of Buddhists (67), shamanists (8) and evangelicals (26) increased faster than other groups, whose overall numbers surpassed 230.[54] Unfortunately for scholars, neither the 2010 nor 2020–2021 census includes questions about religious affiliation. However, a 2019 comparative Buddhism study of young people shows 36.3 percent identifying as Buddhist in Buryatia and 34.4 percent as Christian (Badmaev et al. 2020).

Religiosity monitoring, always difficult, has masked the messy and dramatic competition among proliferating shamanic groups, registered and unregistered, such as Tengeri (also Tengri, named for Sky Gods), founded in 2003, that hosted me in 2010, and the more established All-Buryat Association of Shamans Böö Mïrgel (The Shamanist Faith), founded in the 1990s. Other delightfully named shamanist groups include Khese Khengereg (Rambling Drum); Altan Gadahan (Polar Star); and Aga-based Khükhé Münkhé Tengeri (Eternal Blue Sky). In contrast are traditionalists of priest-led communities who worship local mountain spirits yet reject the term *böö* (shaman).[55]

Statistics cannot adequately depict the splintering of Buddhist communities (*Sangha*) into Buryat, Mongolic, and Tibetan orientations, nor their range from antipathy to synergism with shamanic groups. About forty Buddhist temple complexes have been revived in Buryatia. At the individual level, Tibetan Buddhists, who have no word for missionaries beyond their idea of teachers, have a concept of *icchantika*, a rare person who is beyond the enticement of Buddhist teachings, resistant to its philosophy and reincarnation wisdom. While some incorrigible Buryat shamanists may qualify, most can be enfolded into the Buddhist *Sangha*.

Local variegated Buddhist histories add to the diversity. At least some Eastern Buryat lamas were proselytizing Buddhism by the eighteenth century. It is often called Lamaism in Russia, although the Dalai Lama discourages this geographically differentiating term that stresses practitioner-priests over lay practice.[56] Buddhism gradually took hold in Trans-Baikalia, merging with and partially supplanting shamanist practice. A dramatic example is the sacred site in the Tunka region marked by a giant boulder overlooking the river Khandagait, said to be a hearth of all Mongolic peoples, where for centuries Tengeri rituals were held honoring Chingis Khan as a warrior-leader turned Sky God. These rituals were supplanted and merged with Buddhist practice when the Khandagaityn (Khoimorsk) Datsan was founded in 1916.[57]

A complex system of elegant, well-supported monasteries thrived until the late 1920s–early 1930s. At their peak, some ten thousand Buryats flourished as lamas, including priest-scholars, healers, and artists. Literacy spread in Tibetan and Mongolian, with the historian Dorzhi Banzarov and ethnographer Matvei N. Khangalov among the most famous Buryats of the nineteenth century. The repressed linguist, lama, and diplomat Agvan Dorzhiev and Tibetan medicine specialist Zhamsaran Badmaev became icons of eastern orientation in the twentieth century.[58] All four, especially M. N. Khangalov, for whom the Ulan-Ude history museum is named, have been valorized in the post-Soviet period as Buryat hero-spiritual leaders. A more controversial hero was the lama Lubsan Samdan Tsydenov, who established a short-lived Buddhist state in Trans-Baikalia

(1918–1922) and proclaimed "Buddhism is a refuge of the national spirit" (Tsyrem-pilov 2016, 26–28; Garri 2014, 71).

Soviet repression against Buddhist leaders and temples was protracted.[59] By 1935, 44 large and 144 smaller Buddhist temples had been closed. A haunting passage from the Buryat émigré Nicholas Poppe (1958, 190), in the propagan-distically titled *Genocide in the USSR*, highlighted the Soviet destruction of Bud-dhism: "The end of the Agin Monastery, which was liquidated in about 1934, was particularly tragic. At first it was simply closed, and the lamas were for the most part arrested or sent to the concentration camps in Turukhan Krai." The Soviet film crew of *Descendant of Genghis Khan* exacerbated the devastation: "One of the episodes in the film showed a procession of lamas carrying sacred books. The 108-volume work, *Gandzur*, was withdrawn from the monastery . . . when the books were no longer needed, they were thrown into a ditch beside the road" (Poppe 1958, 190).

A subsequent crystallizing cause of resentment against Soviet repression of Buddhists is represented by legal proceedings that Buryat elites call the "Dan-daron affair." Beginning in 1972, a series of arrests were made against a circle of Buddhist intellectuals and their friends, centered on the brilliant and idio-syncratic Buddhologist Bidiia (Bidiiadara or Vidyahara) Dandaron, whose life (1914–1974) was cut short violently within the notorious Soviet prison system. Dandaron was a follower of the Tibetan lama Jayaksa-Gegen and the Buryat lama Lubsan Samdan Tsydenov, who died along with his dream of a Buryat Buddhist state in 1922. By some accounts, Dandaron was the reincarnation of Jayaksa-Gegen and became first a pupil, then a spiritual disciple, of Sam-dan Tsydenov.[60] They practiced a theocratic Tantric Buddhism that Soviet authorities considered deviant and threatening. While a student of aviation in Leningrad, Dandaron also became a leader of the *balagat* movement, known as Dharma-raja. Arrested in 1937, he was released and rehabilitated in 1956, becoming a popular scholar in the Buryat Comprehensive Scientific Institute (later Institute of Social Sciences) until 1972. His circle—which included Bur-yats, Russians, Ukrainians, Estonians, and others—was attracted to forbidden-fruit teachings of spiritual brotherhood and Tantric rituals. Enduring a full-fledged show trial in Ulan-Ude, they were accused of "organizing a Bud-dhist sect," violating articles 147 (part 3) and 247 (part 1) in the Soviet criminal code (Zhukovskaia 2010, 203).

Shockingly, participants in Dandaron's circle were falsely blamed for "manag-ing a vast underground Buddhist 'cult' that participated in bloody sacrifices and debauched sex rituals; speculated in illegal 'cult objects'; made attempts on the lives of apostates; and carried out secret correspondence with anti-Soviet emigres and 'international Zionism.'"[61] Dandaron was sent to a labor colony in Buryatia, where he died after being forced to work with a broken arm and leg. Others were arrested, lost their jobs and reputations, or were forced abroad, in a series of ripple effects that extended beyond Buryatia to Moscow (its famed Oriental Institute), Leningrad, and the Baltics. Since many who instigated or were complicit in the 1972–1973 repressions were alive when the Soviet Union collapsed, full rehabilitation of the Dandaron circle remained problematic into the 1990s, although his writings were published.[62] They helped younger Buddhists stimulate an eventual multipronged revival that was simultaneously Buryat and Tibetan in orientation, replete with internal tensions.

The 1930s monastery closures and the 1970s Dandaron affair provide perspective on the far better publicized Étigelov phenomenon, considered by some as a mystical puzzle and others as confirmation of the power of Buryat-Buddhist spiritual enlightenment. Dashi-Dorzho Étigelov (also Itigelev) was a Buryat lama who predicted the Soviet repressions and their eventual transcendence. He died and was preserved in a mummified state in 1927, before he could be arrested. He now sits in lotus position, with ritualized splendor, at the reopened and restored Ivolga Monastery complex.[63] He is greeted on special occasions by crowds and dignitaries, who marvel at his well-preserved visage. Some hope for miraculous cures, while others seek to learn the secret of his embalmment. As per his prescient instructions, his secret tomb was revealed only in 2003, when it was safe to do so, after other premature forays. His return to Buryat believers has become a symbol of Buryat Buddhist regeneration, although the body itself is subject to enormous scientific and theological debate, as well as the strains of adoring worshippers.

The excellent monograph of the anthropologist Anya Bernstein (2013) uses this "rematerialized body" and other fascinating examples of body politics to illustrate tensions between a special, unique path for Buryat cultural sovereignty and a sense of the place of Buryats in the wider Geluk Buddhist world. Buryat cultural striving is exemplified in nationalist discourses that recenter Buddhism northward, privileging Buryat lamas. Bernstein shows (2012, 261) how Buryats at crucial moments in Russian-Buryat power relations have managed to incorporate and render into their own political-religious sphere Russian figures of authority, including in 2009 designating President Dmitri Medvedev as "an embodiment of the Buddhist goddess White Tara." This is analogous to Caroline Humphrey's much earlier insights (1998 [1983], 441) that in the Soviet period, "Rather than an insertion of a Buryat native content into Soviet modes of explanation, we find the reverse: the phenomena of the Soviet world appear, disconnected from their theoretical origins, structured by a Buryat consciousness." We are far from taking Sovietization at its face value here, as Melissa Chakars (2014), lauding pragmatic educational successes, sometimes does (compare Chakars 2019).

By 2020, the long-serving official head of the Buddhist *Sangha* in Buryatia Khambo Lama Damba Aiusheev termed President Vladimir Putin the White Tara (can both Medvedev and Putin have this honor?) and controversially praised Putin's more direct support over that of the interdicted-in-Russia Dalai Lama. During his twenty-five-year service, Khambo Lama Aiusheev managed to get himself in trouble with some Buryats for financial decisions, for conflict with the republic head, and for perceived patriarchal comments about women. At a seemingly innocuous children's dance performance, he mentioned the absence of boys as an "uncultured" manifestation of the "Buryat matriarchate." This provoked a Buryat feminist group called I Am Freedom to award him a mocking "sexist of the year" appellation. His financial support for a "sacred cow" in the form of a Buryat breed of sheep to be distributed to impoverished families has been controversial, as has his critique of the republic head's lavish spending in a restaurant owned by a rival Buddhist group, the Center for Tibetan Buddhism. Revealing a willingness to use his Buddhist platform for political and social issues, Aiusheev also criticized Alexei Tysdenov for his handling of the Ulan-Ude mayoral election and Russification language debates. In the 1990s, he advocated that the precious symbol of Buryat and Tibetan Buddhism, *The Atlas of Tibetan Medicine*, should remain in Buryatia and not travel abroad for restoration or exhibition.[64]

Shamanic revival illustrates alternative directions of conscious Buryat post-Soviet cultural striving, creative adaptation, and reconstructed kinship connections. In 2010, I was privileged to participate in a joyous version of Buryat spiritual revitalization, a recasting and democratization of shamanic animal sacrifice practices (*tailagan*) centered on the mountain God of the Tunka Valley, Bøhø [Bukha] Noyon. It was organized by one of several prominent and sometimes competing shamans' associations, Tengeri. The leader Bair Tsyrendorziev explained that the God was open to supplications from everyone, not just long-established local male clan worshippers. Ancestral spirits manifested themselves in various combinations, as an unprecedented group of twenty-seven extravagantly dressed and masked shamans fell into trance through vigorous, prolonged drumming. Unconventionally, among them were women, including one young Buryat apprentice from Mongolia. A key moment in the innovative daylong ceremony, held in a field under a looming Sayan mountain, came when the God himself was manifest through and within the "crossed over" (entranced) dancing figure of the most prominent, elaborately spinning fringe-flying shaman (Figures 10–11).

Soon after, two sheep and a goat were sacrificed near a cluster of birch branches festooned with ribbons. The cooked animals eventually provided ample sustenance, carefully distributed for all the families and guests in attendance.

FIGURE 10. Buryat *tailagan* ceremony, consulting a shaman. By author.

FIGURE 11. Buryat *tailagan* ceremony, Tunka Valley, shamans dancing. By author. 2010.

After local villagers and other supplicants had a chance to ask the spirits personal questions, the ceremony ended with a mass water purification, a promenade, and a huge bonfire of birch branches.

More recently, some Buryats have been discussing the need for a modernization of Tengeri that would discourage animal sacrifice and emphasize the common values of Buddhism and shamanism, especially values of ecological etiquette. This was the position of the late Soyot-Buryat lama-gelong Danzan-Khaibzun (Fedor Sergeevich) Samaev (1954–2005), a deputy to Buryatia's People's Khural from 1994 to 1998 and founder of the organization Maidar (from Bodhisattva Maitreya, Sanskrit), unifying three Sayan datsans. He insisted: "Buryat-Buddhists must not oppose Tengerianstvo (shamanism). The shamanistic Tengeri and Buddhist worldviews are for the Buryat people two spiritual wings, crucial for orientations in life."[65] Samaev also founded the ecology activist group Akhalar, promoting Sanskrit and Buryat concepts of nonviolence, altruism, and pure living within one's place in the world. Beginning in 1992, the movement's aim was to highlight the integration of Buryat religious traditions with ecological values. Followers began the task of registering and preserving traditional places of ancestral spirit worship in the Tunka and Akha (Oka) regions, especially on mountain peaks. Through message dreams well known in visionary traditions, Samaev himself also recovered Buddhist relics that had been buried.[66] Samaev died in a car crash on July 10, 2005, precisely the day of the annual summer Maidari celebration, a correlation his followers see as more than coincidence.

Samaev's Akhalar and his integrated spiritual and practical teachings continued with his successor, the influential scholar-lama Danzan-Dashi (Vladimir Aiusheevich) Shaglakhaev (2014, 9–10), who explains that "Tengeri and Buddhist approaches together enable understanding of the universe and the interconnectedness of humans to it ... A synthesis of Tengeri and Buddhist gods, each at the appropriate level, enables their responsibilities to be fulfilled, for help [to humans] to be delivered." Idealistically, he elaborated to a colleague in 2015 that precisely the Indigenous peoples, such as "Buryats, Sakha, Tibetans, and Native Americans, who honor nature, fire, water, and the earth with their rituals," are those who can "regulate the extremes of nature," being "the most ecologically oriented" in their values, spirituality, and "life energy."[67]

Sacred extended family homelands are connected to a person's bioenergy and ancestry through the concept of *toonto*, mentioned briefly above and elaborated by Dugarova (2014, 147–49). Lands that are productive and hot (*khaluun gazar*), long-occupied tribal places for pasturage and worship, have meaning beyond usufruct because of their maintenance through humble familial obligations, including yearly rituals (*tailagan*). Abrogation is a sin (*séér*). Dugarova explains (2014, 148) that this special sense of interactive ownership has "today been transformed to a general desire of Buryats to hold onto and revitalize their traditions." Kinship-based lands and waters have become the locus of spiritual awakening and historical memory. These specific places of successful cattle raising then extend outward to a general network of Buryat connections, where the animal world, mountains, forests, valleys, rivers and lakes, and their images all become crucial to current "deep ecological consciousness," because all of nature has feelings and reason (Dugarova 2014, 151–52). Certain protected ancestral images—such as eagle, swan, bear, dog, swallow, snipe, cuckoo, wolf, and fox—have reemerged as significant "totems" through offering rituals, naming, and dreaming.[68]

Powerful examples of recovered ancestral wisdom come through dreaming in Buddhist and more traditional shamanic worldviews. Some Buryat, including those not claiming to be shamans, may be able to tap into matrilineal traditions and awaken channels to deceased grandmothers, exemplified in epics and the kind grandmother figure Manzai Gurmé Ézhi. As elders pass away and people become more uprooted from their villages, fear of losing psychologically healing legacies of rituals, morality, and connectedness has intensified. Some of my well-educated interlocutors in Buryatia and abroad see the wisdom of ancestors as no less effective than the science of literate-based Western societies. When dreaming and telepathic understanding, not well enough understood in Western medicine, are lucent enough to recover family narratives, inherited pain may be transformed into activism and self-awareness.

This healing process correlates with a border-transcending Buryat shamanic tradition of respect for a female Robin-Hood like spirit named Modoon. Modoon is evoked through mediator shamans who channel her with formulaic language by chanting: "I am *Modoon*, the descendant of *Gombo*, Who was not defeated by the power of the empire, Who was not defeated by the ruling king. I am the arbitrary *Modoon*" (Dulam 2010, 28). Modoon's tragic history becomes other Buryats' potential rescue. She was an inspiring shaman who helped the poor, fighting unjust rulers and lords, until she was arrested and burned, together with her shamanic dress and drum. But her spirit survived by hiding under embers, drumming frantically until she could fly out and become a heroic savior. The Mongolian ethnographer Bumachir Dulam (2010, 28) terms her a "sanctuary shaman." Modoon's legend and blood ties activated in dreaming in turn resonate with the chanted testimony-refrain of one apprentice shaman, "I have re-related to my ancestor spirits (*Iigeed ugaa bariad*)" (Dulam 2010, 37).

In sum, some in the new generations of Buryat activists, lamas, and shamans represent far more than an inauthentic "constructed culture" or a passing post-Soviet fad. Their diversity and interactions with each other are evolving and explorative. However competitive within their communities, with each other, and with Russian Orthodox or newer missionaries, they have created associations that appeal to villagers and to some urban, relocated Buryats seeking to reconnect with their mini homelands, their kin, and their nearly lost monasteries. Their rituals are self-conscious eclectic conduits through which an impressive range of Buryat-Mongolic ancestor-oriented values have been contended and rekindled in new ways for new times, without paralyzing nostalgia. They constitute aspects of a series of uneven and fragile attempts at rebuilding Buryat dignity in the shadow of a mountain of attempts to curtail it.

Near the village of Kachug, where the Lena River has its mountainous and rocky beginnings, is a site that was used for centuries as a ceremonial hub. Nearby are petroglyphs, and in the Brezhnev period, as an unauthorized Buryat cultural revival was underway in the region, local authorities tried to nip it in the bud by dynamiting the ceremonial stones that marked the sacred space. Far from curtailing religious practice, they drove it farther underground and stimulated the sympathy of some local Russians for the Buryat community of believers (compare Gusewelle 1994, 66; Karnyshev and Ivanova 2014, 179–81). Such determination and its narration then served as a basis for later post-Soviet resilience, in all its cacophony.

Divergent Nostalgias, Clashing Values, and Uncertain Futures

Several sculptures and multiple reactions to them provide insights into interethnic relations and contrasting values in the splintered Buryat homeland, perceived in its broadest sense. The first sculpture is the previously mentioned towering bronze eagle, placed in 2013 during the Ërdyn Games that biannually bring together Mongolic and Turkic peoples. The eagle's prime spot overlooking the Olkhon-Baikal region gives it a panorama of the Tazheran steppe. Its location and form simultaneously honor Olkhon shamanic ancestors and represent a time-tested Buryat sensibility. Closer to Irkutsk, in the Tazheran steppe, another 2013 statue memorializes a Russian folk hero valorized in the song "Along the Wild Steppes of Zabaikal." He is an escaped prisoner, a *brodiaga* (wanderer, Russian). Some local Buryats consider this a tribute to a ruffian and an insult to the spirits of their sacred land. However, mixed ethnic and predominantly Slavic residents or tourists see it as a rightful tribute to their own ancestors, many of whom were Russian prisoners and exiles, sometimes calling themselves Siberiaki.[69]

These first two symbols of divergent nostalgias pale in comparison to the scandal that erupted in 2015 over a third heroic statue not yet built, but planned by the Russian mayor of Ulan-Ude to feature a Cossack conqueror. He was supposed to represent the republic capital's founder, but Cossack valorization seems to have become a political step too far. Nagovitsyn, then head of the republic, nixed the monument after a public outcry that, among other strategies, evoked the United Nations Declaration on the Rights of Indigenous Peoples. Opponents pointed out that the founders of the "ancient town of Ulan-Ude" were Huns, not Cossacks. During the fray, the sarcastic mayor Aleksandr Golkov retorted to a republic news reporter that he has "only one shortcoming, not [being] a member of the titular nationality."[70]

After delay and debate, another controversial sculpture called *Keeper of Baikal*, by the famed Buryat sculptor Dashi Namdakov, overlooks Lake Baikal from a cliff on the sacred island of Olkhon. Its delivery from an Ulan-Ude warehouse in 2017 was delayed due to protests against lack of environmental oversight, the need for an appropriate review process, and the possibility that it violates ancient shamanic values while purporting to champion them. The sculpture is a monumental bronze tree that resembles a shaman-protector with branches constituting his crown. The activist Andrei Ershov, leader of the movement For a Sacred Baikal, protested its placement and fears accelerated ecotourism. The dispute landed in court, revealing contrasting visions of how to create and represent a usable past.[71]

Another case of clashing values also centers on the sacred island of Olkhon in Lake Baikal, site of many rituals and recent protests, where I was told in 2005 that shamanist, Buddhist, and Russian Orthodox believers were in active competition with each other. Ritual objects were repeatedly disappearing from the sacred cave and beach, near its famed Shamanka Rock that abuts the island like a prow (Figure 12). Especially hard to place with any permanence was an icon of St. Nicholas the healer, which reputedly was stolen from a niche in the cave, recovered, and stolen again. Some local Buryats suspected, but could not prove, that the shaman-keeper of the island, Valentin Khagdaev, was behind the thefts. Some also resented Khagdaev for insisting on strict gender segregation, forbidding women in the most sacred parts of the cave. Nonetheless, Khagdaev, and not the local Russian Orthodox priest, regularly presented himself to tourists and anthropologists as more modern and tolerant in his analysis of interethnic relations.[72]

A personally embarrassing vignette reveals potential tensions just under the surface of everyday life in the Greater Buryatia region. In 2005, I touched down on Olkhon Island in a small private propeller plane with a group sponsored by New York's American Museum of Natural History. We had just flown over the majestic sacred rock Shamanka. To my horror, the Russian pilots, who had bragged of their flying experience in the Chechnya wars, set the plane on a grassy

FIGURE 12.   Olkhon Island sacred tree with prayer flags near cave entrance. By author.

plateau just above the sacred rock, close to its access path. "Couldn't we have found somewhere less sacred to put our noisy, intruding plane on?" I stuttered in shock. The two macho pilots just laughed, and our usually competent part-Russian, part-Buryat guide simply shrugged. I feared that my chances for a meeting with the island's keeper-shaman and main historian, the above-mentioned Valentin Khagdaev, were slim, and that we had likely offended many villagers. If shamanists were to be believed, we had also offended the local spirits of the land. It was an inauspicious start that ended several days later in a violent storm that some locals attributed to our disrespect. It did not bode well for the dramatic increase in economically needed commercial tourism on the island and in the republic as a whole.

The battle for commercialization of Olkhon and of Lake Baikal continued into 2017, when a scandal broke out concerning the illegal sale of plots for potential Olkhon lake-front dachas to Chinese buyers. This had been going on semisecretly for nearly a decade but came to a head with a local youth protest against the sales and a shamanic ceremony evoking Tengeri. Ekaterina Uderevskaya, a community council member affiliated with Buryatia's environment oversight department, allowed herself to say on camera to Russia's *Vremya* TV program: "The People's Republic of China has launched full scale development of lands near our sacred Lake Baikal. It is a result of the carelessness and of criminal acts committed by our officials."[73] Fancy villas are being constructed on $500,000 plots of land. In a touching civic society response, a few local officials think they can talk potential and actual buyers out of their investment by appealing to their good will. Some local Russian and Buryat loggers and builders have threatened to boycott the construction sites, even if it is against their economic interests.

Relatively more positive trends are also visible. The thrilling resurrection represented by the unearthing of the Buddhist monk Étigelov, no matter what interpretation one chooses of his bodily preservation and return to Ivolga, can be compared to the hopes raised by some ecology activist successes in the region. These are resonating phenomena that are made stronger, not weaker, by the participation of people of multiple ethnicities in their synergistic movements. They represent not only deep connections to the land but also renewed spirituality on personal and community-building levels. Their histories speak to a strong Buryat sense of rightful recovery from past outrages at the nexus of religion, environmentalism, and politics. Their stories are not over, but local spirituality is probably not enough to save the Baikal region from further economic despoliation, political manipulation by power sources far from the region, and from hemorrhaging outmigration of some of the "best and brightest" young Buryats.

For many Buryats—despite the region's gold, jade, and charoit—few resources are left to share or develop in sustainable ways. Local priorities are low in hierarchies of decision making. While the Russian governor of the amalgamated Zabaikal krai attempts to lease extensive lands to wealthy Chinese or Mongolians, some local Buryat leaders still dream of reunited territories absorbed into the existing Buryat Republic. Most are far from secessionist, wishing merely to recoup the loss of their lands within a legitimate Federation of Rossiia. Legacies of poverty, politics, and demography are not in their favor. Others, mostly Moscow-based Russian economists and politicians, are calling for an amalgamated macroregion that would not be a republic at all, creating a prescription for a further loss of Buryat sovereignty, making any self-rule hard to recover once the borders are legally changed and the territory renamed.[74] This issue is revisited in the conclusions to the book.

In the context of an already splintered people struggling with cross-border communities and multidirectional diasporas, a macroregion would create conditions for accelerating assimilation processes that have been subtly resisted for centuries. Nonetheless, a countertrend of Buryat in-migration to the truncated republic provides some hope for renewal in the form of the talented and worldly youth of Greater Buryatia. Some young people, whether trained in Moscow as academics, in Mongolia as business persons, in the West as scientists, or in Tibet or India as Buddhist lamas, continue to return to their republic homeland in a pattern that needs to become sustainable for the republic to survive and thrive.

REPUBLIC OF TYVA (TUVA)
A Borderline State with Demographic Advantages

Let's return to the name Uriankhai! From ancient times we called ourselves Uriankhaians.

—Igor Irgit, *Tuvinskaia pravda*, September 7, 2017

On the question of identity crystallization, I agree that the language politics of 2015–2016 fully fits as an example . . . All that is tied to the Native language is very important. People feel very strongly."

—Zoya Anaiban, sociologist, personal communications, June 4, 2015, June 1, 2020

Don't go back to Tuva. There's too much crime there and you will be targeted because you don't look Tuvan.

—Russian economist, personal communication, June 10, 2016

My grandfather was a [nomadic] camel herder. He owned 320 camels before Tyva was incorporated into the Soviet Union in 1944. You cannot even imagine what that was like. It was another world.

—Zoya Kyrgyz, musicologist, personal communication, October 12, 2015

Tensions between cultural politics and development issues have been growing with increasing urgency in the past decade in the Republic of Tyva (Tuva), as in other republics of Russia. High across the Sayan mountain range into the Upper Yenisei basin of Siberia, the Republic of Tyva borders Mongolia. Its complex and controversial history of relations with the Russians has in part been driven by its geographic isolation. This chapter explores the degree to which Tyvans, a Turkic-language-speaking people with an overwhelming demographic majority in their own republic, have been able to consolidate their identity as an ethnonational group.[1] This depends on their ability to negotiate use of their regional resources and maintain much-needed subsidies from Russia while preserving their cultural, ecological, and spiritual values.

Significantly, Tyvans are among the few non-Russian peoples of Russia, along with the Chechens and Chuvash, who constitute a substantial majority within the current borders of their "titular republic." Their health and poverty indicators are openly discussed as alarming (Chubarova and Grigorieva 2016). Given that citizens of the republic are among the poorest per capita within Russia, with economic hardship subsidies that make them highly dependent on Moscow's support, how autonomous can Tyvans be?

The Republic of Tyva, despite considerable internal diversity, provides a key case for exploring contingent dimensions of relative and nested sovereignty within Russia. I examine here the shifting dimensions of what aspirations are plausible for a non-Russian group within Russia, as the centralizing state has become increasingly less federal and more authoritarian. As emphasized in the introduction, most Siberians are not currently secessionist, and it is unethical for outsider analysts to attribute secessionist sentiments to any ethnonational group or leader. However, some in Tyva indeed advocated secession as the Soviet Union was breaking up in 1991. This chapter helps to explain why by integrating historical, sociological, and cultural identity field and research data.

A premise of the book is that in post-Soviet Russia political emphasis on republics named for particular nationalities has been helpful for ethnonational mobilization, enabling limited and uneven advocacy for social, cultural, and ecological rights.[2] "Liberal nationalism," as defined by Yael Tamir (1993), and termed "ethnonationalism" by Walker Conner (1994), are aspirational concepts far from outdated but difficult to realize in Russia's current political environment. I argue that when federal relations are balanced, negotiated, and reciprocal, legitimate federalism such as that advocated by the Tyvan director of the republic's national museum, Kadyr-ool A. Bicheldei, can mitigate nationalist polarization reflected in secession claims in fragile federal states. A major danger—alarmingly illustrated by the 2014 annexation of Crimea, current conflagration in East Ukraine, and simmering unrest in the North Caucasus—is the potential for out-of-control political violence.[3] A spiral of violence can result if and when sovereignty bids are repressed harshly. Border republics like Tyva, with a Mongolian border longer than that of Buryatia, are particularly vulnerable.

This chapter places Tyva in the context of Russia, and of Russian nationalism, by reviewing historical legacies, secessionist dynamics, language activism, ecological advocacy integrated with homeland discourses, and religious-spiritual revitalization. Conclusions revisit and expand on issues of federalism, sovereignty, leadership, spirituality, and identity.

Historical Legacies and Revision

Tyva is literally and figuratively a borderline state, given its historical legacies. Despite celebrations of the centennial of its affiliation with Russia in 2014, it legally was only a weak "protectorate" of the Russian Empire, called Uriankhai Territory in 1914, after Chinese and Mongol rule over the area disintegrated. One of the strongest pleas for a return to Uriankhai identity, expressed in a provocative *Tuvinskaia pravda* article in 2017 by the Tyvan activist Igor Irgit, is quoted above. His reasoning, a vivid example of rhetoric meant to galvanize nostalgia, is revealing:

> We continue to be called Uriankhaians by the Chinese and Mongolians, indeed by all who had contact with our ancestors. It is a term of respect that dates to the times of Chingis Khan, when it was associated with our glorious warriors. These warriors were elite divisions in his armies. Uriankhai soldiers did not get drunk. They did not kill children, nor insult anyone, being inculcated for good deeds. They always fulfilled their military objectives. They respected their elders and helped them in everything. It is not surprising that our people respected them completely and gave them full authority. Indeed, our people cherished our warriors and showered them with honor titles and war monikers, such as lion—*arzylan*; elephant—*chaan*; wolf—*boru*; falcon—*nachyn*; eagle—*burgut* and more. Soldiers wore badges of honor, usually of silver . . . [We give badges to our commanders, as a thousand years ago; we sing hymns with pride] . . . With such rituals, a person comes into awareness and respect for one's homeland, taking on responsibilities for one's elders and children, for kin and close ones . . . I very much hope that my historical roots can be preserved. I wish for my sons to be proud of their historical name—Uriankhaian![4]

Understandably, Russian reaction against this brand of Tyvan-Uriankhai patriotism was swift. Despite Igor Irgit's attempts to align his plea with high officials such as Tyva's President Sholban Kara-ool and Russia's Minister of Defense Sergei Shoigu, some Russians see his position as a suspicious attempt to return to China's sphere, when Tyvans were merely "slaves" under China's rule. Although Irgit has correlated his name change suggestion to that of the Yakuts reformulating their self-identity back to their historical ethnonym Sakha, the Russian ethnographer Boris Myshliavtsev retorts that "not one Tyvan calls himself an Uriankhai," and that it was historically a geographical term. More serious, Russian critics of the idea, which is not likely to be adopted any time soon, fear that it represents a socially disruptive appeal to those Tyvans who may want to Latinize their alphabet or orient themselves to China, Mongolia, and other parts of the increasingly affluent Asian community. Political analysts such as Anatoly Savostin consider the name change ploy to be a desire to escape Russia's orbit, fearing it could stimulate Chinese and Mongolian claims for return of territories that they once controlled.[5]

In 1911, Russian officials first explored using Uriankhai as a buffer zone with China and Mongolia. Recent Russian propaganda has magnified the significance of the resulting protectorate status. The chaos of Russia's 1917–1921 civil war in the region led to attempts by Mongols, pan-Mongol Buryat patriots, and Chinese warlords to retake Tyva, but Tyvan leaders declared independence in 1921. It became a separate country—Tannu (Taiga)-Touva (1921–1944), with its own monetary unit called *aksha* and collector-worthy stamps (Figure 13).

Tyva officially joined the Soviet Union in similar timing (World War II and its aftermath) as the much higher-profile Baltic States. Much of the early to mid-twentieth-century history is disputed, as recent Tyvan historians acknowledge, although many agree that, while not part of the Soviet Union, Tannu-Touva leaders created a client state, a revolutionary "people's democracy," with Soviet interests in the area cemented by a 1926 treaty.[6]

FIGURE 13.   1927 Tannu-Touva stamp [postage was issued 1921–1944]. Open source.

When President Vladimir Putin arrived in Tyva for the centennial celebrations, he glossed over the brief moment of Tyva's relative sovereignty and emphasized the region's "unification with Russia" (*edinenie*, Russian) in 1914, as well as its subsequent ability to maintain its own culture: "As a result of Russia taking Tuva under its wing, the local people managed to retain their national identity, culture, language, and the faith of their ancestors." He elaborated: "This land has enormous natural resources that we are yet to develop as we create new production facilities and new jobs"—a point received as a mixed blessing by those in the crowd leery of the track record of Russian newcomers. Subsequent interviews with Tyvans based in the republic and abroad have confirmed that many considered the celebrations "a good excuse to have a multiday extravaganza." However, as one interlocutor dryly put it, they were celebrating "not particularly accurate history."[7]

The celebration itself was an "ordered from above" occasion made to fit into a pattern that other republics, marking longer accession or incorporation histories, also experienced during multiple Putin administrations. The purpose of these public acknowledgments, complete with gift-edition revisionist histories of interethnic relations, seems to be ritualizing gratitude. However, local leaders—especially the Tyvan head (earlier president), Sholban Kara-ool—used it as an opportunity to discuss development, economic subsidies, a new rail line, and employment problems with Putin directly. It became an occasion to welcome back to his homeland the well-connected "native son" Sergei Shoigu, the previously successful minister of emergency response who became minister of defense in 2014.[8] It also helped buttress the youthful Kara-ool's popularity, since he was a controversial presidential appointee. His background as a businessman who made his fortune in alcohol sales is widely critiqued. His excellent relations with President Vladimir Putin, who gave him an Order of Friendship medal in 2017, are emblematic of Tyva's current mainstream politics of dependency on Moscow. (Putin took a widely publicized summer vacation with Kara-ool and Shoigu in Tyva in 2017 and returned to celebrate his sixty-seventh birthday in 2019, walking on a Yenisei River cliff at the border with Mongolia.)

An ironic aspect of recent revisionist history touting legacies of harmonious relations between Tyvan and Russian leaders is that the keynote presentation at the "scientific conference honoring the hundredth jubilee," called "United Tuva in United Russia," was by the famed Tyvan politician and patriot Kadyr-ool Bicheldei. In his address, Bicheldei tried to put a positive spin on Tyva's status within Russia while acknowledging past difficulties, saying, "The road has been opened for further decisions regarding the resolution of social and economic problems of the republic." A linguist by training, ousted as minister of education, Bicheldei's post-Soviet career has mirrored a process of deradicalization and pragmatism that has characterized some Tyvan leaders.[9] In the early 1990s, he led a popular front called Khostug-Tyva (Free Tyva), although he was far from the most separatist within various hothead factions of that party. Emerging from the opposition, he then became a responsible member of the Supreme Council and by 1994 the head of the Tyvan parliament, the Grand Khural. Fluent in multiple languages, he transformed into a statesman and speaker of the parliament for many years under the first popularly elected post-Soviet Tyvan president Oorzhak Sherig-ool. A news report from 1992 mentioned that Sherig-ool and Bicheldei had postponed a referendum on Tyva's secession from Russia, since they "managed to persuade the 'radicals' that the republic's economic position was so difficult that survival without Russia was an illusion" (Kniazkov 1992, 3).

For me, Bicheldei, whom I have met and admire, symbolizes the potential for dynamic young protest organizers to calm down and become wise elder statesmen. However, some consider he has "sold out" to a neo-Soviet establishment and others claim he pocketed money in a corrupt building contract scheme as minister of education. In 2015, for his sixty-fifth birthday, he was honored by his home region Ulug-Zhem *kozhuun* (in Tyvan glossed as "region" and historically associated with kinship collectives). An annual conference was established, called Bicheldei Readings, on current events and issues deemed important for the education of potentially rebellious middle-school youth. The idea behind the meetings is to inspire talented young people to aspire to higher education. The theme of the 2017 conference paralleled the Year of Ecology proclaimed throughout Russia.[10] In 2018, attuned to popular mood, Bicheldei presided over the opening of an exhibit in Tyva's national museum dedicated to the Uriankhai warrior-prince Subedei-Maadyr. By 2020, Bicheldei was rumored to be maneuvering to bring Sherig-ool back into the presidency in the 2021 elections, an uphill battle given Russia's post-coronavirus strategies and constitutional amendment ramifications discussed in the conclusions.

Secession, Displacement, and Demographic Dynamics

Why did some Tyvans advocate secession when the Soviet Union broke up? Answers lie in their history of Sovietization and in one of the most embittering but little-known conflagrations of late Soviet and early post-Soviet history. Incorporation into Russia as a mere "autonomous oblast" in 1944 meant loss of some traditionally claimed lands, many resources (including gold, uranium, and coal), and much dignity. While limited collectivization, in the form of "production associations," began earlier on a gradual basis, massive, destructive reorganization of the pastoral economy and settlement of Tyvan herders did not begin until the late 1940s. A decade later, some unaffiliated Tyvan herders nomadized on territories they considered theirs by clan collective use rights, and some minority Todja herders managed to avoid full settlement through the Soviet period.

Intellectuals, especially active lamas associated with Tyva's once thriving Buddhist community, were punished in a second wave of repression. (Prior repressions occurred in the 1920s, when lamas, nobility, and merchants fled the region to Mongolia and beyond.) Tyva became an autonomous republic inside the Russian Federation only in 1961, when the Khrushchev "thaw" enabled redressing at least some perceived political injustices.

As the Soviet Union was collapsing, pent-up interethnic tensions in Tyva burst into violence against Russians in particularly startling ways. Serious interethnic violence occurred in May–July 1990 and recurred sporadically in the following five years. The initial incidents were concentrated in areas of high unemployment and relatively recent Russian settlement. For example, in the summer of 1990, after a dance-hall brawl, young Tyvans rampaged in the industrial town of Khovu-Aksy, the site of a cobalt plant. Local Communist Party leaders, especially Grigory Shirshin, accused the nascent popular front of fomenting ethnic pogroms against the Russian population to ensure the Tyvan demographic majority. Others insisted that the authorities themselves had an interest in provoking, identifying, and jailing discontented youths to at least temporarily pacify and discredit hotheads. In Kyzyl, the capital, where Tyvans were a minority, Tyvan youths reputedly attacked several non-Tyvan-speaking Russians after probing their language abilities. In the settlement of Elegest, messages were placed under Russians' doors, suggesting that families leave within a month. Houses there were raided and burned. At the remote mountain lake of Sut-Khol, three Slavic fishers, including a boy, were murdered, reputedly for trespassing at a sacred site but possibly due to a personal dispute. Grieving Russians brought the bodies to Kyzyl, where a crowd of mourners, nearly out of control, was persuaded to vent anger into a microphone. One Tyvan observer recalled: "It was terrible to see the funeral procession. From Russians, we heard 'But we taught you to wash yourselves and cook kasha!'"[11]

By midsummer, black beret troops of the Ministry of the Interior were sent to quell the disturbances, angering Tyvans further and exacerbating polarization that increased nationalism on both sides. Russians, estimated at over ten thousand, fled in the early 1990s along the Abazinsk Tract toward Khakassia. Nearly all the residents of the economically depressed town of Ak-Dovurak left, including some Tyvans, although local officials begged skilled workers and professionals to stay.

A recollection from a Tyvan friend sheds light on this turbulent period: "During the disturbances, at the height of the protests, organizers of Khostug Tyva were sitting in the main square in Kyzyl with banners that included 'Russians go home.'" My friend was called over by a school acquaintance and urged to join the protest. But s/he rejected the offer, rebutting with: "Next you'll be coming after métis, mixed people, and I'm one of them . . . My mother was Russian. What do you mean Russians go home? That makes no sense—many have lived here for generations." When I asked about the standard analysis that it was mostly Russian professionals who left, and who had been dominating the Soviet-period politics, I was told: "Sure, plenty of Russian professionals left, but that is not the only kind of Russians, plenty of workers left . . . I don't know how many, what proportion. It could have been more than ten thousand. We don't really know the numbers."[12]

In mixed ethnic villages such as those in the Todju district, where several generations of Russian families had lived peacefully and Russians grew up knowing the Tyvan language, no conflict occurred. This shows that local context studies of interethnic relations are crucial to avoid overgeneralizations about entire republics or regions.

Some of the Russian workers who left are now nostalgic for their lost Tyvan homeland. They say they left not simply due to interethnic conflict but especially due to the economics of collapsing Soviet infrastructure. Examples include Russians from the town of Shagaan-Aryy (also called Shagonar). The name, glossed as White Bright Field, is disconcerting since it was the home of an asbestos plant. Some left before the Soviet Union collapsed, partly because they were out of work as the dangers of asbestos mining and the collapse of the industry became a worldwide phenomenon. (A Soviet town in the Ural Mountains was named Asbestos.) Some left because they felt less comfortable in Tyva than they had before the "disturbances." Many resettled in a town in Krasnoyarsk krai, over the mountains, in a dirty coal-mining valley with a lot of humidity and discomfort. "They miss Tyva," explained a colleague, "and sometimes come back to hunt and relax. They now live in Dudinka, but they've nicknamed it Tuvinka."[13]

The inaccurately termed "refugee situation" and other factors increased the Tyvan majority in the republic, from about 64 percent in the final 1989 Soviet census to over 70 percent by 1997. According to the 2010 census, Tyvans constituted 82 percent of their republic, or 249,299 out of a sparse total of 307,930. By 2020, Tyvans were over 40 percent rural, and their portion of the republic population was rising.[14] Many other ethnic groups—including Russians, Ukrainians, and Kyrgyz—make up the rest. In 1990, while demographics were discussed, the mostly young people who indulged in violence and ethnonational hate speech were motivated by a range of frustrations. A synergistic "perfect storm" of causes, some similar to conditions in other republics, combined to mutually reinforce each other and make parts of Tyva in the early 1990s exemplars of ethnic relations gone wrong (compare Horowitz 2000, 4–6).

In the Soviet period, extractive, semicolonial economic policies, large proportions of Russian settlers after 1944, and growing unemployment among Tyvan youths coincided with the demise of traditional Tyvan pastoralism under harsh sedentarization programs, the mandatory Russifying education of Tyvans in Soviet boarding schools, and the undermining of Tyvan spiritual values. Urbanization and industrialization created contexts in which newcomer Russian professionals lived better, or were perceived to live better, than Tyvans. A squatters' movement of impoverished Tyvans in Kyzyl increased tensions. Some Tyvans saw Russians as a linguistic and demographic threat, and they blamed Russians for ecological destruction in factory towns like Khovu-Aksy and the asbestos-producing Ak-Dovurak. This was compounded by their history of quasi-independence followed by perceived downgrading through incorporation into the Soviet Union. Communist Party cooption of some local elite kinship-linked leaders was increasingly viewed as mismanagement, and Moscow administrators' "divide and rule" tactics began to backfire. By 1990, when OMON troops massively overreacted in what locals saw as police work, backfiring was taken to a new level of resentment against "Moscow's federal level" interference.[15]

Fudging history, one recent Tyvan interlocutor seemed to be in self-denial when arguing that Tyvans had not perpetrated violence against Russians as the Soviet Union was breaking up. Minimalizing the role of the OMON troops, s/he explained: "There was no violence as the Soviet Union collapsed. But many of the Russians left because they felt threatened. They felt that the majority Tyvans were nationalist and might separate. And so, we lost many of our educated cadres. For example, some of the best doctors left." S/he was nostalgic for the stability of the Communist period, reminiscing: "It was good in our youth. We had what we needed. People got a good education. Tyvans and Russians got along fine. There were Russian specialists who taught Tyvans. In school we learned about Western classics, but it was all a distant myth." S/he added that paradoxically, "The whole West was demonized at the same time we learned about their classic Greek and Roman history as roots of civilization."[16]

The legacies of interethnic tensions continue to fester. For Russians still living in the capital Kyzyl, they have become daily, ordinary insults: "A Russian grandmother asked some children who screamed each day under her window to pipe down. The young ten- to twelve-year-old [Tyvan] kids talked back to her: 'You [informal *ty*], as long as you are still alive and still living here, are the one to be quiet. This is our land.'" The commentator went on to ask: "Where does this come from? Clearly from their parents, from the adults."[17] Young Tyvans in turn are living with uncertain futures, with declining interethnic marriages, increasing unregistered common law marriages that end in an accelerated rate of divorce, and failing social safety net programs leading to cycles of impoverishment (Anaiban 2016).

One Tyvan in 2020 clarified: "Specific acts of violence against Russians targeted as Russians have not been that many or that typical. One could even say that Tyvans have suffered more than Russians because the disintegration of the Communist Party meant that the republic has been without real leadership or governance." This political view was then adapted to sympathize somewhat with leaders responsible for something they cannot control: "The powers have been struggling with an unfamiliar phenomenon since those [Soviet Union breakup] days: widespread appearance of petty groups of unorganized criminals." Many of the criminals on the street have been too poor to own serious weapons, either in 1990 or today. My interlocutor added, "in the past five years far more doctors and teachers have left than in the whole history of [twentieth-century] Tuva."

In sum, by the late 1980s a fractured opposition began to develop, when emerging Kyzyl bureaucrats and intellectuals took advantage of Gorbachev's glasnost. The OMON troops ordered by Moscow in 1990 gave the popular front just the ammunition they needed to turn an eclectic and small elite into a more galvanized nationalist secession movement. Rhetoric included hopes for the return of some Uriankhai lands now in Krasnoyarsk krai, as well as historical valorization of earlier times, when Tyvans were ruled by a combination of a nobility (whose leader was a *noion*) and a Buddhist elite (whose leader was the Khambo Lama). This triggered romantic nostalgia of Svetlana Boym's (2001, 41) negative retrospective type. Finally, a folk memory of cultural and political affinity with the Mongols, made rosy with time, meant that some leaders and youths could suggest a turn toward Mongolia for post-Soviet support.

Turkic and Mongolic Identities Synergized into Language and Economic Politics

Politically, culturally, and economically, the Mongolian connection is simultaneously logical and problematic for Tyvans, given that Mongolia has been struggling to lift itself out of impoverishment and resolve complex reform politics. Further, Mongolian cultural affinities and exchanges are perceived as stronger with Buryats than Tyvans, at least some of whom would like to catch up. After a 2015 announcement that Kyzyl has a new exchange program with the city government of Moscow, local commentators quipped, "Why Moscow?—Ulan Bator is closer." Tyvan cultural roots are numerous, embedded in a context of diverse mountain valley economic adaptations and local sociopolitical divisions. Far from "primordial," these roots provide some background for recent nationalist discourse.

Tyvans formed from several Turkic groups, as well as Turkified Mongols, Samodeic, and possibly Ket speakers (Wixman 1984, 201). Tyva (Tuva, Touva) was used as an ethnonym before the tenth century, perhaps as a division of Uighur peoples. The Tyvan language, earlier called Uriankhai, is classified as Uighur-Tukui (old Uighur), in the Uighur-Oguz division of Northern Turkic, within the Ural-Altaic family. It has loan words from Mongolian, and by the eighteenth century, Tyvan elites used Mongolian and Tibetan literary languages associated with Buddhism.

An interlocutor of mixed Tyvan-Russian background brought these complexities alive for me in 2020, explaining that visually Tyvans look like many different Asian groups: "However, we are all Tyvans, no matter what. We live in a valley—like a big kettle . . . It is not important what someone looks like. Some of us look like we are from Philippines, some like Vietnamese, some like big squat Mongolians." Spicing romance with history, s/he added: "In the past we were the hiding place for people who were fleeing big warrior armies, perhaps Chingis Khan's. We had no fences, no borders, but that natural mountain valley kettle." This is why "we ended up with lots of clans—something like twenty-seven to thirty . . . They include Oiuun (meaning play); Oorzhak; Mongush; Ondar (similar to Uighurs), Seljak (similar to Seljuks of Central Asia), Kyrgyz (you know we in Altai are the ancestors of the Kyrgyz)." While acknowledging such distinctions with pride, the conclusion was, "We try to take care of each other."[18]

Tyva is one of the few republics in Russia where it is as common to hear the local language on the streets of the state capital, Kyzyl, as it is to hear Russian. The two official republic languages, Tyvan and Russian, mentioned in that order, are enshrined in article 5 of Tyva's 1993 Constitution, which also guarantees that the republic "observes the rights of all nationalities to the preservation of their native language, ensuring the conditions for their study and development."[19] Therefore, the republic's Tyvan intelligentsia reacted with shock and anger to 2015 federal-level instructions from the Ministry of Education that a "common educational space" be fostered throughout the country using new history and Russian-language textbooks. In Tyva, Russophone officials of the local education ministry controversially complied by recommending that non-Russian languages be taught with the same number of hours as "secondary foreign languages."[20]

The politics behind this Moscow-based stimulus to privilege the Russian language and ensure the continued spread of Russian civilization were reflected in a turbulent meeting held in Kyzyl on May 25, 2015, organized by the republic's All-Russia Popular Front and including members of Tyva's government and Ministry of Education. Although the meeting was multiethnic, it was led by Russian speakers and ethnic Russians, who appeared to be seizing an opportunity to recoup perceived Russian losses. Some at the meeting suggested that in republic schools, "the study of Tuvan is occurring at the expense of Russian."[21] They bewailed the poor quality of Russian speaking, especially in village schools where Tyvan children are taught in their native language. "Tuvan," they proclaimed, using the Russified term for the language, should compete with English or Chinese, not with Russian.

After the meeting, urban and rural Tyvans responded on the internet and with an open letter signed by sixty-seven leading intellectuals and endorsed by the "office of the Khambo Lama." Among many points in the letter, signatories emphasized that plans to downgrade the Tyvan language violate Russia's federal 1993 Constitution. Authors of the letter insisted that Tyvan parents must not be forced to shift their children to non-Tyvan languages and explained, "We do not have the right to threaten the Tyvan language, but rather must do everything to preserve it and its over 1,500-year history." They argued that "any language is the main factor in ethnic identification, and Tyvan is no exception. It is the pride of the Tyvan people, ensuring the maintenance and development of their spiritual culture: shamanism flourishes within it, as do followers of Buddhism."[22] A year later in 2016, an Association of Teachers of Tyvan Language and Literature was created in the republic, with 150 initial members. Earlier, such a formal association and defense of the Tyvan language had not been considered necessary.

The language policy protest and defense of Tyvan has passionate resonance because Tyva is one of the last republics in Russia where Russification has been gradual or minimal, particularly in rural areas.[23] The heartfelt reaction of rural and urban Tyvans perhaps may stave off radical reforms toward Russification in the schools for a time, but increasing numbers of incoming Russians due to railway and other projects may change the equation. Thus, this battle, expressed in the terms of a wounded elite, may presage further tensions. Advocates of a "common educational space," including President Putin and his minister of education, are attempting to literally pave the way for further economic development in the relatively underexploited republics. They have a huge stake in blurring the lines between cultural and economic policies. Previous reassurances of Moscow officials that language politics would be left to the republics have eroded.

Development, Ecology Activism, and Social Priorities

A major front where cultural sensitivities clash with short-term economic gains is the realm of ecology and advocacy for sustainable development. When 2017 was declared the Year of Ecology in Russia, advocates in the republic decided to try to use the often-hollow official propaganda to their advantage. The literal and metaphorical place where Russification has been most resisted is in the widespread emotional Tyvan defense of their homeland as sacred territory worth preserving for future generations, a refrain heard from Indigenous organizers in many other countries (e.g., de la Cadena 2010; Simpson and Smith 2014). Clear mountain streams and rugged mountain roads are dotted with sacred springs, and huge cairn-like piles of rocks (*ovaa*, Figure 14), similar to the *oboo* discussed in the chapter on Buryatia. They are sites of numerous bright-colored ribbon offerings, left by prayerful travelers and locals alike, of multiple generations. My memory remains strong of these exquisite sacred sites where picnics take on ritual meaning, and they are mentioned in nostalgic discussions with Tyvans who have left their homeland.[24]

The exhilaration felt at these places of extraordinary beauty is occasionally marred by mines, some abandoned after the Soviet period and some more recently exploited. My interlocutors have pointed to ecological concerns as part of the tensions between Russians and Tyvans in 1990, and certainly ethnic as well as generational differences concerning out-of-control development have been prominent (compare Humphrey and Sneath 1999, 304). At the end of the Soviet period, several gold-mining projects, the notorious open-pit Ak Dovurak asbestos plant, a cobalt industrial complex, and a thermal electric power station

FIGURE 14.   Ovaa sacred stones, outskirts of Kyzyl. By author.

were functioning. By the end of the 1990s, the power station and one gold mine were operating, with others planned to be refurbished or built on new sites.

Few local laws are in place to protect against wildcat development, and the republic, unlike most other republics in Russia, does not have a ministry of environmental protection, although it does have a state environmental protection committee. Forestry has been relatively undeveloped due to inaccessibility of resources, but that has been changing in the past ten years. Part of Tyva's extensive forests were affected by the ripple effects of the Sayano-Shushenskaia Dam construction, and its dramatic 2009 hydroelectric plant collapse on the Yenisei River that killed over seventy-five people, inundated villages, and destroyed forests in neighboring Khakassia.[25] Most alarming, federal-level financing for ecological protection was radically cut in Russia's 2015 budget, and has been deteriorating since.

Tyva's relatively underutilized resources have meant that less ecology activism was stimulated than in some Siberian regions, although cobalt, coal, gold, rare earths, and asbestos development in company towns like Elegest have certainly contributed to fears about ecological despoliation. A man who left but periodically returns to his coal-dependent hometown drew a frightening picture of its devastation: "The coal industry and our coal heating is such that when you drive to our town you see a wall of black air in the distance, and then you drive through it. It is influencing everyone and of course affects our health. But there's nothing that really has been effective in stopping it." He added: "People running for local office may promise to do something, but their hands are tied. Everyone knows that if they complain, they will simply be replaced by someone more compliant, whether they are in the energy distribution system or are an ordinary person trying to live a decent life."

In the relatively untouched, multiethnic Todju district, nearly 90 percent of the area is categorized as "state forest fund lands," making it vulnerable to exploitation and possible insider-privileging auctions by state officials. A government project to improve water transportation on the Upper Yenisei has enhanced timber industry activity in the region (Donohoe 2009, 34). Illegal logging and arson cover-ups could be devastating here, as elsewhere in Siberia. This is the homeland of the particularly endangered group of nomadic reindeer herders and hunters, the Todja, as well as Tyvans, old-settler Russian families, and newcomer Russians and Chinese (Plumley 2020).

Compounding threats to ecological well-being is the opening of the long-awaited rail line through the Eastern Sayan Mountains, to Kyzyl and the Elegest coal fields to its south. The problematic line from Kuragino was begun in 2007 when President Putin pounded in a silver spike, but delays and financing have plagued construction ever since. Coal extraction and processing are among the dirtiest of all of Russia's industries, and its leadership is reputedly among the most corrupt. A notorious case already mentioned was the mixed ethnic, mostly Native, Yenisei village that was burned, allegedly so that a Russian coal company could take over a mine without Indigenous opposition (Balzer 2017, 12). Cobalt "recultivation" has begun at the TuvaCobalt factory, and a much-needed mercury clean-up is planned for the Terling-Khaia plant. Construction has begun on a controversial ambitious electricity line across the Altai-Sayan Mountains from Khakassia through Tyva to Mongolia, joining Tyva more fully into the Russian energy space, and linking Buryatia and Lake Baikal in a network.[26]

Most of the brave ecology activists resisting megaprojects are Tyvans worried that development is occurring at the expense of sacred mountain lakes and for the benefit of outsiders hoping to make easy money. The poetic name of one prominent activist group reveals its values: The Heart of Nature, led by the Tyvan A. E. Adygbai. It is a linguistic play on Tyva's geographic fame as the "Heart [Center] of Asia," manifest in the stag-crowned obelisk balanced on a world globe adorning the center of Kyzyl on the banks of the Yenisei (Figure 15).

Other groups combatting poorly monitored development include Art, led by A. N. Kuksin; and the regional branch of the political party Green Alliance, headed by V. M. Mel'nikov.[27] The Sacred Earth Network's Southern Siberia Initiative has enlisted several Tyvan environmentalists from Tuva State University

FIGURE 15. Center of Asia park, bank of Yenisei, Kyzyl, with Tyvan youth. By author.

for joint projects with the Ubsunur International Center for Biospheric Research, the State Committee for Environmental Protection, the Forestry Management Ministry, and the Tourism Department. Representatives of the less official, nongovernmental Oktargay Environmental Club, and the sociopolitical movement Salgalga have also been involved.[28] However, the threat of coopted civic activism is great, as informal groups become GONGOs—government-organized nongovernmental organizations. As we have seen in previous chapters, groups with outside financing have been dubbed "foreign agents."

Regular conferences on ecology have been held in Tyva, especially in the 1990s, but their early promise of having a systematic regulatory function has diminished under recent political administrations. Among the 1990s politicians advocating for sustainable development, republic rights, and mining regulation was the chemist and Tyvan deputy to Russia's Duma Kara-Kys Arakchaa, who had impressive experience working for the State Committee for the North (Goskomsever) in Moscow. But when she returned to Kyzyl, her political career in the People's Party of Sovereign Tyva was repressed. As head of a laboratory complex in Tyva, she has become an advocate for sacred spring (*arzhaan*) water therapies.

Lack of ecology oversight has been particularly bad for rural regions, where people are dependent on government subsidies and reluctant to jeopardize them. In the 1990s, 90 percent of Tyva's budget came from federal funds (Arbachakov 1999). That figure has gone up under successive Putin administrations, and Tyva was misnamed an "Arctic subsidy" recipient, despite its location on the Mongolian border, far south of the Arctic. By 2020, the Arctic subsidy loophole had closed, but important federal government support remained for cattle raising, meat processing, tourism, mines, rail, and road projects. Tyva was proclaimed a potential "window to Asia" with its ambitious Kyzyl-Khandagai-Borshoo-Ürümchi (China) road corridor project, passing through the former Buryat *okrug* Ust-Orda.[29] Activists opposing this and other Chinese-investment-linked "new silk roads" projects were threatened with the loss of not only their own jobs but those of their close family members.

Ecology education has focused on experimental eco-lyceums organized by teachers hoping to combine spiritual awareness with ecology sensitivity, featuring "return to traditional values" as a theme. Environmental education has become an important part of secondary school education programs, sometimes combined with "participation in rituals at sacred springs and trees" (Radkau 2008, 294). Professor Lilia Kyrgyzovna Arakchaa at Tuva State University in Kyzyl has developed a program glossed as "Ecological Culture of the Tuva People and Environmental Awareness and Education," in part to train teachers in local schools in environmental education using local cultural traditions to intrigue children.

While acknowledged as a valiant effort, it has received little official support and runs mostly on volunteer efforts.

Some federal and republic nature preserves are protected under the republic's weak environmental affairs programs. A nature preserve called Taiga was established in 2009 in the Western Sayans, at the Uyuk Ridge, land of the Scythian "Valley of the Kings" archeological site, where a tourist-bait "shamanic labyrinth" augments an outdoor museum complex. The rich Scythian gold art found there has been spirited to St. Petersburg's Hermitage Museum, creating resentment, but locals revel in the elaborate king-and-queen compound burials found with horse sacrifices. Some of the thousands of finds have been copied to provide a sense of pride in the wealthy Scythian culture that Herodotus made famous.[30] In addition, the Ubsunur Hollow, a UNESCO-sponsored biosphere reserve on the border of Tyva with Mongolia, is at once a protected zone, a burial-mound-filled archeological site with Scythian, Turkic, Hunnic, and Buddhist relics and a tourist attraction. Ecotourism has become a buzz word that shows a degree of official environmental consciousness without binding regulation.

Local and international activism has achieved protections for three important sites in the past several years: the medicinal springs at Ush-Beldir (*Tere-Khol kozhuun*, in Tyvan), a sacred mountain site Shui (*Bai-Taiga kozhuun*), and the park Shanchy (*Chaa-Khol kozhuun*). New parks are planned, since UNESCO has designated Tyva one of two hundred areas deserving special world ecological attention. But such protected zones will not be enough to stem the coming tide of development. The Ministry of Natural Resources and Ecology in the republic reveals its priorities in the title. Similarly, the Tuvan Institute of Complex Use (*osvoenie*) of Natural Resources, far from contributing to sustainable solutions, seems to have a "fox guarding the chicken coop" approach to development. Wolf regulation programs exist but are ineffective, and thus far contests to create local ecological monitoring projects have been sporadic at best.

In an interview in his parliament office, Kadyr-ool Bicheldei confessed that many Tyvans were worried about the influx of Russian workers insensitive to Tyvan cultural values that any new railroad connecting Tyva (Kyzyl) to Krasnoyarsk would bring.[31] He stressed that federal relations were a matter of constant negotiation, with the need for economic development beyond crude, poor-quality coal. Employment, he explained, was uppermost in many leaders' minds, sometimes at the cost of ecological protection. Perceptions that local Russians lived better than Native Tyvans needed to be changed. "We have learned to love stability," he insisted, adding "we want peace and global interconnections as a basis for economic growth." Bicheldei named the republic's most serious problems as (1) alcoholism; (2) youth unemployment; and (3) narcotics trade from abroad. He saw these as interrelated and serious at urban and rural levels.

Resorting to metaphor, he described Tyva as having its own "microclimate," like a little kettle placed high in the mountains, but like all microclimates, it is still integrated with larger regional and global forces. His concerns resonate today, especially since Tyva has become a pass-through or production region for narcotics moving to other parts of Siberia. Some also fear that many young people are too preoccupied with everyday survival to care about ecological activism.

In sum, the Republic of Tyva, remaining highly dependent on Moscow subsidies, could be poised to become a more high-profile part of Russia. This is partially due to the unpredictable friendship between President Vladimir Putin and his defense minister Sergei Shoigu. But it also has more structural ramifications, including building military bases with high-employment ripple effects. Tyva may be a border state for Russia, but it is "peripheral" only in a strict geographic sense. In the geopolitical mapping of many of its people, it is conceptualized as the "Center of Asia." It has potential for sustainable development, including of rare earths wanted by China, although that could be squandered, given the current harsh pan-Russia economic environment, coronavirus impacts, and exploitive China trade agreements. It has potential to have its own multilateral international relations, given its strategic geography near China and Mongolia. Most important, it could have greater-than-average sovereignty within Russia, if its leaders can use their current political access, historical legacies, and four-fifths-majority Indigenous population to argue for a more secure way of life as a federal republic.

Tyvans resent the attributions of high crime rates, of "Muscovites saying Tyvans are armed and dangerous on the basis of a few robbery incidents, that Tyva itself is dangerous." They retort: "Look at Moscow—it is dangerous there." While my interlocutors may be correct that organized crime and gangs are no worse than elsewhere in Russia, young and poor urbanites have been known to pick on perceived weaker "marks" from rural areas, only to find that "rural youths are tougher, have better survival skills, from being hunters, fishers."

The Russian economist's warning I had perceived to be somewhat racist in 2016 (an epigraph of this chapter) sadly was rendered more realistic in 2017, when the Moscow political economist Yakov Mirkin declared Tyva to be one of at least fifteen "national disaster zones" in Russia. He revealed that Tyva's 2015 gross domestic product (GDP) per capita was 66 percent lower than in Russia as a whole, at the level of "third world" countries like Bhutan and Papua New Guinea. Residents' life expectancy by 2017 was 63.1, on average, and men's life expectancy had dipped to 58 years, among the world's worst statistics. The crime rate was among Russia's worst, at 2,682 annually per 100,000 residents, or "two thirds more than the average for the country."[32] In such conditions, it is hard to judge degrees of local loyalties to Moscow officials. Compounding bitterness and controversy, some Tyvan analysts began blaming Tyvan poverty on their own "ethno-psychological roots" rather than federal budget cuts, high-level corruption, and lack of support for private businesses. By 2020, Tyvans were admitting in their press and personally that their republic had become "perhaps the poorest in Russia." Poverty statistics render the high "happiness indicators" of Tyvan subjective well-being (at 86 percent) methodologically suspect or indicative that many Tyvans have priorities divorced from material well-being, or perhaps both (compare Obydenkova and Libman 2015, 123; Tarbastaeva 2018a).

Spirituality: Buddhism and Beyond

To whom and toward what can Tyvans turn? Tyva is best known for its mountainous beauty, its spiritual sanctuaries, and the fascinating eclectic mix of Buddhist and shamanist spirituality in its rural communities. Many Tyvan spiritual leaders have long looked east to Mongolia and Tibet, rather than north to Moscow, for inspiration and support. However, their frequent isolation has meant that they have also developed spiritual lives born of local connectedness to the land and local understandings of their religious roots. A substantial 2019 survey of Tyvan youth revealed that 68.3 percent considered themselves Buddhist, in the sense of a flexible nondogmatic cultural loyalty (Badmaev et al. 2020, 38).

A Tyvan word usually glossed as "religion," *chüdülge*, encompasses shamanism and Buddhism as well as perceived "outsider religions."[33] It includes shamanic practices in part because some leaders of this "traditional archaic religion" have conformed to and encouraged Russian (and European) discourses that privilege organized religions over eclectic, individuality-based spirituality (compare Pimenova 2013, 126–33; Balzer 2012, 202–7). Some leaders frame Tyvan shamanic cosmology and rituals as epitomizing a "pure ur-religion"—for example, the scholar-folklorist-turned-shaman Kenin-Lopsan. His is a nostalgic view, given how much has been changed and adapted over many centuries of pluralistic cultural mixing in Inner Asia.

Buddhist cultural valorization gained a significant, bittersweet boost in 2014 with the death of the sixth Tyvan Khambo Lama installed in 2010—Tensin Shultim, born Nikolai Kuular—and the subsequent lavish ceremonial enthronement of a new, young Khambo Lama—Lopsan Chamsy Giatso, born Bair Shyyrap in the village of Kungurtug in 1976. Both lamas had made pilgrimages to Tibet and had training in India. The new leader studied for many years at the Goman datsan, in southern India, rather than the northern datsan and monastery complex of Dharamsala, associated with His Holiness the Dalai Lama. From 2009 to 2014, he led the Chyrgalan Khuré of Tere-Khol', in his birth region. One of five contenders, he was elected in 2014 in an emergency meeting of the Buddhist community of Tyva, centered in Kyzyl's Tsechenling Khuré.

The highly official enthronement in 2014 was attended by hundreds of believers, many Buddhist guests, Tyvan state authorities ranging from the republic head and parliament members to local officials, as well as the highest representatives of other religions in Tyva, including the Russian Orthodox bishop of Kyzyl, Feofan. Events were divided between rituals and official speeches. The dignified ceremonies, captured on film for posterity, included sutra chanting, a yellow silk path leading to the raised throne, the Khambo Lama's entrance and prostration, his oath to serve the Buddhists of his native land, and Buddhist music with horns and drums. The Buryat Did Khambo Darba Ochirov garnered spontaneous applause when he emphasized that Soviet authorities had tried to divide and rule the Buddhist community along ethnic lines, but that Tyvan, Buryat, and Kalmyk members of the Buddhist *Sangha* (community) had not let them succeed (compare Bernstein 2013). Local musicians, some associated with pre-Buddhist Tengri and shamanistic beliefs, graced the celebration.[34]

In 2015, politicization of Buddhist international contacts accelerated with the expulsion from Tyva of its long-term-resident and much revered Tibetan lama of the Geluk school Shiwalha Rinpoche, who had been acknowledged by the Dalai Lama as the eighth reincarnation of an eighth-century Indian monk-scholar, Shantideva. Although born in Switzerland, Lama Shiwalha Rinpoche had trained in the Sera Monastery of India, educated to the highest *geshe* level. He considered one of his past lives to have been a Siberian lama and had applied for citizenship in Russia. Honored in Tyva as a particularly dynamic revitalizer of Tibetan Buddhism, he had opened a temple and stupas throughout the republic. For eleven years, he helped to train many new monks, working especially with the Buddhist activist association Enerel (Compassion), headed by Aneta Oorzhak. While Federal Security Service (FSB) officials based in Moscow labeled him and his assistant Lobsang Tsering security threats, the head of the republic Sholban Kara-ool called on Moscow authorities to reconsider the deportations amid widespread consternation among thousands of followers. Shiwalha Rinpoche's defenders widely proclaimed: "How can a man who teaches us love, compassion, and unselfish help to others be dangerous?"[35]

The Buddhist community again was caught in politics in 2019, with the election of the eighth Khambo Lama, the late Jampel Lodoy (earlier Apysh-ool Sat), who had been previously elected Khambo Lama in 2005. Son of a herder, he later became head of the important republic-owned Buddhist temple complex Ustuu-Khuré, site of folk music festivals as well as meditation. The seventh leader, Lopsan Chamsy Giatso (Bair Shyyrap), so eloquently and elegantly installed in 2014, was deposed in a secret ballot that may have turned on his attempts to keep Buddhist decision making about the advanced training of young lamas in India independent of the government of Tyva and Russia. In the new norm for ordinations, the eighth Khambo Lama was celebrated in December 2019 with the attendance of Russian Orthodox priests, Buryat lamas, Buddhist dignitaries from Mongolia but not India, shamanist and secular representatives. The head of Tyva, Sholban Kara-ool, explained in a lengthy speech during the installation ritual at the secular House of Folk Arts, home of Kyzyl's Ministry of Culture, "the Khambo Lama will start his activities with renewed energy and new perspective. The leadership of the republic is always ready for collaboration. We are carrying out our work to complete the construction of a Buddhist complex consecrated by His Holiness the Dalai Lama. We need unity to complete this important task."[36] In 2020, not politics but the coronavirus caused yet another, ninth Khambo Lama, Gelek Natsyk Dorju (Sergek Olegovich Saryglar), to be installed with a less elaborate ceremony at the Tsechenling Khuré. He is younger than his predecessor and trained at Ivolga (Buryatia).

Tyva's Buddhist revival had begun in the late 1980s, when poorly trained local lamas emerged from hiding into the exuberance of open worship and rebuilding of temples throughout Tyvan territories, including parts of Krasnoyarsk. Before the Russian Revolution and civil war in the region, the largest Buddhist monasteries had been in the Chadan Valley, and the whole greater Uriankhai region had twenty-two thriving Khuré with over three thousand lamas. Revival was led by a reconstituted Buddhist Society of Tyva and was stimulated by the widely celebrated visit of the Dalai Lama in 1992. When I met Nikolai Kuular in 2005, before he became the sixth Khambo Lama (Figure 16), he stressed that the Buddhist community was still waiting eagerly for a return visit of the Dalai Lama, and that they were frustrated by Moscow officials' concessions to Chinese pressure concerning a planned visit to celebrate the opening of a new Khuré.

Under President Putin, the Dalai Lama continues to be barred from Russia. Pressure from China has increased, indirectly resulting in surveillance of the Kupenchetso Buddhist Center and the Tyvan Tibet Support Group, among the many in Russia organizing celebrations of the eightieth birthday of the Dalai Lama in 2015. In 2020, his eighty-fifth birthday was widely celebrated online. As elsewhere in Russia, Tyvan Buddhists have needed to maintain a delicate balance between autonomy and cooperation with secular authorities.

While the local shamanic community is notoriously splintered, it appears united in the opinion that official republic endorsement of religion favors Buddhism, rather than shamanism or Orthodoxy. This is in part correlated to perceived public perception of the popularity of Buddhism over shamanism. A survey from the early 1990s indicated that about 43 percent of Tyvans considered themselves Buddhists, while only 3 percent claimed shamanism as their main religious

FIGURE 16.   Nikolai Kuular, 2005, before he became Khambo Lama in 2010. By author.

practice, and more recent surveys have revealed an increase in self-identifying Buddhists (Lindquist 2012, 80; Pimenova 2007; Badmaev et al. 2020). In the past two decades, situational and flexible approaches to rituals that were earlier kept underground became increasingly visible.

Rituals focus on personal healing in emergencies, as well as the importance of supplication to local spirits and regional gods of pre-Buddhist Tengri worship. They are centered at the cairns and ribbon-festooned trees that are constant features at natural sites of special beauty, on mountain peaks and at sacred springs throughout Tyva (and Buryatia). Supplication continued through the Soviet period, hidden to various degrees and never fully squelched because local Soviet officials themselves continued to observe some rituals with their families in private.

By the early 1990s, a full-throated shamanic revival had begun in Tyva, led in part by the famed folklorist and shamanic practitioner Mongush Kenin-Lopsan and since 1993 linked to the global shamanic revival.[37] Interestingly, Tyva's head of state has visited Kenin-Lopsan on his birthday for many years, revealing that the republic's shamanists are recognized at least somewhat. In 2017, Minister of Culture Aldir Tamdin, noting that Kenin-Lopsan had spread word of Tyvan folklore, history, and shamanic practice "to all corners of the earth," honored his birthday and praised his newest book *Sud'ba shamanki* (Fate of a Shaman) at a presentation in the Aldan-Maadyr (Sixty Warriors) National Museum of Tyva attended by many of the Tyvan elite, including some healers in shamanic dress wearing feathered headdresses.[38] The book, in the form of a popular novel, memorializes Kenin-Lopsan's grandmother, who was called Déér Khami (Heaven Shaman) and was repressed by the Soviets.

Mongush Kenin-Lopsan proclaimed himself as supreme leader of the shamanists when he established the main shamanic society Düngür (Drum) in the 1990s. By 2004, he had been challenged in this symbolic and organizational leadership by Kara-ool Dopchun-ool, a well-connected kinsman of the current president Sholban Kara-ool, and the founder of the rival splinter association Adyg Ëren (Bear Spirit). Dopchun-ool earlier had been one of Kenin-Lopsan's most trusted directors, earning a title from him of Great Shaman (Ulug Kham), until their public rivalry put the entire concept of a coherent shamanic society able to regulate and repudiate "charlatans" into question. By 2020, Dopchun-ool had become "Supreme Shaman of Russia and the Republic of Tyva." Today, several organized shamanic societies demand dues and networking solidarity from their regional and Kyzyl-based members.

In the late 1990s, Tyva's first president, Oorzhak Sherig-ool, reputedly asked a community of shamanic healers led by the group Düngür to help to end a period of drought that had been plaguing the region. This, as well as the connectedness to the land through myriad sacred spirit-imbued sites, shows the degree to which shamanic concepts and rituals permeate Tyvan society at all levels. Far from threatening and demonic, as some Russian Orthodox Russian nationalists claim, shamanic beliefs and values correlate to an expressed, deep ecological connectedness that we also have seen in the Buryat and Sakha cases.

Among the most famed Tyvan shamans of the post-Soviet period was the late healer Ai-Churek Shiizhekovna Oiun (Figure 17), known widely as Ai-churek (Benevolent Spirit Heart), founder of another shamanic group, Tos Déér (Nine Heavens), and a protégé of Kenin-Lopsan. Their healing center, for over a decade located near the center of Kyzyl, down the street from the monument to the Center of Asia, was created out of a former high school, with sacred sculptures, a large central eagle image, yurts, a shamanic world tree (*kham-yiash*) and colorful streamers in its front yard.

By 2016, symbolically as well as physically the center had been moved to the edge of Kyzyl, but it continued to receive clients. Although Ai-churek died under tragic and mysterious circumstances, her prayers and drumming disks live on to comfort believers. One explained: "When she chanted prayers and drummed, she

FIGURE 17. Ai-churek with author, 2005, at her curing center in Kyzyl. Used with permission by Aldynai Seden-Khuurak in author's camera.

sometimes sounded like the Kyrgyz *Manas* [epic singing]. I can envision everything portrayed in those prayers. Her drumming also evokes images for me. Her powerful *Ydyk Ydyktaar* is a blessing for fertility—for the health and well-being of the clan."[39]

Although Ai-churek's practice focused mostly on personal clients and training new shamans, some of her practices and her legacy have been ecology-oriented. She came from a remote village where connections to the rhythms of seasons and of the land were normal, although she readily admitted that as she was growing up people thought she was crazy. She explained to me in 2005: "The *algysh* I sing today come from absorbing the chants of my childhood, and from nature. Those called by the spirits can become suicidal if they don't listen to the call to begin to help people themselves" (Balzer 2012, 206). She listened, helped one of her own schoolteachers transcend personal problems, and eventually grew into a shaman with a formidable reputation for empathy healing.

International connections for Tyva have arrived in several unusual ways, given its isolation and its poverty. Tyva as a potential exotic tourism "brand" came to be associated with Kenin-Lopsan's insistence that Tyva had maintained a pure, ancient, and authentic version of shamanism. He claimed that its power was accessible through the many texts of his published *algysh* (prayers) (1995), as well as through the well-traveled shamanic representation of Ai-churek, using connections to Michael Harner's Foundation for Shamanic Studies. One of Kenin-Lopsan's most appealing formulations began as a rebuttal to the then minister of defense of Russia, Sergei Ivanov. It posited archaic shamanism as an ur-religion of humankind: "The Wise Men bringing offerings to Jesus Christ were shamans, or in effect, the first priests of paganism. The shamanic religion is the first religion of the peoples of the world, the source of spiritual cultures of all ethnoses. The ancient Turks, from whom great peoples sprang . . . were shaman-ists."[40] He bragged that "since 1993 in Tyva, international symposiums of scientists and shamans have been attended by authoritative specialists on shamanic studies from Austria and Germany, Switzerland and Belgium, Italy and America" (Kenin-Lopsan with Likhanova 2006).

Synergistically, seekers of new forms of world music discovered the phenomenal skills of Tyva's throat singers, whose traditions of multiple voices sung at once by one person were developed through the reverberations of herders in mountain valleys as well as their harmonizing with babbling brooks. During the Soviet period in 1988, the first throat singer to emerge from Tyva was the late Gennady Chash, featured in a Smithsonian folklife festival, where I had the privilege to introduce him to the public. Not accidentally, he was a pioneer of ecology activism in the republic. An earlier version of creative collaboration was the Tyvan singer Gendos Chamzyryn with the British experimental musician Tim Hodgkinson, whose insights into shamanic music and art centered on the Tyvan concept of *küsh* (strength, force, energy) (Hodgkinson 2005–2006; compare Beahrs 2019). In part through the efforts of ethnomusicologist Theodore Levin and Tyvan scholar Valentina Süzükei (2006), the group Huun-Huur-Tu became a worldwide sensation. A biannual festival of throat singing has become a pilgrimage phenomenon for international spiritual travelers. Younger musicians include the pathbreaking women's group Tyva Kyzy and the charming men's group Alash. A founder of Huun-Huur-Tu, Alexander Bapa, has created the company Pure Nature Music, and established the group Chirgilchin, featuring a woman who sings Tyvan traditional songs without throat singing.[41] Their poetic name means "shimmer in the air over the steppe," revealing the subtlety of language reflected in natural observation.

Tyvans furthered the reputation of their music with an acclaimed 2015 music festival of Ustuu-Khuré (also Ustuu-Hure) held in the Ubsunur Hollow Nature Preserve. A 2017 version was called Khoomei in the Center of Asia, and honored the late great singer Kongor-ool Ondar, one of my hosts in 2005. Ondar's image was memorialized in a bronze, life-sized sculpture in Kyzyl, valorizing not only him but his art (compare Süzükei 2014). The 2019 Festival of Live Music and Faith, a celebration Tyvans already are nostalgic about, was held in the town of Chaldan.[42]

In private conversations over the past decade, Tyvans have confessed their concern that Russian Orthodox resurgence and Protestant missionizing have been muddying the "previously simple and pure" spiritual and cultural landscape of Tyva. Protestant outsiders, including some American missionaries active and controversial since the 1990s, may provide more choice for some young Tyvans searching for new options in a confusing, competitive religious market. However, one unpopular American missionary couple was asked to leave by the head of the republic. Most urban Tyvans I have met remain tied to their Buddhist heritage as their main spiritual identity. They add ad hoc shamanic practices to this as they need them, neither smoothly syncretizing nor agonizing over potential contradictions. One interlocutor, using an economic metaphor, joked that invitations to shamanists to attend Khambo Lama ordinations or music festivals at temples amounted to "Buddhist raider behavior."

In Tyva, personal donations for newly renovated and flourishing Buddhist temples and toward the training of recently declared lama apprentices have become a norm. Local and national-level politicians, including Sergei Shoigu, visit Buddhist temples for publicity photo ops, whatever their inner convictions may be. In 2015 in Russia's national-level press, a fuss was made over Sergei Shoigu's crossing of himself at a Russian Orthodox Easter ceremony, with speculation that he had converted due to the war with Ukraine. Probably not. Rumors among Russians have circulated since Sergei Shoigu became minister of defense that he does not speak his native Tyvan ("Tuvan"), with some Russians claiming he is fully Russified. Probably unfair. His high profile, and that of his sister Larissa, a deputy to Russia's Duma, merely magnifies what many non-Russians in Russia enact—situational identities exquisitely calibrated for multiple social and political contexts.

Slippery Slope Federal and Interethnic Relations

Trouble in Russia's Defense Ministry training programs was exposed in a shocking incident in the summer of 2017, when a massive interethnic brawl broke out in an army garrison in the Urals village of Elan. Putting the defense minister truly on the defensive, the "bloody fighting" involving Tyvans caused Shoigu to rush to the training center where it occurred and resulted in at least two court cases, about fourteen serious injuries, and a commission of inquiry that included military lawyers and representatives of the famed Mothers of Soldiers nongovernmental organization.[43] While details were and remain disputed, most accounts mention that the majority of knife-and-fist wielding fighters on one side were just-graduating and drunk Tyvans, and the majority on the other side were Russian soldiers, also drunk, with a few officers. A group of about sixty Tyvan, Khakas, and Dagestani career contract soldiers had completed a three-month advanced training program and were possibly on track to become officers. Local and nonlocal Russian superiors had trained them using, as is customary, quite harsh techniques. The level of the program indicates that the notorious tradition of draftee hazing, called *dedovshchina* (Russian, rough gloss—grandfather onslaught), was less a factor here, although in such programs "minority" ethnic groups often stick together and perceive Russian officers to be unnecessarily crude and punishing. In the spark that set off the brawl at Elan, a Russian officer allegedly asked a Tyvan trainee to fetch running shoes from under his bed. Obscene insults were exchanged, and the graduating trainee refused the task. As they came to blows, others piled on—until approximately sixty non-Russians were fighting close to a hundred Russians. They hardly fit the epic imagery of "Sixty Warriors" that graces the nostalgic name and iconography of the Tyvan National Museum.

Several aspects of this case have rung alarm bells, placing in perspective the plea of Igor Irgit for Tyvans to return to the benevolent warrior values that he claims were prevalent in romanticized Uriankhai times. Young Tyvan recruits with knives, as well as restless Tyvan street toughs committing robbery against Russians in Kyzyl, do not conform to the samurai-like values that their elders had expected of them. The atmosphere of the Russian army is hardly conducive to socialization into graceful warrior-statesmen, nor is the threat of being sent into a messy hybrid war in East Ukraine that is increasingly unpopular with many republic citizens. Tyvan (Buddhist) soldiers, with a reputation for being more reliable than temperamental (Muslim) draftees from the North Caucasus, have shown themselves to be just as susceptible to anger when pushed as everyone else.

This anger-triggering incident has revealed what many have long understood, that the Russian army mirrors and magnifies social divisions in Russia's society, including interethnic tensions. The tensions come at a particularly awkward time of general demographic decline for Russians within Russia, health precarity, and increasingly strained federal relations between Moscow and the republics.

A Tyvan friend who frequently travels to Moscow explained in 2020 that he uses his identity as a citizen of Russia strategically. "Sometimes I say I'm a Rossiiane—sure. But sometimes I feel more Tyvan." Because of his Asian looks, he added: "In Moscow, they will constantly stop you . . . The police ask for your documents, thinking you are from Central Asia . . . But I say I'm a Rossiiane—why are you hassling me? And show my documents proving I'm from Tyva, and they calm down and leave me alone . . . Otherwise, if I were Kyrgyz, they could ask for money or haul me in for infractions."

Tyva, at once central and remote, has had various moments of polarization and depolarization in relation to Moscow, influenced by shifting conditions within federal and pseudofederal Russia. Dmitri Gudkov, a Russian opposition politician and analyst in Moscow, in 2016 observed with sorrow that most Russians had no idea where Tyva's capital, Kyzyl, is on a map, or even whether it is a city or a region within Russia. Many were far more preoccupied with nationalistic, empire-building assertions that "Crimea is ours" than with taking care of what is already established within "multiethnic Rossiia's" federal boundaries, places like impoverished Kyzyl. "Look at your own real country," he suggested, "That is what needs to be given aid."[44]

"Federal" often means something different to administrators in Moscow than in the regions, especially the republics—creating built-in structural tensions. Pragmatic republic leaders, who have strained for a negotiated federalism ("states' rights") but have been buffeted by the pushes and pulls of centripetal and centrifugal forces, have emerged by necessity in all the Siberian republics, including post-Soviet Tyva. Since President Putin came to power, the process has been more centralizing than decentralizing, with "federal" usually meaning assertion of top-down authority. This was exacerbated in 2017 when President Putin denied a renewal of federal-level treaty relations to Tatarstan, sending a ripple of fear through the republics.[45]

Analyzing Tyva's relations with Moscow authorities reveals dynamics of what the renowned historian of China Prasenjit Duara (1996) has called the "hard and soft boundaries" of interethnic relations. "Soft" boundaries are those that are flexible, enabling ethnic awareness without harsh nationalist enmity and with a fluidity characteristic of many multiethnic communities through time. Many kinds of soft boundaries are possible and have been normal for post-Soviet Russia in Far Eastern Siberia. However, once enmity is triggered, it is difficult to soften hardened boundaries.

Leadership and Nostalgia

Deradicalized leaders like Kadyr-ool Bicheldei may provide unusual cases of valiant leadership. Yet his all-too-human fall from grace in a murky Education Ministry construction money scandal makes him far from comparable to towering models like Nelson Mandela and Mahatma Gandhi. Once ethnonational idioms of enmity or unfairness based on nationality become entrenched, a dangerously polarized nationalism can feed on itself. "Ethnic entrepreneur" discourse, including but not limited to hate speech, can spin into a mass-level resonance and resistance to central authorities. Entrepreneurs of division do not exist in a vacuum, and it is crucial to take the conditions that foster them into consideration.[46]

Some Tyvans are nostalgic for the pre-Soviet period when traditional values included diplomacy, defined broadly as understanding the effectiveness of tact, something they find missing in today's discourses. The following educational narrative, told in 2020 by a father who prefers anonymity, is worth recounting in its entirety:

> Tyvans in the old days were really natural diplomats. There's the story of the old herder whose horse was stolen by a young brash brigand. The old man realized what had happened and followed the tracks of the young man, finally coming upon his yurt and glancing to see his horse tethered in the distance. The old man entered the yurt as a traveler from afar and smiled at the young man, who said, having made eye contact and knowing precisely what was going on, "Please sit down and have some tea. You look upset—what has happened?" The old man explained, "I fear my best horse was eaten by some wild animal. I'm upset about it—and fear my horse is gone forever." "Oh dear," said the young man, "Please sit down and calm yourself." To his helper, he said "please go get that new horse and choose another one as well for this old man." This way, everyone's pride was salved. No one came running in ranting and raving about a stolen horse—and the old man ended up with two horses.

At the level of Russian-Tyvan relationships, many Tyvans feel tact and diplomacy have been replaced by colonial and neocolonial misunderstandings. Tasting degrees of sovereignty and then having it pulled back delegitimizes center-periphery "soft boundary" relations.[47] Such actions from a so-called "federal" government can put a republic and its people(s) on a fast track to polarization. In the past decade in Siberia, various ethnonational groups have had different degrees of cultural mobilization, and various conditions for enabling cultural life to flourish. Tyva has been in a relatively advantageous cultural if not economic position, despite recent language politics and the deportation of a popular lama. These caveats indicate alarming trends.

Having a relatively sovereign republic infrastructure makes a huge difference in how cultural and territorial rights are asserted. Negotiated territorial borders of perceived homelands are crucial (compare Nadasdy 2017). Some Tyvans have explained that they bitterly feel the loss of lands they held when they controlled "Uriankhai krai," and until 1944 were legally separate from Russia. An urban interlocutor in 2020 explicitly cited this transitional time period before lands were taken away: "I am nostalgic for the period when, just as Tyva was entering into the Soviet Union in 1944, my own relatives were in high positions. One was minister of justice—and some had their own 'gold accounts' (foreign currency).

We had more say in what was going on in Tyva vis-à-vis Mongolia and Russia then, because Russia was trying to court us into the Soviet Union."

While historically based borders for Tyva could be larger than they currently are, today's republic leaders have declined to press for border changes, knowing this would be seen as provocative. Tyvan leaders have developed a sense of limited sovereignty within existing borders, while chafing to various degrees at the delimitations. In the process of negotiating a delicate balancing act with Moscow, some have lost the respect of their people. One friend in 2015 explained: "I myself was in Khostug-Tyva [Free Tyva] in the '90s. These days, I don't have much patience with our Grand Khural [parliament]. They are all puppets [Russian, *kukli*]."

Swallowing disillusionment has become a familiar pattern, along with turning away from politics to family and spiritual life. Yet Defense Minister Sergei Shoigu is widely admired. A typical Tyvan reaction to my bringing up his name has been: "Shoigu—he's the only noncorrupt minister. People tell jokes about him—that he has no car or home of his own. But he proudly says: 'I have my small homeland [Russian, *malaia rodina*]. I can always go back.'" One analyst added the following twist: "Some people say he is a fool, because he is being used by the government in Moscow. They [Putin and his people] keep him close, since it is a good way to keep Tyva loyal. Our people love Shoigu, and are proud he is in Moscow, that he has become the minister of defense. Me—not so much. I don't care."

Self-generalizations about one's people are common in Tyva. As one Tyvan interlocutor explained: "The Tuvan [Russian pronunciation] people have always been rebellious. That's why Russians need to keep someone high in the power circles—to keep us loyal." The common denominator in my interviews since President Putin came to power is a sense that Moscow authorities are perceived to be manipulating the Tyvan leadership, and the republic as a whole. Rather than being an exception, as a close friend of President Putin, Sergei Shoigu sometimes is seen as a particularly high-class puppet—or more accurately, an elite hostage— to keep Tyvans engaged in Russia. Several days after I heard the proclamation that Shoigu was the only truly "clean" minister, newspapers in Russia mentioned that Sergei Shoigu and his extended family own several large mansions.[48]

Sovereignty, Indigeneity, and Activism

What's in a name? The politics of naming the republic territories for their titular people have created a strong, patriotic ethnonational identity with and within a specific homeland. In other words, somewhat arbitrary definitions have come to take on a reality of their own over time.[49] Whenever a Russian nationalist politician such as Vladimir Zhirinovsky or, more alarmingly, any Russian official close to President Putin, makes claims that the republics should be abolished and "consolidation" of regions should proceed more intensively for a more streamlined, efficient federation, leaders in the republics feel the heat of local cultural and business elite discontent. Tyva is no exception. Sovereignty appetites have grown with the experience of republic administration, in negotiations with the Center, and from owning names that have become more than abstractions over time. This is reflected in fury over appointments of perceived outsiders to positions of authority in the republics. It makes the Tyvan activist Igor Irgit's call for renaming Tyva by its pre-Soviet Uriankhai designation particularly provocative. Some take it as a move to draw closer to Mongolia and China. A friend pointed out that the original coat of arms of Tyva depicted a horse and rider facing east toward a rising sun, and that it was later turned to face west (Moscow).[50]

Activism in Tyva links concerns about rapid development, ecological protection, and an urgent wider sense of the need for homeland preservation. Some of this dynamic parallels processes that occurred as the Soviet Union was imploding. It may be relevant to recall that following independence in some fledgling post-Soviet states, ecology activism became more muted, probably due to economic necessity.[51] As we have seen in the Buryatia case, ecology movements may be at once multiethnic yet represent the salience of ethnonational identity assertion—these need not be contradictory, given the dynamics of "soft boundary" interethnic relations. Republic leaders in Tyva, some more effective than others, have attempted to negotiate with central authorities over conditions for sustainable development in contexts of increasingly palpable climate change, economic impoverishment, and dependencies. Unfortunately, some republic authorities have been complicit in serious losses of rights for Indigenous "smallnumbered" peoples, especially the Todja, caught in development and corruption binds. Different kinds of indigeneity and shifting degrees of power possibility must be acknowledged.

Spiritual revitalization is evident in a nexus of land claims, sacred site recovery, ecology advocacy, and temple renovation. Language programs and other aspects of cultural revival have required increasingly greater political interactions, as successive Putin administrations have consolidated power. Correlated to demography and history, the Tyvan language has been less threatened than titular languages in most republics. However, recent curtailment of its status in the school system has infuriated Tyvan intellectuals. As elsewhere, intellectuals use the discourse of endangered languages to express discontent with centralizing, standardizing education policies. In Tyva, spiritual authenticity also has been contested and has resulted in dissension among shamanic groups, whose advocates come from rural as well as urban backgrounds. Russian Orthodox revival has come into tension with shamanic revival and Protestant Christian mission-izing. As elsewhere, the main audiences for Protestant proselytizing have been children of mixed ethnic marriages, but these are fewer in Tyva than in other republics. For Tyvans, the politics of Buddhism, resurrection of temples, and pro-motion of cultural ties to Mongolia and India have been especially salient, popu-lar in rural and urban contexts. The Buddhist *Sangha* as well as the shamanist communities provide ample room for talented lamas and shamans to be trained in their respective traditions, rising from impoverished rural backgrounds into leadership. Religious advancement becomes an expression of activism.

Demographic proportions matter. Tyvans are in a better (if that is the right word) position to be more assertive in their discourse, given their four-fifths majority and their history of being a quasi-independent state. Tyvan leaders have reclaimed their own stamps, seal, Buddhist symbolism, and historical ability to play off Russia, Mongolia, and China. A trend toward Tyvan monoethnicity has accelerated, as Russians and others, feeling discomfort as minorities, have been leaving the republic for better labor markets. Some settle elsewhere when their children move for higher education. The head of the republic has attributed Rus-sian outflow to a poor quality of life and instituted a policy for skilled Russians to be provided better living arrangements to entice them to stay (Tarbastaeva 2018b, 74). Such "affirmative action" breeds resentment.

Tyvans to uneven extents have been able to stimulate competitive farm-ing, cattle raising, dairy, and other local economic markets, while maintaining selected traditional cultural practices as a strategy. The Buddhist scholar Inna Tarbastaeva (2018b, 78)—whose background merges Tyvan, Khakas, and Korean roots and whose native language is Russian—boldly summarizes Tyvan "call-ing card" cultural strengths as "native language maintenance, nomadic way of life, shamanism, buddhism, sacred rituals, throat singing, and national-style wrestling."[52] Eerily echoing yet adapting Soviet propaganda, she argues that any people (ethnonational group) is better off economically and creatively when in a multiethnic environment. More optimistically, she suggests that Buddhist values may help young Tyvans adopt a "small is fine" people-focused localized approach to improving their combined spiritual and economic well-being (Tarbastaeva 2018a).

In Tyva, as elsewhere, activists have emerged to complain that their sons should not be sent to wars they did not begin and do not support. This hap-pened during the first and second Chechen wars and has occurred recently dur-ing not very well-reported protests against fighting in Ukraine. Arguments often emphasize the importance of not losing much-needed population and fertility potential, considering the relatively small numbers of a given Indigenous people. However, in Tyva during the second war against secessionist Chechens, the novel argument was made that Tyvans needed to stay home to augment their police force, since crime rates in the republic were too high! Recently, the Tyvan activist Sayana Mongush, a former Grand Khural deputy, has used the word "genocide" to describe losses of non-Russians fighting in East Ukraine. Russians have followed suit with their own genocide language against Tyvans, a point returned to in the conclusions to this book.

As Tyvans search for ways to preserve their people, borders, language, and spirituality, they increasingly have been drawn to polarizing discourses of purity, authenticity, and nostalgic longing for an imagined golden age that may not have been so golden in the turbulent twentieth century (compare Boym 2001, 41). Some have expressed retrospective nostalgia for a lost sovereignty that was not really so independent in their Uriankhai period. But others seem to represent a more prospective nostalgia, especially those active in language protection, spiritual revitalization, and ecology efforts. In Tyva, which style of nostalgia becomes galvanizing remains open to debate and critical for effective choices that could mitigate interethnic polarization.

CROSSOVER TRENDS

Eurasianism, Competition, Cooperation,
and Protest

> **Our group is called On the Path of the Ancestors, and we have trav-
> eled in the past decade to Buryatia, the Altai mountain region, Mon-
> golia.**
>
> —Lydia Shamayeva, Sakha language school director, December 16, 2019

> **You must see this with your own eyes. Better yet—be in this wonder-
> ful moment.**
>
> —Buryat musician Gombo Dambiev, on opening of the multicultural
> festival Yokar Nights, Theater Baikal, July 2016

> **Constant contacts exist between wiki-media specialists from Udmurt-
> ia, Chuvashia, Tatarstan, Buryatia, Tyva, as well as other represen-
> tatives of minority languages of Russia . . . [they are] practical and
> morale building.**
>
> —Letter from Sakha Wikipedia founder Nikolai Pavlov-Khalan,
> September 23, 2016

> **It is well known that in the years of Soviet power, trips to sacred
> places were discouraged or if they occurred were hardly sacral.
> Today, it is different: the meaning of many cult places is returning to
> its original intent. They are becoming not only places of worship but
> sites of religious tourism, pilgrimage sites.**
>
> —Tyvan scholars Marina and Evgeni Mongush, writing of sites
> in Tyva and Buryatia, 2015

Many in the republics within Russia are straining for cross-republic and transnational connections beyond their ethnic communities. Some have found them
in the paradoxical refuge of the internet, while others create exuberant music
festivals or travel to sacred sites in nearby republics. Some have become cynical,
giving up on elections and political activism while nonetheless sharing networks

they carefully define as cultural rather than political. Others continue to fight to save forests, taiga, and rivers, interconnected places that crisscross regional administrative boundaries within Russia.

The famed and youthful Russian opposition politician Ilya Yashin warned me in 2016 that "ecology movements won't pull people together—these are protests that are local in nature. We are looking for crossover issues that can rally people more broadly. Our anti-corruption campaign is our best bet" (personal communication, June 10, 2016). However, anticorruption efforts also are more effective when locally targeted, and people in the regions of Russia sometimes resent initiatives begun in Moscow or St. Petersburg, whether official or from the opposition. A key question becomes how communities coalesce, culturally and socially, to form connections that move beyond the boundaries of specific republics within Russia. While this has political implications, stimuli for multileveled identity affiliations are potentially more broadly significant than any single ecology, anticorruption, or anti election fraud campaign.

Russia's 2016 parliamentary elections generated record low numbers of voters throughout the country, and subsequent elections have continued the apathy trend. Yet 2021 campaigns reveal that debates about societal concerns are still possible, especially at local and regional levels. This has occurred in revived single-mandate districts and during campaigns by regional heads of governments and mayors, despite the preponderance of candidates running as members of President Putin's party of power United Russia, and despite the lack of television time allowed for opposition parties. Ignored by the official media, unauthorized small and medium scale street demonstrations continue to erupt in unexpected places, in fraught conditions with sometimes chilling ramifications. How can these disparate and contradictory political and societal trends be better understood?

This chapter examines significant connections and tensions characterizing multileveled horizontal and vertical ties crucial to any federal system and to the health of a struggling civil society. I seek to expose some fault lines of a federalism that is slipping away, but more importantly, to reveal that people-to-people connections continue to be made, sometimes joyously, as in the case of cultural festivals, sports events and online conferences.

My argument is that these ties and multiethnic local events need not be secessionist in nature or subversive. Rather, they constitute the very sinew that could help Russia and its citizens through times of political trouble, economic sanctions, corruption, health crises, and general chaos. Discourses among Turkic and Mongolic peoples of Eurasia about civilizational commonalities are becoming a possible means toward recovering broader senses of collective self-worth.

Piecing together cross-republic relationships and their diverse motivations is difficult precisely because some officials in Moscow perceive them as threatening, while for many in the republics, connections made at personal, everyday levels require no special theorizing about wider society-wide resonance. Some material for this chapter comes from casual, accidental conversations that have revealed important connections. In the past seven years, I have learned to ask explicitly about cross-republic ties, finding that popular interest in broad definitions of kinship sometimes have sparked deeper networks. Attention to one's ancestry, following kinship roots wherever they may lead, is one of several channels that have generated creative cooperation and sometimes unexpected trouble (compare Shnirelman 1996; Shimamura 2014; Tishkov 2020). In some cases, as the saying goes, "the personal may become political."

I emphasize cultural and historical connections. These are most visible in historical perceptions of commonalities through Eurasianism, a trend that has become fashionable in all three republics featured here. It is a Eurasianism that differs from that of the 1920s' founders of "classic" Russian Eurasianism, such as Nikolay Trubetskoy, and from the Eurasianism of the Soviet dissident-turned-nationalist-hero Lev Gumilev.[1] However, Gumilev has been valorized by some Sakha, Buryat, and Tyvan intellectuals, among many other non-Russians of post-Soviet Asia, in part because he has been astonishingly misunderstood. Far from treating non-Russians of Eurasia as equal partners in an endeavor meant to improve the cultural, social, and economic lot of all peoples, Gumilev's theories of *passionarnost'* (passionate cultural attainment) singled out the Russians as culturally superior leaders of the continent, warning that only some peoples (specific ethnic groups) could intermarry successfully with each other. On close reading, his was a chauvinist and hierarchical worldview, little better than the Communist Party approach to non-Russians as "younger brothers." This has not stopped certain Turkic and Mongolic leaders, including intellectuals and artists, from touting Gumilev, including the internationally acclaimed Buryat artist Dashi Namdakov.[2] Gumilev's once-banned multivolume works have become something like a bible—so rich in cultural detail and stories that people are able to strategically pick and choose what they want from his eclectic body of work.

Opinions among my interlocutors diverge concerning whether citizens in the republics should have greater communication with each other. Are any of the republics, or trends within them, models for the others? What are local understandings of terms like Eurasianism, Siberia, Far East, Siberiaki, pan-Turkism, and pan-Mongolian? How are concepts linking individuals in the republics transformed into action? What are the transmission belts of nationalism and nostalgia, transnationalism, opposition, and power?

A striking movement exemplifying widespread interest in these themes is that of shaman Alexander, whose popular individual initiative synergized shamanic ideas with political protest in multiple regions in 2019. As mentioned in the introduction, his journey to Moscow was cut short by authorities in Buryatia only after he became a domestic and international internet sensation. Alexander attracted considerable numbers of followers on a quasi-pilgrimage he described as intended to peacefully purge and purify Russia from President Putin. He hoped to reach Red Square by walking along a route that would accumulate sympathizers and enable him to "exorcise" the corruption of the Kremlin by having Putin acknowledge his culpability and abdicate power. As one Sakha friend explained after his arrest, "the reason Alexander became so popular is that he was saying things that many were feeling but did not dare express."

Debates concerning mutual cultural heritage of languages, epics, and shamanic perspectives are ongoing wherever Sakha, Buryats, and Tyvans meet, sometimes sparked by discussion of shaman Alexander. In the post-Soviet period, noteworthy cultural exchanges include cross-republic film, music, art, and sports projects, as well as conferences and youth workshops. Regional economic connections logically follow, although they are sometimes discouraged by Moscow officials fearing loss of administrative control and leery of local initiative privatization or foreign instigated interference. Economic strategies linking individuals in the republics, or their leaders, have led to complex, not always cooperative, energy, mining, railroad, tourism, and logging projects. We begin here with economic issues, move to revisionist Eurasianism, revisit Turkic and Mongolic language politics, and highlight youth festivals. Spiritual revitalization represented by Buddhism and the Tengri movement are discussed. We culminate in analysis of shaman Alexander's dramatic albeit aborted efforts.

Economics, Fires, and Federalism

A positive example of cross-republic joint economic endeavors is the cooperation of Tyvan and Buryat partners, using Tempus funding, enabling them to develop a higher education program to stimulate the safety, production, and marketing of traditional food products. It encourages Indigenous businesses and includes Kazakh partners. Named TradPro, it focuses on "the traditional food cultures of Tuvan, Buryat, Kalmyk and Kazakh nomadic-pastoralists." Its funding application identified an important entrepreneurial small business gap to be filled, using a cultural appeal:

> The variety of livestock raised in these regions includes cattle, sheep, goats, horses, yaks, reindeer and camels, offering an unparalleled range of traditional meat and dairy products from free-range, grass-fed livestock. However, traditional meat and dairy producers operate on a very

small scale and cannot meet the consumer demand for quality traditional food products. TradPro will help develop the expertise necessary for small-scale producers to ensure that their products meet safety standards and are able to reach a wider market. The project has the added benefit of promoting the cultural sustainability of these closely related peoples and their national cuisines, which contributes to the vitality and diversity of our global cultural heritage.[3]

Another fascinating example of cross-border cooperation is the annual Tyva-Mongolia border market called Tsagaan-Tolgoi, held since the late 1990s, recreating a tradition that was begun in the tsarist period. Its 2017 version, on the Mongolian side in the aimaks (subregions) of Zavkhan and Uvsanur, granted special three-day permits for Tyvans to enjoy the crafts, light industry, and products sold and on display. Based on a cultural exchange agreement as well as economic interests, preparation for the market in Tyva called on "border nomads, border patrols, customs officers, migration and intelligence organs to mobilize for cooperation with their counterparts."[4] There has been less incentive for a comparable Tyva-Buryatia market on their shared border, perhaps due to the impoverishment of both republics. However, Tyva, Buryatia, and Sakha each have programs to stimulate local animal breeds, and these are appropriately suffused with pride in successful animal husbandry traditions.[5]

Russia's economy continues to be highly reliant on natural resource extraction, with oligarchical "winners" rarely residing near their wealth sources. This has ramifications for regional ecology and often involves opaque public-private business deals. As mentioned in the chapter on Sakha, local communities have resented the high-level Russia-China gas pipeline Power of Siberia (Sakha Republic-Primorskii krai), since energy wealth is perceived to be siphoned off to China while communities along the pipeline's path continue to use cheap and polluting coal. Few mechanisms exist for Russia's civil rights leaders and environmental activists to provide a unifying umbrella to effectively influence or protest such "done deal" transregional projects. However, in 2019, Lev Ponomaryev's group For Human Rights was legally reconstituted to include regional environmental activists. Their coalition has some potential to join disparate communities together in targeted negotiations for economic benefits and reparations. Whether their network evolves into organized opposition and mobilized civil society is a crucial question, particularly given the heightened sensitivity and high stakes of pipeline politics in Russia, as elsewhere.[6]

Competition and tensions are reflected through further examination of cross-republic relations, given that internal border questions and jurisdictional ambiguity within Russia, in the Soviet and post-Soviet periods, have been more common than many realize. Geographical contention between Buryatia and the Sakha Republic has manifested itself in concerns over pipeline routes and the locating of a chemical processing plant, mentioned previously. These disputes reflect the worries of local communities that they may be stuck with their neighbor's rejected projects. In addition, a revealing link between national self-identity and economics is the competition between the Sakha Republic and Greater Buryatia over which entrepreneurs can claim and market the purple stone "charoit," sacred to local Indigenous peoples, that comes from the Char River, near the republics' poorly defined borders.

Increasingly serious are questions of jurisdiction and resources for fighting forest fires that know no republic or regional boundaries. This has been a slow-burning issue through the post-Soviet period, reaching peak emergency awareness in 2019–2021. In the 1990s, forest fires burned out of control on the Sakha-Chukotka border due to disputes over jurisdiction. In summer 2019, particularly in the Northern Krasnoyarsk region, Sakha Republic, Irkutsk area, and Zabaikal krai, crossing the megaregions of the Siberia and Far East Federal Districts, devastation was over 6–7 million square acres, and smoke reached Alaska.[7] Russia's emergency services, using military planes and personnel, were unable to fully control the burning for months. Local people, especially in Irkutsk, added fuel to the fire by accusing Chinese migrant workers of having set the conflagrations to cover up illegal logging operations. While this may have been among the causes, other factors included wide violations of safety rules, bungled attempts to clear areas for resource extractions, loss of Indigenous control-burn practices due to all-Russia laws, lightning strikes, and climate change. In sum, in a time of competition for federal resources among the regions, forest fire emergencies have sparked further divisions as well as some attempts to cooperate across administrative divisions. Most administrators rue any ethnicization of the conflagrations, recognizing that Russian, Sakha, Buryat, Tyvan, and Évenki local communities all have suffered huge financial and human tolls.

Internal border tensions pale in comparison to the separatist dangers that constituted the first and second post-Soviet wars and insurgencies in the North Caucasus (compare Roeder 2018). Worried about the Chechnya war, in 1995 the then presidents of the republics of Tatarstan, Bashkortostan and Sakha wrote a joint appeal to President Yeltsin, titled "For the Consistent Democratization and Federalization of Rossiia." It is an idealistic document worth reading today, but the reform hopes of its signers have been dashed and the cooperation that allowed it to be written undermined. The text in part proclaimed:

> The republics are concerned by the inadequate representation of their interests in the legislative and executive organs of power. The funds for

opening and maintaining national schools and for developing culture are lacking today; to this day, there are no special channels on television and radio covering the life of the peoples of Rossiia. . . The question of the integrity of the country can be resolved for a time using force, but in the long term, this will lead to the opposite.[8]

Today, cross-republic political activities entailing public and sometimes more secretive interactions are difficult to decipher. They are discouraged and down-played by Moscow authorities, unless they take place in officially approved Federal District contexts overseen by presidential representatives. Before these mega-regions modeled on military security districting were established by President Putin, presidents of republics were much freer to jointly advance specific group interests with the federal center. However, informal consulting on cross-republic strategies regarding Moscow-derived policies and legal issues does occur. Local debates about the appropriateness or effectiveness of elections at various levels are frequently more open than some of those same debates in Moscow and St. Petersburg. We can discern patterns concerning increased public anger over elec-tion falsification, fear of police discrimination against those of Asian appearance, and cynicism about the glorification of Russia's role in local histories.

Federal-level decrees may be received and activated in various ways. When Tatarstan's bilateral agreement with Moscow was not renewed in 2017, anguished messages of resentment flew among the intelligentsias of various republics, includ-ing Sakha, Buryatia, and Tyva. Similar solidarity, with ripple effects beyond the elites, is reflected in protests against the 2020 centralizing and Russifying changes to Russia's Constitution, discussed in the book's conclusions.

Eurasianism Redux: From Lev Gumilev to Genghis Khan

Several years ago, riding a wind-swept ferry across the Lena River with a Sakha man who was soon to become a high official at a local university, he suddenly said: "What do you think of Lev Gumilev? Don't you think we need a new post-Communist ideology—and that Eurasianism could be it?" Having heard such arguments many times, I was not surprised. I asked him why he would put faith in the eclectic writings of a Russian who had a far from sympathetic understand-ing of local Sakha, or more broadly Turkic, colonial history (compare Etkind 2011). Wasn't this just a neocolonial twist on legitimizing Russian hegemony? No, he explained, this was a chance for the cultural roots of many different peo-ples' contributions to "Rossiia" to be acknowledged, even if the multiculturalism it delivered was imperfect. While it was not likely to become a way for ethnic

Russians to tap into their "inner Mongol" (as a Western historian has claimed)—my interlocutor felt Eurasianism represented a significant acknowledgment that Russia's "unique path" is partly due to its many centuries of Asian connections.[9] He was delighted that President Vladimir Putin had evoked Eurasianist ideology in public appearances, something the president has continued to do sporadically and strategically.

The romance of Asian cultural influence can be seen as a form of self-Orientalism, and that was what this university administrator seemed to be at once exhibiting and yearning for. The Buryat economist Nikolai Atanov explained similar sentiments at a 2013 international conference "Meeting at Lake Baikal: Burden of the Past, Challenges of the Future." He ended a presentation titled "The Eurasian Platform as a Basis for Symmetrical Cooperation among Post-socialist Countries of East Asia" by proclaiming: "It is appropriate to rework the issue of Eurasian identity on a theoretical-methodological basis, including its economic ramifications . . . Eurasian mutual benefit can be derived through Eurasian solidarity, joint adaptation to modern realities of globalization and regionalization, so that a practical and theoretical base can be laid for greater economic integration" (Atanov 2014, 68–69). Citing Gumilev, Atanov envisioned greater inter-republic solidarity within the Russian Federation, as well as expanding contacts among Central Asian states of the Former Soviet Union, seeing these as multiple levels of the same Eurasianist ideology. He was particularly impressed that President Nursultan Nazarbayev of Kazakhstan had in 1996 authorized the main academic university in the then newly established capital Astana (now Nur-Sultan) to be named the L. N. Gumilev Eurasian National University.

Using cultural rapport and diplomacy to create economic and political synergies is certainly nothing new. The delicate issue here is the degree to which these synergies are authorized in Moscow, and sometimes coopted by Russia's pseudofederal officials. Several somewhat contrasting cases of art, film, and archeology politics illustrate the potential and the difficulties.

In 2014, the Republic of Tyva unveiled a monumental sculpture by the Buryat artist Dashi Namdakov called *The Royal Hunt at the Center of Asia*. It was strategically placed at the heart of the capital Kyzyl, on the bank of the Yenesei River where Tyvans have long and proudly claimed their land precisely marks the Center of Asia. Attending the opening ceremony were the artist and many senior officials, including Tyva's native son/local hero—Russia's Defense Minister Sergei Shoigu, as well as Republic President Sholban Kara-ool. Dashi's website proclaims his Eurasian concept for the installation as depicting the embodiment of mythical nomadic figures: "the spirit of shamanic ancestors, the mystery of early Buddhist culture, the signs and symbols of ancient art" are brought to life.[10]

As Dashi has explained, the sculpture features a magnificent amazon-like queen and a falcon-bearing king, each on horseback, representing "nomads of Eurasia" whose roof is "the sky above them" (Figure 18). "The rider's souls 'breathe' the boundless immensity of the steppe on which they are galloping . . . [since] the steppe is the center of creation, defining the essence of existence for the sculpture's personages."

This blatant essentialism, meant to charm, ironically magnifies one of the public relations messages that some Russian authorities have been trying to project. As the Buryat art critic Maria Tagangaeva explains (2015, 52–53), it underscores "Russia's otherness, traditions, and special path, which the [Occidentalized] West 'cannot understand with the mind.' . . . [It] enables the 'vitality' of Russian culture and the 'richness' and 'diversity' of the culture of the 'peoples populating Russia' to be demonstrated."

Born in 1967 in the village of Ukurik, in the now-abolished Ust-Orda Buryat Autonomous Okrug, Dashi is a fascinating transnationalist, with homes in London, Italy, and Moscow. Many of his sculptures are forged in Italy. A 2015 project called *Soul of Asia* took him back near his homeland in the Irkutsk region. Another of his sculptures, called *Genghis Khan*, has conquered Hyde Park, London. President Putin, as well as the German politician Gerhard Schroeder and the actress Uma Thurman, are advertised as among the many wealthy collectors of his work. Dashi has described himself to a journalist using primordialist ideas reminiscent of Lev Gumilev: "I am an Asiatic person in my roots . . . and I have assimilated the experience of the European artistic school . . . In upbringing and

FIGURE 18.   *The Royal Hunt at the Center of Asia*, Kyzyl, by Dashi Namdakov. Used with permission by artist Dashi Namdakov.

in my genetics I am right in the center of Eurasia. This is why I consider myself a Eurasian person in the most direct sense. It is more than the mechanical sum of Oriental and European starting points, but an elevating symbiosis. I feel that the whole continent is in me at once" (Sal'nikova 2008, 37). Dashi, who works in many media besides sculpture, refers to his semimagical imagery depicting ancient Scythians as a "reincarnation" of the "spiritual Orient."

Dashi's popularity has spawned imitators across Russia, including in the republics of Sakha and Tyva. Yet it is film projects that he and others have created that truly cement the vogue of Eurasianism in its most romantic, idealized form. Dashi was a designer on the art film *Mongol*, released in theaters in 2007, produced in cooperation with Russian heartthrob actor and script co-author Sergei Bodrov Sr. The film employs Eurasianist themes and tropes directly, as acknowledged by Bodrov: "Genghis Khan answers the question of what the Russian land is and whence it came! His passion produced enormous changes in the mentality of Rus."[11]

For perspective, valorizing Genghis Khan had become an international phenomenon. His reputation experienced high-profile revision when he was named "Man of the Millennium" by *Time Magazine* in 2000. Myriad new histories of his significance appeared in Russia, Mongolia, Europe, and the United States after the Soviet Union collapsed. As early as the late 1980s, a group of Mongol historians visiting Washington's Woodrow Wilson Center tried to convince a packed audience that a kinder, gentler Genghis Khan was rarely aggressive but usually a defensive and savvy negotiator as he made his way across Central Asia marrying women of many tribes and promoting talented individuals.[12]

Into this fray charged the Sakha theater-director who became his republic's longest-running minister of culture of the post-Soviet space (from 1991 to 2014), Andrei Savich Borisov. While still a minister, with multiple resources at his disposal including from UNESCO, Andrei decided to create a blockbuster film on the early life of Genghis Khan (Temujin). Called in Russian *The Secret Genghis Khan* and in English *By the Will of Genghis Khan*, it appeared in 2008–2009, to mixed reviews. Its hero was played by a Tyvan actor (Eduard Ondar), and Temujin's mother was played by the legendary Sakha actress Stepanida Borisova, Andrei's wife. "Why didn't you create a film with a Sakha hero-ancestor?" cried some Sakha nationalists. "Why did you stress his personal life and the trauma of his wife being captured by enemies?" cried Eurasianist historians looking for sweeping lessons. "Why wasn't the film more accurate ethnographically and historically?" asked Russian intellectuals.[13]

Andrei, who is a friend, explained that he wanted to use the creative filmmaking itself as a bonding experience for many actors of various Far East nationalities—Tyvan, Sakha, Buryat, Éveny, Évenki, local Russian, Mongolian, and more. He wanted the film to represent, indeed symbolize, an inspiring collaborative, cross-cultural project that humanized a tortured young man who had become a notorious legend, the very epitome of a savage warrior. Striving to blow stereotypes, Andrei sought to reveal a group-psychology history of how tribes and clans that were once splintered could become consolidated through the personality of a strong leader.[14] He was fully aware of its potential resonance in chaotic post-Soviet identity-searching times. Filmed in numerous locations, from the Verkhoyansk (sacred Kiḣylyakh) mountains of the Sakha Republic to the Baikal region, Tyva, and Mongolia—the protracted and complex money-hemorrhaging project created a synergistic comradery among most of those involved.

A Sakha villager in the Srednaia Kolyma region, having played a hunter and warrior as an extra in the film, told me the experience was exhilarating and life changing. A Buryat colleague recalled that the vast tent-filled film sets and gorgeous scenery while living on location in camps made everyone feel as if they were reliving history. Collaborating on such a monumental project enriched the imaginations of participants at all levels and empowered them to think of epic mythmaking as an ongoing, improvisational, multicultural process, the opposite of filmmaking with a Soviet-style frozen, preapproved propagandistic script.

Digging deeper into history, some intellectuals and middle-class people of Sakha, Buryat, Tyvan, or mixed ethnic backgrounds have become fascinated by popular archeology, sacred sites, and linguistics. A quarterly journal called *Narody i religii Evrazii* (Peoples and Religions of Eurasia), based in the Altai since 2007, has a readership beyond academia. Archeology tourism has become fashionable for affluent non-Russians of the Far East and Siberia. A Sakha doctor in the bureaucracy of the main hospital in Yakutsk told me in 2016 that he and many of his friends have been thrilled to go on tourist trips to Tyva, because they can feel their common roots through the glory of ancient gold-filled Scythian burials of the Western Sayans, at the Uyuk Ridge, the "Valley of the Kings." "Have you been there?" he asked eagerly, and was delighted with my affirmation, agreeing that it is a shame much of the precious gold finds were taken to St. Petersburg's Hermitage Museum for "safekeeping." But he was more interested in the sacred burial land itself. This natural and cultural preserve (called Taiga, protected since 2009) has become a pilgrimage site for many looking for ways to be proud of their past. The doctor also emphasized Turkic-language solidarities, explaining "this is our common heritage with Tuvan and Uriankhai Sakha ancestors." Other Sakha friends feel rapport with Tyvans for keeping alive Turkic rituals of respect for nature spirits at sacred springs, blessing gnarled trees with prayer ribbons, and celebrating seasonal change during the spring New Year holiday Shagaa Bile.

I have long known of Sakha interest in the Central Asian archeological culture labeled "Sak" and, as editor of the journal *Anthropology and Archeology of*

Eurasia, have occasionally made gentle fun of the wider phenomenon that I call "Everyone wants to be Scythian."[15] In the past ten years, a club with its own t-shirt has formed, called "the new Scythians," through the Lev Gumilev Center of Eurasianism and Scythology. Cultural and genetic roots seeking is an understandable phenomenon, and many Tyvans welcome a steady stream of intellectually engaged distant kin. Tyvan tourist guides emphasize with pride the importance of written Turkic language origins, evident through the ancient Orkhon script found on rune-filled tall stelae memorializing fallen warriors.[16] In 2020, a teenaged Sakha student expressed astonishment during one of our fire-pit gatherings that early Turkic peoples had their own written language and impulsively exclaimed: "Why weren't we taught this in grade-school in Yakutsk?"

One manifestation of pride in archeological discoveries is the near-cult status of the Sakha historian Anatoly Ignatevich Gogolev, whose books on "Uriankhai Sakha" roots discuss origins in the Kurykan culture of the Lake Baikal region. Anatoly, who was my postdoctoral academic mentor in 1986 at Yakutsk State University, carefully analyzes multiple sources of Yakut-Sakha culture, including Turkic, Mongolic, and Tungusic. But the multiethnic Kurykan state that flourished just before the arrival of Genghis Khan has especially captured the imaginations of some Sakha and Buryats. Anatoly's lifelong research helps to answer the intriguing question of how a predominantly Turkic-speaking people like the Sakha could have landed so far north along the Lena River. As my doctor-interlocutor explained: "The peoples around Lake Baikal were indeed mixed in the Kurykan period—and many fled north in the wake of Genghis Khan. The genes of his military personnel were spread far and wide—but you can say that our Turkic Sakha ancestors were the conquest refugees of their day,. . . settling farther north and encountering other peoples—Tungusic, Paleo-Asiatic."[17]

Historical symbolism is strong in the official seals of the post-Soviet republics within Russia, and most were selected in highly competitive art submissions during the 1990s. As we have seen, the official seal of the Republic of Tyva has a flying horseman dashing across a sky with a sun in the righthand corner, valorizing a legendary hero. The state emblem of Buryatia has Lake Baikal imagery, along with sun and Buddhist symbolism including a trident, despite the official Moscow-based guidelines for the seals discouraging religious symbols. Significantly, the seal of the Republic of Sakha features an image of a cliff drawing (carving) of a horseman holding a pole with a banner, and some see the horseman as more peacemaker than warrior. It comes from the cliff art of Irkutsk oblast, in the territory of the abolished Ust-Orda region. [See three seals on cover.] This famous horseman is called the "Shishkinsk pictograph," named for the specific place it was found along the Upper Lena River, along with other precious cliff art dating from the Neolithic and Bronze Age periods. Originally discovered in the eighteenth century during the Great Northern Expedition of Gerhardt F. Miller, the site was documented by Alexei P. Okladnikov (1970) in the twentieth century as having had over two thousand images, with about seven hundred remaining.

The Shishkinsk site has become the locus of an important interregional preservation campaign, since it was recently vandalized (!) and is vulnerable to pollution, road construction, natural erosion, forestry projects, and climate change. Sakha, Buryat, and Russian representatives are collaborating to save the site and its famous imagery in a project partially funded by the Sakha government, led by Yuri Kuprianov. Whether accurate or not, most see the horseman as symbolizing early Turkic warrior society, and his image has landed on some of the bills of the Kazakh money, *tenge*. Buryats too have proclaimed the site invaluable for deciphering their ancestry and use its symbols liberally on their souvenirs. The popular site has become an outdoor museum requiring tourist control. One of its advisors, my Sakha colleague Uliana Vinokurova, has summarized: "the cliff art and runic writing [of Orkhon] are thus among the sustainable lynch-pins of commonality among the Turkic-Mongolic peoples of Eurasia."[18]

Turkic-Mongolic Language Politics and Russian-Slavic Backlash

Since the Soviet Union collapsed, language revitalization projects have been key to the political and cultural recovery of non-Russians' self-worth in each republic of Russia. News of morale-boosting prizes for seemingly obscure histories of linguistic correlations spreads widely, by word of mouth and the internet. For example, news of the awarding of a Turkish cultural prize for Gerasim Levin's *Historical Ties of the Yakut Language to Ancient Turkic Languages (7th–9th Centuries)* was celebrated not only in Yakutsk, where the author is the assistant director of the "museum of literacy," but also in Buryatia and Tyva. A Yakutsk based online conference in 2021 celebrated the languages and cultures of the peoples of Eurasia.[19]

Since historically complex demographic balances vary widely in the republics, it matters greatly whether demographic proportions favor non-Russians. In the three republics featured here, these proportions are "all over the map." Contemporary Tyvans are a substantial majority, Sakha constitute a narrow majority, and Buryats are a small and shrinking minority, especially given the gerrymandering of their territory. Each of these republics passed laws designating dual state languages in the 1990s, and school systems in each republic responded in the first post-Soviet decade with increased education in non-Russian languages at all levels (compare Osipov 2015). Statistics, as evident in the individual republic profiles, have shown improvements in rural and urban non-Russian language learning, even though a shortage of schools featuring non-Russian language and cultural programs in capital cities in the past decade has meant that parents sometimes line up overnight to enroll their children in coveted programs. Russia's language politics has swung back toward discouraging republic "titular languages," as the Ministry of Education, under President Putin-appointed leadership as of 2016, has emphasized standardized and intensive training in Russian.

The trend was given accelerated motivation by a Russian protest movement launched in the context of 2016 Duma election campaigns. A group calling itself "defenders of the Russian language in the national regions of Russia" launched an appeal "to the country's political parties and movements."[20] While the group has been particularly strong in the Turkic-language-prominent republic of Tatarstan, it has significant representation in Buryatia and some weight in Tyva. Their declaration began, "we want to turn your attention to the sad situation with regard to the study of Russian, which can be seen in a number of national republics of Russia." It elaborated that republic governments have been able to make their "titular languages" required subjects in the schools even when the "non-Russian linguistic milieu" is weak, and even when parents [read Russians] do not want their children to spend time on these languages. The appeal requests changes in Russian Duma legislation to make Russian required everywhere as the majority state language "and the study of non-Russian languages voluntary." Such legislation has undermined republic authority and violates the spirit of cultural sovereignty in the republics, as the Russian signatories well know. The appeal itself has exacerbated interethnic tensions and raised the profile of language politics to all-time highs in post-Soviet Russia.[21] Its goals were furthered by President Putin's constitutional amendments of 2020.

Language politics are multileveled as well as interactive and reactive. Underlying the defense of one's native language—whether Russian, Sakha, Tyvan, or Buryat—is often a sense of linguistic and cultural commonalities that transcend the barriers of specific republics. The phrase mentioned above, "Turkic-Mongolic peoples of Eurasia," highlights this metasolidarity. On the Russian side, sensitivity to the pain of "losing Ukraine and Belarus" after the collapse of the Soviet Union is being worked through by certain pan-Slavic defenders, following in the wake of the famed writer Alexander Solzhenitsyn. These pan-Slavists would like to see a larger Slavic-based state and have cheer-led the 2014 takeover (or for them, "recovery") of Crimea. Among their organizations is the Imperator (Emperor) Fund for the "preservation of historical legacy," whose secretary is the spin-master publicist Vladimir Stanulevich. Shifting levels of identity—activated more or less in certain situations for Slavic, Turkic, and

Mongolic peoples in interaction with each other—can be called transnational rather than fully international. They are appealing on a civilizational basis, in contexts that need not be confrontational but unfortunately sometimes become so (compare Tishkov 2020).

Intentionally nonconfrontational are republic-based and steadily expanding native-language Wikipedia and dictionary projects. The Sakha Republic, Buryatia, and Tyva have their own morale-building, fully interactive wikis based at universities—and some of the entries they choose to feature for "insiders" are illuminating. In the Tyvan version, links are provided to other Turkic-language sites, including Sakha-language sites.[22] The Buryat language project celebrates the *buryād xelen* version of the Buryats' Mongolic language, with numerous articles on Buryat history, symbols, Buddhism, and Mongolian contacts. Alternate language instructions for interaction are in English, not Russian.[23]

The Sakha language project, begun in 2006 by the young linguist Nikolai Pavlov, has as its slogan "Ahaghas bilii" (Toward Open Knowledge). As with the Western model Wikipedia, each article includes an invitation for discussion and editing, and an additional forum enables adding articles and comment. The project includes on its main page references to other popular Sakha sites, such as a local districts (*ulus*) forum, Yakutsk online, Yakut youth, and the Sakha diaspora's Sakha Open World site.[24] Significantly, it too has links to other Turkic-language wikipedias. Some of its articles feature profiles of Turkic historical figures who were repressed in the Soviet period. However, a site advisor emphasized in 2016 that it is important "only because its articles are in the Sakha language, that the project supports Sakha language speakers and readers."

A rapturous poem-prayer (*algys*) on the main Sakha wiki page sets the tone:

Саргы-дьаалы Сахам тыла,	My free-flowing Sakha Language
Айхал-алгыс Сахам тыла,	My word-image-filled Sakha Language
Уруй олук Сахам тыла,	May my Sakha Language flourish
Күн бэлэҕэ Сахам тыла,	My Sakha Language, a present from the Sun
Эйигин мин ынырыаҕым,	To you I will greet,
«Ийээ!» диэммин хаһыытыаҕым.	Loudly calling you my Mother!
Тоҕойдору туораан ис,	Go without meandering,
Арҕастары ааһан ис,	Surpass inequality,
Саргы дьайаан Сахам тыла,	May you freely flow
Сарыал санаа—Сахам тыла!	Like rays of the Sun, my Sakha language

Bootur Toburuokap [Petr N. Toborokov, war hero poet, 1917–2001][25]

Students from each of the republics study in the capitals of the other republics, sometimes creating lasting bonds and burgeoning multilingual, multiethnic family ties. For example, Tyvans and Sakha study in Ulan-Ude, and some Buryats are studying in Yakutsk. While their projects are not necessarily predictable at the respective universities, informal conversations indicate that sometimes the students are unhappy and homesick, especially Buryats going north to Yakutsk. Nonetheless, in each capital are *zemliachestvo* (home community) support groups enabling diaspora connections and adaptation. Some Tyvan students are getting their Kandidat degrees in Ulan-Ude, requiring considerable scholarly interaction.[26]

A Moscow-based 2016 combined "scientific and practical" conference recruited scholars from the Turkic-language-speaking republics of Tatarstan, Bashkortostan, Tyva, and Sakha. It was called "Modern Problems of Turkology: Language, Literature and Culture," and its sponsors included the Eurasian Association of Universities. It attracted experts from Russia and Central Asia working on themes of "expanded silk road" tourism, as well as linguistics and "culturology." The intent behind the project appears to have been a desire to bring several generations of Turkologists together in a setting where Moscow scholars could be privy to, if not control, the agenda. Sessions included a retrospective on renowned Kazakh-Turkic activist Olzhas Suleimeinov, a sharp critic of Russian colonialism, who received a prize during the conference, and the more prospective "psychology of pedagogy in Turkic language training of youth."[27]

Civilizational solidarity has been stimulated through youth projects. Non-Russian elders worry that young people are losing their Turkic or Mongolic sense of self-worth through Russification and through the globalizing influences of the English-and-games-saturated internet. One relevant project—not limited to Sakha, Tyvan, and Buryat youth—has been the multiyear interregional Etnova Forum, playing on the Russian words "Ethnos" and "New." Describing their goals as an ethnic-tourist program to stimulate young people's interest in their own cultures, they have met regularly since 2000. The project began as a culture camp of relaxation and fun in Khakassia, to help stimulate Turkic identity and pride in minority languages. They have provided workshops in ethnocultural crafts, pedagogy, volunteering, social work, horse tourism, new media, and youth theater and directing. Participants from Sakha, Buryatia, and Tyva, some of whom I know, have been enthusiastic; they hope that funding from various republics as well as Moscow continues. Pre-pandemic "trainers" included Russians as well as non-Russians, and the forum, usually held in August, has been nicknamed "Warm Siberia." In 2016 and 2017, the forum met in Khakassia and received a Russian Event Award from the federal Ministry of Tourism. It broadened to incorporate youth from all over Russia, and in 2016 included a German delegation. Thus, some of its initial impetus seems to have shifted, or perhaps been hijacked. One of the themes of the 2017 forum was "military-patriotic upbringing."[28] By 2020, the forum was on hold, and young people were exploring other options.

Youth Camps, Sporting Competitions, Festivals, and Art with Historical Resonance

An important way to galvanize youth is through sport. An upbeat, Russia-wide "healthy way of life" campaign has been associated with several Putin-sponsored youth organizations and summer camps that have tried to become the successors to the Young Communist League (Komsomol).[29] One dynamic young Sakha businessman (aged thirty-five) whom I met in 2017 mentioned that he had gotten his start as a youth leader of Russia's "young people's parliament," which organized sport, travel, and study groups. As long as he stayed in sports and business, he was well supported, but the minute he developed an interest in local politics without allegiance to President Putin's United Russia party he felt thwarted, even threatened. He had never thought of himself as oppositional but was pushed to the point where he felt he had been placed in that category.

While Putin-sponsored groups and campaigns have had some representation in the non-Russian republics, their main events and camps, such as the notorious "free love" happenings run by Nashi at Seliger Lake, have been overwhelmingly Russian and perceived as such by Turkic- and Mongolic-speaking young people. "Putin's patriotic camps" have not resonated with most Buryat, Sakha, and Tyvan youths, some of whom have told me that they would feel endangered in such rally-like, anti-Western environments. More appealing for those interested in marathons are grueling international foot races held on the ice of Lake Baikal. Also popular are the motor bike and car racing at Lake Baikal, cleverly called the "silk way rally."[30]

A delightful alternative for Turkic and Mongolic youth in the past several years has become the Ërdyn Games held on the shores of Lake Baikal, with sacred mountains visible in the distance. Termed an "international ethnocultural festival," these games have combined sport, music and dance performances, prayers, and history lessons. Their Russian gloss, for advertising purposes, is "Igry narodov Evrazii" (Games of the Peoples of Eurasia). The events are sponsored by Sakha and Buryat local governments, especially Irkutsk oblast. Former Sakha Minister of Culture Andrei Borisov, mentioned above, helped establish the games in 2001 with the Buryat cultural historian and activist Dashinima Sanzhevich Dungarov and Sakha organizer Vladimir Davidovich Ivanov. Held in 2005, 2011, 2013, 2015–2017, and 2019, with the eighth in 2021, the games are called *Ërdyn naadan* in Buryat, named after the traditional Buryat summer festival that the Buryat folklorist-ethnographer Matvei Nikolaevich Khangalov described in the nineteenth century.[31]

Nadaan is similar to the Sakha summer solstice celebration *Yhyakh* and the Tyvan summer ceremony *Nadaam*. Traditionally, these were moments in the sacred and social calendar when multiple hierarchical and competitive kin groups could coalesce in one large, fertile, and majestic mountain valley. They provided opportunities for families to cement kin and marital alliances, with matchmaking, engagement ceremonies, and weddings sometimes accompanying the celebrations. Some of this social and personal networking has continued in the current incarnation of the games, in more modern and less controlled form. They especially celebrate the solidarity of Sakha and Buryat youth, although by the 2016 games, Tyvan young people and delegations from Mongolia and Canada also attended.

The Buryat name for the modern games stems from an extinct volcano near the river valley Anga, at the Aia Bay of the sacred Olkhon region, a site where three legendary heroes were said to have competed with each other. Repressed in the Soviet period, the festival was revived in the 1990s and took its current more elaborate transnational form beginning in 2001 (Figure 19). The multi-day festival features archery, wrestling, running, rope pulling, weightlifting with rocks, horse racing (in Buryat *mori-urildaan*), and other sports competitions that were beloved before the 20th century. One called *néershaalgan* involves beating a sheep's backbone; another, *shadainaadan*, cracking a ram's bone. Craft master classes, craft markets, and food emporia are available. Competitions for genealogical recitation and epic singing are held, with winners receiving luxurious prizes and personal acclaim. In 2016, a nostalgia-imbued parallel conference was held to discuss "how to preserve traditional games."[32]

Several common Turkic and Mongolic cultural practices with similar names resonate throughout the festival: circle dancing with singing called *yokhar*, jaw harp (*khomus*) playing, prayer-giving (*algysh* in Tyvan and Sakha), and fire offerings by a priestly figure, sometimes called a "white" (or pure) shaman.

In 2016, a multicultural art exhibit called "Spirit of Asia" was coordinated with the youth festival, including participation by the renowned Buryat sculptor Dashi Namdakov. Various regions also erected special "exhibit yurts" to highlight their local art. While the intent behind the festival has been to bring to life somewhat romanticized "traditional" cultural practices, its complex, multievent dynamics feel contemporary and fresh. Young people are as likely to dance to rock music, or "new age shamanic rock," as they are to dance circle dances, beat bones, and chant poetry.

Every generation has been enjoying a renaissance of folk arts, through handicraft heritage projects and art that capture the spirit of national motifs without

FIGURE 19.   White Shaman overlooking the Ërdyn Games. Permission correspondence with festival organizers. Image on open source https://fotovmire.ru/
sajany-foto.html/bajkalskij-shaman-s-bubnom. Original on https://ok.ru/erdgames.

mimicking. Each republic featured here has a national art museum with a range
of contemporary art, enabling exhibitions that include the work of each other's
best artists. Released from the binds of socialist realism, these artists, many of
them young, creatively use old media in new ways (horse hair tapestry), depict
Indigenous people in new predicaments (figures falling through watery chaos
representing climate change), valorize nature through hyperrealism, or illumi-
nate epic heroes with humor and irony. Stone and bone carvers have flourished;
the "GranPri" (a play on Grand Prix) in bone carving was won by the Ulan-Ude
artist Bato-Munko Chimitov at Yakutsk's 2020 Kulakovskii Friendship Center art
fair. The Sakha precious metals sculptor Alexander Manzhur'ev had a personal
exhibition in Kyzyl, and was proud that his art was displayed along with Scythian treasures. Sakha, Buryat, and Tyvan jewelry making has revived, especially
silver working that streamlines and adapts traditional styles, such as my favorite
ear picker ornament. Fantasy dressmaking, turning folk costumes into dream-
like surrealism, has become a marker of festival and theater clothing in all three
republics, especially Sakha and Buryatia.[33]

Jaw harp playing and the throat singing called *khomei* continue to have special
meaning for many elders and some Sakha, Buryat, and Tyvan youth. In 2017 in
Kyzyl, young people were visibly reverent at a memorial to the great Tyvan musician Kongor-ool Ondar and were crucial to the unveiling of his depiction in a
bronze, life-sized sculpture.[34] The charming city center statue, already laden with

meaning, had further significance because it was collaboratively designed by a young Tyvan artist (Syldys Oiudup) and created in the workshop of the Buryat sculptor Alexander Mironov. In addition, the international museum based in Yakutsk dedicated to the jaw harp (Muzei i Tsentr khomusa narodov mira) regularly hosts concerts, festivals, and conferences that have included musicians from the republics of Sakha, Buryatia, Tyva, and beyond. It also sponsors school programs to promote enthusiasm for folk music, as does the Museum of Music and Folklore in Yakutsk.

Striving for Spiritual Connections: Buddhism, Epics, and Sky God Worship (Tengri)

Delving beyond officially endorsed forms of Eurasianism, exemplified by the Eurasian Association of Universities, we find trends that reveal revitalization of common Turkic and Mongolic spirituality. This is evident in the renaissance of Buddhist thought, practice, and leadership in the republics most associated with Russian Buddhism—Kalmykia, Buryatia, and Tyva. A fascinating collaborative sociological survey of 709 students in these republics by eminent Buddhist activist-scholar colleagues has shown young people's interests in and identification with Buddhism to be mainly as a "provider of spiritual-moral values" (Badmaev et al. 2020). While student ignorance of the historical sources of Buddhism (India, Tibet) is exposed, perhaps the most relevant data to emerge from the study is a predominant agreement that the historical legacies of Buddhism in Buryatia and Tyva make these Asian regions of "traditional Buddhism" different from the rest of Russia, and special. An overwhelming majority of students rejected the idea that "Buddhism is close to Russian culture and mentality." Intriguingly, a quarter of the Tyvan students and a third of the Buryat ones saw "Yakutia" as a Buddhist region, perhaps due to perceived potential for kindred-spirit collaboration. At least some may have been aware that Buryat Buddhists have established a temple outside Yakutsk, although their activities, publicity, and record of conversions have been modest.

At a combined political and civilizational level, common Turkic and Mongolic ties in the past have been termed "pan-Turkism" (or "pan-Turanism") and "pan-Mongolism." That historical labeling masks more subtle, multiple levels of Turkic and Mongolic identities and activism. New variations of Turkic and Mongolic solidarities are far from the same movements that overly paranoid early Soviet government officials saw as an existential threat in the 1920s and 1930s.[35] Today's incarnations include the dissemination of loosely unifying pre-Christian polytheistic concepts called Tengrianstvo (Tengrism, Tengri, Tengeri), a form of pan-Turkism. These could again create Russian paranoia and backlash if misunderstood as secessionist or destructively nostalgic. The power of nationalist ideas comes in many forms, and their tango-like interaction in response to each other have created unexpected passions unlike Gumilev's version of *passionarnost'*.[36]

In June 2010, I was asked to perform one of the most embarrassing "participant observation" rituals in my quarter-century of intermittent fieldwork in the Sakha Republic. The setting was a nearly finished Tengri temple on the outskirts of the summer solstice festival grounds near Yakutsk. Creators of the Yhyakh ceremonial complex called Three Birches (Us Khatyn) had refused to let the organizers of the temple have a visible presence inside their extensive grounds, and so the hike to find the temple across a meadow was arduous. When I arrived with a jaw-harp musician friend, we were greeted warmly by the temple's designer, builder, financier, and chief priest—a vigorous white-haired elder-businessman, Vasily Nikolaevich Atlasov, whom I already knew. Part Évenki and part Sakha, Vasily ushered us into the spacious eight-sided building reminiscent of the form of an old-fashioned Sakha winter house (*balagan*) but also modeled, Vasily proudly mentioned, on "Ivan the Terrible's church of Blagaveshensk on Red Square [Moscow]."

The temple, smelling of fresh wood, had a packed earthen floor, not yet covered with boards, and a huge hearth to the right of the main entrance. This was when the encounter turned awkward, as Vasily invited me to kneel before their roaring fire to introduce myself to their god with a food offering. Usually I was comfortable with making fire spirit offerings, something I had been doing regularly since 1986. This was somewhat different—not a "feeding" of the mediator fire spirit (*iot ichchi*) to reach specific deities in an extended pantheon but rather "a gift of honor for the God Tengri of the temple." My chocolate squares would be fine, our priest assured, unlike some Sakha purists who insist on Sakha traditional foods. However, I needed to do this humbly kneeling in the dirt by the fire and "by twisting my body into a swastika position." "How could I do this?" I stuttered—and when he demonstrated I smiled politely and tried to explain that my long, diaphanous, white Yhyakh clothes would probably render this obeisance difficult. Besides, I added nervously, "I'm not comfortable with anything associated with the swastika." Vasily reassured me that I could offer the chocolate with a bow and explained that their swastika was not the symbol co-opted by the hated Aryan-valorizing Nazis but rather the original ancient Central Asian Turkic symbol that had also been adopted in Hindu ritual practice. He added that the runes I had seen painted on the outside of the building were not from the "Orkhon script of the Altai Mountains," but rather from a still more ancient version of the Turkic "Uighur script."

After I had honored the fire spirit, we recovered our rapport. By then, an entourage had formed of Vasily's main "ideologist-consultant," the Sakha historian Andrei Krivoshapkin (pseudonym Aiynga, or blessed), and another worshipper, Nikolai Kurilov. They escorted us to the central iconography of the temple—a huge movable-parts, zodiac-like apparatus raised in the middle of the floor that resembled a wheel of fortune. Andrei expounded on their syncretic new-old religion: "We are getting back to our roots through this temple by honoring the Turkic people as well as the religion of the Cossacks who came here in the seventeenth century. The word 'Tengri' itself is very misunderstood—it means Light and is the name of our Sun God." "Not Sky?" I asked. "No—that is a common misconception. It is our God, our main god, but also a God with a family, like the Christian trinity—Father, Son, Holy Ghost." Nikolai explained other familiar concepts:

> Our idea of Tengri includes the ancient ideas of dualism—night and day, darkness and light. White light sun is the fire . . . We also honor the colors—especially the seven primary colors of the rainbow [that are seen on the iconic wheel]. We take what we know from many religions and construct our concepts out of their knowledge of facts, [their wisdom] . . . We also are working on the level of collective consciousness.

Aside from literally reinventing the wheel with popular spiritual tropes, who are their co-worshippers and how unique is this "new religious movement" found far to the north of the original Turkic-language speakers' homelands? A small yet influential group of the Sakha intelligentsia has gravitated toward this temple and helped Atlasov sponsor several other temples in the republic. The main temple is affiliated with musicians who have revived the beloved *khomus* mouth organ, or "jaw harp," and they sometimes give concerts of traditional music in the temple. Another key player is the Yakutsk-based historian Lena Fedorova, director of the International Fund for Research into Tengri, as well as associate director of the Olonkho [Sakha epos] Theater. The popular Lena Fedorova has organized "international culturological expeditions" to Central Asia, Siberia, Mongolia, North India, Nepal, Tibet, and "Xinjiang-Uighuria." Her contacts include like-minded scholars and activists in Altai, Tyva, Kazakhstan, and Kyrgyzstan, where a more full-blown Tengri worship has developed.[37]

Another channel for Tengri proselytizing has been numerous conferences on the Turkic epics, including *Olonkho* in Sakha and *Manas* in Kyrgyz. A jovial competition seems to have evolved, with each group claiming its epics are longer or older. I have attended several conferences and celebrations of the epics in the past decade where Sakha, Tyvan, Altai, Kyrgyz, and other scholars and epic singers have reveled in the revival of a nearly lost art. An entire center for the study of epics has been established at the main university in Yakutsk. The slippage from scholarship to worship of pre-Christian, pre-Buddhist Tengri is palpable at these conferences. At minimum, its "ancient wisdom worldview" is evoked for its possible lessons for today, especially regarding ecological consciousness for the preservation of sacred lands.

At a conference in 2013, the elder-statesman historian Vasily Nikolaevich Ivanov, head of Sakha's Olonkho Studies Center, admitted to me during a three-way conversation with a folklorist from Kyrgyzstan that indeed the "Turkic epics have been used to enhance political self-identification." Our Kyrgyz colleague was dashing in his signature Kyrgyz white felt hat with black applique, reminding me that Turkic solidarity is sometimes subtly signaled by the fashion for non-Kyrgyz men well outside of Kyrgyzstan to wear the pointed white hats. Later, Vasily Ivanov reinforced with me his delight at meeting the Turkic colleagues who had come for the conference, noting that they had helped deepen his understanding of the Sakha epics and that he had been pleased to share with them the poetic opening ceremony prayers of that year's summer solstice festival, officially dedicated to the Sakha *olonkho*.

Tengri has captured the imaginations of scholars and youth of Mongolic backgrounds as well, including Kalmyk and Buryat. A special journal issue "Humanities Research of Inner Asia," published in Ulan-Ude in 2017, was devoted to the "role of Tengeri and Northern Buddhist ideas of Ekaian (the 'Unified Circle') in the ethnocultural genesis of Turko-Mongolian peoples of Inner and Northeastern Asia."[38] Going further, a romantic statement (originally in Russian) from a web commentary celebrating traditions of "Nomads of the Great Steppe" dated June 28, 2016, emphasized blood solidarity tropes:

> In our blood and soul we carry the sacred legacy of our ancestors. We cannot know them as an unbroken line to the past. But they live on in us, and in our blood spread all over the whole world. This is precisely what makes our blood sacred. It is what enables our parents to give us not only substance but consciousness. To reject one's spirit and the souls of one's ancestors is to reject oneself. Each person must be enabled to find within oneself the best parts of one's legacy, to gain through that will and bravery. Blood is the carrier of life, the secret to one's creativity. Your blood and sacred soul are where the Will of the God Tengri lives.[39]

Tengri worship's status as a new religious movement is fragile but growing in several republics and Central Asian states. Post-Soviet conceptions are explicitly legitimized as adopted from pre-Christian, pre-Buddhist, and pre-Islamic times, and a full-fledged pantheon rivaling that of Greek or Nordic civilization is touted. This is supported by quotations from Herodotus, in conference presentations, and in a growing popular literature on early Turkic civilization, such as books by Lena Fedorova (2012) and Andrei Krivoshapkin (1998). In sum, the Tengri revival offers potential for seekers of new, wider kinds of ideological community, sometimes selectively combined with Buddhist and shamanic ideas. However, it could be abused by charismatic leaders who may use dangerously essentialist metaphors of blood and belonging to create insider vs. outsider solidarity. From blood tropes to chauvinism is one small step. From perceived chauvinism to backfiring repression is another.

Shaman Alexander and His Protest Journey to Moscow

In his 2018–2019 meteoric rise to national and international attention, Alexander Prokopievich Gabyshev, also called "shaman Alexander," "Sasha shaman," and "Sania," came to mean many things to many people. For some, he is a potent symbol of protest against a corrupt regime led by a president he calls "a demon." For others, he has become a coopted tool in some part of the government's diabolical security system, set to attract followers so that they can be exposed and repressed. Some feel he is a "brave fellow" (*molodets*), "speaking truth to power" in a refreshingly articulate voice devoid of egotism. Others see him as misguided and psychologically unstable, made "crazy" by a tragic life that includes the death of his beloved wife before they could have children. Some accept him into the Sakha shamanic tradition, arguing his suffering and two–three years spent in the taiga after his wife's death qualify him as a leader and healer who endured "spirit torture" in order to serve others. Others, including some Sakha and Buryat shamans, reject him as a charlatan whose education as an historian was wasted when he became a welder, street cleaner, and plumber. These and many other interpretations are debated by my Russian and non-Russian friends with a passion that at minimum reveals he has touched a nerve in Russia's body politic. It is worth describing how Alexander, born in 1968, describes himself and his mission as a "warrior shaman" before analyzing some of the comments of his high- and low-profile followers and critics, in order to place him in historical context.

Picture Alexander on foot pushing a gurney and surrounded by well-wishers, walking a mountainous highway before being arrested by masked armed police for "extremism" in September 2019. Among over a hundred internet video clips of Alexander's epic journey from Yakutsk to Ulan-Ude via Chita, is an interview from *Shaman on the Move!* (June 12, 2019):

> I asked, beseeched God, to give me witness and insight. . . . I went into the taiga [after my wife had died of a dreadful disease ten years ago]. . . . It

is hard for a Yakut [Sakha person] to live off the land, not regularly eating meat and fish. . . . I came out of the forest a warrior shaman. . . . To the people of Russia, I say "choose for yourself a normal leader, . . . young, competent." . . . To the leaders of the regions, I say "take care of your local people and the issues they care about and give them freedom." . . . To the people, I say "don't be afraid of that freedom." We are endlessly paying, paying out. . . . Will our resources last for our grandchildren? Not at the rate we are going . . . Give simple people bank credit . . . Let everyone have free education and the chance to choose their careers freely . . . There should not be prisons. . . . But we in Russia [*rossiiane*] have not achieved this yet, far from it . . . Our prisons are terrifying. . . . At least make the prisons humane. . . . For our small businesses, let them flourish before taking taxes from them. Just take taxes from the big, rich businesses. . . . For our agriculture, do not take taxes from people with only a few cows. . . . Take from only the big agro-business enterprises.[40]

In this interview and others, Alexander made clear he is patriotic, a citizen of Russia, who wants to purify its leadership. "Let the world want to be like us in Russia," he proclaimed, "We need young, free, open leadership." While he explains that "for a shaman, authority is anathema," he has praised the relatively young and dynamic head of Sakha Republic: "Aisen [Nikolaev] is a simple person at heart who wants to defend his people, but he is constrained, under the fear of the demon in power [in the Kremlin]." Alexander acknowledges the route he has chosen is difficult, and that many will try to stop him. Indeed, he has begun his "march to Moscow" ("eight thousand kilometers") three separate times, once in 2018 and twice in 2019, including after his arrest when he temporarily slipped away from house arrest in December 2019, was rearrested and fined. In 2021, he was detained yet again before he could try to leave Yakutsk, this time on a white horse with a caravan of followers. His announcement of the new plans, with a photo of him galloping on his white horse carrying an old Sakha warrior's standard, mentioned that he would begin his journey by visiting the sacred lands of his ancestors in the Viliui (Suntar) territories, "source of my strength," and encouraged followers to join him, since "truth is with us." Their route was planned to pass through sacred Altai.

Alexander has often explained that "for freedom you need to struggle." Into 2021, he hoped to meet his goal of reaching Red Square to perform his "exorcism ritual." But his arrests and reconfinement in a psychiatric clinic under punishing "close observation" conditions make that increasingly unlikely, especially given massive crackdowns on all of President Putin's opponents, including Aleksei Naval'ny and his many supporters. One of Alexander's most telling barbs critiques the "political intelligentsia," who hold "too many meetings" and do not accomplish enough. He tells them: "It is time to stop deceiving us." Yet he considers that numerous politicians in Russia, across the political spectrum, would be better alternatives than the current occupant of the Kremlin.[41]

Among Alexander's most controversial actions before he was arrested was a rally and ritual held in Chita in July 2019, with a microphone-equipped stage under the banner "Return the Town and Country to the People". After watching the modest and articulate Alexander on the internet for months, I was amazed to see him adopt a more crowd-rousing style, asking hundreds of eclectic multiethnic demonstrators to chant, "That is the law" (*Eto zakon!*) even before he told them what they would be answering in a "call and response" exchange. He bellowed, "give us self-determination," and the crowd answered, "That is the law." He cried, "give us freedom to choose our local administrations," and the crowd answered, "That is the law." His finale included "Putin has no control over you! Live free!"[42] Only after this rally did I begin to wonder who, if anyone, was coaching him and why. Had he changed in the process of walking, gaining loyal followers, and talking to myriad media? The rally, with crowd estimates from seven hundred to one thousand, had been organized by the local Communist Party opposition. Local Russian Orthodox authorities denounced it and suggested that Alexander was psychologically unwell. Alexander himself simply said, after his arrest, "It is impossible to sit home when a demon is in the Kremlin."

How and why is Alexander using discourses of demonology? He seems to be articulating Russian and Sakha beliefs in a society that can be undermined by evil out of control. When he first emerged from the forest, he built a small chapel-memorial in honor of his beloved wife and talked in rhetoric that made connections as much to Russian Orthodoxy as to shamanic tradition. He wears eclectic t-shirts that reference Cuba and the petroglyph horse-and-rider seal of the Sakha Republic, plus one made for him called "Arrive and Exorcise" by the Novosibirsk artist Konstantin Eremenko that renders his face onto an icon-like halo (Figure 20).

Another image depicts him as an angel with wings. He has called himself a "Holy Fool," correlating his brazen actions and protest ideology directly to a Russian *iurodivy* tradition that enabled poor, dirty, beggar-like tricksters to speak disrespectful truths to tsars, including Ivan the Terrible. His appeals to God are ambiguous—purposely referencing the God of Orthodoxy and the Sky Gods of the Turkic Heavens (Tengri) in his speeches. Some of his interviews have been with paint on his face, a thunderbolt zigzag under his eyes that he calls a "sign of lightning" derived from his spiritual awakening after meditation in the forest. He claims, as a "warrior shaman," that he is fated to harness spirit power to heal social ills in a way that even great warrior-khans of the past like Chingis Khan could not do. While his emphasis has been on social ills that begin with the top leadership, he also has been willing to pray and place healing hands on

FIGURE 20.   Shaman Alexander in t-shirt by K. Eremenko, December 16, 2019. Used with permission by Konstantin Eremenko.

the head of a Buryat woman complaining of chronic headaches, who afterwards joyously pronounced herself cured.

During his trek, on camera and off at evening campsites, Alexander fed the fire spirit pure white milk products, especially *kumys* (fermented mare's milk), while offering prayers in the Sakha "white shaman" tradition that he hoped to bring to Red Square for a benevolent ritual not only of exorcism but of forgiveness and blessing. He chanted: "Go, Go, Vladimir Vladimirovich [Putin]. Go of your own free will . . . Only God can judge you. Urui Aikhal!" He expressed pride that some of the Sakha female shamans and elders have blessed his endeavor.

A more critical delegation of Buryat shamans accosted him and his followers on their way to Ulan-Ude. The Buryats represented the Tengeri Society, the group that hosted me in 2010. They warned that they were worried Alexander's politicized claims about banishing Putin could redound against the entire shamanic revitalization movement, as well as the ancient world view of Tengrianstvo that they were trying to recover. They feared that their group and others could be labeled an extremist cult, especially since Alexander (or a youth in his entourage with the pseudonym Raven) reputedly had cursed the children of a police officer when the policeman expropriated a donated car from Alexander's followers. The delegation accused Alexander of "violating the canons of harmonious, light-giving shamanism" by possibly provoking civil disharmony, courting a violent outcome by advocating the demise of President Putin. They doubted that Putin would leave office peacefully of his own accord and were concerned about Alexander's vague references to a mass civil disobedience action if he did not. The groups parted uneasily, with the Tengeri Society shamans emphasizing they had conducted a sensational camel sacrifice to "reinforce the authority of Russia." This too became a viral and controversial internet video, enhancing rather than mitigating some Russians' perceptions that shamans of the Far East were resurrecting a dangerously "primitive" pagan past. By March 2020, Tengeri had also led a shamanic ritual to dispel the coronavirus from Russia and predicted its dissipation.[43]

Russian observers, including well-known politicians and eclectic citizens commenting online or on camera, have had wildly divergent reactions to Alexander, sometimes laughing and mocking his naïve, provincial, or perceived weirdo (*chudak*) persona. But some take him seriously, including the opposition politician Leonid Gozman, President of the All-Russia movement Union of Right Forces. Leonid, admiring Alexander's bravery, sees significance in how many supporters fed and sheltered him along his nearly two thousand kilometer trek before he was arrested. Rather than resenting him for insulting Russia's wealthy and powerful president, whose survey ratings have plummeted, Alexander's followers rallied and protected him with a base broader than many opposition politicians have been able to pull together.[44]

Anticorruption hero Alexei Naval'ny featured Alexander on one of his online 2019 TV programs, giving him a platform and some backhanded compliments by correlating Alexander, [President] Putin, and [Defense Minister] Shoigu all as "terrible Satanists." Naval'ny, dripping sarcasm, suggested the possibility that Putin and Shoigu might themselves engage in a ritual by "smearing themselves with blood of some deer," and "dancing around a fire" to rid themselves of the "Yakut warrior-shaman," since "Russian authorities are themselves a community of insane people who are crazy about esoterica: red threads, astrologists and more." Naval'ny's summary implied "we have come to this" while attempting to rid ourselves of "Putin's tyranny."[45]

Some relatively independent Russian pundits have praised Alexander as Russia's plain-speaking "Forest Gump," while more official Russian political analysts have used Alexander's opposition to inaccurately discredit and ethnicize his movement. For example, using the Russian term for the Sakha, one warned,

"Yakuts seem to have set off a slow bomb." In contrast, some Russian Siberians such as Yaroslav Zolatarev applauded Alexander as the potential leader of a new version of Siberian regionalism.[46]

Back in his homeland, on Sakha TV President Aisen Nikolaev commented with sympathy on the stress and pressure that "resident of Yakutia" Alexander had been under. Nikolaev regretted the way people like Alexei Naval'ny and Mikhail Khodorkovsky (?) had "used" Alexander to "destabilize the country for nefarious reasons," becoming the excuse for "people landing in jail defending him." In a measured tone with ominous implications, he added that he hoped Alexander would have "no further health concerns," and that it was "good that he has returned home" since his arrests.[47]

Nikolaev's references to Alexander's possible illness under stress point anyone knowledgeable about Russian history to the sad legacy of political abuse of psychiatric diagnoses, used against dissidents, including shamans, in the Soviet period and earlier (compare Balzer 2012, 51, 108; Bloch and Reddaway 1984; Reddaway 2020). Indeed, after Alexander's arrest in Buryatia, psychiatric "experts" brought from Moscow examined Alexander in Yakutsk, and his many well-wishers feared he would land in a clinic for a legally indefinite sentence. But competent lawyers were found, and a second round of expert psychiatric diagnosis vindicated him and spared him until 2021 from unwanted drugs.

During a period of closely monitored liberty in 2020, Alexander was able to reconnect with his Sakha and Eurasian roots in a small community ceremony. He participated in the placement at an extended family compound outside Yakutsk of a memorial post (sérgé) rimmed at the top with rune-like Turkic symbols representing the spiritual power of Sky Dieties. One friend commented that it was an important healing for him to commune with his ancestors through prayer-blessings (algys) and offerings of kumys. I observed in this partially filmed private ritual that he donned a traditional Sakha man's waistcoat adorned with silver for the occasion and was supported by members of the republic's Tengri Society.

Alexander went from house arrest to further arrest and incarceration in a mental health clinic in 2020. He appealed his December 2019 arrest and 2020 incarceration to the European Court of Human Rights, and his case was accepted. In 2021, his additional forcible detention under murky circumstances involved at least fifty policemen, after he had announced his renewed campaign, violating release terms. While some whisper that they fear for his life, others hope he escapes with fines and the ability to continue his marathon movement unmolested.

Alexander's valiant, charismatic effort has been halted, and we have enough temporal distance to preliminarily assess its meaning as a plateaued spiritual revitalization movement with political significance. Sakha shamanic concepts include the compelling idea that especially after age forty, after several bouts of spiritual testing (*étéénei*) requisite for being "chosen by the spirits," a true shaman can become a powerful healer and wise elder-leader (Chirkova 2002; Basilov 1997). Alexander has described enduring spiritual testing in the forest through deep grief, humble prayer, and heart-soul-mind-body (*kut-siur*) suffering after he turned forty. I suspect he intended his "long walk" and his self-awareness as a shamanic holy fool to stimulate a social mobilization process exposing opposition to President Putin. I wonder if Alexander really expected to fulfill his dream of entering Moscow with a peaceful parade of followers ready to witness his lighting a purification fire in Red Square. His value thus far has been his ability to raise consciousness and stimulate open debate about the precarious condition of Russia's society and leadership. He has tapped into amorphous simmering resentments and gelled them into simply expressed coherence. His walk inspired followers using Russian and Sakha cultural symbols, concepts, and legacies, conjured by his agile mind that could highlight the original meaning of the old Russian term *khodiataistvo*, literally a petition or appeal brought on foot to a leader in Muscovy. Initially I correlated his uncanny confidence with the Russian "holy fool" and "carnival" traditions before learning that he had done so himself in interviews that simultaneously captured people's fancy and entertained.

Why should we be surprised that a Siberian postmodern internet-viral shaman could use multiethnic social codes so resourcefully? As with most religious revitalization movements in times of trouble, interactive political ramifications are exacerbated when perceived by authorities to be destabilizing. The degree to which shaman Alexander's movement will have success or authenticity will depend on whether his voice is suppressed long enough for people to forget his words, whether he is made a martyr, and whether he takes his social and political critiques to a new level of programmatic ethical principles and practice (ritual), as have many new religious movement leaders before him.

Other colorful shamanic leaders have been based in Siberia. In the late 1990s, I followed and participated in the syncretic spiritual revitalization movement of Anatoly Yurevich Mikhailov, a tall young Sakha-Russian charismatic high-school dropout who called himself Kyta Baaly (Place of Plenty). Beginning in his homeland, the Megino-Kangalas *ulus*, his popularity spread to the capital, Yakutsk, but fizzled when his ambitions caused him to proclaim himself the son of the highest Sakha Sky God, as well as Jesus Christ, on Sakha TV (Balzer 2012, 185–90). His platform was nationalistic although nonchauvinist, calling for return to "pure Sakha values," including polygamy to increase the Sakha population and alcohol abstinence to encourage Sakha fitness. His movement never reached the organizational or sustainable level of the dream-inspired Altai Mountains leader Chot Chelpan(ov), who with his daughter in the early twentieth century founded an anticolonial religion called Burkhanism (or Ak Jang, the White Faith) that integrated aspects of Buddhism, Russian Ortho-doxy, and shamanic faith (compare Sherstova 2010; Vinogradov 2010, 245–57). Another less well-known yet fascinating spiritual-political resistance move-ment came out of nineteenth-century Western Siberia with the mobilization of a Khanty-Nenets shaman-warrior called Vavlyo Neniang (Vauli Piettomin), who stole from the rich to sustain poor reindeer breeders. He was one of sev-eral Siberian Robin Hoods (Balzer 1999, 75–98). Today's Nenets hero-activist is Eiko Serotéto, a young and dynamic reindeer breeder and leader who has emerged with a movement "in the name of Nature" called Voice of the Tundra (Magomedov 2020).

Allowing for a broad range of definitions of religion and spirituality, each of these cases deserves to be added to the burgeoning anthropological and religious studies literature on "new religious movements," growing so rapidly that some Japanese scholars created the acronym NNRM—new new religious movements—to refer to second-generation phenomena and serial "cargo cults" (Daschke and Ashcraft 2017). I find that the famed anticolonial, antimissionizing Indigenous religions of Native North America are the most appropriate for comparisons to the Siberian cases, perhaps because these are the movements I know best. These include the Seneca's (Haudenosaunee) Code of Handsome Lake, as analyzed by Anthony F. C. Wallace (1956, 1969), and the multi-Indigenous Plains Indians Ghost Dance, more appropriately termed Nanissáanah, sparked by the Paiute leader Wovoka (Jack Wilson) in 1890, recorded and analyzed by James Mooney ([1896] 1965) and many others (e.g., Treuer 2019).

The Seneca's struggles turned into a movement that restructured individual and community consciousness and behavior to shape cultural change, while the Nanissáanah in its Lakota version was repressed so forcefully at Wounded Knee that it lives on as an inspiring legend rather than a new religion. They are authentic in their own ways, although perhaps in retrospect Handsome Lake's messages may be considered more socially enduring than Wovoka's. Alexander is less revolutionary than either Handsome Lake or Wovoka, and more mod-est in his aspirations as a leader of consciously constructed sustainable cultural change. Outsider anthropologists need not rush to make deity-like judgments about which spiritual epiphany mixed with political and economic strategies is a suspiciously manipulative "invention of tradition" and which cultural change program eventually deserves to be recognized as a revolutionary "new religion." Although they may topple specific leaders and elites, even violent revolutions are rarely as culturally cleansing as their leaders claim, and traditions are generally made more authentic when critiqued, reconsidered, and adapted in each generation. These are contextual "matters of degree" we will return to in the book's conclusions.

Steps and Missteps on Uneven Terrains

Shaman Alexander's populist appeal for commonsense leadership, as well as the Tengeri-based sincerity of other religious leaders, is geared toward encouraging new lifeways within Russia without advocating separatism from it. These fledgling, galvanizing movements may stimulate shamanic, pan-Turkic, or Turkic-Mongolic identities. They are mostly oriented toward sharing variously defined cultural rather than political solidarities. Many spiritual leaders using eclectic references are neither propagating nor dreaming of political power for themselves, although actions like Alexander's have political resonance. Some in the Tengeri, epic revival, art, and Eurasianist movements seem to be looking for creative outlets for their frustrations that in Russia today little can be accomplished through political impetus from below. As we have seen, Eurasianism among some non-Russians may become a form of regime support, far from oppositional. In another trend, some thwarted politicians are advocating a new ideology for business and cultural ties that they are terming "Turkish Spring."[48]

In the past decade, cross-republic connections from below have been built on personal ties, created in part through professional contacts and tourism that is frequently pilgrimage-oriented. A Sakha friend commented somewhat sadly that "the process is going on only on the level of personal and professional communication [rarely official] . . . although it might be possible to write a whole article on this using views from inside the process."[49] Many long for more contacts, but finances to support them are shrinking, as are discretionary funds for personal travel, sports, festivals, exhibits, and film projects.

To prevent further political radicalization and polarization, productive cross-republic trends described here, as well as the broader civilizational identities they represent, should be encouraged rather than nipped in the bud. Yet the opposite has occurred. Transportation has become prohibitively expensive throughout the entire Far East, and indeed all of Russia. Shockingly, small claims business lawyers in Yakutsk who need to present materials to courts of appeal in Khabarovsk or Vladivostok are complaining that travel expenses render building effective cases increasingly challenging. Their enthusiasm for pursuing risky appeals that expose government officials or uneven tax policy is shriveling. Difficulties are exacerbated when travel is beyond one's republic or administrative region. For example, administrative-structural differences between "Siberia" and the "Far

East" make it harder to connect on special academic, ecological, art, and professional projects. In one example, editors organizing a book project on "ethnocultural processes in the Far East" needed to leave out Buryats and Tyvans because they were not technically part of the Far East, despite important socioeconomic linkages, historical legacies, and desire to collaborate.

What do artificially imposed structural-administrative divisions, meant to orient everyone to Moscow in a "power vertical," mean for the ways that local Russians (sometimes calling themselves Siberiaki), Sakha, Buryats, and Tyvans relate to Moscow officials, and to each other? While contextual variation makes broad generalization risky, some patterns can be discerned. Historically, the vast distances between Siberia/Far East and the rest of Russia have led to interesting semantic-psychological formulations, such as Siberians calling the Moscow-oriented territory of Russia west of the Urals "the mainland." Cultural distancing historically provoked clichés about the "freedom-loving wild East" of Russia, and contemporary conditions enable pride in a combined Siberian/Far Eastern identity to be correlated with relative degrees of personal freedom. Yet crippling and humbling economic dependencies on federal "unitary" governance (read subsidies) are built into the system. The system is functioning poorly, creating cynicism, unemployment, distrust of legal protection, and just-under-the surface social unrest that sometimes breaks out in unexpected ways (compare Saxer and Andersson 2019).

Infrastructure project support from Moscow is repeatedly delayed. Roads and rail lines are advertised as built but take years to be completed. A rail bridge over the Lena River was discussed when I first did fieldwork in Yakutsk in 1986 but still has not been built, even though parts of the town were demolished to make way for it. How can local residents not see this, whether or not their official TV stations cover such blatant failures? A survival skill for country-wide TV journalists is when in doubt cover-up, don't cover. Occasionally the problem is simple ignorance—a TV-24 program in 2017 identified the Sakha Republic as part of Japan. A bridge co-funded with Chinese money on the Chinese-Russian border was literally hanging in the air near Khabarovsk in 2016–2017 because Russians had not come through with funds for their (10 percent) side of the project. The whole corrupt affair became the butt of region-wide joking that used the failure as symbolic of Moscow officials' incompetence.[50]

The beauty of clear streams dancing down majestic mountains is appreciated by residents and visitors of all three republics featured here, regardless of ethnic backgrounds. While not completely pristine, these territories include some of the most extensive underdeveloped and hard-to-access natural wonders on the planet. A Sakha shaman-healer once half-seriously told me that he is grateful to mosquitoes because they keep developers away. But more seriously, local people differ on the pace, amounts, and strategies for how rivers, mines, and other resources should be harnessed—and how much development is right for the country. These debates have been prominent in local election campaigns. Opinions rarely conform to a simple equation: Native = Leave Nature Alone; Russian = Develop as Fast as Possible. A preponderance of local Indigenous people favor cautious, sustainable, and consensual development. They wish for more genuine, not pro forma, consultations with Moscow officials and within their own larger regions, for better long-term planning in their perceived-as-fragile homelands.

Siberia was first called "a country in reserve" in the Soviet period by a worried biologist-turned-activist named Zev Wolfson (1980, 1992), who used the pseudonym Boris Komarov (Boris the Mosquito). He decried the roughshod Soviet Progress mentality that placed "Man above Nature," but eventually gave up and moved to Israel. Instead of mass cross-fertilization and valorization of his ideas, his heroism was lost in daily life struggles as the Soviet Union broke up. People in Siberia since then have been waging more isolated battles, as the introduction to this chapter quoting opposition politician Ilya Yashin mentions. In 2016, representatives of Russia's Green Party (affiliated with Greenpeace Russia) were arrested for trying to mobilize their own fire brigades to fight out-of-control forest fires in Western Siberia. Their crime? Organizing without authorization and accepting money from foreign sources. Meanwhile, Russia's 2017 budget included a 10 percent cut for the Ministry of Emergency Response (which handles forest fires), the very ministry that popular Tyvan native son Sergei Shoigu headed before he became minister of defense. By 2019–2021, as discussed, forest fires had devastated much of Siberia in swaths comparable to the more highly publicized Australia and Amazon disasters. Some say Russia's dire cutbacks for fire protection can be correlated to Western sanctions over Russia's aggression in Crimea. Something that is harming local people is being used as propaganda to place blame not on Russian officials and Russia's policies but on a generalized enemy termed "The West."[51]

Returning to an issue raised in the introduction to this chapter—can any of the republics or trends within them be considered as models for the development of horizontal and negotiated federal ties? The pressures of vertical power are too great for any one republic to buck central authority blatantly, despite frequent accusations by Moscow elites that the heads of the republics are corrupt ethnocrats with their privatized "ethnocracies." Rather, leaders have developed strategies of lobbying the federal center for pet projects, sometimes with cross-republic or international ramifications. These include funding for energy, road, mining, and pipeline projects. Crucially, they encompass expensive cultural programs such as sports and youth festivals. Out of the republics featured here, probably rich and pivotal Sakha Republic has had the best leverage for its cultural projects,

Northern subsidies, and development plans. But its elites worry that their ability to determine their own agendas has been slipping.

Some republic leaders have been more effective than others in linking their priorities to lobbying efforts in Moscow. In turn, Russian authorities often impose conditions, many of which are nontransparent. A steady stream of officials from various republics have visited Tatarstan because Tatar leaders are perceived to have "gotten the most" out of Moscow officials.[52] This is due less to Turkic solidarity than to practical ramifications: some Moscow officials themselves are part of the large Tatar diaspora in Moscow. However, perception of Tatarstan's success has declined significantly since its failure to renew its "bilateral treaty" with Moscow in 2017. This has created ripple effects of fear in the republics, a topic developed further in my conclusions.

As in the 1990s, interactive politics involves playing the "ethnic card" when possible—but Tyvans, Sakha, and Buryats are increasingly in less strong positions, despite the fame of Sergei Shoigu. "We need more officials in Moscow," a Sakha friend once confided. But fewer, rather than more, non-Russian officials have served in Moscow in the past decade. And the privileging of "titular ethnic republics" over Russian regions was never as effective or enshrined in law as Russian nationalists alleged and mythologized (compare Osipov 2015).

Many talented non-Russians, feeling isolated and not well enough empowered by central state authorities, are turning their attention to their own homelands, in a dynamic that may spell fewer cross-republic, transnational ties, at least in the short-term. The coronavirus has exacerbated this inward turn yet also made people aware of the potential for creative online networking. Eventually, as presidents of the republics of Tatarstan, Bashkortostan, and Sakha warned back in 1995, untended smoldering fires, while not as dangerous as those out of control, could reignite with potentially devastating consequences. Crackdowns on admired local leaders could backfire. Conclusions further the argument that authorities would do well to embrace rather than discourage transnationalism and cross-fertilizing cooperation based on civilizational commonalities, since these can transcend a backward-looking nostalgia that focuses on victimization, bitterness, and reaction.

FEDERALISM, CULTURAL DIGNITY, AND NOSTALGIA

People in Russia would revolt if they were not allowed to use the internet and WhatsApp freely.

—Indigenous friend, half humorously, May 30, 2020

I truly fear the abolishment of our republic. This has been threatened before, but the campaign to turn it into the Baikal Republic is now being led by Buryats and Russians who may not understand the full implications of what they are doing.

—Buryat colleague, September 18, 2016

Free land giveaways will lead to ecological disaster!

—Placards in Sakha and Russian carried by demonstrators in Yakutsk representing the group *Sir* (Land), June 8, 2016

The whole world has been straining for ties with Nature after losing them. Tengrianstvo revival does this for people—it is needed as never before. It's not about politics and power but priorities.

—Andrei Savich Borisov, former minister of culture, Sakha Republic, June 27, 2020

Predictions of doom are not far from the lips of many in private conversations in contemporary Russia, although before the coronavirus pandemic one would not know this from watching neo-Soviet propagandistic TV or reading rigged opinion polls. The virus broke any illusions that all was well, while the country's leadership failed to offer sustainable ways for Russia to escape the liminal period citizens all over the world were experiencing. Just prior to the pandemic an increasingly authoritarian President Putin sought to adapt Russia's Constitution to allow him additional presidential terms beyond 2024 and to consolidate recentralization. If he could use approved constitutional amendments as a referendum on his rule, he could stave off revolt by citizens increasingly discontented with lost social safety nets. Even before the virus struck, the amendments package included crucial sweeteners promising better health care and ecological oversight in the regions of Russia.

Against the advice of some preeminent Russian social scientists, a formula privileging the Russian people and culture was slipped into the amendments. Particularly offensive to non-Russians is article 68: "The state language of the Federation of Rossiia on all its territory is the Russian language, as the language of the state-forming people, entering into a multinationality union of equal-rights peoples of the Federation of Rossiia." The concept that the Russians were the only "state-forming" people was among the reasons for protests and resignations of various deputies in several republics, including Sulustaana Myran (For A Just Russia party) from Sakha's Il Tumen parliament.[1]

Russia's current regime has offered a familiar tradeoff, promising social protection in return for decreased political rights. In the context of the pandemic and the ploy to extend presidential rule, the regime sought to enhance Vladimir Putin's fading Good Tsar image by proposing vastly increased funding for social and health services. As of 2021, promises have not been fulfilled, Putin's image as a strong take-control savior has been damaged, and local politicians, including heads of republics, have stepped into the breach with uneven results.

Encroachment on political, cultural, and human rights has accompanied erosion of territorial guarantees, particularly in the frontier zones of the Arctic and Far East. In 2016, President Putin's administration announced that it was ready to give away small plots of land (a hectare) in the Far East to those Russian citizens who would work the land or use it to improve the tourism industry. Its widely touted intent was to populate a perceived underpopulated area with Russian citizens, countering feared Chinese migration. This is why the Cossack Yuri A. Bugaev, on a Far East land claim trip, bragged to the journalist Andrew Higgins: "This is not just for adventure but to save Russia."[2] While the controversial Duma law that set land reform in motion included provisions for privileging locals before Russian "mainlanders," the legislation nonetheless stimulated a firestorm of protest among residents of the vast Far East, especially Indigenous families in the Sakha Republic.

Many in the republic were appalled that they would yet again lose control over their territory in unpredictable ways emanating from Moscow. Some Sakha Il Tumen deputies traveled to Moscow to talk with Duma members, hoping to return triumphantly to their republic with an exemption. Rumors flew that Egor Borisov, then head of the Sakha Republic and a loyal member of Putin's United Russia party, opposed the law. However once the law was in place, Borisov quelled opposition by proclaiming that Sakha citizens would be given first chances at the land, and that the law would not threaten existing farms or stimulate industrial farming projects because the individual plots being given away were too small. Protesters filling a main square of the capital, Yakutsk, in March 2016, when the weather was far too frosty for normal street demonstrations, showed how angry the Sakha activists had become.

Similar complaints against land redistribution continue to be voiced through-out the Far East, especially by Indigenous groups that see themselves as repeat-edly exploited, rapidly losing territory and rights. A crucial technicality—that Buryatia and Tyva are not officially in the Far East but in the Siberian Fed-eral Region—has exempted these regions. The ability of the Russian Federa-tion Duma to make laws that infringe on regional jurisdictions is nonetheless decried by activists and in corridors of local authority. Since the coronavirus has frozen massive resettlement, including by Chinese workers, some Indigenous citizens hope they have a reprieve on accelerated development projects they do not explicitly approve. Fear of uncertainty amplifies the sting of lost representa-tive governance.

People in the republics who resist voting in elections or referendums are well aware that their republic leadership is tied to Moscow's purse strings, and that many "strings attached" have become frayed. Residents may worry about different issues or feel the resonance of certain issues variously. In resource-poor Tyva, people remain especially dependent on Moscow subsidies. In Bury-atia, people debate whether their republic is in danger of being abolished, how much pollution Lake Baikal can withstand, and whether monocompany towns can survive. In Sakha, many complain they are on the brink of unprecedented industrialization without adequate ecological oversight. Nearly all spurn new migrants, whether temporary workers, Chinese businessmen, Russian devel-opers, Cossacks seeking land, or Russian-Ukrainians fleeing war in Eastern Ukraine.

Despite the bravado of official propaganda touting President Putin's approval ratings, citizens of Russia live in an unstable society where mass protests against election fraud at the level of 2011–2012 numbers are no longer possible, where republic puppet leaders are called heads of administration rather than presi-dents, and where administrative-structural constraints mean that people seek to hold on to cultural rather than political sovereignty. The Republic of Tatarstan's inability to renew its bilateral treaty with Moscow in 2017 sent chills down the spines of many citizens of the "non-Russian republics," as indeed it was meant to do. The pathos of recent times is that no one seems to know exactly to what to realistically aspire—dreams are disparate and sometimes destroyed for peo-ple who tasted a degree of political and economic sovereignty and then saw it yanked away from them.

Indigeneity and sovereignty are contextual and contingent. Therefore, lessons of this book are multifold. Key interrelated themes include:

(1) When self-worth stems from broad civilizational identities, it tends to mitigate more strident and chauvinist senses of nationalism.

Eurasianism, Turkic and Mongolic cultural pride, and Arctic solidarities are forming in relation to each other, diverse nationalisms, and Indigenous loyalties. Flexible situational identities are normal for citizens of Russia, as elsewhere.

(2) Identity can be crystallized through shattering events that force people to realign and rethink their loyalties. While this may eventually be productive, it can be painful, as when bilateral treaties are revoked, language laws privileging one people over another are instituted, nonviolent activists are jailed or detained in psychiatric clinics, and/or a quasi-federation (like the former Soviet Union) falls apart.

(3) Genuine, negotiated federalism, rather than formal or fake federalism, can be a major driver mitigating interethnic tensions and non-Russians' fears of Russification. Ongoing federal processes can result in viable nested sovereignties, or degrees of sovereignty, concerning land and intertwined economic and political rights.

(4) Republic structures and support help to consolidate the human rights of Indigenous ethnonational groups through hard-won named territories. They may not be equal in their resources or subsidies, resulting in asymmetry, but they are integral to Russia's historical legacy. Unilateral abrogation of republic-based rights or reallocation of their lands constitutes a serious breach of trust.

(5) Authoritarianism may be tempting, as indicated by those who regularly express dreams of a "Good Tsar Savior" in opinion polls that often omit the republics of the Federation of Rossiia. However, authoritarianism can backfire when a regime does not deliver on promises, and paternalistic programs and patronage fall through. While non-Russians tend to feel this failure sooner and more intensely than others in Russia, it is an endemic and growing problem for all *rossiiane* (citizens of Russia).

(6) Ecology movements in Russia have the potential to address crucial local concerns, as well as to become a networking basis for interconnections that unite a broad base of activists hoping to represent and widen civil society. This is a locus of civic activism that at its best encompasses Russians and non-Russians cooperating with each other and with the state. Those ecology activists who see problems as systemic are more likely to work together on crossover issues that transcend local protests.

(7) Movements for social and political change, especially among Indigenous communities, have become more egalitarian and creative in how they generate and valorize leaders. Leaders in turn can be galvanized by this process. Leadership means interaction with society at many levels.

Efforts to foster a broader base, beyond a small influential intelligentsia, are evident in accelerated use of the internet, youth empowerment, and the ways more women have become active in Indigenous movements not only in Russia but around the world. Reactive, ethnically exclusive men's groups have also emerged.

(8) Reminiscing and reflecting on better times can be one of many paths toward survival for Indigenous communities. Prospective nostalgia can be pragmatic without chauvinism or revenge seeking. It often involves a process generating serious societal debates about selected usable pasts, especially given generational change. Recovered or reconstructed pasts, also called traditions, may or may not incorporate various kinds of inspiring spirituality, intensified ritual, and creative symbolism.

To further unpack these themes, particularly the last one, a visible place for analysts to start is understanding some of the debates surrounding historical monuments. This should not surprise. We know from US experience how Civil War memorials and Christopher Columbus have become "iconoclash" (Latour 2002) magnets in American society.

Moving Targets of Study, Creating and Moving Monuments

The length of my field time in Siberia, which I have visited periodically since 1975–1976 if I count my Western Siberia studies with the Ob-Ugrian Khanty (Balzer 1999), has made me aware of shifting trends in which heroes and key historical moments are valorized, as well as my reactions to these shifts. Debates surrounding the symbolism and mythmaking of monuments constitute an important lens magnifying social change.[3] The very word *pamiatnik* (memorial monument) in Russian is intriguing because it incorporates the material, often huge sculptures, as well as nonmaterial sites of spiritual and memorial meaning. Here I feature changing approaches to physical sculptures residing in prominent public contested spaces. Public monuments and their symbolism have appeared almost as punctuation marks in this text to make a point and move on. It is worth reviewing their galvanizing potential and emotional loads, beyond their artistic merit.

For May Day in 1986, I was firmly requested to show up on the formal viewing stand under the statue of Lenin in Lenin Square, Yakutsk, to see the parade celebrating the working class along with the far-from-working-class Communist Party elite of Yakutia (Figure 21). My "scientific advisor" Anatoly Gogolev, who also had little choice in the matter, was to accompany me.

FIGURE 21. Yakutsk State University parading at May Day in Lenin Square, Yakutsk, 1986. Banner proclaims, "Greetings to the Brotherly Peoples of the USSR!" By author.

It never dawned on us that within a decade that square and a larger one nearby would be the scene of very different kinds of demonstrations, although some of those marching under the university's banner in 1986 had just been involved in a student protest over an interethnic brawl that had ended with police repression of the students. The larger-than-life-sized Lenin statue, with right arm raised to the sky, looking like those everywhere in capitals of the Soviet Union, had an aura of permanence and confidence that made it inconceivable that its very existence could be questioned.

In 1992, a "frenemy" (not all my Sakha interlocutors are friends) visited me in Cabin John and played a dirty mind game. He declared with a sly grin that after the collapse of the Soviet Union, the statue of Lenin in Yakutsk had been removed, and wondered what I thought. While I believed him, my intuition told me to be cautious, and so I said something like "it is up to the people themselves to decide such things," although I probably looked pleased. It took until the following summer to discover that he had been pulling my leg. The statue was still in the square, and a typical response from those whom I asked about it was: "Why should we hide our Soviet past? It is clear that Lenin is part of our history and we cannot erase him. We just need to know more about the past." These were the days when everyone was talking about "filling in the white spots [blank spaces] of history" and getting beyond the ubiquitous Soviet propaganda they had grown up with and mostly accepted.

My friends were more interested in another dramatic, potentially cathartic switch in the urban landscape: removing a bust of Russia's first secret police chief Felix Dzerzhinsky and changing the name of the main street that bore his name to that of the Sakha intellectual and early ethnographer A. E. Kulakovskii. They lost the name change battle, and Dzerzhinsky remains on his pedestal, but they gained a new statue of Kulakovskii and a smaller street near the university was named for him. Subsequently, a new, more alarming trend developed: the appearance of five Stalin statues in the republic in the past decade, including one small but resonating bust currently in front of a private bank in Yakutsk that the mayor narrowly averted from placement in Lenin Square.[4]

In the decade between 1986 and 1996, I systematically interviewed everyone I could about a Great Fatherland War victory memorial near the Lena River embankment that includes a giant column with a warrior-horseman flying off its side (Figure 22). Opinions were evenly divided over whether the huge dramatic multivocal figure was Manchari, a Robin-Hood-like nineteenth-century folk hero (Communist-approved) or a more distant Sakha ancestor Niurgun Bootur, from the *olonkho* epic of the same name. Each interpretation valorized a Sakha leader, and the statue remains beloved by local Sakha and Russians, although some resent that it was not created by a Sakha artist.

In subsequent years, when I remember to ask, I have found that perceptions remain split about the winged horseman's identity, but that more people say he is the epic hero Niurgun than the forest brigand Manchari, who stole from the rich to give to the poor. Manchari's reputation has become slightly tarnished, although a 2017 sports competition in the Upper Viliuisk region was named for him.

As mentioned in chapter 1, controversial Cossack sculptures have appeared in the post-Soviet period in the Sakha Republic, the first valorizing the purported founder of Yakutsk, the Cossack Petr Beketov, without acknowledging that a trading center and settlement of Sakha people was already on the site of Yakutsk in 1632. The bearded Beketov, leaning on an ax and seated on logs, is

FIGURE 22.   Niurgun Bootur/Manchari monument. Great Fatherland War Victory Square, Yakutsk. By Maria Koryakina June 2020 for author.

meant to portray a farsighted builder. Nearby is an ornate new Russian Ortho-dox mini-chapel, and down the street near the Lena River embankment is a renovated Russian Orthodox church and seminary complex. While Beketov is offensive to many Sakha because of his violent and wily conquering of Yakut princes, a more insidious recent statue depicts the Cossack Simeon Dezhnev with his Sakha mistress/wife Abakaiade, looking like a stereotyped Pocahontas in a braid, with their child. (Dezhnev, married to someone else, famously left her for territories farther east.) In the late 1990s, a Sakha friend took me to see these statues and to commiserate that city planners had not held more hearings about them. In travel brochures, the Dezhnev-Abakaiade monument is billed as representing "the first interethnic marriage between a Russian settler and his Yakut wife, and also their child—the symbol of the coming together of the two peoples."[5] It appears that well-meaning planners, worried about the demise of

Soviet propaganda concerning the "brotherhood of the peoples" and aware of the decline of interethnic marriages in the post-Soviet period, sought to create a monument to assimilation.

In the Buryat Republic, sculptures have been equally controversial and represent a range of cultural-political constituencies. In addition to Lenin, monuments include the bronze eagle placed overlooking Lake Baikal during the 2013 Ërdyn Games, pleasing most Buryats. *Keeper of Baikal*, the towering bronze tree sculpture on the sacred island of Olkhon by native son Dashi Namdakov, is for some Buryat critics less a spiritual symbol than a tourist attraction. Ecology activists and shamanists fear it violates the delicate balance between ecological awareness and commercial exploitation inherent in recent intensification of ecotourism and branding on Olkhon Island and in Buryatia in general (compare Comaroff and Comaroff 2009).

A political decision in 2015 by then head of republic Viacheslav Nagovitsyn narrowly averted a scandal when he cancelled yet another Cossack monument, meant to portray Cossacks as the founders of the old fort town of Ulan-Ude. That version of history is blatantly inaccurate, given that the town existed well before the Cossacks' arrival. The Russian mayor who had wanted the statue built in turn protested that local Buryat intellectuals were chauvinist in their rejection of his version of history and in their personal attacks on him. Mayoral offices and publicity are often more contested and open than other politics in Russia. In the Sakha case, a popular, tolerant Sakha mayor of Yakutsk was able to block a Stalin bust, while in Buryatia a nonliberal, less popular Russian mayor of Ulan-Ude failed to place a Cossack image in a prominent place, appealing to a different political-demographic constituency. A clever way to monitor interethnic relations in divided Buryatia and elsewhere is to watch the ups and downs of sculptures.

Tyva, with its over-two-thirds majority Tyvan demography, has been spared plots to glorify Cossacks, although they do have an association in the republic. The familiar Lenin in the main square still stands, juxtaposed with a new museum building featuring graceful Asian slanted roofs and Buddhist references. A young Tyvan girl was mocking Lenin's pose when I caught her in a photograph in 2005. New post-Soviet sculptures have appeared in Kyzyl, including the recent popular monument to the elder statesman throat singer Kongor-ool Ondar, famed for his role in the film *Genghis Blues*. More blatantly political is the sculpture in a residential park of a heroic robed male figure with hands down and clenched, called *The Unburied*, honoring "those sacrificed to political repression."[6] An additional emblematic sculpture within Kyzyl's main Yenisei embankment park is called *My Home*, depicting a nomad with his camel and implying that all of Tyva's natural beauty is "homeland."

Debates were stimulated in Kyzyl by the decision to destroy or remove traditional buildings, including a shamanic healing center, to create the spacious park on the Yenisei River embankment commemorating the Center of Asia, Eurasianism, and the hundredth anniversary of the "coming together" of Russia and Tuva. As we have seen, since 2014 its main attraction is *The Royal Hunt*, by the renowned Buryat sculptor Dashi Namdakov. This elaborate sculpture has "put Kyzyl on the map," as Tyvan authorities who commissioned the sculpture had hoped. Tyvans ignore a rival Center of Asia in Yongfeng, China, near Ürümchi, that boasts its own sculpture. They flexibly choose their own interpretations of *The Royal Hunt*, with more seeing it as honoring legendary ancestors rather than political relations with Russia. Nearby, the Soviet socialist-realist brutalist globe with obelisk (1964) that had dominated the waterfront before royalty came back in fashion was replaced by a Center of Asia globe and pyramid, held up by mythical lion-like beasts (chimera) that recall Buddhist iconography. Near Kyzyl, in a sacred grove, is a more natural marker: an enormous heart-shaped rock that has been proclaimed by Ai-churek and her shamanist followers to be the true "heart of Asia."

Towering over Kyzyl's valley, formed by the confluence of the Great Yenisei (Bii Khem) and Little Yenisei (Kaa Khem), on a mountain slope is the Kadarchy Monument, valorizing a vibrant herder with upturned toes on his felt boots and a pole across his shoulders. He is a hovering romantic reminder of the Tyvan nomadic past.

When do public monuments ignored for years become contested or mocked? Perhaps when societal shifts reveal deep rifts in already unstable ground, much like the melting permafrost of climate change that produces sink holes and methane gas. What had been unquestioned fixtures of a background landscape may become potential hot-button symbols surfacing for discussion, if not destruction. Just as salient, we live in an internet age when news of Confederate horsemen removals or Christopher Columbus toppling in multiple cities travels fast, including across oceans to Australia. In 2017, a Sidney statue of Captain James Cook was defaced as protests swelled against his moniker as "discoverer" of Australia. In 2020, the Russian fur merchant Alexander Baranov was voted to be escorted off his Sitka pedestal into an Alaskan museum.

"Contagion effects" can go in multiple directions, enhanced by accumulation of pent-up grievances triggered by local conditions. Such synergistic combinations are accompanied by a growing savvy about what Indigenous movements may accomplish when the world is watching. Glasnost and the collapse of the Soviet Union created openings for debates about Lenin, Felix Dzerzhinsky, Stalin, interethnic relations, Cossack "discoverers" of land long occupied, numerous unsung Indigenous s/heroes, along with subsequent exposure for at least some

Siberians to a whole range of new political and cultural worlds, sparking passion and potential protest. The images and figures that endure are those of leaders honored for defending their people against perceived outsiders, such as the Uriankhai warrior Subedei-Maadyr in Tyva, Gésér in Buryatia, and Niurgun Bootur in the Sakha Republic.

Cultural Dignity: Does Buddhism Make You Stronger?

What galvanizes people in this age of eclectic cultural smorgasbord exposure? Non-Russians of the republics of Sakha, Buryatia, and Tyva sometimes divide their compatriots into those who are forward-facing and pragmatic, as opposed to those who are stuck in preoccupation with the Soviet past. They argue, depending in part on their generation, over whether shreds of Soviet practices and the logics of "collective benefit through personal sacrifice" are worth recovering (compare Oushakine 2009). A counterpoint dynamic involves processing deeper cultural-historical pasts to consolidate transnational solidarities into concepts of current cultural-political identity and broader community building. People are aware that cultural identities have political ramifications. This is why discourses of "Turkic-Mongolic peoples of Eurasia" become a possible means toward restoring broader senses of collective self-worth, as emphasized in the previous chapter. Liberal nationalism that is not premised against others, and transnationalism based on civilizational commonalities, may become means of transcending common local critiques that disparage nostalgia for the past as paralyzing.[7]

For Indigenous individuals and groups, whether in the intelligentsia or not, dwelling on histories of Russian colonialization and Sovietization may produce narratives of debilitating regret. Self-victimization does occur, including justification of Russification and accepting official narratives of Russian cultural superiority. More creative, productive responses are developing, as my republic profiles and some of the crossover trends reveal. This is why I have titled this book "galvanizing nostalgia," to show that alternative critical analyses of history are possible in Russia. Homegrown optimistic, prospective use of nostalgia may stimulate cultural pride at various levels without leading to extremism.

An example of brilliantly using selective history to stimulate cultural pride as well as transnational solidarity between Tyvan and Buryat-Mongolian people entirely avoids focus on Russians, emphasizing a moment in early twentieth-century pre-Soviet history when Tyvan and "Mongolian" warriors successfully attacked the Kobdo Fort (1911–1912), one of the border strongholds of the dwindling Chinese Qing empire. Billed today as a "national liberation movement," this moment of nonpacifist valor by two ostensibly Buddhist peoples was celebrated at a 2017 roundtable in Kyzyl, along with "chasing Chinese traders from Tuva."[8] Potential relevance to current multiethnic relations is clear, although coded at several levels for plausible deniability.

When the Soviet Union collapsed, the influential Harvard historian Edward (Ned) Keenan (1991) provided a powerful metaphor with a compelling theory behind it: that the Soviet period was merely thin and cheap linoleum that with wear eventually exposed higher-quality, longer-lasting floorboards of Russia's multicultural history. Of course, much had changed, and some of what was revealed included periods of ethnic tensions as well as harmony, especially in the border areas the historian Alfred Rieber (2014) calls "shatter zones." A key aspect of Keenan's argument was that post-Soviet non-Russian intelligentsias have a right to process their own histories, in all their beautiful and terrifying complexity.

A similar refrain emphasizing lasting cultural values over many genera-tions has reemerged in Native intelligentsia discussions of social history. Uliana Vinokurova's (2017) comparative article summarizing "values at the beginning of the twenty-first century" suggests that a combination of local and ethnic val-ues remains crucial for the Sakha. Strong customary law guiding interpersonal and territorial relations has encouraged a sense of fairness across generations. Vinokurova claims: "A tendency toward verbal etiquette, agreements based on oral guarantees, a concern for one's moral reputation, a struggle for free access to clan lands, and civic social behavior" have prevailed in Sakha consciousness. She explains that this is why free speech and information as practiced for centuries meant that its violations "coalesced into a sense of being wronged, of injustice, culminating in the violence of the red terror and repression."[9]

"Why were some republic elites more repressed than others?" asked a Sakha friend recently. When I turned the question around, my interlocutor sug-gested that Buryats had been more repressed than Sakha—although both were persecuted—because "Buryatia had a stronger religion [Buddhism] and more ties with kin on the other side of border." Russians, s/he explained, perceived the numerous and "ideologically alien" Buryats as potentially strong and thus Buryats were targeted more, as a greater threat to the Soviet Union. Today, a simi-lar rationale on the part of some local and Moscow officials may be driving the petition to create a Baikal Republic, replacing the Republic of Buryatia, dropping the name of its titular Indigenous people. Current motivations are more nuanced than those in the Stalinist era.

The Buryat man leading the petition to amalgamate Buryatia, Irkutsk oblast, and Zabaikal krai into a single Baikal Republic is Evgeny Buianin, head of the Buryat branch of Russia's Rodina (Homeland) party.[10] For him, positive tradeoffs are involved in this campaign, which may fizzle given that signatures have been slow to accrue and many among the elites of Buryatia oppose consolidation. Buianin's arguments include the promise that Buryatia's rock-bottom economic performance compared to other Russian regions could improve, that Russian and Buryat would both be official languages in the merged megaregion, and that the earlier abolished districts of Ust-Orda and Aga will be part of the territory. For President Putin, such an enlarged territory on Russia's border could be harder to control, although amalgamation of the unwieldy and unequal regions and republics of the Russian Federation periodically has been part of his rhetoric.[11]

Why select Buryatia to help consolidate Russia as a unified, nonfederal state? Native intelligentsia inside and outside Buryatia speculate that Buryats are perceived as particularly feisty, although some Buryats themselves hasten to explain this is not their self-perception (nor mine).[12] Several of my interlocutors discussing this threat affirm that Buddhism may have given Buryats an extra dimension of strength and self-confidence, whereas shamanistic and Russian Orthodox backgrounds left other groups more susceptible to acculturation. In these conversations, Buryats are proclaimed to have maintained greater political dynamism, including at the levels of institute and university politics, than Sakha and Tyvans. Yet many in Buryatia are extraordinarily wary of separatist discourse, of being perceived as disloyal. In Buryatia independent journalists have been beaten, local historians have lost their jobs, and foreign researchers have reported relatively more persecution than in other regions of Russia. Some suggest that this reflects local officials' attempts to prove their loyalty to Moscow.[13]

Buddhism has become a significant transnational, civilizational outlet for increasing numbers of believers in Russia, particularly in the republics of Kalmykia, Buryatia, and Tyva, as well as their surrounding territories. In the past decade, a small Buddhist community has become part of the religious mosaic of the Sakha Republic, not only for the Buryat and Tyvan diaspora living there but also for a few Sakha and Russian converts. One of its leaders is a monk from Buryatia, and others were trained at its famous and thriving Ivolga complex, visited regularly by all post-Soviet leaders of the republic. As we saw in chapter 4, a survey of 709 students in the "Buddhist Russia" republics indicates increasing fascination with Buddhism among young people as a way to express traditional family and moral values while being progressive, "a resource to enable feeling free as individuals in the marketplace of religion" (Badmaev et al. 2020, 35–39).

In Buryatia in 2016, a gorgeous giant thirty-three-meter-high Sakyamuni Buddha image was painted on a cliff near the village of Baian-Gol in the Khori region (Figure 23). "Broadening the sacred geography of Russia," local residents completed it "miraculously fast," according to Aleksandr Lobsan of the local Buddhist *datsan*. Celebrations were led by Lodo Rinpoche, an emigrant from Tibet since 1993, who announced, "the Buddha image has become a symbol of our pure intentions." He emphasized the importance of the Dharma, "brought into being two and a half thousand years ago and still relevant in our world today."[14]

In a reactive counterpoint, persecution of certain Buddhists has intensified at the same time as the previously insular, defensive Buddhist community has been increasing in numbers and activating transnational connections. A sense of oppression has extended beyond complaints that the Dalai Lama has not been allowed to visit Russia since 1993. While new Buddhist temples have been erected or restored in Buryatia and Tyva, new antiterrorist laws (named for Duma Deputy Irina Yarovaia), created to guard against Muslim extremists, have been deployed to keep Buddhist leaders associated with the Dalai Lama out of Russia or to hassle some who have visited. As with Shiwalha Rinpoche in Tyva, attempts were made to expel a prominent and beloved Buddhist monk from Buryatia, a case appealed several times. As the editor of the journal *Buddhizm Rossii* [Buddhism of Russia] Andrei Terent'ev drily commented, "It is a matter of considerable concern that incorrectly formed invitations could be correlated

FIGURE 23.   Sakyamuni Buddha image Khori, Buryatia. http://www.burunen.ru.

with terrorism."[15] Discrimination is particularly painful when Buddhists of Buryat backgrounds from the Dalai Lama's community in Dharamsala wish to visit their ancestral homeland.

Predictably from my fieldwork, less controversy and more official support for the Buddhist community has occurred in demographically Tyvan-dominated Tyva. Culminating the annual Tyvan *nadaam* celebration in 2016 at the village of Chaa-Khol, an exciting temple was opened where the centerpiece image is a restored bas relief Buddha from the thirteenth century, originally set in a niche on a cliff. Local Tyvans reported that the temple was rebuilt in record time (again), due to their "strong desire to have their own *khuré* [temple]." It was rebuilt on the same territory where a temple had been constructed in 1811 and later destroyed during Soviet antireligious campaigns.

In rhetoric emblematic of what I mean by galvanizing nostalgia, the republic head and local believers used the term "reincarnation" to describe the temple's spiritually mandated reconstruction. Sholban Kara-ool exulted: "Our new temple has appeared, placed on the site of our old [destroyed] one at Chaa-Khol after many years. It is possible, as [we] Buddhists say, that this is nothing less than a reincarnation."[16] Despite serious local poverty, volunteer contributions and the republic government spurred construction in less than a year. Hundreds of believers attended the opening ceremonies, featuring ancient Tyvan Buddhist rituals. The celebrated Khambo Lama Lopsan Chamzy was accompanied by an impressive entourage of monks and youthful apprentice monks.

To return to my provocative section title—it may not be Buddhism itself that makes one stronger, despite its perennial messages of inner strength and ancient, pure Dharma paths. Rather, the drive to create community on the basis of spiritual and historical heritages with renewed meaning has become a significant, relatively viable substitute for openly oppositional political activism (compare Guchinova 2021). This is far from the militant Buddhists, exempting themselves from pacifist teachings, who have arisen in Burma (Myanmar), pockets of Tibetan-exile India, or Sri Lanka. While many in the republics use the phrase "cultural sovereignty" to describe their somewhat curtailed local aspirations, an appropriate corollary would be striving for cultural dignity, signifying openness to cultural connections and reincarnation possibilities in multiple senses. Cultural sovereignty within a given republic is important to ensure the legal rights that enable religious and linguistic flourishing, but its subtext is a turning inward, potentially encouraging insularity that may be unwise or impossible to sustain in a globalizing world. Expansion of pan-Mongolic Buddhist communities and pan-Turkic Tengri communities reveals renewed dynamism and suggests alternatives to Russification.

Shamanic worldviews also are available to be activated and revived in new ways, although the extent of Soviet repressions has made it impossible to precisely reproduce eclectic shamanic practices. A post-Soviet shamanic revival has developed with uneven results in all three republics, riding a wave of nostalgia for healing seances, lost folk wisdom, and spirit-driven energy (Balzer 2012). In Tyva, the republic where shamans (*kam*) and the scholars who follow them have made the boldest claims to conserving *kamlanie* as an "archaic religion," acknowledging lost powers has led to a search for effective prayers (*algys*) and to new ways of using inherited shamanic gifts for creativity in music and arts (Levin with Süzükei 2004). In 2016, at the same time local Tyvans were celebrating the opening of the new Buddhist temple in the village of Chaa-Khol, the villagers of Shui Bai-Taigin were unveiling a memorial to the late Tyvan composer Khuresh-oola Damba. His poignant quote from 1971 distills the spirit of creative galvanized nostalgia: "I was never able to see the séance of an actual shaman. I did not even see shamanic 'action' on the stage recreated by actors. The drum in their hands sounded very differently. I wanted to convey my own impressions in music."[17]

Ecology Activism, Indigeneity, and Sovereignty

In the introduction to this book, I asked, "Under what conditions is it possible for ecology movements to be transformed into wider civic society activism?" This has become a key question, given that some of my interlocutors in and from the republics have despaired that their ecology movements are failing, despite seemingly approved, legal public and private strategies of protesting development perpetrated in their regions without their consent. President Putin's naming 2017 the Year of Ecology is particularly ironic for them. The basic Indigenous activist mantra, "nothing about us without us," meaning insistence on UN standards of "free and informed consent," often has been violated in Russia. "Usual suspect" blame is attributed to corporate greed and corruption of officials and businessmen, sometimes including members of the Indigenous community. Addressing the consequences rather than the root causes of ecological disasters has become a norm (compare Henry 2010, 2018; Plantan 2022).

The 2017 flooding of the diamond mine Mir in the Sakha Republic, owned by the wealthy ALROSA Company, was a quintessential example of perfidy, with 8 people missing, a disputed number dead, and 142 rescued.[18] Some of the rescued miners explained they were trapped underground for over thirty hours in an area that was too unsafe to be mined in the first place. Experts and activists had warned there was a near-certain danger of flooding if side walls were breached. Examples of ALROSA's disrespect for local communities are accumulating, beginning with its open-pit diamond mine at Mirny that became the second largest in the world and caused extensive damage to the Viliui water system. ALROSA's project to exploit the Ust-Nakinsk diamond deposit, located inconveniently in a Special Ecology Protection Zone, is threatening the Markha River and forests in the Niurba region.[19]

Conditions for an effective ecology movement include long-term committed publics in rural and urban areas, protest mobilization in emergencies without fear of arrest, access to media at multiple levels, interethnic cooperation, adequate understanding of local ecological contexts for subsistence and sustainable living, leadership at many levels including urban activists, and institutional support through empowered republic and federal-level environmental protection agencies. As Harley Balzer has pointed out, civic society generation and renewal works best with public-private, state-citizen partnerships (Balzer 1996, 300–303). Indeed, the terms "civil society" and "civic society," often used interchangeably, usefully may be differentiated to emphasize degrees of "from below" and "collaboration with state" interaction. International awareness and support are helpful, sometimes crucial, but have been increasingly curtailed with the designation of many groups as "foreign agents."

Ideal conditions for ecology activism are rare anywhere and have been particularly elusive in Russia. One of the most surprising wins has been the 2020 sacred Kushtau Hill case in Bashkortostan's southern Urals, where multiethnic and multigenerational activists were able to stop a limestone mining project with the intervention of the republic's governor.[20] However, Bashkir activists were then arrested as nationalists in an old systemic pattern of at least partially fixing a problem while arresting those who call attention to it. Of the cases featured here, the Sakha Republic has come closest to fulfilling some conditions at various moments, partially due to the very resource wealth that has caused it to have more than a fair share of development and the emergencies that accompany it. As Vera Solovyeva (2/23/2021) wrote to her PhD committee member, social anthropologist Mark Goodale: "There is a huge cultural revitalization back in my homeland. People in my Republic are returning to their ancestral beliefs. This means that they finally begin to understand who they are and start to discover their inner strength, which was almost broken by all those events in our recent history. It is difficult to stand up for our rights and there may not be enough time. We don't know for sure, but we need to try."

Discouraged activists feel an understandable pessimism as they fight on multiple fronts against irresponsible mining, illegal logging, forest fires, and coke processing, plus covered-up nuclear testing mistakes compounded by proliferating pipelines and chemical processing plants built in permafrost. Yet these activists have accrued considerable experience in dealing with authorities at multiple levels, bringing lawsuits and informing the media. A silver lining may be that the more extensive the experience of post-Soviet activism becomes, the better the chance for these movements to help to build civic society. However, two further underfulfilled conditions related to addressing underlying causes of Indigenous discontent should be acknowledged. First, political rights, as outlined in the UN Declaration on Indigenous Peoples, must be more widely understood, including by Indigenous groups themselves, and legally enforced. Second, the efforts of Indigenous activists and intellectuals to effectively use and adapt traditional knowledge and ecologically oriented worldviews should be recognized, accepted, and encouraged without paternalism (Kimmerer 2013).

Uliana Vinokurova (2017, 92) views "sensitivity to ecological risk as constituting one of the strongest mobilizing values of the Sakha." In addition to the importance of stimulating an "ecosystemic society," she emphasizes values that support traditional dualities in key dynamic partnerships: male-female, human-animal, personal connectedness to places of residence for sustenance, and person-social interconnectedness under extreme conditions of the North.

Permeating shamanic, Tengri, and Buddhist worldviews is the basic philosophy of an integral ecological relationship of human communities with Nature. Practitioners advocate walking gently on the land that one is meant to pass through without owning or despoiling. Native ethnographers claim, in an interesting crossover trope I have heard several times, that the footwear Tyvans, Buryats, and Sakha once wore had upturned toes to avoid digging holes in Mother Earth. "And look at our mines now," Buryat and Sakha interlocutors sigh. Token offerings of respect to the earth are expected when shamanic healers gently pull their medicinal plants from the ground, as I have witnessed on many foraging trips. Hearth and camp fires are "fed" food offerings to express humble gratitude to local spirits and dieties for one's sustenance.

An affectionate, heartfelt rapport of Indigenous people with the land and its resources has become a cliché that some cynics mock by pointing out trash left by local youth at sacred sites. Yet Indigenous activist youth groups have made a point of creating work brigades to clean up such sites. Many young people are aware of ecological values, even in their breach. A sense of husbandry of land and animals, rather than ownership of them, has characterized Native Siberian approaches in the past. Nostalgia for this self-proclaimed "traditional worldview" is widely expressed, especially when local people watch bulldozers they do not control destroy meadows, marshes, and forests. Nostalgia is easily referenced after trauma, whether a specific ecological disaster or a world-shattering pandemic.

Most ecology activists, whether Native or Russian, understand that the days of romantic, isolated caretaking are long over, having become overidealized in tropes of a "golden past." They see that their best chances for saving parts of the land, lakes, and river systems require deed-based legal ownership, a form of complicity in an hegemony they did not create, during negotiations over development projects. In Russia, even this is difficult, for the state owns all resources beneath the land's surface. When a diesel oil tank exploded, leaking over twenty thousand tons into the Norilo-Piasinskii water system near the company town of Norilsk (owned by Norilsk Nickel) in the Arctic in 2020, activists and citizens across Russia decried lack of maintenance on tanks vulnerable to permafrost melting.[21] Within the republics, residents can and are asking for greater oversight and participation in state-dominated companies. Some demand local referenda to approve major development projects, especially those infringing on nature preserves, Special Ecology Protection Zones, and sacred lands. The interrelationship between conservationist ecological sustainability and cycle-sensitive spiritual-religious worldviews is openly expressed by many in the republics beyond the core activist community.

Given their long-term spiritual significance, sacred sites, including graves, have become central to ecology activism among many Indigenous groups throughout the world (compare Nadasdy 2017, 238–39; Sponsel 2012). The Native ethnographer Marisol de la Cadena (2010, 335) reminds us that the Republic of Ecuador's 2008 Constitution includes rights for Mother Nature: "*Pachamama*, where life becomes real and reproduces itself, has the right to be integrally respected in [her] existence." This has some distant analogy with the Republic of Sakha having a Ministry for the Protection of Nature, since the word for "nature" in Sakha, *aiyylgha*, itself contains the word for "spirit." Each republic has some environmental protection oversight, with varying degrees of effectiveness. Protections require strengthening but are being weakened.

In the larger Western context, indigeneity has come to mean holding on to what is left of "our land," as in the case of the Northern Canadian Yu'pik territory of Nunavut (literally glossed "Our Land") that took nine years and a generation of Native lawyers to negotiate. Those born on territories where Native subsistence activities predominate are acknowledged as First Nations in Canada. Such legal protections have eroded in Russia, existing mainly on paper (Novikova 2014; Balzer 2017; Solovyeva 2018). Urban indigeneity is especially problematic, based primarily on self-identity and community building (Forte 2010; compare Brown 2003). In the case of Canada, enormous devastation with resulting health hazards has been documented on First Nations (Sai'kuz) land associated with the Tar Sands and linked Keystone XL Pipeline projects.[22] In this interconnected internet and Skype era, Native Siberians, including Sakha and Buryat friends, have watched debates about the Keystone XL project and the Dakota Access pipeline protests at Standing Rock in real time. They have rejoiced at the several hiatuses in the Dakota and Keystone pipeline construction in the United States, mourned court case losses, and observed with fascination the growing solidarity coalitions of Native groups with some local ranchers.[23]

While Siberian colleagues and friends do not expect similar large-scale collaborations to interrupt development projects in the Far East anytime soon, they have begun to access the resources and prestige of the United Nations Program on Indigenous Peoples in New York and Geneva. Some consider themelves part of a global Indigenous movement that has generated an inkling of empowerment, the chance to go over the heads of their governments in the name of Indigenous human rights and transparency. They appreciate that UN bylaws protect First Nations of many different sizes and political status, enabling recognition of the rights of those with "titular republics" within Russia, as long as they do not have their own nation state.[24]

An intriguing debate erupted at my dinner table in 2016 (after a fire offering) as I was hosting a multiethnic group just returned from the annual UN Forum on Indigenous Peoples. Perhaps inspired by their experience in New York, my guests spoke quite frankly. One ecology activist, shifting from third to first person, proclaimed:

> The Sakha people will win—it is in their fate to finally be free. The land can't simply be taken from them—they are at the edge of their ability to withstand everything that has happened to them. But this can't go on. It could get violent. People could take up arms—like in Chechnya. But we are not Chechens. We really do want to make sure everything is done peacefully, legally. This is why I decided to take the whole issue of the "free land law" [Far East Hectare] to the UN. People were criticizing me—saying that we can protest, or write on the internet—but we're not really accomplishing anything—why don't I take my complaint to the UN? It became a kind of "last resort."[25]

Reversing the stereotype of the younger generation being more hotheaded, a young woman had a more cautious, philosophical approach: "I think things will change when the generations change ... We need to not keep being 'against things'—the [planned] chemical factory, the land grabs, nuclear issues in the republic—but 'for something.' For ourselves. For our values, our Sakha values. We need to change our psychology—and then other things can change. It starts with ourselves."

"No, no" insisted another, "this has to be a community [effort], a popular thing. You can't just work on yourself. That seems too selfish, too much like in the West with the focus on individuals." The soft-spoken young woman healer defended herself: "That's not what I meant. First you change your own psychology—then you work with your community for what needs to be done. But it all needs to happen based on our own traditions. I'm not rejecting that. Indeed, it is our spirituality that I'm most concerned about. If this can be changed, then community and national level issues will fall in place."

Conversation then turned to an interesting mix of spirituality, ecology, senses of "fate," and discussion of protest strategy and leadership: "It is in part through the 'hidden world' of the spirits that change for the better will occur. More people need to recognize that there is a spirit world, beyond our everyday world, and this will make them more sensitive to preserving our ecology." The elder-activist had the last word, after I asked about leadership: "I don't think we need some new charismatic leader. That might be too dangerous. But we do have people working behind the scenes. That is how those demonstrations, the protests against the land grabs and the chemical processing plant have been shaping up." Everyone agreed that local elections, if they were free and fair, might also help.

Most ecology protests have focused on immediate development concerns, especially the despoliation of Lake Baikal and the Lena River, themselves important indexes of Far East Siberian natural beauty and renewable resources. In Tyva, some reject the incoming rail line, associated with coal and population increases, despite the prosperity it may bring. Residents of the entire Far East also worry about underground nuclear testing and fallout from rockets sent from Kazakhstan's Baikonur base. More broadly, some scientists and others have become increasingly vocal about the ripple effects of pervasive climate change, which has led to extensive permafrost thawing and release of methane gases in the North that disproportionately influence the climate of the whole planet.

In the past decade, as in Alaska, some villages in the Far North have had to be relocated due to increased flooding. In 2007, a prescient Sakha colleague originally from Srednaia Kolyma shared her concerns about global warming: "More numerous and serious floods seem to be accompanied by broader health and ecological problems . . . with thawing, diseases we never had in the North are likely to flourish, even smallpox." Indigenous leaders in the region—of Sakha, Éveny, Évenki, Chukchi, and Yukaghir backgrounds—have been trying to raise alarms at numerous levels concerning interrelated issues of political, economic, and ecological change. Unfortunately, the issue of climate change has become especially politicized, since it is associated with foreign researchers. An official scolded a friend in 2015: "Foreigners arrive saying they are studying 'global warming' but end up studying the politics of ecology activism. They then say negative things about us."[26] In 2020, a top FSB general used the coronavirus as an excuse to "protect Indigenous peoples" against foreigners—who, he claimed, only pretend to study the Arctic and Indigenous peoples but actually work to thwart development of the Northern Sea Route.[27]

Beyond commonalities of sacred site protection, spiritual depth, and climate change alarm, how does Indigenous activism in Russia correlate with the perceptive reinterpretations of indigeneity that have become prominent in the Americas and Europe? The theme of "emergent indigeneities" (Fortun, Fortun, and Rubenstein 2010) plays on Michael M. J. Fisher's (2003) *Emergent Forms of Life and the Anthropological Voice* by highlighting the moving target nature

of what we study and how we analyze it. Important further directions for reinterpretations of colonial and neocolonial legacies, and the shifting conceptual
boundaries of indigeneity, have come from the Native American anthropologists Kim TallBear (Sisseton-Wahpeton Oyate) (2013, 2016), Audra Simpson
(Mohawk) (2014, 2016), and Paul Nadasdy (2017).

Kim TallBear (2016, 24–25), based at the University of Alberta, of Sioux-
Dakota background, provides a passionate plea for rethinking US history so
that "'making kin' can help forge relations between Peoples in ways that produce
mutual obligation instead of settler-colonial violence upon which the U.S. continues to build itself." She suggests that broken treaties originally negotiated in good
faith by Natives are the familiar outcome of spirals of violence based on uneven,
racialized power relations disguised as mutually "sovereign" and national. Warning that legacies of racism and violence are still with us, she explains (2016, 24):
"We see small tolerances for say Indigenous languages, the beating of drums and
burning of sage in carefully contained moments. But this represents an idea that
Indigenous people should be included in a nation that is assumed to be a done
deal, its hegemony forever established."

Such plain talk (addressed to American anthropologists for their annual professional meeting) has resonance with my Siberian friends, hoping to build vibrant
Indigenous societies without enduring patronizing hypocrisy concerning Native
rights. Aside from the ethnographic detail that Siberians too consider sage sacred
and offer it to their fire spirits, can "making kin" (including fictive kin) mitigate
social tension? As we have seen, it can and did in the revisionist histories of Genghis Khan, as told by Indigenous scholars and filmmakers. More currently, we can
look at patterns of interethnic marriage and see that they have been declining since
the breakup of the Soviet Union in all three republics featured here. This has been
particularly the case in Tyva, where several recent waves of Russian out-migration
have made interethnic marriages and strong mutually obligated fictive kin friendships increasingly unlikely. Ironically, the Russian husband in a Tyvan-Russian
marriage pitched an analogous argument in a private conversation in 2016, saying that "more interethnic marriages between Tyvans and Russians would better
ensure the peace in Tyva." But when it is politically connected Russians, however
well meaning, pushing for interethnic marriage on their terms, Natives have the
right to yet again become suspicious. The powerful message, that kin relations
may be better than unequal, unenforceable treaty relations, is only effective when
mutual respect and consent are at the core of the relationships, personal and sovereign, negotiated every day, as the messy, deeply humane novels of the Ojibwa
writer Louise Erdrich (e.g., 1984, 2016, 2020) demonstrate.

Better understanding of the messiness of resistance is what the incisive
Columbia University-based anthropologist Audra Simpson advocates in her

pathbreaking monograph *Mohawk Interruptus* (2014) and her essay (2016) on "ethnographic refusal." Describing the ways Mohawk (Iroquois) negotiate the US-Canadian border using their Mohawk passports, Simpson shows how sovereign nations can exist within each other without the smaller, Native one being negated. This is highly pertinent to the Russian context, where Indigenous groups are far better off when they have their own "titular" republics than when they have smaller districts or no politically recognized territory at all. Yet who does the "recognizing"?

Simpson shows that alternatives to hegemonic recognition can be found in the complex dynamics of multicultural politics. Like Nadasdy (2017), she correlates Native connection to their ancestral lands, to "place," with specific remembered, bonding events in history. Place-history-toponym interconnections have been crucial to recoveries of self-worth described in this book. However, the distortions built into any system of hierarchical definitions of indigeneity and citizenship make Simpson's warnings about settler-state power, and how we write about it, alarming. The costs of changing Indigenous senses of loose and flexible solidarities toward European-style nationalism can be great, as Nadasdy (2017) analyzes concerning Yukon First Nations in *Sovereignty's Entailments*. "Coevalness" is frequently denied in subtle and blatant ways during negotiations about degrees of sovereignty (Nadasdy 2017, 261). For structural injustice to be unbent and mitigated, it must be understood at many levels of interaction.

Sadly, a pattern of Russian monitoring of Indigenous Siberian leaders traveling to the UN has resulted in tensions reminiscent of some described by TallBear, Simpson, and Nadasdy. In one dramatic 2015 border case, recounted by the person against whom it happened, a Russian official ripped a visa necessary for the leader to travel abroad, shrugged, and returned the passport with a malicious smile. Several Native leaders from across the North, as well as from republics featured here, have resorted to political asylum abroad. Increasingly in the past five years, UN programs—for example, on language defense, land claims and ecology—have fallen hostage to official policies of specific member countries, including Russia. "Nested sovereignty," or matrioshka sovereignty, built into federal states like Russia and Canada functions only with good will and legal protections for Indigenous rights that are consistent and trust building.

Separatism and Its Discontents: Beyond Rhetoric, Regaining a Sense of Proportion

During President Putin's regime in Russia, Moscow has hosted at least two congresses that convened motley crews of separatists from countries around the world. Somehow, Russian authorities failed to invite as guest speakers anyone from Russia itself, whether from the North Caucasus or the Far East. One of these surrealistic affairs took place in 2016, prominently featuring advocates of Texas's separation from the United States. Giving platforms and TV time to politicians representing various radical fringes was a famous intelligence device in the Soviet period that President Putin, a former KGB operative, has revived. The trick has induced me to reflect on the serious consequences of blowing separatist politics out of proportion and jamming information waves with mixed messages or diametrically opposed explanations of events. Yet genuine, negotiated federalism is precisely what would make the republics less threatening to central authorities.

Moscow officials, in public and in private conversations, routinely magnify separatist claims within Russia, probably as an excuse to persecute opposition leaders they find offensive, accusing them of nationalist or religious extremism and terrorism. In the case of the North Caucasus, where an insurgent "mountain brothers" Caucasus Emirate has threatened lives of civilians, arrests may be justified if done with superb intelligence and pinpoint accuracy. In stark contrast, surveillance and arrests of unarmed phantom separatists are unnecessary and self-defeating in Far Eastern Siberia. The late, moderate Russian sociologist Leokadia Drobizheva (2005, 2011, public appearances up to 2020) often warned that separatism could begin from "the center" rather than the "peripheries" if unjustified crackdowns make non-Russians in the republics too angry and polarized. The history of post-Soviet Chechen/North Caucasus wars shows a spiral of radicalization that perhaps could have been stopped (Baiev 2004; Akhmadov and Lanskoy 2010; compare Dunn and Bobick 2014). I recall with worry my Sakha interlocutor fresh from the UN who proclaimed: "We are not Chechens. We really do want to make sure everything is done peacefully, legally." But can they? What is the scope for legal dissent? Is there any justification for accusations of separatism in the republics featured here?

Ostensibly federal structures to protect legality and human rights exist in Russia today. The Constitution of 1993 provides basic outlines for a new, post-Soviet Russia that could have lasting, democratically oriented influence. It continues to be evoked by non-Russian leaders in the republics (Andrei Borisov, Viacheslav Markhaev, Kaadyr-ool Bicheldei) but has been superceded by 2020 amendments that curtail protections for individual liberties and Indigenous communities' group rights. A system of regional ombudsmen remains in place, and it is regularly used for defense of individual citizens in cases of civil rights violations, especially concerning labor, housing, and children. Russia has paid compensation to those who have won appeals in the European Court of Human Rights (Strasbourg), including Chechens. Some Sakha have applied for a European appeal over the "Far East Hectare" land giveaways, although Russian authorities have signaled that their own Supreme Court of Appeals should take on more cases so that they do not reach Strasbourg. Shaman Alexander's case is before the European Court, while a 2020 Russian Duma law has increased restrictions on shamanic practice. Tyvans and Buryats have appealed decisions within Russia concerning Buddhist monks, and Buryats are fighting Chinese land rentals in Zabaikal and land sales on Olkhon Island. These appeals and many others show that the multilevel court system is being used and taken seriously, despite its sluggishness and unevenness (compare Hendley 2017).

Russian experts on federalism increasingly warn that institutions have been steadily gutted over the past twenty years, beginning with the election process and encompassing the media, courts, and various federal administrative processes. Lobbying for economic and social programs on a haphazard basis has put republic leaders at risk, especially given their shrinking opportunities to generate international funding independently (compare Hale 2014; Petrov 2013; Zubarevich 2015, 2017). In Duma, mayoral, and regional executive elections in Russia, little competition has been allowed. From Sakha Republic, one elected Duma deputy, Fedot Tomusov, is not of the United Russia party but is associated with the mildly oppositionist For a Just Russia party. Another candidate, the former minister of culture Andrei Borisov, was prevented from running for the Duma in 2016 on technicalities found in his signature collection. The popular mayor of Yakutsk Sardana Avksentieva was pressured to resign in 2021 but was allowed to run for Duma deputy. In 2020, unexpectedly massive street demonstrations were sustained for months over the arrest of the popular governor of the Far East Khabarovsk region Sergei Furgal. As Nikolay Petrov (2017, 28) summarizes: "[In Russia's Asian North], over the course of 25 years, governors were steadily disempowered, as were regional elites in general."[28]

At the level of Sakha, Buryat, and Tyvan families responding to societal disruption and economic hardship, discontent is expressed "at the kitchen table," as it was in the Soviet period into the mid-1980s (compare Ries 1997). Families have split over whether they support Crimea's annexation, and some have agreed to stop talking about it to keep familial peace. Yet many are loyal to the concept "We are of multiethnic Rossiia [*rossiane*]." The comparable phrase for multicultural regional orientation in the Sakha republic is "We are Yakutians [*yakutiane*]," and in Buryatia "We are Baikalians [Baikalskii]." Tyvans, given their demographics and political history, do not have a comparable patriotic formula signaling their presence inside Russia with one semantic sweep, but one can listen carefully for whether an interlocutor self-identfies as a "Tyvan" (closer to the indigenous pronounciation) or a Tuvan (closer to Russian and to the Russian spelling of their ethnonym). In Tyva, one rarely hears of the blatantly independent movement Khostug Tyva (Free Tyva) that was unevenly popular in the early 1990s. It is today acknowledged as unrealistic given China's increasing stregnth in the region.

Non-Russian citizens who wish to express patriotism by voicing discontent publicly or through approved channels increasingly find loyal-opposition-style dissent difficult. A Moscow-based Federal Agency for Nationality Affairs (mis-translated as Agency for Ethnic Affairs on its token English website) was recon-stituted in 2015 within the "regional development" buraucracy. It was founded by Igor Barinov, a Russian ex-intelligence official with sympathies that reputedly lie more with ethnic Russians than non-Russians. This is the familiar "fox guarding the chicken coop" approach to environmental protection and interethnic rela-tions. Ethnic Russians in the republics are given increased scope for nationalist expressions. For example, Russians and Tyvans continue to argue over the scale and meaning of interethnic conflict in Tyva from 1985 to the early 1990s, to the point where a group of Russians has demanded that "mass Tuvan violence" be considered a "genocide" against Russians.[29]

Key concerns among non-Russians from all three republics include issues of interethnic violence and prejudice in "mainland Russia" west of the Urals. Some Sakha, Buryat, and Tyvan parents are afraid to send their children to universities in the major Russian cities due to street violence against Asian-looking youth. Indigenous citizens are lumped with Central Asian migrants (compare Reeves 2013). Interethnic brawls and some targeted skinhead violence against Asians have created an atmosphere of mutual accusation and fear in certain Moscow and St. Petersburg neighborhoods, exacerbated by the notorious street killing of the Sakha chess champion Sergey Nikolaev, first reported as Buryat. Siberians have been caught in violence among soccer fans, with serious casualties resulting. Native girls have been assaulted in Moscow and St. Petersburg. Rumors abound, because these are not incidents accurately reported on local TV, and thus con-cerns become magnified. No rumor, a close Sakha friend explained that Russian toughs had shoved him nearly onto the tracks of the Moscow metro; he was saved only because his train arrived as he struggled. His attackers were not grabbing his computer but him.

Tension does not amount to a massive desire for separation from Russia. When people at their kitchen tables discuss the chances for Russia to break up, most express alarm at the idea. But it is a possibility that has been raised more in the past five years than in other years since 1991. I know families where members differ on whether a breakup is possible, and they may differ on the likelihood of disintegration along regional or ethnic (republic) lines. However, it is one thing to speculate and analyze dangers of breakup and another matter entirely to wish for the disintegration of one's state. For most in the older generations, one mega-political breakup in their lifetime is plenty. Many, knowing what happened in Chechnya, recognize that bloodshed could occur if authorities in Moscow decide to crack down on perceived separatist demonstrations. One dangerous scenario would be the organization of multiple social and ecology-based protests in various republics and regions of Siberia at similar times, causing central authorities to believe they are more coordinated than they actually are. Militarization of the region could ensue, creating dangers of polarization where previously they had been fewer. The coronavirus lockdown and subsequent transition may have made this scenario less likely, although street demonstrations continue to vie with more ingenious networking for change.

My Indigenous interlocutors especially fear republic boundary restructuring, diluting demographic proportions, violating their sense of homeland, and thus provoking the long-term festering resentments that in theory restructuring is meant to quell. The danger of Russia's disintegration was discussed openly in the press in 2017, the centenary year of the Russian Revolution. This included the exposé of an administrative plan to restructure republic borders and statuses after President Putin's 2018 election. The political scientist Vladimir Gelman (2017) specifically tried to dispel fears of disintegration in an article that was revealing for raising the specter at all. He argued that the greater danger is that "entrenched political and economic monopolies in the regions will impede the country's political democratization and economic development."[30] In an informal conversation (personal communication, September 14, 2017), he confirmed that he wrote his article to calm general fears, but that the circulating anonymous plan advocating internal border restructuring is plausible and disturbing. In 2020, central authorities tried to amalgamate Nenets Autonomous Okrug with Arkhangelsk. When local leaders fought back, these plans were shelved. In 2021, other restructuring proposals, potentially further undermining Indigenous sovereignty, were discussed.

After Russian Minister of Education Olga Vasilyeva provocatively defended Stalin, Oleg Kashin, a brave Russian opposition journalist who was beaten nearly to death for his reporting, worried that the country has not yet fully shed its Stalinist approach to state control, and that the social "swamp" of Stalinist acceptance has been "bubbling."[31] Like many liberal Russians, some of whom have emigrated, Kashin yearns for a country where official rejection of the Stalinist inhumane state is completed, and not left hanging (compare Etkind 2013). Crackdowns on doctors who exposed coronavirus statistics, rescued the poisoned opposition politician Alexei Naval'ny, or tried to help shaman Alexander auger poorly for this vision.

Rethinking History, Galvanizing Nostalgia

It is healthier for a struggling civic society to have its leadership galvanize nostalgia rather than fear and anger. However, as Svetlana Boym (2001) presciently reminded us, much depends on what kind of nostalgia is evoked. The type she termed "retrospective nostalgia" can indeed provoke fear and anger by fanning fires of chauvinist nationalist antimodern mythmaking. While its "restorative" qualities might sound enticing, its lure is laced with illusions of grandeur and attributions of conspiracy. In American society we have examples of nostalgia proclivities represented by different kinds of popular culture manifestations. A productive example is the extravaganza rap musical *Hamilton*, a resurrection of our "founding fathers'" (and mothers') democratic birth pains that takes discourse about the country's origins away from right-wing politicians, rendering it healthy, debated, and mainstream again. A vivid contrast is the political grandstanding represented by the slogan "Make America Great Again!" (Consider the difference between this and President Obama's future-oriented slogan "the audacity of Hope.") Those who hide behind slogans of "respect for ancestors" while justifying police brutality or violence over removal of Civil War statues are playing precisely on the most dangerous kinds of nostalgia—racist ones. As we emerge from the ripple effects of the global pandemic, we are more sharply conscious of how important it is to select what in our personal and collective pasts may be used to motivate socially responsible adaptive prioritizing.

To analyze the more positive, prospective use of nostalgia, Svetlana Boym (2001, 27) turned to Walter Benjamin, explaining that for him "every epoch dreams the next one and in doing so revises the one before it." Benjamin (1969, 170) wrote: "it is precisely the modern which always conjures up prehistory." His scorn for concepts of Progress and inevitable historical causality was rooted in critique of his times, the early twentieth century, as he mocked paradoxical, experimental flailings at revolution, including Russia's. As Boym put it (2001, 27), "Nietzsche's happy cows or Marx's primitive communities held little fascination for Benjamin . . . Benjamin's modern hero had to be at once a collector of memorabilia and a dreamer of future revolution."

When I began this book project, I was looking for modern, or postmodern, post-Soviet s/heroes. I expected to focus more on specific leaders of the republics featured here and to examine the interrelationships among leadership, society, and cultural change. Instead, I produced profiles of places and issues, including some cameos of people with leadership potential. The "dictatorship of law" conditions created in President Putin's Russia have not enabled charismatic leaders to flourish in Sakha, Buryatia, and Tyva, although they were beginning to emerge in the chaos of the immediate post-Soviet period (compare Stoner-Weiss 1997; Smyth 2006). Maverick figures such as the Tyvan historian-linguist Kaadyr-ool Bicheldei, the Buryat historian Vladimir Khamutaev, the Buryat ecology activist Sergei Shapkhaev, and the Sakha theater and film director Andrei Borisov have been thwarted, albeit to various degrees, and not arrested as would have happened in the Stalin era. Ominously, the Sakha shaman Alexander has been incarcerated in a psychiatric clinic for political activities. Less high profile, but quietly influential, have been women civic society leaders, including the Russian Lake Baikal activist Marina Rikhvanova and the Sakha Save Lena! founders Ekaterina Evseyeva and Valentina Dmitrieva, concerned about the environmental legacies they are leaving for their children. The Sakha activist Antonina Gavrilyeva is another inspiration, as her 2016 letter to the UN Indigenous People's Forum quoted in the introduction shows. All are socially aware activists far different from the Putin-supported Chechen warlord Ramzan Kadyrov, who has flourished in the past decade.

Some of my Siberian interlocutors emphasize the worth of movements that are organic and popular enough to not require leaders as figureheads but instead empower many activists working together and separately in ad hoc, effective, and flexible ways. They reference ancestral wisdom wedded to science, discovery, reverence and mutual respect. Such grounded and relatively democratic movements for furthering Indigenous rights and ensuring ecologically informed lifestyles are analogous to what David Treuer (2019, 332–38) has described for the coalition of Indigenous at Standing Rock, including many women activists.

Andrei Borisov, the former minister of culture of the Sakha Republic, in 2020 recalled his hopes for a new civic society-stimulating organization with a multivocal name, Él Iité, glossed from the Sakha language as "advancing the state of the people through socialization." He began it in the context of a 2016 campaign for Duma deputy that was derailed, but its ideals live on in a loose society of several hundred and in a weekly TV program in which Andrei interviews diverse rural and urban activists. Él Iité was formed to create multiethnic solidarity and to refresh broad-based leadership into becoming more natural, sincere, and less rigid than the current cultural, political, and economic establishments. Since the name puns on the word elite in Russian and English, it has been widely misunderstood. Andrei envisions the concept as bridging generations and linking with informal organizations striving for civic society in all of Russia. In 2016, acknowledging imbalances in Russia's current societal values of selfish wealth accumulation, he tapped into the familiar galvanizing and popular rhetoric of Eurasianism: "Civilization is simply unthinkable without the history of the Turkic-Mongolic peoples. Indeed, Rossiia is a unique state bridging Europe and Asia, it is the heart of Eurasia."[32] Since the 1990s, Andrei has attempted to inspire citizenship and community building at the grassroots level using his vision of history. By 2020, reminding me of his own roots as "Sakha, Cossack, and Tungus," he was looking forward to the opening of the Arctic Center of Epos and Arts in Yakutsk in 2022–2023: "We are an ancient Turkic people, yes. But for a thousand years we've been in the North. We are really Northerners." His faith in plural identities and "from below" activism reminds me that the concept of Indigenous in Russian—*korennoi*, meaning "rooted"—can be multipronged.

History is magnified whenever we write about it. Dangers of distortion, as Audra Simpson (2014) and many others have pointed out, are rife regarding Native peoples' interaction with "settler states." Resurfacing rejection of Christopher Columbus's "discovery" of a long-occupied "new world" highlights the need to constantly critique our relationship to history and position ourselves regarding toppled s/heroes. Anthropology is always unfinished, and sometimes cutting-edge (Biehl and Locke 2017; Appiah 2020). Hopefully, we raise our consciousness and our consciences in reflective and engaged anthropology.

Debates in our society and in anthropology have heightened my awareness of the seriousness of purposeful historical manipulation by some Russian leaders. In the past, I might have dismissed as mere ceremony the repeated jubilee-ization that touts the history of various republics' forcing/joining/absorption into the Russian Empire. Today, I see retrofitting history as a disturbing trend orchestrated from Moscow and imposed on non-Russians—a symptom of twenty-first-century variations on colonization. I wonder how recent historical events that occurred within the current lifetimes of many observers, such as the interethnic tensions that were accompanied by violence and repression in Tyva, so quickly could become enormously propagandized, invoking accusations of genocide. Understanding that social history construction is about both memory and forgetting (Ricoeur 2004; Grant 2009), I find discourses that encourage competing or selective victimization psychologies particularly disturbing. Precisely these revenge-seeking versions of "my people must not be hurt again" are what lead to justifications for changing or abolishing republic borders, a particularly dangerous road to polarization and possible violence.

Nearly every concept featured in this book has been discredited in the social science literature at some point—identity (too vague, too situational to matter); nostalgia (too emotional and imprecise even when parsed into typology); sovereignty (too unobtainable at local, personal or cultural levels in our globally connected world); indigeneity (land-based but also urban); democracy (too Western model-imposing); autonomy (too tied to Soviet terminological falsehoods); ethnicity, nationalism, ethnonationalism (idioms masking the realpolitik of global economic politics and causation); civilization (too sweeping and prone to theories of "clashes"); liberal (too much like neoliberalism); (N)native rights (too token and controlled by human rights legal discourse from above); (C)culture (too holistic, better to use its adjective cultural); tradition (too artificially fixed to convey cultural change); religion (a European construct).

Yet we must use accessible language to be understood, and what gets trashed by one generation of scholars often is picked up and adapted by another. While acknowledging that many of these critiques may be fair at times, I nonetheless use these terms and others strategically and contextually here. It is attention to the messy contexts of history and to multiple self-identities that really matter. The toggling interaction of transnational crossover trends like Eurasianism with various forms of ethnonationalism appears to have intensified in Russia in the past decade. I have set this interaction into the context of newly emerging forms of indigeneity.

As I was writing this book, a notice about research on the phenomenon of nostalgia came into my email, from the journal *New Scientist*, headlined "How Nostalgia Makes Us Human" (Burrell 2016). Psychologists have discovered that nostalgia can be good for you in small, nonparalyzing doses, as the cartoon at the beginning of this book hints.

Notes

INTRODUCTION

1. Alternative names have developed for the republics and their "titular peoples" over long-term interethnic interactions. Yakut is the historical name used by Russians for the Turkic-language speaking people who call themselves Sakha. Yakut is not pejorative, as some proclaim, but rather may originally have derived from a term Tungusic peoples used to describe Yakuts and their homeland to early Russian explorers. Buryat is the name for the Mongolic-speaking people whose communities spanned territories now in Russia, Mongolia, and China. An alternative Library of Congress transliteration is Buriat. Tyvan is the historical name for the Turkic-language-speaking people of the Altai-Sayan Mountains, and this spelling more accurately reflects the way they pronounce their name. From this derived the Republic of Tyva in the early 1990s, although it is more frequently called Tuva in Russian.

In Russian geopolitical terminology, Siberia refers to a vast territory east of the Urals but is conceptualized as stopping at the Far East. European tradition enables me to refer to Western and Eastern Siberia, with Eastern Siberia extending to the Bering Sea.

2. For Indigenous peoples and politics comparisons, see especially de la Cadena and Starn 2007; Dean and Levi 2003; Forte 2010; Nadasdy 2007, 2017; Neizen 2003; Tidwell and Zellen 2017; Treuer 2019.

3. These claims are controversial among some non-Russians, although my liberal nationalist friends in all three republics accept "old-settlers" of intermarried Slavic-Native backgrounds as legitimately Indigenous. Some analysts invoke the "hybridity" of these groups to demonstrate ethnogenesis of new ethnic groups, such as the Dolgan, consistent with old-fashioned Soviet ethnos studies (Bromlei and Kozlov 1989). On the 2010 Siberiaki census debate, see https://globalsib.com/10185/, April 14, 2011 (accessed 5/30/2020). Compare Balzer (1994a), the Russian historian Nina Minenko (1975), the sociologists Anisimova and Echevskaia (2012), and Jeanmarie Rouhier-Willoughby (2015). Rather than using the more accurately transliterated *sibiriaki*, I spell the ethnically based term "Siberiaki" to correlate with the conventional English geographical term "Siberian."

4. Compare Laruelle 2018. A famous example is the Manezh Square 2010 Moscow riots, analyzed by Viatcheslav Morozov (http://www.ponarseurasia.org/memo/what-happened-manezh-square-ideology-institutions-and-myths-regarding-anti-migrant-riots-2010 [accessed 5/20/2020]). On polarizing dangers of "pure-bloodism" or advocacy of genetic purity, compare among many diverse cases, Ippei Shimamura (2014, 350–54) on Mongolia and Audra Simpson (2014) on Mohawks and the work of Victor Shnirelman.

5. For coverage of this top-down initiative that some activists find hypocritical, see https://www.iucn.org/news/eastern-europe-and-central-asia/201703/year-ecology-russia, March 21, 2017 (accessed 3/25/2017).

6. On how federalism is used, abused, and analyzed in Russia, see Alexseev 1999; Balzer 1998; Cameron 2012; Chebankova 2008; Fish 2005; Giuliano 2011; Gorenburg 2003; Graney 2009; Hagendoorn et al. 2008; Herd and Aldis 2002; Khakimov 2002; Kolstø and Blakkisrud 2004, 2016; Lankina 2004; Osipov 2017; Pain 2013; Prina 2016; Protsyk and Harzl 2013; Roeder 2018; Stoliarov 2001; Tishkov and Shabaev 2019; and Triesman 1999. For comparison with Canada, see Solomon 2005.

7. While Galina Starovoitova and Leokadia Drobizheva had differences in pragmatic approaches before Starovoitova was assassinated in 1998, their liberal democracy positions in retrospect converge. Starovoitova unjustly but widely was blamed, as President Yeltsin's first nationality advisor, for instigating a laissez faire attitude toward the republics, encapsulated in the famous phrase "take all the sovereignty you can swallow." It was meant to invite a negotiated balancing of federal and republic jurisdictions based on diverse economic realities within Russia's asymmetrical federalism, not to be an invitation to secede. Drobizheva, first as head of the Institute of Sociology (Academy of Sciences, Moscow) and later as a member of President Putin's Council for Interethnic Relations continued influential into 2021. For "Law Defining Regional Authorities' Responsibilities regarding Interethnic Relations," see the Kremlin website (http://en.kremlin.ru/events/president/news/copy/19460, October 22, 2013 [accessed 5/20/2020]).

8. Regional specialists within Russia concur: for example, Petrov 2012, 2017; Starinova 2019; Zubarevich 2015.

9. For details of the treaty, see Balzer and Vinokurova 1996. Compare Triesman 1999.

10. Examples include Barth 1969; Brass 1991; Brubaker 2004; Connor 1994; Eriksen and Jakoubek 2019; Horowitz 2000; Pachenkov 2006. Barth's pathbreaking edited volume (1969) was less attuned to the conflict-generating dynamics of constructing ethnic boundaries than is the fifty-year anniversary volume of Eriksen and Jakoubek (2019).

11. Compare Balzer 1990, 1994b; Beissinger 2002, 147–99; Humphrey 2008, 257–380; Khazanov 1995; Montgomery 2005, 257–81. See also Bernstein 2013, 6n5.

12. On this eye-opening drama, see chapter 1 on the Sakha Republic. See also Argounova-Low 2012, 85–105, including mention (94–95) of my unjustly alleged provocateur role.

13. Humphrey's argument adapts those of Alain Badiou, the sociologist Bruno Latour, and the anthropologist Marilyn Strathern. While Badiou focuses on major catalytic and revelatory events, Humphrey emphasizes the "decision-event" that "leaves open a space for the unexpected, whether this works consciously or unconsciously" (2008, 375). See also Grant and Ries 2002.

14. These highly public examples are mine, not Boym's. Their chauvinist writings and speeches have chilled non-Russians throughout Russia, including Siberians. For a sample, see Dugin 1999. Rogozin has advocated greater Russian military presence in the Arctic, made claims on Alaska, and helped found the youth group TIGRs, a Russian acronym for Tradition, Empire, State, and Motherland. "Rogozin's TIGRs" (novayagazeta.ru/politics/69747.html, August 30, 2015 [accessed 09/01/2015]) is no longer available, but Paul Goble's discussion of it is (http://windowoneurasia2.blogspot.com/2015/08/rogozins-tigers-come-out-of-bunker.html, August 31, 2015 [accessed 6/15/2020]).

15. Nostalgia for the Soviet period has been monitored for over a decade by the Levada polling center, the best independent survey organization in Russia. However, its late founder, the eminent sociologist Yuri Levada, once told me he regretted that they pay too little attention to the republics. Levada polls led by Karina Pepiya showed an increase in nostalgia for the Soviet period up to 75 percent in a Russian-focused sample by 2020, as reported in the *Moscow Times* (https://www.themoscowtimes.com/2020/03/24/75-of-russians-say-soviet-era-was-greatest-time-in-countrys-history-poll-a69735 [accessed 3/26/2020]).

16. The identity of these interlocutors needs to remain anonymous, since I have heard directly only the Sakha side of the debate, and I did not witness it. The anthropologist is also known for his respect for the literacy-based religions of Judaism and Buddhism.

17. The non-European cases covered in the original edited volume examined Victorian India and colonial Africa. Terrence Ranger (Hobsbawm and Ranger 1983, 212) explained, "The invented traditions of African societies—whether invented by the Europeans or by

Africans themselves in response—distorted the past but became in themselves realities through which a good deal of colonial encounter was expressed."

18. During 1985–1986, I was on the official US-USSR cultural exchange for over a year, with two extensions. I spent half of 1985 in then-Leningrad begging to be allowed into the field in the Far East and finally achieved my goal in early 1986. I use openly taken handwritten notes as a basic, traditional method of putting interlocutors at ease, in conjunction with recordings, photographs, and film when given permission.

19. I was probably the first to call the Soviet Union "affirmative action" oriented regarding Native peoples, a controversial point later taken up on a much larger scale by Terry Martin (2001). Compare Balzer 1990, 1999.

20. See my "credits, claims, and confessions" for further names. I credit friends and consultants when they wish to be known and leave vague those who have requested anonymity. For more on field approaches, see my "Sacred Trust" chapter in Balzer 2012, 15–33.

21. On specific interview contexts and timing in Buryatia and Tyva, see chapters 2 and 3.

22. Co-theorizing also is exemplified in the quirky and brilliant connections that the anthropologist of Iran, India, and Singapore Michael M. J. Fischer (2003, 2009, 2015) encapsulates in his conceptions of "emergent forms of life," his book *Anthropological Futures*, and his attention to finding channels of creative dignity with his interlocutors.

1. SAKHA REPUBLIC (YAKUTIA)

1. Personal communications; http://nazaccent.ru/content/16181-rodnoj-yazyk-kak-roskosh.html, May 28, 2015 (accessed 6/6/2020).

2. "V natsional'nykh respublikakh schitaiut lishnym zhalet' russkoiazychnykh pisatelei," http://asiarussia.ru/news/8068/, June 24, 2015 (accessed 6/21/2020). Constitutional changes are analyzed in the book's conclusions.

3. Vitaly Obedin, *Yakutsk vechernyi* journalist, October 2014. *Sakhalar*, the plural of Sakha, also designates a mixed Sakha-Russian group who have lived in the republic over multiple generations and identify more with Sakha than Russians.

4. While 2010 census data asserted that 450,140 people know the Sakha language out of a total of 478,085 Sakha in all of Russia, these data are disputed. For census data, see http://www.gks.ru/free_doc/new_site/perepis2010/perepis_itogi1612.htm (accessed 6/13/2020). Interviews in the past decade with Russians based in Moscow in charge of the census and with Sakha linguists have made me skeptical of the accuracy of the 2010 census, and the 2020–2021 census was put on hold. Compare Anderson 2015; Chevalier 2017; Ferguson 2019; and Mestnikova 2010a. Akulina Mestnikova (2010b, 228) mentions that UNESCO's interactive *Atlas of the World's Languages in Danger* includes the Sakha language as well as languages of Russia's numerically small peoples of the North. The work of Darima Badmatsyrenova and Anna Elivanova, based in Neriungri, on multiethnic language practice in the republic is relevant, as is the 2021 wonderful interactive Sakha-Russian dictionary created by V. V. Migalkin (https://edersaas.ru/slovar/; accessed 4/19/2021).

5. I am grateful for those Sakha who vouched for me as an ethnographer in 1986 and averted my deportation. I have collected stories of these protests from friends and colleagues who were affected by them and from others who want me to know their versions of what happened. Sometimes I am stopped on the streets of Yakutsk with such narratives. For perspective, see Balzer and Vinokurova 1996; Argounova-Low 1994, 2012.

6. Uliana Vinokurova reports that Mikhail Nikolaev appointed a range of scholars and practitioners with various political points of view. They took about a year to read as many constitutions of United Nations members as they could find, regardless of size or continent. See also Oleg Sidorov's (2017) biography of Mikhail Nikolaev.

7. Another controversial statue in Yakutsk is of the Cossack Simeon Dezhnev with his Sakha mistress and child, discussed in the book's conclusions. Few Sakha visit either statue. The Russian "peaceful incorporation" perspective is exemplified by Sergei Podyapolskiy and Anastasya Podyapolskaya (2016).

8. I am grateful for insights and hospitality in 2010 to Viktor Petrovich Struchkov and his horse-herder neighbor Jaako Gavrilovich Sleptsov. The Mitrofan stories epitomize the reverse of Soviet propaganda about rich kulaks exploiting workers. Mitrofan and his sons were repressed in the 1920s, although Mitrofan provisioned the Red revolutionary Pankratov.

9. I learned of this trip from discussions with several participants in 2010. See Ksenofontov 1937, a foundational text for Sakha identity and history seekers; Balzer 2015; and http://ilin.sakhaopenworld.org/ (accessed 5/20/2020).

10. Demographers' concerns about the official census have been expressed for all three censuses of the Putin presidency, as covered periodically in my journal *Anthropology and Archeology of Eurasia* (https://www.tandfonline.com/toc/maae20) and https://riss.ru/demography/demography-science-journal/5271/, March 31, 2014 (accessed 12/18/2019).

11. Personal communications, 2015–2021. Controversy surrounding this issue prevents me from revealing my sources.

12. http://publication.pravo.gov.ru/Document/View/1400201910100003?index=30&rangeSize=10 section on demography, 32–34. October 4, 2019 (accessed 6/5/2020).

13. Balzer 2014. The mosque on the outskirts of Yakutsk was controversial when first built in the early 2000s, but its moderate imam (willing to shake women's hands including mine) reassured neighbors that they would not have a loud, disruptive "call to prayer."

14. Rosstat 2018 and earlier data are available at http://www.gks.ru/bgd/regl/b19_14p/Main.htm (accessed 5/3/2020), with thanks to Robert Orttung, email of May 3, 2020. See Arutiunova 2020 for survey data showing differentials in how Sakha and Russians in the republic perceive grievances with potential to stimulate protest.

15. Mir A. Umchanov, personal communication, July 10, 2010. The word in Sakha for "hare" is *kuoba*. It took several more years before the Chinese gave up entirely, returning to the republic's central regions to lease land. Compare this to the Chinese in the Zabaikal region and country-wide outrage over Chinese leasing "Russian" lands, discussed in chapter 2. See "Gubernator Zabaikal'ia: Kitai uchel daleko vpered" http://asiarussia.ru/news/8072/, June 25, 2015 (accessed 6/13/2020).

16. Compare Burnasheva 2019; Larsen et al. 2014; and Fondahl et al. 2014 on the Sakha Republic having multiple levels of Arctic identity. See also the Soviet propaganda film *Kepsé Yakutia!* (1972), https://www.youtube.com/watch?v=yDB36vMjF4w 3/24/2014 (accessed 6/13/2020), and Liubov Borisova's 2019 award-winning feature film *Nado mnoiu solnste ne saditsia*, https://www.youtube.com/watch?v=8VKWsdT8Ezg, September 18, 2019 (accessed 6/13/2020).

17. "Glava Yakutii vystupil s predlozheniiami po razvitiiu Arktiki," http://news.ykt.ru/article/33024 6/27/2015 (accessed 6/13/2020).

18. The felicitous phrase "reluctant entrepreneur" is Aimar Ventsel's (2015). See for context Argounova-Low 2007; Crate 2006, 93–144; Ferguson 2021.

19. The activist report was used by the Sakha Republic's parliament, Il Tumen, personal communication, April 16, 2009. Important data from the farmers' protest letter is no longer online, "Fermery Yakutii trebuiut otstavki glavy respubliki," http://www.vesti14.ru/ru/13/politics/243, July 6, 2015 (accessed 7/7/2015).

20. Official responses to the farmers' protest letter highlighted grants to young farmers.

21. Economic downturn is clear from https://www.yktimes.ru/ekonomika/ekonomiku-yakutii-okonchatelno-perekosilo, July 23, 2019 (accessed 6/15/2020).

22. This peak proportion included nontransparent addendums to the agreement that differentiated local-level and republic shares. Compare more public reports from the 1990s citing 20 percent share in "Siuzhet nedeli/Almaznye brat'ia," https://www.kommersant.ru/doc/13103, November 19, 1996 (accessed 12/13/2019); and the 2000 revocation (Decree no. 1191) of the 1991 and 1997 Yeltsin agreements, http://kremlin.ru/acts/bank/555/print, June 27, 2000 (accessed 12/13/2019).

23. On the accident-waiting-to-happen and flood ramifications, see http://yakutsk.ru/news/society/chto_i_trebovalos_dokazat_bez_publichnykh_slushaniy_nyurbinskiy_rayon_daet_razreshenie_na_razrabotku/, February 14, 2017 (accessed 9/1/2017). On ALROSA, see "Nastoiashchie yakutskie brillianty zasiiaiut v Evrope," http://www.1sn.ru/133931.html, March 24, 2015 (accessed 6/13/2020). In 2016, Finance Minister of Russia Anton Siluanov was reelected as chair of ALROSA, with Republic Head Egor Borisov designated as first vice-chairman. The federal government owns 33 percent of the company, with the republic holding 25 percent and local municipalities getting 8 percent. Remaining shares ownership is not transparent, and a site indicating this information is no longer available.

24. On Évenki gold mining, see Vitaly Alekseev, "Évenki zaimutsia zolotodobychei," http://www.gazetayakutia.ru/component/k2/item/3712 (2013 [accessed 3/21/2013]). On Kankun, see http://www.yakutia.rushydro.ru/file/main/yakutia/company/investprojects/17376.html/Kniga_2.pdf (2011 [accessed 6/13/2020]); and Vera Solovyeva's 2013 UN report at http://unsr.jamesanaya.info/study-extractives/index.php/en/cases (accessed 5/16/2013).

25. Varvara Zakharovna Kyrillina, director of the Verkhoyansk regional museum, 2010. On the crater, see http://sakhalife.ru/batagayskiy-proval-vyizov-uzhe-nevechnoy-merzlotyi/, September 19, 2017 (accessed 9/20/2017). An earlier crater, growing deeper each year in the area, is called the Batagai "megaslump." See https://www.cambridge.org/core/journals/quaternary-research/article/div-classtitlepreliminary-paleoenvironmental-analysis-of-permafrost-deposits-at-batagaika-megaslump-yana-uplands-northeast-siberiadiv/6E1CDD9631CF354F08444B50DD2EBE4D, February 16, 2017 (accessed 6/24/2020).

26. On Anatoly Chomchoev and his Test Ground of Cold, see "Small Energy Breakthrough in Early XXI Century," http://localenergy-apec.ru/files/conf/Anatoly-Chomchoev.pdf (2012). See also the joint-stock company SakhaEnergo, which promotes alternative energy including wind power, http://www.sakhaenergo.ru/ (accessed 6/13/2020).

27. Tuimaada-Neft is a joint-stock company (http://tuneft.ru/ [accessed 6/13/2020]) connected with the pipeline company Sakhatransneftegaz. See also http://investyakutia.com/en/posts/947-v-iakutii-mozhiet-poiavitsia-nieftiepierierabatyvaiushchii-zavod, April 23, 2015 (accessed 6/6/2015). Makarov's Il Tumen site (http://iltumen.ru/node/791 [accessed 6/6/2015]) is no longer active.

28. President Putin approved the line extension in 2020, reported by Diane Pallardy with map, https://www.icis.com/explore/resources/news/2020/04/30/10503185/gif-inside-story-power-of-siberia-2-s-new-route-makes-russian-gas-supplies-to-china-more-feasible (accessed 6/15/2020). Compare Rossneft's site (http://www.rosneft.com/news/pressrelease/19062015.html [accessed 6/22/2015]). For analysis, see Sidorstov, Ivanova, and Stammler 2016; Stammler and Ivanova 2016.

29. The Ministry for Nature Protection in the Sakha language is Sakha Respublikatyn Aiyl5yny kharystabylyn ministiérstibété. See https://www.sakha.gov.ru/; https://minpriroda.sakha.gov.ru/news/front/view/id/2892807 and http://www.nature.ykt.ru/RIAC/RedBook/HOME.htm (all accessed 5/5/2021). For 1990s Russian Federation context, see State Committee 1997.

30. http://savelenariver.org/index.php?option=com_content&task=view&id=118&It emid=1 (accessed 6/6/2015). The major site chronicling ecology activism is http://www. eyge.ru/index.php (accessed 4/30/2021), from Эйгэ (Surroundings) in Sakha. A weekly Sakha language news supplement is «СахаЭкос» (SakhaEcos). See "Greens of Yakutia" https://web.archive.org/web/20100112021526/http://greenyakutia.ya1.ru/ (accessed 4/30/ 21); and the site of the activist Uhhan (Ivan Nikolaev) (http://uhhan.ru/news/2014-09-01-10442 [accessed 6/13/2020]). See also archives 2008–2013 at http://www.eyge.ru/project. php?id=16, and http://savelena.ykt.ru/index.php (both accessed 6/16/2020). A Save Lena! protest letter addressed to Russian President Dmitry Medvedev in 2008 moved to http:// www.wood.ru/ru/lonewsid-22987.html (accessed 6/18/2020). For an industry perspective on the safety of the pipeline, see http://www.pumpsandsystems.com/topics/seals/ mechanical-seals/oil-gas-project-sets-new-standards#sthash.AV8xhdUN.bnQK43KS. dpuf, December 17, 2011 (accessed 6/13/2020).

31. Ramifications, including a lost and found notebook, are discussed in the introduction.

32. These are August 2019 communications that need to remain anonymous. See also the work of Vera Solovyeva and Vera Kuklina (2020) on climate change ramifications and Indigenous knowledge.

33. The "Clean City-Clean Planet" conference was held under Northern Forum auspices: https://www.northernforum.org/en/members/directory/89, August 12, 2014 (accessed 6/13/2020).

34. On the committee, see http://www.sakha.gov.ru/node/246334 (accessed 6/22/2015). The youth group in Sakha is Amma kyrgalyn ychchata imeni O. P. Ivanovoi-Sidorkevich.

35. The Day of the Lena River is sponsored by the pipeline company Sakhatransneftegaz, http://sakhalife.ru/2-iyulya-den-reki-lena-3/, June 28, 2017 (accessed 6/13/2020).

36. Examples include A. I. Matveev, https://youtu.be/Njs4VUNlSjU, February 16, 2019 (accessed 3/11/2019); and A. I. Sivtsev, https://www.youtube.com/watch?v=4coSZ UTFAiA&feature=youtu.be, February 16, 2019 (accessed 3/11/2019). V. P. Korotov summarized ecology activism in Niurba.

37. These demands were unfulfilled. See taigapost.ru/news/fedot-tumusov-za-otrav lenie-vilyuya-dolzhen-otvetit-ministr-ekologii-yakutii, August 26, 2018 (accessed 8/31/ 2018), covering Tumusov and the local demonstration on the banks of the Viliui.

38. The account of the two villages is from Alexei Petrovich Rozhin in 2010, confirmed in 2017 by the healer Mikhail Mikhailovich Postnikov, also from the region. The survey data is from 2015 by the Sakha sociologist Yury Zhegusov, presented at a George Washington University conference. He admitted, "public perception of climate change and its impacts in the urban environment is site-specific and does not always agree with the [relevant] meteorological observations." Vera Solovyeva's (2018; 2021) survey research in villages in Northern Sakha Republic, including the Arctic, indicates increasing concern about climate change.

39. From his website, http://EgorBorisov.Ru (accessed 6/5/2015), no longer available.

40. This reliable source has lived periodically in the republic for over ten years in a mixed ethnic marriage. The number of villages is similar to the number I have heard from other sources.

41. Official information was available at http://www.sakha.gov.ru/node/246462; and http://www.sakha.gov.ru/node/246428 (both accessed 6/29/2015).

42. The main rally on May 27, 2015—including an outdoor concert and speakers such as the organizers Rudolf Mikhailov, Ivan Rufov, and Ivan Shamayev, as well as the woman's group leader Evdokiia Reshetnikova, and Minister for Nature Protection Sakhamin Afanasev—was broadcast by *Vesti Yakutii* at https://www.youtube.com/watch?v=hCehk PObILo (accessed 7/9/2015). Many young people and representatives of various religious

groups were part of the crowd. Egor Borisov's response was broadcast on May 27, 2015. The announcement for the rally was at https://www.youtube.com/watch?v=urM8DUzfDW4 (accessed 7/10/2015).

43. This issue has become too sensitive to reveal sources for the quotations, from oral and email interlocutors.

44. From the farmer's protest, "Fermery Yakutii trebuiut otstavki glavy respubliki," http://www.vesti14.ru/ru/13/politics/243, July 6, 2015 (accessed 7/7/2015, no longer available). An interview with Ernst Berezkin, http://www.vesti14.ru/, July 15, 2015 (accessed 7/18/2015) is also no longer available.

45. Solomonov 2000; Ministry for Nature Protection, http://www.nature.ykt.ru (accessed 6/20/2015). Information on the "1995 Federal Law on Specially Protected Areas" was published in a report of the State Committee of the Russian Federation for Environmental Protection (1997). This law defined the main protected zones as *zapovedniki* (strict reserves), national parks, *zakazniki* (reserves), and natural monuments.

46. For categories and numbers of protected areas, see Ministry for Nature Protection, http://www.nature.ykt.ru (accessed 6/20/2015); and http://www.sakha.gov.ru/node/448 (accessed 7/13/2017).

47. Personal communication, June 2007. For poetic comparison, see Ackerman 2009. For a profile of the reserve, see https://www.cms.int/siberian-crane/en/page/monitoring-eastern-asian-population (accessed 6/15/2020).

48. A PBS special on Siberian cranes' destinations into China terms it the "longest bird migration in the world," https://www.pbs.org/video/disappearing-lake-4pzwix/, episode 4, November 13, 2019. On Chinese in the Arctic, see, for example, https://www.nytimes.com/2019/05/24/climate/china-arctic.html (both accessed 4/9/2020).

49. Personal communication, June 2013. See its UNESCO site, http://whc.unesco.org/en/list/1299 (accessed 6/13/2020).

50. Personal communication, fieldnotes July 16, 2010, while hiking.

51. The congratulations by Ivan Makarov is from the site of Sakhatransneftegaz http://www.oaostng.ru/?q=company/news/5658 (accessed 6/27/2015).

52. Personal communication, fieldnotes, June 26, 2013, interview in Ministry of Culture offices.

53. As with other aspects of Yhyakh, timing of the traditional New Year has been disputed, with some Sakha considering it was earlier, in spring rather than the summer solstice. On Yhyakh and the creation of its recent versions, see the dissertation of Liudmilla Nikanorova (2019), and the monographs of Ekaterina Romanova (1994, 1997). See also the work of the ethnographer Anatoly Gogolev (e.g., 2002). Compare Balzer 2013.

54. Personal communications and emails, summer 2015, with friends increasingly preferring anonymity. Compare Romanova and Ignateva 2012; Nikanorova 2019.

55. Uliana Vinokurova, email July 2, 2015. See also Vinokurova 2011.

56. Andrei Borisov, extended phone call June 27, 2020. Andrei added: "We know from legend about Ellei. We wanted to reproduce this sense of history."

57. Villiam Yakovlev, personal communication May 27, 2014. Villiam's parents named him for William Shakespeare. Compare Vinokurova et al. 2009; Yakovlev 2009.

58. Fieldnotes, June 20, 2013. Borisov, whose 2010 inauguration I attended, seemed to be looking straight at my notes, as I sat nearby with the family of his minister of culture. His folksy self-presentation on a range of issues, filmed while driving around Yakutsk, is at https://www.youtube.com/watch?v=MQpM-dB0xYg 9/5/2014 (accessed 6/13/2020).

59. Egor Borisov's reelection in 2016 as the vice-chair of the diamond company ALROSA was perceived by at least some of his Sakha constituents as epitomizing the beholden and trapped nature of his relationship with Moscow. ALROSA's violations of ecology, law, and human rights are described at https://meduza.io/feature/2017/08/10/

my-tak-zakrichali-nas-ves-mirnyy-uslyshal (accessed 1/19/2020); http://yakutsk.ru/news/society/chto_i_trebovalos_dokazat_bez_publichnykh_slushaniy_nyurbinskiy_rayon_daet_razreshenie_na_razrabotku/, February 14, 2017 (accessed 9/1/2017).

60. The group Ус Тумсуу, meeting regularly for men's solidarity rituals, is known for organizing a spontaneous mass demonstration in Yakutsk after a Sakha girl was allegedly attacked by a Kyrgyz migrant in 2019, searching for an Ingush man blamed for a Sakha death at a wedding in 2020, and accompanying police on anti-illegal migrant raids. See https://sakhaday.ru/news/spory-vokrug-rejdov-us-tusuu-po-nochnym-zavedeniyam-ne-utihayut?from=copy; http://yakutiafuture.ru/2020/12/19/innokentij-makarov-kim-da-ki%d2%bbite-buolbataxpyn-bejem-ki%d2%bbibin/ (both accessed 5/7/2021); and https://news.ykt.ru/article/119048 (accessed 4/20/2021).

2. REPUBLIC OF BURYATIA

1. "Vystuplenie glavy Respubliki Buryatii 'Den' buryatskogo iazyka,'" https://glava.rb.ru/see-news/, October 28, 2014 (accessed 7/15/2015; missing 5/14/2020).

2. For examples of media coverage, see "Aleksei Tsydenov ofitsial'no stanet glavoi Buryatii posle 13 sentiabria," https://www.baikal-daily.ru/news/19/270929/, September 11, 2017 (accessed 9/12/2017); "Biografiia Alekseia Tsydenova," https://ria.ru/20170207/1487349738.html (accessed 5/12/2020). For profiles, see https://newbur.ru/n/43272/, July 10, 2017 (accessed 9/12/2017). On singing with a Turkish choir, see http://baikal24.ru/text/14-07-2017/tureckogo/, July 14, 2017 (accessed 9/12/2017).

3. Natalia (Budaeva) Arno, December 1, 2016. Many Buryat friends and colleagues interviewed since 2015 prefer anonymity. For perspective on language politics, see especially Graber 2020.

4. For analysis, including the official view defending Igor Shutenkov's election with 52 percent of the vote, see "Glava Buryatii prizval protestuiushchikh priznat' itogi vyborov mera Ulan-Ude," https://ria.ru/20190911/1558551938.html (accessed 5/14/2020); https://www.themoscowtimes.com/2019/09/11/protest-erupts-in-far-east-russia-after-pro-kremlin-candidates-victory-a67213 (accessed 5/14/2020).

5. This video (https://youtube.com/watch?v=Y5avTS5H7o0 [accessed 7/15/2015]) is no longer available. See Aleksandra Garmazhapova, "O 'voenykh buryatov,'" http://echo.msk.ru/blog/garmazhapova/1585974-echo/, July 16, 2015 (accessed 5/14/2020); Paul Goble, "Moscow's 'Putin's Militant Buryats' Video Clip for Ukrainians Backfires in Buryatia," http://windowoneurasia2.blogspot.com/2015/07/moscows-putins-militant-buryats-video.html, July 17, 2015 (accessed 7/17/2015).

6. My interpretations of this controversial history are formed from conversations with Buryat interlocutors beginning in 1989. Kathryn Graber and Joseph Long (2009) were in the field during the okrug amalgamation process. Compare Bernstein 2013; Chakars 2014; and, by Buryat historians, Buraeva 2005; Chimitdorzhiev 2004; Khamutaev 2008, 2012; Vostrikov and Poppe 2007.

7. Sergei Bazarov, "Ne buryaty, a buriaadmongoly," http://asiarussia.ru/blogs/22072/, July 1, 2019 (accessed 7/3/2019). Compare Shimamura 2014, which emphasizes politicized ethnic differences between Buryats and Mongols in Mongolia, in part due to Mongolians of Mongolia claiming more exclusive rights to Chingis Khan's ancestry and legacy. Mongolian approaches were on display during a 2002 Smithsonian exhibit titled "Modern Mongolia: Reclaiming Genghis Khan." A dominant theme was Genghis Khan's "foundation for building a true democracy."

8. Irina Nymatsyrenova, "V Ulan-Ude proshel piket za vosstanovlenie Ust'-Ordy i Aginska," http://www.infpol.ru/news/society/108673-v-ulan-ude-proshel-piket-za-vosstanovlenie-statusa-ust-ordy-i-aginska/, February 7, 2013 (accessed 2/9/2013).

9. "Buryatiiu i Zabaikal'e predlozhili ob"edinit' v edinyi okrug," http://baikal-daily.ru/news/19/109675/, December 25, 2014 (accessed 12/28/2014); Paul Goble, "An Economic Move toward a Greater Buryatia?," https://windowoneurasia2.blogspot.com/2014/12/window-on-eurasia-economic-move-toward.html (accessed 12/28/2014).

10. On renting land to Chinese, a move favored by Zabaikal Governor Konstantin Il'kovskii, see "Gubernator Zabaikal'ia: Kitai ushel daleko vpered," http://asiarussia.ru/news/8072/ (accessed 6/25/2015). Land leases to Mongolians are more popular. On amalgamation, see the interview with the Buryat State University economist Margarita Namkhanova, "Buryatiiu i Zabaikal predlozhily ob"edinit' v edinyi okrug," http://www.baikal-daily.ru/news/19/109675/ (accessed 12/25/2014).

11. In-migration into the republic was projected to decline in an official report on socioeconomic indicators for 2021–2022 put out before the pandemic worsened trends: https://egov-buryatia.ru/minec/activities/directions/strategicheskoe-upravlenie/strate gicheskoe-planirovanie/prognoz-ser-rb/, October 3, 2019 (accessed 6/5/2020).

12. "O vliianii Mongolii na Buryatiiu, ili spasibo russkim natsikam," http://asiarussia.ru/blogs/8370/ (accessed 7/30/2015). Alexei Tsydenov's 2018 visit to Mongolia included plans for numerous tri-lateral projects including China, https://www.montsame.mn/en/read/133183 (accessed 2/18/2020).

13. Official sources for republic subsidies and per capita incomes include *Statisticheskii ezhegodnik*, *Regiony Rossii*, and the prime minister's site on investment and subsidies in the Far East and Baikal area. Confirmation is from the Moscow State University economist Natalia Zubarevich, personal communication, May 14, 2015.

14. The source, http://hro.rightsinrussia.info/archive/abuse-of-psychiatry/nizovkina/ released, February 28, 2012 (accessed 3/12/2015) was removed by June 9, 2020.

15. Compare "FPLB Participates in Celebrations of the 350 Anniversary of Buryatia Joining Russia," http://baikalfund.ru/eng/news/article.wbp?article_id=b4e99bc9-f9b7-4ff0-841b-08379bcdbd45 (accessed 6/8/2020).

16. On Khamaganov's death in a possibly induced diabetic coma, see https://www.svoboda.org/a/28375607.html, March 17, 2017 (accessed 6/6/2020). On the attack, see http://www.rferl.org/content/opposition-journalist-buryatia-assaulted/27126448.html, July 14, 2015 (accessed 7/30/2015).

17. On the protests, see "Iz-za natsional'noi politiki na mitinge potrebovali otstavki glavy Buryatii," http://nazaccent.ru/content/14752-iz-za-nacionalnoj-politiki-na-mitinge-potrebovali.html; "Ot konflikta v BGU do nedoveriia k vlastiam Buryatii ozhidaemo 'povernul' miting v Ulan-Ude," http://ulanmedia.ru/news/society/08.02.2015/419778/ot-konflikta-v-bgu-do-nedoveriya-k-vlastyam-buryatii-ozhidaemo-povernul-quot.html (both accessed 2/17/2015); Paul Goble, "Buryat Protest over University Appointment Leads to Demand for Ouster of Republic Head," http://windowoneurasia2.blogspot.com/2015/02/buryat-protest-over-university.html, February 9, 2015 (accessed 2/9/2015).

18. On Bair Tsyrenov's protest, see "Deputat Bair Tsyrenov i 'magicheskoe kryl'tso' Khurala," http://gazeta-n1.ru/news/53721/. On "Russia's abandoned Far East," see http://www.rosbalt.ru/russia/2017/08/08/1637045.html (both accessed 6/8/2020). A link on the corruption scandal in the Natural Resources Ministry, http://newsbabr.com/bur/?IDE=163789, was removed by June 8, 2020.

19. https://egov-buryatia.ru/press_center/vystupleniya-glavy-buryatii/detail.php?ID=58935, February 22, 2020 (accessed 3/12/2020).

20. Tat'iana Ivashchenko, "Izuchenie buryatskogo iazyka: kak dobrovol'nost' stanovitsia problemoi," https://regnum.ru/news/society/2316840.html, September 4, 2017 (accessed 9/12/2017). The 2014 language program was titled "Preservation and Growth of the Buryat Language" and was given financial support through 2016.

21. See the epigraph of this chapter quoting Yeshen-Khorlo Dugarova-Montgomery. See also Abaeva 1998; "Celebration of the White Month: Sagaalgan comes to Baikal," https://1baikal.ru/en/istoriya/prazdnik-belogo-mesyatsa-na-baykal-prikhodit-sagaalgan (accessed 6/8/2020).

22. "Sayan Elders" was a gift manuscript already translated into English in 2000, when Bair Dugarov was my houseguest. For more on *Gésér* in Buryatia, see Bazarov 2006; Ratcliffe 2019. On the related *Gésar* revival in Mongolia, see Rubin 2015.

23. Data on epic, festival, and genealogy revival is from fieldwork. On language history, see Graber 2020; Montgomery 2005. Compare Chakars 2014, 265; Dugarova 2014, 152–53; Khilkhanova and Khilkhanov 2004.

24. Malanova and Vasil′eva 2007, 1. I am grateful to Tatiana and Dharm Hall for the 2020 gift of this glimpse into Buryat spiritual worlds through art.

25. I am grateful to Uliana Vinokurova, July 31, 2015, for this field observation. She explains that the monument was placed for the 2013 Ërdyn Games, celebrating Eurasian nomadic peoples. On the games, founded in 2010, see chapter 4.

26. This is a distillation of Zoja Morokhoeva's position, gleaned from many discussions and her presentation at Georgetown University when she was a Fulbright scholar working for a semester with me in 1995. See Morokhoeva 1995, 1998.

27. Personal communication, October 25, 2007. See Marina Saidukova, http://www.snob.ru/profile/28033/blog/71698 (accessed 11/18/2014), including on the unjust repression of her family, caught in a massive crackdown in 1940 as Mongolia sympathizers (https://snob.ru/profile/28033/blog/75748/, accessed 4/21/2021). See also "Sait buryatskogo naroda," http://www.buriatia.org (regularly accessed 2014–2020), featuring Buryat youth.

28. Personal communication with Irina Urbanaeva during the International Congress of Slavic Studies, Harrogate, July 22, 1990. See Urbanaeva 1994. The song and comment from Elena are from my 2005 field notes.

29. Compare Balzer 2012, 196–202; Dugarova 2014, 152–53; Humphrey 2002, 202–20; Quijada 2008, 1–22; Quijada 2019; Quijada et al. 2015, 258–72.

30. A 2015 *tailagan* is at "V Irkutskoi oblasti provedut buryatskii obriad pokloneniia reke," http://nazaccent.ru/content/tag/тайлаган (accessed 5/5/2021).

31. The phrase is discussed by Dugarova 2014, 152–54, and confirmed by interlocutors. Lists of kin-tribal groups vary in their order, partly depending on personal affiliations. Alphabetical here, these are the groups Abaev 2014 rails against in the epigraph as having *aimak-ulus* (tribal-local) ambitions.

32. On why it is a World Heritage Site, see "Lake Baikal," http://whc.unesco.org/en/list/754 (accessed 5/20/2020).

33. On certification of ecologically protected sites, see Shagzhiev 2015. Compare "Siberia's Sacred Lake Baikal," http://www.sacred-sites.org/threatened-sacred-sites/lake-baikal-2/lake-baikal-siberia/ (accessed 12/20/2019); RAIPON reports prepared before 2013; https://www.youtube.com/watch?v=-sGbLOhp1AM 7/16/2013 (accessed 12/20/2019).

34. https://egov-buryatia.ru/about_republic/geografic-and-weather/osobo-okhran yaemye-prirodnye-territorii/index.php?sphrase_id=990122 (accessed 5/6/2020). Most were established before 2012. Compare Henry 2010.

35. "V Ust′-Kutskom raione vysokopostavlennykh chinovnikov poimali za podzhogami lesa," http://www.ust-kut24.ru/?p=72454, April 28, 2020 (accessed 4/29/2020); https://tayga.info/154495, April 29, 2020 (accessed 5/6/2020). Illegal logging coverup has been a motive for arson in Siberia but is probably not relevant in this case.

36. I was honored to first meet Sergei Shapkhaev in 1989. For an obituary, see "Izvestnyi ekolog Sergei Shapkhaev skonchalsia v Buryatii," http://tvatv.ru/news/1/326810/?utm_source=yxnews&utm_medium=desktop&utm_referrer=https%3A%2F%2Fyandex.

ru%2Fnews (accessed 9/23/2019). His legacy continues with Save Baikal (SpasiBaikal), https://tayga.info/baykal (accessed 5/6/2020).

37. Compare its site, https://www.asi.org.ru/ngoprofile/047f5653b183292-139/, and the official Irkutsk designation, https://irkobl.ru/sites/ngo/public_faces/226180/ (both accessed 5/6/2020). See also Sarah Beckham Hooff's "Environmental Policy and Politics of Lake Baikal," https://geohistory.today/policy-politics-lake-baikal/ (2010 [accessed 8/11/2015]).

38. Data are from interviews with activists. On Baikal Environmental Wave, founded in 1992, and its co-founder Marina Rikhvanova (with Jennis Sutton), see http://baikal wave.blogspot.com/ (accessed 4/21/2021, for information up to 2010 with a warning of subsequent website server confiscation); Gleb Fedorov, http://rbth.com/science_and_tech/ 2014/09/16/saving_siberias_crown_jewel_state_program_aimsto_clean_up_l_39809.html (accessed 10/1/2014). See Pacific Environment's website, http://pacificenvironment.org (accessed 5/20/2020); Anna Nemtsova http://www.thedailybeast.com/articles/2013/11/09/ marina-rikhvanova-s-quest-to-save-russia-s-lake-baikal.html, November 9, 2013 (accessed 8/11/2015). See "Tvoi Irkutsk," http://www.irk.ru (accessed 5/20/2020), for updated coverage.

39. The grant is through the fund "Lake Baikal." See https://tayga.info/152465, February 25, 2020 (accessed 5/6/2020). Project coordinator is Inna Anikienko, a member of the young scientists' group Baikal Initiative.

40. On the plankton *epishura*, studied by an international group of scientists, see https://baikaldimensions.wordpress.com/2013/08/07/circumbaikal-cruise-preparations/ (accessed 8/23/2015). A 2017 review is https://1baikal.ru/en/ekologiya/what-can-be-done-with-the-legacy-of-the-baikalsk-pulp-and-paper-mill (accessed 5/20/2020).

41. Petr Netreba, "Kto vyigral i kto proigral ot sokrashchenii gosraskhodov," RBK-daily *RosBusinessConsulting*, https://www.rbc.ru/newspaper/2015/03/04/56bd135a9a794 7299f72c2cb, March 3, 2015 (accessed 5/14/2020).

42. Compare Dampilon 2011; Metzo 2009a; Metzo 2009b, 119–40.

43. Fieldnotes August 4, 2010. Compare Zhukovskaia 2004, 2010.

44. Compare Balzer 2012; Bernstein 2012; Morokhoeva 1995.

45. I am grateful to Uliana Vinokurova, July 31, 2015 for this Tunka Valley report.

46. Varfolomeeva 2019, 163. The Veps scholar Anna Varfolomeeva's excellent fieldwork in Akha for Central European University compares differential indigeneity in Karelia and Buryatia. Her material on Akha beautifully augments my field sources.

47. Its archive site is http://www.erkhe.narod.ru/index_ru.html (accessed 9/23/2019), Duu Ugékh Érkhé [Justice That Gives Voice] in Buryat. I am grateful to Zoja Morokhoeva, personal communication, August 19, 2015, for information on Érkhé. A March 4, 2007, protest letter after the hate-crime stabbing death of the young Buryat banker Nikolai Prokopiev, addressed to President Putin, remains on the site, http://erkhe.livejournal.com/ (accessed 5/20/2020). See http://radjana.livejournal.com/; http://sarvarupa.livejournal. com/49950.html (both accessed 6/9/2020).

48. Marina Saidukova, personal communication, October 25, 2007. See the site www. buryatia.org (accessed 5/20/2020) for analyses of current issues. See also Saidukova-Romanova 2007.

49. Fieldnotes, July 5–6, 2011, Petrazavodsk, Ninth Congress of Ethnographers and Anthropologists. The Buryat ethnosociologist was Oiuna Zhimbaevna Gonchikdorzhieva, presenting "Sovremennye mezhetnicheskie otnosheniia v selakh Buryatii."

50. Pavel Boronoev (2018, 10–16) cites data indicating suicides in Buryatia are double the national average. In a March 6, 2015, *Interfax* article, "Russians More Crisis-Resistant Than Europeans—Psychiatrist," Nikolai Neznanov, a psychiatrist at the Federal Supervision Service for Health Care, rationalized alarming data on high suicide rates in Russia,

especially for Finno-Ugrian and Buryat males, citing 60–70 cases per 100,000 per year in recent years, when the world average is 8–12.

51. Leisse and Leisse 2007, 784. This survey by European scholars asking blatantly political questions is unusual. Permission for foreigners to conduct surveys in Buryatia is difficult to obtain, and several more recent projects have been cancelled or curtailed. Compare Hagendoorn et al. 2008.

52. On the 2018 suicide case of Mergansana Amar, see https://crosscut.com/2019/06/asylum-seeker-vowed-never-return-russia-his-death-ice-custody-sent-him-back (accessed 9/23/2019).

53. See Anya Bernstein's excellent 2006 film *In Pursuit of the Siberian Shaman*, documentary educational resources, http://www.der.org/films/in-pursuit-of-siberian-shaman.html. Early in the film a Tatar interlocutor explains, "We all live on sacred Buryat land."

54. See Timur Badmatsyrenov (2015, 106), who explains that Buryats more often than Russians in the republic see themselves as religious, https://cyberleninka.ru/article/n/religioznaya-situatsiya-i-religioznye-soobschestva-v-respublike-buryatiya/viewer (accessed 5/20/2020). Compare Badmaev et al. 2020; Holland 2014.

55. See also Balzer 2012, 196–202; Bazarov 2000; Humphrey 2002; Quijada et al. 2015; Weir 2018; Zhukovskaia 2004.

56. For context on Buddhism in Russia, see Abaeva 1998; Badmaev et al. 2020; Balzer 2010; Bernstein 2013; Quijada 2019; Tsyrempilov 2009, 2013, 2016.

57. I am grateful to Uliana Vinokurova, July 31, 2015, for her fieldwork that deepened my understanding of a sacred site I had visited in 2010 without grasping its significance.

58. As Robert Montgomery points out (personal communication, June 7, 2020), Matvei Khangalov was a baptized Irkutsk Buryat with a Russian education. Zhamsaran Badmaev was also called Petr Badmaev and was an adviser to Nicholas II. Thus, some Buryat intellectuals were exemplars of Russian Orthodox cultural influences rather than Buddhist ones. See also Gusev and Grekova 1995; Kuz'min 2014; Montgomery 2005.

59. Early members of the repressed—to various degrees—Buryat Buddhist intelligentsia include the Tibet specialist Bazar Baradin (1878–1938); the journalist Mikhail Bogdanov (1878–1919); the Mongol specialist Gombozhav Tsybikov (1873–1930); the folklorist Tysben Zhamtsarano (1881–1942); and Bato-Dalai Ochirov (1875–1913). I am grateful to Robert Montgomery (November 25, 2019) for insights into their legacies. Leisse and Leisse (2007, 770) provide comparable repression figures for the Russian Orthodox community. For Russian Orthodox history in the region, see Murray 2013.

60. Montlevich 1992, 107. A Buddhist account of Samdan Tsydenov, the "last Dharma King of Buryatia," whose last name is the same as the head of the republic, is https://www.tsemrinpoche.com/tsem-tulku-rinpoche/great-lamas-masters/lubsan-samdan-tsydenov-the-dharma-king-of-buryatia (accessed 2/20/2020). This multisourced narrative plausibly claims that Tsydenov at least temporarily saved many Buryat Buddhist lives from Soviet revolutionaries by creating his "refuge kingdom."

61. Appropriately, Robert Montgomery (2005, 276) terms these Soviet slanders "surrealistic." Natalia Zhukovskaia first described the Dandaron tragedy to me on May 6, 1993. See Zhukovskaia 2010, 202–4.

62. For his work, see Dandaron 1995, 1997. Among those affected by and writing about the "affair" when and where they could, see Piatigorsky 1975; Semeka 1974, 1991. See also Baraev 1994, 84–91; Montlevich 1992, 107; Montlevich 1993, 42–45.

63. The popular power of the Étigelov phenomenon is confirmed in numerous conversations. Dramatic coverage on Dashi-Dordzho Étigelov (also Itigelov) is widespread, for example, "Poslanie Khambo Lami Étigelova," directed by Yamzhina Vasileva for the TV company Arig Us, 2012, https://www.youtube.com/watch?v=-yPsNh3PHcc (accessed 7/15/2015). See also Bernstein 2013; and Quijada 2012, 2019.

64. Despite their differences, Tsydenov congratulated Aiusheev on his twenty-fifth anniversary as Khambo Lama. The Khambo Lama's authority is distorted in the press to the extent that it is difficult to judge whether his religious conservatism amounts to male chauvinism, since he is defended by Buryat women in his community. On the feminist scandal, see Aleksei Belov, "Patriarkhat i ovtsy kak skrepy buryatskogo buddizma," http://www.ng.ru/ng_religii/2020-02-18/12_481_buddhism.html; on relations with Tsydenov, see Ekaterina Ermenko, "Alekseia Tsydenova obvinili v raskole," https://www.kommersant.ru/doc/4142054 (both accessed 3/29/2020). For positive views, see Amogolonova 2015; Bernstein 2013, 101. For a mixed assessment, see Garri 2014, 92, 348. On *The Atlas of Tibetan Medicine* in Buryatia, see Avedon 1998; Liudmila Klasanova, https://www.buddhistdoor.net/news/museum-of-history-of-buryatia-holds-20th-anniversary-exhibition-of-the-atlas-of-tibetan-medicine (accessed 3/29/2020). On controversy over its travel, see Quijada 2019, 135; Zhukovskaia 2010, 219.

65. The quote is from Uliana Vinokurova's conversation with D. Shaglakhaev in July 2015 in Sayan, as he cited his mentor (personal communication, July 31, 2015). My data on Lama Danzan-Khaibzun Samaev was augmented by Zoja Morokhoeva (personal communication, August 19, 2015). See also the Tunka website on sacred places, http://tunkarb.ru/obitel-sagaan-ubgena/?commentId=190 (accessed 3/29/2020).

66. The movement's motto was "akhimsa-altruizm-ariun" [nonviolence, altruism, pure living]. On the treasure-recovery and Ter tradition in Buddhism, see Germano 1998, 53–94. On its resonance within the Buryat Buddhist revival, see Bernstein 2013, 91–98.

67. The quote is from Uliana Vinokurova's July 2015 fieldwork in Sayan. See also Dorzhigushaeva 2002; Shaglakhaev 2014. For context, see Filatov 2014; Karnyshev and Ivanova 2014.

68. The term "totem" has a long, controversial history in anthropology, to the extent that I would avoid it if my interlocutors were not using it themselves. Its adjectival form "totemic" is often more appropriate. Compare the animism literature, including the perspectivist incarnations of Descola 1994; Viveiros de Castro 2014; and Willerslev 2007.

69. I am grateful to Uliana Vinokurova, July 2015, for pointing out these contrasting sculptures, and for interviews in 2015 that highlighted various reactions to them.

70. This seemingly minor incident has serious implications, given how polarized and mutually insulted people became over it. See "Kto raskachivaet mezhnatsional'nye otnosheniia v Buryatii?," http://asiarussia.ru/news/8408/ (accessed 7/23/2015); Paul Goble, "Buryats Invoke UN Declaration on Indigenous Peoples to Block Monument Honoring Cossacks," http://windowoneurasia2.blogspot.com/2015/07/buryats-invoke-un-declaration-on.html 7/23/2015 (accessed 7/23/2015).

71. See "Ustanovku skul'ptury 'Khranitel' Baikala' perenesli na oktiabr'," http://irkutskmedia.ru/news/622157/, September 13, 2017 (accessed 9/13/2017); https://www.irk.ru/news/20170913/sculpture/, September 13, 2017 (accessed 9/13/2017). See also Dashi's website, http://www.dashi-art.com/, and discussion of another of his famous statues (in Kyzyl), *The Royal Hunt*, in chapter 4.

72. Compare Balzer 2012, 196–202; Bernstein, *In Pursuit of the Siberian Shaman*, which features Valentin Khagdaev and includes an amusing splicing of the Russian Orthodox priest juxtaposed to the shaman, http://www.der.org/films/in-pursuit-of-siberian-shaman.html (accessed 7/23/2015).

73. "Coast Busters: Building on Sacred Lake Baikal Land," https://www.rferl.org/a/russia-baikal/28575045.html?ltflags=mailer (accessed 6/27/2017). On the "destruction of sacred forest on Olkhon," see http://fedpress.ru/article/1823480 (accessed 5/20/2020). On development on Olkhon, see https://www.washingtonpost.com/world/2021/04/01/russia-baikal-tourism-environment/?itid=ap_isabellekhurshudyan (accessed 4/21/2021).

74. A petition for a Baikal Republic is one variation on amalgamation, discussed in Conclusions. See Bernstein (2013, 213–14) on support for amalgamation by the Russian Duma deputy Boris Gryzlov, echoed by the Buryat State University economist Margarita Namkhanova, "Buryatiiu i Zabaikal predlozhily ob"edinit' v edinyi okrug," http://www. baikal-daily.ru/news/19/109675/ (accessed 12/25/2014). Some amalgamation proposals are trying to differentiate economic zones from political ones, but it is difficult to see how this can be sustainable.

3. REPUBLIC OF TYVA (TUVA)

1. Tuvan is a Russified form of the more accurate Tyvan ethnonym. On the language and language politics, see especially Anderson and Harrison 1999; Ondar 2011; Seden-Khuurak 2003; Tanova 2006.

2. Compare Anderson 1991; Baiburin, Kelley, and Vakhtin 2012; Balzer 2010, 2017; Humphrey 1998; Tal'taeva 2001; Vinokurova 2017, 2018.

3. I am not suggesting structural or moral equivalents concerning underlying causes of these cases. See especially Roeder 2018. Compare Dunn and Bobick 2014; Hagendoorn et al. 2008; Protsyk and Harzl 2013.

4. Igor Irgit, http://tuvapravda.ru/?q=content/vernyom-nazvanie-uranhay, September 7, 2017 (accessed 9/22/2017). Paul Goble's "Calls to Restore the Chinese Name for Tuva Rile Russians," http://windowoneurasia2.blogspot.com/search?q=Tuvans&max-results=20&by-date=true, September 19, 2017 (accessed 9/22/2017), alerted me to this example of the book's theme. Compare Ostrovskikh 1899.

5. On Russian reaction, including quotes from Boris Myshliavstev and Anatoly Savostin, see the anonymous editorial in https://regnum.ru/news/polit/2323276.html, September 18, 2017, with excellent accompanying photographs (accessed 9/22/2017).

6. For samples of twentieth-century Tyvan history, see Alatalu 1992; Anaiban 1998–1999; Aranchyn 1984; Dulov 2013 [1956]; Kabo 1934; Mongush 1993; Potapov 1964. See especially Bicheldei 2014.

7. For official news coverage, see http://www.tuva.asia/news/tuva (accessed 5/20/2020). See also the websites of President Vladimir Putin and Head of the Republic of Tyva Sholban Kara-ool. Most interviews with Tyvan interlocutors after September 2014 need to remain anonymous.

8. See Sergei Shoigu et al. 1997, 2005, 2006–2007, 2007–2008. On him, see Rzhevskii 2005.

9. See Bicheldei 2010, 2014. I have collected data and news reports on Kaadyr-ool Alekseevich Bicheldei since the early 1990s and interviewed him in his parliament office (the Grand Khural) on June 14, 2005. Sadly, his pragmatism may have taken a turn toward corruption, given that in 2017 he was accused, while minister of education in 2013, of having manipulated bids for an Academy of Sciences institute building. He was removed from the ministry and yet allowed to become director of the national museum. On the corruption trial and denunciations, see "Bitva za bablo: Kak Bicheldei ochistil karmany gosudarstva," http://risk-inform.ru/article_7006.html, no. 46 (November 21, 2017); "Zatiazhnyi boi . . .," http://risk-inform.ru/article_8000.html, no. 19 (May 21, 2019 [both accessed 1/23/2020]).

10. "V Khaiyrakanskoi srednei shkole Tuvy proshli ocherednye Bicheldeeskie chteniia," https://www.tuva.asia/news/tuva/8989-bicheldeevskie-chteniya.html, March 31, 2017 (accessed 4/4/2017).

11. Data come from anonymous interviews in the past twenty years, and especially from an unpublished Institute of Ethnography report given to me in 1991 by its lead author, the late Maria Ia. Zhornitskaia, who headed a crucial government-ordered

fact-finding trip. Her report was "Natsional'naia situatsiia v Tyvinskoi ASSR i Khakasskoi AO (mai–iiun' 1990 g.), written with carbon copies in December 1990.

12. These 2020 recollections must be uncredited due to their sensitivity.

13. This speaker, originally from Shagonar, prefers anonymity.

14. Sociodemographic data and projections were published for 2020–2024 at http://gov.tuva.ru/press_center/news/politics/42193/?clear_cache=Y, April 16, 2020 (accessed 6/5/2020). Fuller official data published in 2012 are at http://www.gks.ru/free_doc/new_site/perepis2010/perepis_itogi1612.htm (accessed 6/5/2020).

15. Zhornitskaia 1990 report. For context, see Anaiban 1998–1999; Anaiban 2005; Anaiban and Balakina 2015; Balakina and Anaiban 1995; Boiko 1983; Lamazhaa 2012; Pimenova 2007.

16. The setting for this conversation was Delphi, Greece, 2015.

17. Viktor Petrov, a Russian journalist who grew up in Tyva, considers Tyva's isolation and ethnic tensions dangerous: "Tuvinskaia iama" (The Tuvan Pit), http://svpressa.ru/blogs/article/152246/ (2016 [accessed 8/23/2017]). He complains of a twenty-five-year outflow of disillusioned and scared Russians, including his family and friends. Compare the memoir by Roman Senchin (2012).

18. The speaker prefers anonymity. The parentheses on clan explanations are the speaker's, as is the word "clan." See also Balzer 2019.

19. For the October 1993 Constitution, see the website of the Republic of Tuva, http://gov.tuva.ru/, under documents (accessed 1/23/2020).

20. For language statistics and background, see Anderson and Harrison 1999. For language politics, see http://tuva.asia/news/tuva/7984-otkrytoe-pismo.html, June 2, 2015 (accessed 5/20/2020). See also Baldanov 1998.

21. See Paul Goble, "Tuvans Protest Plan to make their Native Tongue 'Second Foreign Language' in Republic Schools" http://windowoneurasia2.blogspot.com/2015/06/tuvans-protest-plan-to-make-their.html, June 2, 2015 (accessed 6/3/2015).

22. The document was published as Bavuu-Siorion, M. V. et al., "Open Letter," http://www.tuva.asia/news/tuva/7984-otkrytoe-pismo.html, June 2, 2015 (accessed 5/15/2020).

23. On the teachers' association, see https://www.tuva.asia/news/tuva/8571-tyva-dyl.html, March 31, 2016 (accessed 5/15/2020). On the history of Russians in Tyva, see Tatarintseva and Mollerov 2017. Compare Viktor Petrov, http://svpressa.ru/blogs/article/152246/ (2016 [accessed 8/23/2017]).

24. Compare Levin with Süzükei 2006, 29, including a musical prayer at an *ovaa*, track 2, DVD.

25. An October 4, 2009, report on the disaster was published by the Federal Environmental, Technological, and Atomic Supervisory Service (Rostekhnadzor) but soon removed from its website. See instead http://engineeringfailures.org/?p=703#sthash.uFaq6YGx.dpuf (accessed 1/13/2016).

26. See https://www.tuvaonline.ru/2017/09/05/oleg-budargin-lep-iz-hakasii-cherez-tyvu-mozhet-proyti-v-mongoliyu.html (accessed 9/20/2017); https://www.tuvaonline.ru/economy/ (accessed 1/13/2016). For a 2015–2020 plan to improve Tyva's ecology, clean up the most egregious Soviet legacy sites, and create more protection zones, see https://www.tuvaonline.ru/2014/10/21/v-tuve-planiruyut-pereizdat-krasnuyu-knigu-i-sozdat-novye-zakazniki-i-zapovedniki.html (accessed 6/15/2020). For development plans through 2030, see https://medium.com/@RBaisarov/massive-developments-underway-in-tuva-f731521933b9 (accessed 4/22/2021).

27. Zoya Anaiban, personal communication email, March 18, 2015.

28. The effort began well under the Sacred Earth Network's Russian representative Alexander Arbachakov in 1999 but has been less successful in recent years. Some

groups and activists named in Arbachakov's report remain engaged—for example, Lilia Kyrgysovna Arakchaa, http://sacredearthnetwork.org/Newsletters/ENews13p1.html#anchor541264, July 29, 1999 (accessed 5/20/2020).

29. The road corridor project was touted, among other places, in a feature magazine article "Republiki Tyva: Tsentr Azii," *Rossiiskaia munitsipal'naia praktika*, no. 4 (2017): 63–95, without mentioning that Kyzyl and Ürümchi compete for the distinction of being the "Center of Asia," http://www.promweekly.ru/archive/rmp/2017/RMP_4_2017.pdf (accessed 3/17/2021).

30. This complex, seen in 2005, has become more elaborate. See Olga Gertcyk, https://siberiantimes.com/science/casestudy/features/f0212-focus-on-tuva-stunning-treasures-and-macabre-slaughter-in-siberias-prehistoric-valley-of-the-kings/, February 11, 2016 (accessed 5/20/2020).

31. Personal communication, June 14, 2005.

32. http://kasparov.ru/material.php?id=597E2C1D3F79B (accessed 8/1/2017). Compare Konev and Lomachenko 1998; Government statistics 2004, 2010.

33. Aldynai Seden-Khuurak, personal communication, February 15, 2005; see also Seden-Khuurak 2003.

34. Much visual evidence of the 2014 enthronement disappeared by May 2020. My description also comes from observers who attended. For context, see Poppe 1958.

35. See https://www.buddhistdoor.net/news/russia-orders-buddhist-leader-shiwalha-rinpoche-to-be-permanently-deported, October 7, 2015 (accessed 5/19/2020). Chinese political pressure, due to Shiwalha Rinpoche's association with the Dalai Lama, was said to be the cause.

36. The reassertion of the Khambo (also Khamby) Lama as head of the Buddhist community was made official in 1997. On the 2005 consecration, see https://www.tuva online.ru/2005/04/02/kambylama.html (accessed 5/20/2020). On politics of number eight, see https://vcatuva.ru/news/2019/12/19/8870.html; http://savetibet.ru/2019/12/21/tuva-kamby-lama.html; https://www.tuvaonline.ru/2019/12/01/nastoyatel-hrama-ustuu-huree-dzhampel-lodoy-izbran-kamby-lamoy-tuvy.html (all accessed 2/3/2020). On the ninth installation, see https://www.buddhistdoor.net/news/ninth-kamby-lama-elected-in-tuva-republic (accessed 4/22/2021).

37. Data on shamanic politics is based on fieldwork in Tyva and with Tyvans abroad. It fits with an excellent summary by Ksenia Pimenova, although she refrains from calling Kenin-Lopsan a shaman. She notes his self-proclaimed title "president for life of all Tuvan shamans" (Pimenova 2013, 133). My interviews with Kenin-Lopsan plus observations at a symposium in Garmisch, Germany in 2000 indicate that by 2000 he went beyond pride in his shamanic ancestry into full-regalia shamanic ritual with a drum. For views of shamanic practices and glimpses of the beauty of Tyvan natural surroundings as spiritual inspiration, see Svetlana Stasenko's 2017 film *Shamanic Lessons for Beginners* from Passenger Studio, and my review (Balzer 2020).

38. Compare http://nazaccent.ru/content/23715-v-tuve-prezentovali-knigu-sudba-sha manki.html 4/10/2017; https://www.tuva.asia/news/tuva/8996-kniga.html 4/7/2017 (both accessed 5/20/2020). See Kenin-Lopsan 1995, 2006, 2010, 2017.

39. Personal communication, December 29, 2019.

40. The quote from Kenin-Lopsan is from his chastising public letter against a slur by Minister of Defense Sergei Ivanov in 2006 associating shamans with fakery, published by Kenin-Lopsan with Likhanova 2006. Compare Calazans, Van Alpern, and Wunderlich 1997. In the United States, fascination with Tyva was expressed by the Friends of Tuva movement and the delightful film *Genghis Blues*, https://www.youtube.com/watch?v=-_xlbCq0WTw 2013 (accessed 5/19/2020).

41. See https://www.youtube.com/watch?v=8aUTLrKGnTw, March 23, 2010 (accessed 5/19/2020); https://www.pnmartists.com/ (accessed 5/19/2020).

42. To follow these events and related ones, including free online *khomus* lessons from masters during the coronavirus pandemic, see https://en.tuvaonline.ru/ (accessed 5/19/2020).

43. My sources are mostly official Russian sites and news coverage, with added perspective from friends knowledgeable about Tyva. For Russian coverage of this incident, see https://meduza.io/feature/2017/08/03/v-sverdlovskoy-oblasti-proizoshla-massovaya-draka-kontraktnikov-v-tsentralnom-voennom-okruge-schitayut-chto-eto-bytovoy-konflikt (accessed 9/20/2017); https://ura.news/news/1052299414, August 3, 2017 (accessed 9/20/2017); https://www.nakanune.ru/news/2017/8/3/22478334/ (accessed 9/20/2017); https://www.nakanune.ru/news/2017/8/9/22478883/ (accessed 9/20/2017). Compare Paul Goble, "Clash between Tuvin and Ethnic Russian Soldiers at Training Academy Turns Violent," http://windowoneurasia2.blogspot.com/2017/08/clash-between-tuvin-and-eth nic-russian.html (accessed 8/3/2017).

44. Gudkov also pointed out that Tyva, at 168,000 square kilometers, is bigger than Austria or Hungary, and six times larger than Crimea, at only 28,000 square kilometers. See his http://www.mk.ru/politics/2016/01/02/ironiya-imperii-ili-kyzyl-nash.html (accessed 1/3/2016). Compare Viktor Petrov, http://svpressa.ru/blogs/article/152246/ (2016 [accessed 8/23/2017]).

45. See also conclusions to the book; Paul Goble, "Putin's Regional Amalgamation Plan Faces Court Challenge," http://windowoneurasia2.blogspot.com/2015/03/putins-regional-amalgamation-plan-faces.html, March 9, 2015 (accessed 3/9/2015); and Rafael Khakimov, "Moskva lish' by grabit' i otnimat'," https://www.idelreal.org/a/30259693.html, January 18, 2020 (accessed 1/22/2020).

46. Compare Balzer 1999; Balzer, Petro and Robertson 2001 on "cultural entrepreneurs"; and Giuliano 2011.

47. This argument is inspired by Prasenjit Duara (1996). Compare Thomas Eriksen and Marek Jacoubek's (2019) revisiting of Fredrik Barth's theories of ethnic boundary dynamics as based on social interaction rather than specific kinds of cultural content.

48. The interlocutors cited in these political quotes must remain anonymous. On Shoigu in the news, see https://jamestown.org/program/russias-defense-minister-shoigu-coro navirus-and-relentless-military-modernization/, March 25, 2020 (accessed 4/23/2021); http://www.spectator.co.uk/2015/12/silent-strongman-sergey-shoigu-is-the-real-force-behind-russias-military-aggression/ (accessed 9/20/2016); and https://24smi.org/celebrity/367-sergej-shojgu.html (accessed 5/20/2020). For a 2017 review of his career, see https://www.tuva.asia/news/tuva/9030-shoygu-v-smi.html (accessed 8/24/2017).

49. This point, a theme of the book, is similar to one that Brian Donohoe (2012) has made concerning the significance of naming for Russia's Indigenous peoples' changing legal claims. Our independently reached arguments correlate at various levels of ethnonational-territorial categorization within Russia, but republic identity and loyalty are especially salient.

50. The 1933–1939 Tyva People's Republic seal had the sun behind rather than in front of the rider, and from 1941 to 1962 the rider was reversed. From 1962 to 1992, when Tyva was an "autonomous republic" inside the Soviet Union, the rider disappeared in favor of a hammer and sickle. The post-1992 seal again has a dashing rider facing the sun, presumably east. My friend's 2020 comment, "Look closely—there was a time when on this seal the rider pointed to the east, and then they changed it to point to the west," uncovered an even more complex story. See this book's cover and "Gerb Tyvy," https://ru.wikipedia.org/wiki/Герб_Тывы (accessed 5/5/2021).

51. On ecology activism and its relationship to nationalism, compare Dawson 1996; Donohoe 2009; Henry 2010, 2018.

52. Listing generalized, eclectic traits as culturally sustainable potentially renders them frozen in time and commensurate. However, Inna Tarbastaeva, based in Novosibirsk and born in Tyva, has the background, education, and political awareness to be sensitive to varied ways in which these "calling card" strengths may change or be used strategically. She combines insider and outsider analysis, problematizing categories of "emic," and "etic." Personal correspondence, March 2, 2020.

4. CROSSOVER TRENDS

1. Nikolay Trubetzkoy in 1925 famously proclaimed, "By its very nature Eurasia is historically destined to comprise a single state entity," quoted in Trubetzkoy 1991, 164–65. See Gumilev (1912–1992) 2009. Compare Bassin 2016; Clover 2015; Laruelle 2008. The founding congress of the political movement Eurasia, led by Alexander Dugin with forty-nine delegates from forty-eight regions of Russia is at http://eurasia.com.ru/stenogramma.html (accessed 6/2/2020).

2. See especially Tagangaeva 2015. In addition, a statue honoring Lev Gumilev has been erected in Tatarstan.

3. I am grateful to Brian Donahoe for sharing details of this project, email, August 22, 2017. See also http://www.supagro.fr/tradpro/?lang=en# (accessed 8/2/2016). On the significance of food sovereignty and the "slow food" movement for Indigenous people, see Whyte 2017; Mihesuah and Hoover 2019.

4. See http://gov.tuva.ru/press_center/news/economy/32353/, August 21, 2017 (accessed 8/22/2017, missing 4/26/2021).

5. In Sakha, a valued breed of small cattle is called *ynagha*, in Buryatia the breed sponsored by the Khambo Lama is Mongolian. In Tyva, yak breeding is also being revived.

6. Announcing the coalition, Lev Ponomaryev applauded activists who were "forgetting their fear," and stated, "We know at a minimum that thirty regions in the country have seen civic protest against ecological problems," https://www.svoboda.org/a/30303054.html (accessed 12/6/2019). It is doubtful that protests could reach US Standing Rock or Canadian Trans Mountain levels of multiethnic Indigenous solidarity mobilization.

7. For comparative coverage, see Kendra Pierre-Louise, "The Amazon, Siberia, Indonesia: A World of Fire," https://www.nytimes.com/2019/08/28/climate/fire-amazon-africa-siberia-worldwide.html (accessed 9/4/2019). For perspective on Siberia in the context of international scholarship on Indigenous knowledge, climate change, and ecology, including issues of controlled or "cultural burns," see Solovyeva 2021.

8. "Za posledovatel'nuiu demokratizatsiiu i federalizatsiiu Rossii (Poslanie Presidentu Rossiiskoi Federatsii B. N. El'tsinu)." *Panorama-forum* 1995, no. 1: 3–4, reprinted in Balzer 1998, 8–11, signed by Mintimir Shaimiev, President, Republic of Tatarstan; Murtaza Rakhimov, President, Republic of Bashkortostan; and Mikhail Nikolaev, President, Republic of Sakha (Yakutia).

9. See Nathans 2016 for a review of several recent books on Russia, including Clover 2015.

10. http://www.dashi-art.com/en/news (accessed 8/22/2017). See also Tagangaeva 2015, 52.

11. Bodrov interview with T. V. Khoroshilova, "Chem sila, brat?" *Rossiiskaia gazeta*, http://www.rg.ru/2006/12/15/bodrov.html, December 15, 2006 (accessed 5/22/2020). He mentioned consulting with a shaman for the film *Mongol*, http://www.imdb.com/title/tt0416044/ (accessed 8/22/2017). Bodrov is known for his 1996 film on the North

Caucasus, *Kavkazskii plennik* (Prisoner of the Mountains). On its cultural significance and tropes, see Grant 2005.

12. I kept notes from the surrealistic conversations I had with them, since this was one of my postmodern, "interpretive anthropology" awakenings, when I realized that a renewed, nostalgic nationalism was shaping post-Soviet approaches, including in Mongolia. Samples of the Genghis Khan boom include Juvaini 1997; Man 2013; Weatherford 2005. See also Shimamura 2014 for an important perspective on why Mongols in Mongolia claim Genghis Khan as a more exclusive ancestor, considering Buryats a separate and less equal group.

13. For the film, see https://www.youtube.com/watch?v=JeDIVeYYOxY. For review samples, see http://news.bbc.co.uk/2/hi/entertainment/7415373.stm; http://www.artsan dopinion.com/2009_v8_n6/genghiskahn.htm (all accessed 8/2/2016). The dream of dramatizing a Sakha ancestor epic hero was fulfilled by Nikita Arzhakov's 2020 Sakha-language film *Tygyn Darkhan*: https://www.sakha.gov.ru/news/front/view/id/3221536; https://www.youtube.com/watch?v=mqY_WpWwpIY; trailer at https://www.youtube.com/watch?v=HzHz7jN6-B4 (all accessed 1/19/2021).

14. This is similar to the idea behind the 2017 and 2019 government-supported Kazakh films *Kazakh Khanate: Diamond Sword* and its sequel *Kazakh Khanate: Golden Throne*, directed by Rustem Abdrashev, set in fifteenth-century "Eurasia."

15. For background, see Basilov 1989. An ambitious exhibit on the "tribal" Scythians in London's British Museum was mounted in 2017. The famed British reviewer Peter Aspden proclaimed them relatively obscure and exotic, albeit known to Herodotus, https://www.ft.com/content/96cca90c-7c63-11e7-ab01-a13271d1ee9c (accessed 8/23/2017).

16. On the Lev Gumilev Center, based in Moscow, see https://www.gumilev-center.ru/about/ (accessed 5/30/2020). On Orkhon (also written Orhun in Turkish), see the magnificent folio-sized reprint volume published in Turkey of V. V. Radloff's famous atlas (original 1892–1899). This volume epitomizes the cultural diplomacy of Turkic civilizational solidarity.

17. See Gogolev 1986, 1992, 1993, 1994, 2002. For comparable Buryat "roots" research, see the work of Bilikto Bazarov and Denis Miyagashev. See also Generalov 1982; Shinkareva 2006. With the doctor and others, probing implications of multiple Sakha aggressions against various local Indigenous communities was awkward. "Paleo-Asiatic" is now a discredited linguistic category with important ramifications for Yukaghir history.

18. Uliana Vinokurova, personal email communication, September 9, 2016. See also Vinokurova 2017. For cliff art documentation and periodization, see Okladnikov 1970. Background includes http://ysia.ru/glavnoe/yurij-kupriyanov-poruchil-aktivizirovat-mezhregionalnoe-sotrudnichestvo-po-sohraneniyu-shishkinskih-pisanits/; "Shishkinskii pisanitsy," https://www.youtube.com/watch?v=_rNW39qY1hk; http://baikaler.ru/guide/sight/shishkinskie_pisanicy/ (all accessed 6/2/2020).

19. The 2021 conference with multiple institutional sponsors was in honor of the eightieth birthday of linguist and jaw harp virtuoso Ivan Egorovich Alekseyev, "Khomus Jubaan." The prize-winning book is Levin 2013. A Baikal-Nauka March 31, 2014 announcement was picked up the same day by https://www.tuva.asia/news/ruregions (accessed 8/22/2017).

20. http://ruskline.ru/news_rl/2016/07/04/etnolingvisticheskij_konflikt/; Paul Goble, http://windowoneurasia2.blogspot.com/2016/07/russias-parties-must-address-fate-of.html (both accessed 8/2/2016). Compare Laruelle 2018, 2021.

21. I was naively flabbergasted at the outcry among Russian colleagues when I published an issue of my journal *Anthropology and Archeology of Eurasia* under the title "Alphabet Wars" (Balzer 2007), highlighting debates about making the Latin alphabet the renewed basis for Turkic language writing in the Sakha Republic and Tatarstan.

Anthropology colleagues in Moscow were furious that I had used "wars" to describe a debate they were hoping to downplay. Soon after, legislation was passed in the Russian Duma forbidding republics to return their languages to the Latin alphabet, something that had been common in the 1920s and early 1930s, as well as forbidding the designation of English as a third republic language. Early in the Putin period, an internationally oriented Sakha friend was fired from his high-level government job for advocating that the republic have three state languages, with English as the third.

22. Note the word "wiki" comes from Hawaiian, meaning "quick." For the Tyvan site, see https://tyv.wikipedia.org/wiki/Кол_арын (accessed 5/22/2020).

23. For the Buryat site, see https://bxr.wikipedia.org/wiki (accessed 5/22/2020).

24. For the Sakha site, see https://sah.wikipedia.org/wiki (accessed 5/22/2020). Other Sakha links include Сайт якутской молодежи, Форумы по улусам, Саха Диаспора, Якутск On-line. See especially https://sakhaopenworld.org/ (accessed 5/5/2021).

25. The author is Буөтур Тобуруокап in Sakha. The translation is mine with the help of Vera Solovyeva, 2017.

26. Brian Donahoe, personal communication, August 22, 2017. The Kandidat degree is between an MA and a PhD in level of qualification.

27. For the announcement and report, see http://www.tuva.asia/news/russia/8790-anons.html; http://www.rad.pfu.edu.ru/newsletter-1/newsletters2016_files/the-first-international-scientific-conference-dedicated-to-the-problems-of-turkology-abmodern-problems-of-the-turkology-language-literature-culturebb (both accessed 8/22/2017). I was honored to help host Olzhas Suleimeinov at Georgetown University in the early 1990s.

28. See http://www.19rus.info/index.php/kultura-i-sport/item/34683-forum-etnova-soberet-molodezh-v-askize; http://xakac.info/news/53993; https://vk.com/ethnova (all accessed 5/22/2020).

29. On Kremlin-sponsored Nashi youth camps, see http://www.thedailybeast.com/articles/2011/08/10/kremlin-s-extremist-youth-camp-in-russia.html, updated July 13, 2017; http://content.time.com/time/photogallery/0,29307,1646809_1416342,00.html (both accessed 5/22/2020).

30. For a taste of the "silk way rally" culturally inflected hype, see https://www.youtube.com/watch?v=dcJ5qS_VLOg&vl=en, February 12, 2020 (accessed 6/8/2020).

31. For the 2017 games, see https://ok.ru/erdgames. For 2019, see https://ok.ru/erdgames/photos (both accessed 5/22/2020). A local ethnographic museum is named for Matvei Nikolaevich Khangalov. See his 1889 classic on Buryat folklore and reprints of his work, including Bazarov 2010. See also Dugarov 1991.

32. Information on the games stems from happy participants and proud organizers, as well as excellent press coverage such as http://www.vesti14.ru/ru/12/cultureandsport/222/ (accessed 7/18/2015); http://www.rodnie-berega.ru/news/78-jordynskie-igry (accessed 9/22/2016); https://ok.ru/erdgames (accessed 8/28/2017).

33. These examples barely scratch the surface of the art revival in Turkic and Mongolic republics. An issue of my journal was devoted to it (Balzer 2015), as is the life work of the art historian Zinaida Ivanova-Unarova (e.g., 2000, 2008), whose June 17, 2020, emails added cases such as Alexander Manzhurev's 2016 show in Kyzyl. Buryats presented a 2017 exhibition, "Liki Gésériady [Images from the Gésér Epos]," at the Yakutsk National Museum, directed by Asia Gabysheva. The Sakha artist Anna Osipova gifted her abstract painting *Tengrianets*, evoking a blue sky, to the Kyzyl National Museum for a 2018 exhibit honoring the Uriankhai warrior Subedei-Maadyr. Artists best representing these trends include Mikhail Starostin (the climate change example), Tuiaara Shaposhnikova (painting), Antonina Fillipova (fantasy clothing) in Sakha; Dashi Namdakov (sculpture), Zorikto Dorzhiev (painting), and Bato-Munko Chimitov (bone carving) in Buryatia; and

Leonid Urjuk (prints), Syldys Oiudup (design), Alexander Baranmaa (sculpture), and Éres Baidyndy (from a carving dynasty) in Tyva.

34. Ondar, "master of a vocal art," was given a *New York Times* obituary by Margalit Fox when he died in 2013, the same year he performed at the Rose Parade (*New York Times*, August 4, 2013, 20). On the memorial, described by interlocutors and widely covered, see https://www.tuvaonline.ru/; https://www.tuva.asia/news (both accessed 5/22/2020).

35. For historical perspective, see Landau 1995; Zenkovsky 1960. For a sample of debates, see Svyataslav Knyazev, "Russia vs. "Pan-Turkism": Problems and Opportunities from Gasprinsky to Hitler and NATO," http://www.fort-russ.com/2015/12/russia-vs-pan-turkism-problems-and.html, December 6, 2015 (accessed 1/9/2015).

36. See also Kolstø and Blakkisrud 2016; and the 2017 *Nationalities Papers* 45(4) book symposium in their honor with participants J. Paul Goode (707–10); Oxana Shevel (710–13); Igor Zevelev (713–16); authors' comments (716–19).

37. Lena Fedorova (2012) is the author of *Spiritual Basis of Eurasianism*. See also Krivoshapkin-Aiynga 1998. On claims of *tengrianstvo* to combat crisis and corruption, see an interview with Kazakhstan's Aidyn Olzhaev, "Kak Tengrianstvo mozhet spasti ot krizisa i korruptsiia?," 365info.kz, October 4, 2015, reposted on the Sakha website of Afanasy Nikolaev, http://yakutiafuture.ru, September 4, 2016 (accessed 9/4/2016).

38. Authors include two lamas—the Buryat Norbu Aiusheev, Khambo Lama of Buryatia's Okin datsan, and the Tyvan lama Roman Ludup (Sundui-Bashki). Scholars include N. V. Abaev, L. L. Abaeva, and T. I. Garmaeva. See Garmaeva and Abaev 2017. Nikolai V. Abaev, cited in the chapter on Tyva, embodies cross-republic cooperation as professor of philosophy at Tuva State University, a deputy to the Grand Khural of Tyva, and head of the Laboratory of Synergistic Research on Eurasia of the Institute of Inner Asia at the Buryat State University in Ulan-Ude. See his profile at https://www.tuva.asia/persons/82-abaev.html (accessed 5/22/2020).

39. "Nomads of the Great Steppe," https://ok.ru/group/52425173303350/topic/65810 042732598 (accessed 8/28/2017), was replaced by similar text on a "Kalmyk customs" site dated July 24, 2016, with the same link (accessed 5/22/2020). Translation mine.

40. See *Shaman idet!* (Shaman on the Move), https://www.youtube.com/watch?v= zPrb_1nWXtE, June 12, 2019 (accessed when released and 3/19/2020). Many videos are listed under "Shaman idet" and "Put' shamana," [Shaman's Path], e.g., https://www.you tube.com/watch?v=W1jE71TAqZw. See also "Shaman protiv Putin" (Shaman vs. Putin), https://www.youtube.com/watch?v=tfTEtiqDf6U, June 24, 2019 (all accessed 7/3/2019). Some Alexander videos have disappeared from the internet since I first saw them. Some are professional journalism, from the Russian TV of Free Europe (RFE under http://svo boda.org) or the relatively independent Russian NTV: for example, "Pochemu Kremlin ob"iavil voinu Shamanu—Grazhdanskaia oborona" (Why Did the Kremlin Fight the Shaman—Civil Defense) https://www.youtube.com/watch?v=M7OVy2ROASQ (accessed 3/15/2020). See also Oleg Boldyrev's interview with the BBC, September 24, 2019, https://www.youtube.com/watch?v=U0LaLhkKj2g (accessed 3/15/2020).

41. Yakutia.com featured over 106 videos in Russian and Sakha under the rubric "I/We Shaman" (https://www.youtube.com/playlist?list=PLmg4mvMyK_WsGBQbMZlZR 2rZ7Z5_J7d9, accessed from 4/2019 to 3/19/20). Alexander described plans for the aborted 2021 journey (https://www.youtube.com/watch?v=YK0LlFAjx3E, accessed 1/15/2021). On his 2021 show-of-force arrest featuring nine police cars and leading to involuntary hospitalization, see https://mbk-news.appspot.com/news/specoperation/; an appeal to the Sakha supreme court was lost (https://credo.press/236169/); and by April his health had seriously deteriorated (https://ria.ru/20210405/shaman-1604221831.html, all accessed 4/26/2021). A private video circulating of his arrest shows police overwhelming

him in bed as if they were expecting a wild animal; he was forced to the floor bleeding, then handcuffed. On his May trial, see https://www.sibreal.org/a/31242513.html (accessed 5/8/21). By July he was sentenced to a closed clinic regime.

42. "Shaman Alexander vystupil s obriadom v Chite" [Shaman Alexander Performed a Ritual in Chita], July 12, 2019, https://www.youtube.com/watch?v=2W0KwRaHexU (accessed 7/14/2019). The Chita rally is excerpted at https://www.youtube.com/watch?v=x81rgbsEgmI 10/15/2019 (accessed 3/15/2020).

43. On the coronavirus dispersal, see http://nazaccent.ru/content/32494-buryatskie-shamany-proveli-obryad-po-izgnaniyu.html, March 16, 2020 (accessed 3/18/2020). On the scandal-provoking camel sacrifice ritual, with a disputed number of two to five camels mentioned or seen on video, see https://www.maximonline.ru/guide/maximir/_article/minutka-divannoy-analitiki-verblyudyi-uhodyaschie/; https://lenta.ru/news/2019/02/21/victim/ (both accessed 3/18/2020). On the Buryat Tengeri Society encounter with Alexander's entourage, see Oleg Boldyrev's BBC interview at https://www.youtube.com/watch?v=U0LaLhkKj2g, September 24, 2019 (accessed 3/15/2020).

44. Personal communication, December 4, 2019; Russian TV interview with Mikhail Sokolov, "Shaman v Moskvu pridet, poriadok navdet?," August 1, 2019, https://www.svoboda.org/a/30087117.html.

45. This Naval'ny video, https://www.youtube.com/watch?v=5MMgfm18znI&y=192s from April 2019, had been removed by March 2020.

46. On Alexander's significance as a Siberian regional leader, see http://region.expert/shaman-prospects/, December 16, 2019 (accessed 12/17/2019). For Western press, see Anton Troyanovski, "'An Exorcism Must be Done': An Anti-Putin Shaman Sets off Unrest," *New York Times*, September 10, 2019, https://nytimes.com/2019/10/09/world/Europe/shaman-putin-dissent.html; Klaus-Helge Donath, "Shamane mit politischer Agenda," *Die Tageszeitung*, July 16, 2019, https://taz.de/Russischer-Aktivist-will-Putin-stuerzen/!5611801/; Andrew Roth, "Siberian Shaman Arrested on Trek to Exorcise Vladimir Putin," *The Guardian*, September 19, 2019, https://www.theguardian.com/world/2019/sep/19/siberian-shaman-arrested-on-trek-to-exorcise-vladimir-putin (all accessed 3/15/2020).

47. "Glava Yakutii i shaman Aleksandr Gabyshev," https://www.youtube.com/watch?v=YZnv1pABj7c&list=PLmg4mvMyK_WsGBQbMZlZR2rZ7Z5_J7d9h&index=13, September 26, 2019 (accessed 3/15/2020). To my knowledge, Mikhail Khodorkovsky has not commented on Alexander, nor supported him financially.

48. See the university analyst Afanasy Nikolaev's blog "Yakutiia—obraz budushchego" (Yakutia—Model for the Future), which picked up a speech from 2015 by the former Orenburg politician-turned-bank-advisor Kamil Bibersov of Ulianovsk advocating greater "Turkish world integration" (http://yakutiafuture.ru/2017/09/12/tyurkskij-mir-dumaet-o-vektore-integracii/?_utl_t=fb . 9/12/2017 [accessed 9/12/2017]).

49. In a sign of the times, I am keeping this August 2016 email communication anonymous.

50. The bridge was finally completed. For contexts of corruption, see especially Åslund 2019; Dawisha 2014; Pomerantsev 2014. See also Harley Balzer's review of Dawisha (https://www.journalofdemocracy.org/articles/stealing-russia-blind/, 2015, accessed 5/5/2021). See reports on Putin's corruption and Ukraine war strategy by PARNAS party members Boris Nemtsov and Vladimir Milov that may have contributed to Nemtsov's assassination in 2015: e.g., https://larussophobe.wordpress.com/2011/04/03/special-extra-the-nemtsov-white-paper-part-v-putin-the-thief/ (accessed 9/12/2017). A pinnacle of anti-Putin corruption exposé is Aleksei Naval'ny's 2021 "Dvorets dlia Putina," https://palace.navalny.com/?fbclid=IwAR25GwypKb-XFSqHt3YiLyF45ASSnZFCL7wKbTJS-DI1FFoIVJIaomkrBhc (accessed 4/26/2021).

51. My sources on the budget and Greenpeace actions must remain anonymous, although some of this has been covered unevenly in the Western press. See Zev Wolfson (Boris Komarov)'s work, especially (1980), from a Russian ms. originally smuggled out of the Soviet Union, and (1992). For excellent background, see Murray Feshbach and Alfred Friendly Jr. (1992); Julian Agyeman and Yelena Ogneva-Himmelberger, eds. (2009); Lada V. Kochtcheeva 2009.

52. Gulnaz Sharafutdinova, personal communications, June 7, 2016; March 13, 2020. See Sharafutdinova and Turovsky 2016; Sharafutdinova 2020. By 2017, Tatarstan lost most of its legal "special case" privileges. Sharafutdinova (personal communication, September 14, 2017) sees long-term step-by-step strategies to erode existing ethnic-based republic privileges and boundaries. Compare https://tlgrm.ru/channels/@metodi4ka/1155 (accessed 9/7/2017); Gelman 2017.

5. CONCLUSIONS

1. For constitutional amendments in Russian, see http://duma.gov.ru/news/48045/ (accessed 5/29/2020). For excellent commentary by the legal scholar William Pomerantz, see https://www.wilsoncenter.org/blog-post/putin-constitution (accessed 5/30/2020). I am grateful for perspective from William Pomerantz, personal communication (March 16, 2020; March 31, 2020), and from colleagues in Russia who request anonymity. See also Pomerantz and Smyth 2021. Details on language policy were omitted from the Kremlin's English-language summary on culture: "The state undertakes the obligation to support and protect culture as a unique heritage of Russia's multi-ethnic nation," http://en.kremlin.ru/acts/news/62988, March 14, 2020. On protest, see https://www.sibreal.org/a/30486181.html, March 12, 2020 (both accessed 3/15/2020). Cautioning against the Russification amendments were Valery Tishkov and Leokadia Drobizheva.

2. Andrew Higgins, https://www.nytimes.com/2016/07/15/world/europe/russia-looks-to-populate-its-far-east-wimps-need-not-apply.html, July 14, 2016 (accessed 6/15/2020). For perspective, including ramifications of climate change, see Ksenofontov and Polzikov 2020.

3. Attention to monuments has accelerated in anthropology and history of East-Central Europe and Russia, for example, in the works of Andrew Graan on Skopje and Kathleen Smith on Moscow.

4. For the politics behind this Stalin's adventures, see Balzer 2015. Compare Verdery 1999.

5. As is common in Yakutsk, the sculpture is referred to as the "Abakayade Memorial," http://wikitravel.org/en/Yakutsk (accessed 5/16/2020). It was created by the Sakha sculptor Eduard Pakhomov, who was also the teacher of the young Buryat Dashi Namdakov. See Ivanova-Unarova 2016.

6. For some tourists who do not read the Russian plaque, he looks like Genghis Khan (http://kyzylorbust.blogspot.com/ 3/30/2016 [accessed 5/6/2016]). This undermines the sculptor's intent to depict a non-Russian, by implication Tyvan, as a symbolic purge victim. Ethnic identity tipoffs are his robe and upturned felt boots. The title *The Unburied* echoes themes of Alexander Etkind's powerful *Warped Mourning* (2013).

7. For theories of liberal nationalism not embedded in fashionable critiques of "neoliberalism," see Tamir 1993. Compare Comaroff and Comaroff 2009. These approaches are far from Samuel Huntington's (1996) "clash of civilizations."

8. "Natsional'no-osvoboditel'naia bor'ba narodov Tuvy i Mongolii 1911–12," https://www.tuva.asia/news/tuva/9011-kobdo.html (accessed 5/23/2020).

9. See also Vinokurova 2018. In 1990s and 2012 sociological surveys of Sakha, Tyvans, and Russians, Vinokurova (2017, 89–90) reports that Sakha were more likely than others to mention ethnic solidarity as crucial for their survival. She suggests this was stimulated

by a need to act on their sense of dispersion across vast territory. Sakha were more likely to have elite professional jobs, with higher education, and to believe in their republic leadership, although the struggle against corruption was acknowledged in high percentages. Language as the key ethnic marker was high for Sakha and Tyvans, with Tyvans scoring 98.5 percent in one survey to 93.8 percent for Sakha. The surveys were guided by Leokadia Drobizheva under the Academy of Sciences Institute of Sociology, enabling me to discuss them with relevant colleagues at the time.

10. See http://infpol.ru/news/society/118543-ulan-udenets-prosit-putina-sozdat-baykals kuyu-respubliku/, September 1, 2016 (accessed 5/30/2020); "Tema ukrupneniia raionov," http://asiarussia.ru/articles/12235/, May 6, 2016 (accessed 6/19/2020); Paul Goble, http://windowoneurasia2.blogspot.com/2016/09/rodina-activist-opens-petition-drive-to.html, September 1, 2016 (accessed 5/30/2010).

11. Arguing against amalgamation are Mekhanik and Ponomarev 2020. A leaked 2018 government plan to consolidate regions, anticipating abolishing certain ethnonational republics, was a trial balloon. Motivated by efforts to curtail Tatarstan's ambitions, it has implications for all the republics. See https://tlgrm.ru/channels/@metodi4ka/1155 (accessed 9/7/2018).

12. As a direct-lineage Franz Boas student through Frederica de Laguna, I am aware of the dangers of cultural overgeneralization on the basis of personality traits and of the notorious war-driven "culture at a distance" history of "culture and personality" studies in American anthropology associated with Ruth Benedict, Margaret Mead, and Gregory Bateson. However, such intellectual proclivities or projections onto others often recur in my fieldwork, and it would be inaccurate to ignore them. Compare Appiah 2020.

13. Details of several thwarted research projects are other scholars' stories to tell. Several Buryat researchers feeling uncomfortable in their homeland have joined the Buryat diaspora in Europe and the United States in the past several years.

14. The same honored monk led rituals to bless a statue in Zabaikal krai, an image of the White Chakrasambary God, also called Burkhan Sagaan Démchog, situated in the national park at Alkhan, already a site of pilgrimage representing Buddhism in its Buryat-Mongol manifestation. See "Buddisty rasshiriaiut sakral'nuiu geografiiu Rossii," http://www.ng.ru/ng_religii/2016-09-21/3_buddisty.html (accessed 5/25/2020). Compare Bernstein 2013, 106; Guchinova 2021.

15. http://www.ng.ru/ng_religii/2016-09-21/3_buddisty.html (accessed 5/25/2020).

16. http://gov.tuva.ru/press_center/news/2016-09-21/3 (accessed 5/24/2020); http://tuvaculture.ru/2794-v-chaa-holskom-kozhuune-tuvy-gde-sohranilos-drevnee-izo brazhenie-buddy-postroen-hram.html, September 21, 2016 (accessed 5/6/2016). Rituals were led by the Tyvan Khambo Lama, born Shyyrap Bair-ool.

17. The quotation is from the excellent journal *Novye issledovaniia Tuvy* (http://www.tuva.asia/news/tuva/8793-dambaa.html, September 23, 2016 [accessed 5/29/2020]). A 2016 conference in Tyva ("Decorative and Applied Arts, Crafts, and Beliefs of the Peoples of Altai-Sayan Mountains," http://www.tuva.asia/news/tuva/8738-remesla.html, July 25, 2016 [accessed 5/25/2020]) featured papers on shamanism, including mine. Since I have written about the shamanic revival in Siberia, I have not focused on it here. See Balzer 1997, 2012, 2013; Vitebsky 1995.

18. The unofficial news site https://meduza.io (accessed 8/30/2017) covered this at the time. For analysis, see Solovyeva 2018.

19. Diamond mining expansion has proceeded. See Solovyeva 2018; Sakha news sources (e.g., http://yakutsk.ru/news/society/chto_i_trebovalos_dokazat_bez_publichnykh_ slushaniy_nyurbinskiy_rayon_daet_razreshenie_na_razrabotku/, February 14, 2017 [accessed 9/1/2017]). The dismissal and house arrest of Niurba ulus head Boris Popov for resisting ALROSA was described in chapter 1.

20. On the halt of the Bashkir Soda Company's limestone mining at Kushtau Hill, designated a protected natural area in 2020, see https://www.rferl.org/a/russia-bashkor tostan-kushtau-hill-enviroment-activists-/30829316.html (accessed 4/30/2021); and Paul Goble "Ufa has Transformed Environmental Protest into National Movement, Sidorov Says" https://windowoneurasia2.blogspot.com/2020/08/ufa-has-transformed-environmental. html, August 23, 2020 (accessed 8/27/2020). For background on how difficult ecology activism has been, one must begin with the colossal Soviet legacy of environmental despoliation (Feshbach and Friendly 1992).

21. Norilsk, in Krasnoyarsk krai adjoining Sakha, has a deplorable ecological track record. On the spill, see https://siberiantimes.com/other/others/news/state-of-emergency-in-norilsk-after-20000-tons-of-diesel-leaks-into-arctic-river, June 2, 2020 (accessed 6/2/2020). Legal access to underground resources may be changing, with new possibilities of timed (rented) exploitation on lands in the Far East Hectare category. For perspective on the incendiary but sometimes accommodating mix of politics of oil, money, and culture in Russia, see Rogers 2015.

22. See Bullfrog Film's 2014 *Standing on Sacred Ground* (accessed 5/30/2020). I was an advisor for the Standing on Sacred Ground project, due to its segment on the Altai Mountains. Nunavut is the target of Chinese investment for gold, zinc, lead, and copper (https://nnsl.com/nunavut-news/chinese-ownership-of-nunavuts-resources-stokes-unease/, May 21, 2020 [accessed 6/18/2020]). I maintain a reference list on indigeneity for our Indigenous studies network at Georgetown, featuring Indigenous scholars and activists as well as research by non-Natives. See https://indigeneity.georgetown.edu/ (accessed 4/28/2021).

23. Appropriate disclosure is that I attended with Native Siberian friends a mass protest against the Keystone XL Pipeline on the Washington, DC, Mall in 2014, led by the Cowboys and Indians alliance. Other US friends were at the months-long Standing Rock protest on Sioux territory in 2016, and I again was with Siberians at the Spring 2017 Standing Rock support march in Washington, DC. See also https://indigeneity.georgetown.edu/ (accessed 4/28/2021).

24. See the UN document http://www.ohchr.org/Documents/Publications/fs9Rev.2.pdf (accessed 9/16/2016). For meticulous comparison of Russian, Ukrainian, and UN laws on Indigenous peoples, see Babin 2014–2015. See also Donahoe et al. 2008 for perspective on Russia's categorizations and their implications.

25. As Siberians have worked more within the UN Forum on Indigenous Peoples, they have increasingly understood how beholden its activities are to member states. Antonina Gavrilyeva has transferred logistics of the fight against the "free land law" to lawyers in Moscow. Far East Hectare is discussed at "Minvostokrazvitiia predlozhit 30 sposobov osvoit' 'dal'nevostochnyi gektar,'" https://lenta.ru/news/2016/08/22/gector/ (accessed 5/23/2020).

26. Anonymity is necessary here. Compare Crate 2006.

27. General Vladimir Kulishev is quoted at https://thebarentsobserver.com/en/secu rity/2020/05/fsb-general-sees-growing-threat-foreign-arctic-researchers-and-indigenous-peoples (accessed 5/28/2020).

28. Nikolay Petrov (e.g. personal communication, September 14, 2017) regularly reiterates his perception of the danger of increased destabilization in the regions. He suggests that under President Putin a 2 percent average arrest rate per year for regional leaders or their key subordinates has been enough to frighten regional elites into compliance with Moscow directives, sometimes against their economic interests or local popularity. He views attempts to change internal republic borders, including in the Baikal region, as consistent with President Putin's efforts to curtail regional prerogatives: "People do not see the unintended consequences of such policies."

29. See Ilya Azar's review of the debates (https://meduza.io/feature/2016/09/15/tuvinskaya-narodnaya-respublika). For Russian views, see http://via-midgard.info/news/panslavyanskoe-molodyozhnoe-obedinenie-tomska.htmandsputnikipogrom.com/russia/50248/vanished-in-tuva/#.V95fva10e-d (both accessed 9/16/2016).

30. I have not seen this plan and have no way of judging its level of threat. Compare https://tlgrm.ru/channels/@metodi4ka/1155 (accessed 9/7/2017); and Gelman 2017. Another recommendation for restructuring the regions to dilute non-Russian demographics and political clout in Sakha Republic and Buryatia surfaced on a consistently provocative website, with the author probably using a pseudonym (Ivan Vladimirov, "Kak nam obustroit yakutov: fakty, tsifry i plan deistvii dlia russkogo national'nogo pravitel'stva," https://sputnikipograom.com/russia/75734/rebuilding-sakha/ [2017] [accessed 8/9/2017]). On entrenched yet negotiated patronage in Russia, see Hale 2014.

31. Oleg Kashin, "A Shadow over a Swamp: How Stalin Became Our Motherland," http://www.slon.ru, August 25, 2016 (accessed 8/27/2016). Compare the riveting, creepy depictions of Pomerantsev 2015, and the analysis of Etkind 2013.

32. The paragraph derives from an extensive phone interview with Andrei Savich Borisov, June 27, 2020, with the exception of this quote, from a *Maxim* interview, "V razvitii institutov grazhdanskogo obshchestva—budushchee Yakutii i Rossii," that went offline (http://www.gazetayakutia.ru/index.php/yakutiya/item/20966-andrej-borisov-v-razvitii-institutov-grazhdanskogo-obshchestva-budushchee-yakutii-i-rossii [2016] [accessed 4/28/2016]).

References

Abaev, Nikolai V. 2014. "Strategiia razvitiia etnokul'turnykh traditsii evraziistva (na primer Respubliki Buryatiia)." In *Obrazy, traditsii i kul'tura mnogonatsional'nogo mira i soglasiia*, edited by A. D. Karnyshev, 112–38. Irkutsk: Irkutskii gosudarstvennyi universitet.

Abaeva, Liubov'. 1998. *Buddhizm v Buryatii*. Ulan-Ude: Buryatskii gosudarstvennyi universitet.

Ackerman, Diane. 2009. *Dawn Light: Dancing with Cranes and Other Ways to Start the Day*. New York: W. W. Norton.

Afanas'ev, Lazar. 2002. *Aiyy suola* [The Road of the Spirit]. Yakutsk: Bichik (in Sakha).

Agarkova, Elena. 2010. "The Baikal Movement." *Institute of Current World Affairs* (May): 1–8. http://www.icwa.org (accessed 5/20/2020).

Agyeman, Julian, and Yelena Ogneva-Himmelberger, eds. 2009. *Environmental Justice and Sustainability in the Former Soviet Union*. Cambridge, MA: MIT Press.

Akhmadov, Ilyas, and Miriam Lanskoy. 2010. *The Chechen Struggle: Independence Won and Lost*. New York: Palgrave Macmillan.

Alatalu, Toomas. 1992. "Tuva—A State Reawakens." *Soviet Studies* 44(5): 881–95.

Alexseev, Mikhail A., ed. 1999. *Center-Periphery Conflict in Post-Soviet Russia*. New York: St. Martin's.

Amogolonova, Darima D. 2015. "A Symbolic Person of Buddhist Revival in Buryatia: 'Our Hambo' Damba Ayusheev." *Inner Asia* 17(2): 225–42.

Anaiban, Zoya. 1995. "Ethnic Relations in Tuva." In *Culture Incarnate*, edited by M. M. Balzer, 102–12. Armonk, NY: M. E. Sharpe.

Anaiban, Zoya. 1998–1999. "The Republic of Tyva (Tuva): From Romanticism to Realism." *Anthropology and Archeology of Eurasia* 37(3): 13–96.

Anaiban, Zoya. 2005. *Zhenshchiny Tuvy i Khakasii v period rossiiskikh reform*. Moscow: Institut vostokovedeniia RAN.

Anaiban, Zoya. 2016. "Sovremennye etnodemograficheskie kharakhteristiki molodezhnykh grupp Tuvy i Khakazii." *Novye issledovaniia Tuvy*, no. 2. http://nit.tuva.asia/nit/issue/view/7/showToc.

Anaiban, Zoya, and Galina F. Balakina. 2015. "Dinamika mezhetnicheskikh otnoshenii i etnicheskikh stereotipov v Respublike Tyva." *Sotsialisticheskie issledovaniia*, no. 8: 93–99.

Anaiban, Zoya, and Svetlana P. Tiukhteneva. 2008. *Etnokul'turnaia adaptatsiia naseleniia Iuzhnoi Sibiri: Sovremennyi period*. Moscow: Institut vostokovedeniia RAN.

Anderson, Benedict. 1991. *Imagined Communities: Reflections on the Origin and Spread of Nationalism*. London: Verso.

Anderson, Gregory. 2015. "Russian Colonialism and Hegemony and Native Siberian Languages." In *Language Empires in Comparative Perspective*, edited by Christel Stolz, chapter 4. Berlin: Walter de Gruyter.

Anderson, Gregory, and K. David Harrison. 1999. Tyvan (Languages of the World). Munich: Lincom Europa.

Angé, Olivia, and David Berliner, eds. 2016. *Anthropology and Nostalgia*. New York: Berghahn Books.

Anisimova, Alla A., and Olga Echevskaia. 2012. *Sibirskaia identichnost'*. Novosibirsk: Novosibirskii gosudarstvennyi universitet.

Appiah, Kwame Anthony. 2020. "The Defender of Differences." *New York Review of Books*. May 28. https://www.nybooks.com/articles/2020/05/28/franz-boas-anthropologist-defender-differences/ (accessed 5/28/2020).

Aranchyn, Iu. L., ed. 1984. *Problemy istorii Tuvy*. Kyzyl: Tuvinskii nauchno-issledovatel'skii institut iazyka, literatury i istorii.

Arbachakov, Alexander. 1999. "Southern Siberia Conservation Initiative's (SSCI) Information Coordinator Reaches Out to Tuvan Environmentalists." http://sacredearthnetwork.org/Newsletters/ENews13p1.html#anchor541264 (accessed 5/3/2020).

Argounova, Tatiana. 1994. *Republic of Sakha (Yakutia)*. Cambridge: Scott Polar Research Institute, University of Cambridge. http://www.spiri.cam.ac.uk/rfn/sakha.htm (accessed 2/3/2015).

Argounova-Low, Tatiana. 2004. "Diamonds: A Contested Symbol in the Republic of Sakha." In *Property as Culture—Culture as Property*, edited by Erich Kasten, 257–65. Berlin: Reimer.

Argounova-Low, Tatiana. 2007. "Close Relatives and Outsiders: Village People in the City of Yakutsk, Siberia." *Arctic Anthropology* 44(1): 51–61.

Argounova-Low, Tatiana. 2012. *The Politics of Nationalism in the Republic of Sakha (Northeastern Siberia) 1900–2000*. Lewiston, NY: Edwin Mellon.

Arutiunova, E.M. 2020. "Predstavleniia o sotsial'nykh problemakh i protestnaia aktivnost' v respublikakh, keis Sakha (Yakutia)." *Rossiia reformiruiushcha-iasia: ezhegodniki* 18, edited by M. K. Gorshkov, 391–406. Moscow: Novyi khronograf.

Åslund, Anders. 2019. *Russia's Crony Capitalism: The Path from Market Economy to Kleptocracy*. New Haven: Yale University Press.

Atanov, Nikolai. 2014. "Evraziiskaia platforma kak osnova simmetrichnogo sotrud-nichestva post-sotsialisticheskikh stran s gosudarstvami Vostochnoi Azii." In *Vstrecha na Baikale: Vremia proshlogo, vyzovy budushchego*, edited by A. A. Bazarov and Ia. Kenevich, 59–69. Ulan-Ude: Buryatskii gosudarstvennyi universitet.

Avedon, John F. 1998. *The Buddha's Art of Healing: Tibetan Paintings Rediscovered*. New York: Rizzoli International, Arthur M. Sackler Museum.

Babin, Borys. 2014–2015. "Rights and Dignity of Indigenous Peoples of Ukraine in Revolutionary Conditions and Foreign Occupation: Evolution of the Statute of Indigenous Peoples of Ukraine, as Legal Grounding for Crimea." *Anthropology and Archeology of Eurasia* 53(3): 81–115.

Badmaev, Valerii, Mergen Ulanov, Chimiza Lamazhaa, Uliana Bicheldei, Vladimir Antonov, and Oiuna Ochirova. 2020. "Rossiia i buddiiskii mir glazami molo-dezhi Tuvy, Buryatii i Kalmykii." *Novye issledovaniia Tuvy: Religiia i sovre-mennost'*, no. 1: 35–49. https://nit.tuva.asia/nit/article/view/904 (accessed 5/20/2020).

Badmatsyrenov, Timur B. 2015. "Religioznaia situatsiia i religioznye soobshchestva v respubliki Buryatiia." *Vlast'*, no. 4, 103–7. https://cyberleninka.ru/article/n/reli gioznaya-situatsiya-i-religioznye-soobschestva-v-respublike-buryatiya/viewer (accessed 5/20/2020).

Baiburin, Albert, Catriona Kelly, and Nikolai Vakhtin, eds. 2012. *Russian Cultural Anthropology after the Collapse of Communism*. New York: Routledge.

Baiev, Khassan, with Ruth and Nicholas Daniloff. 2004. *The Oath: A Surgeon under Fire*. New York: Pocket Books.

Balakina, Galina. 2009. *Strategii razvitiia depressivnogo regiona.* Kyzyl: TuvIKOPR SO RAN.

Balakina, Galina F., and Zoia V. Anaiban. 1995. *Sovremennaia Tuva: Sotsiokul'turnye i etnicheskie protsessy.* Novosibirsk: Nauka.

Baldanov, Saian Z. 1998. *Stanovlenie i razvitie natsional'nykh literatur respublik Sakha i Tyva.* Ulan-Ude: Izdatel'stvo Buryatskogo gosuniversiteta.

Balzer, Harley D., ed. 1996. *Russia's Missing Middle Class: The Professions in Russian History.* Armonk, NY: M. E. Sharpe.

Balzer, M. M., ed. 1997. *Shamanic Worlds.* Armonk, NY: M. E. Sharpe.

Balzer, M. M., ed. 1998. "Federalism and Nationalism: Views from the Republics of Rossiia." *Anthropology and Archeology of Eurasia* 37(2).

Balzer, M. M., ed. 2007. "Alphabet Wars." *Anthropology and Archeology of Eurasia* 46(1).

Balzer, M. M., ed. 2010. *Religion and Politics in the Russian Federation.* Armonk, NY: M. E. Sharpe.

Balzer, M. M., ed. 2015. "Art, Identity, and Ethnicity: Republics of Kalmykia, Buryatia, Altai, and Sakha (Yakutia)." *Anthropology and Archeology of Eurasia* 54(3).

Balzer, M. M., ed. 2019. "Cross-Cultural Influences in the Far East and Central Asia." *Anthropology and Archeology of Eurasia* 58(1–2).

Balzer, Marjorie Mandelstam. 1990. "Nationalism in the Soviet Union: One Anthropological View." *Journal of Soviet Nationalities* 1(3): 4–22.

Balzer, Marjorie Mandelstam. 1994a. "Siberiaki." In *Encyclopedia of World Cultures,* edited by Paul Friedrich, 331–35. New Haven: Hall, HRAF.

Balzer, Marjorie Mandelstam. 1994b. "From Ethnicity to Nationalism: Turmoil in the Russian Mini-empire." In *The Social Legacy of Communism,* edited by J. Millar and S. Wolchik, 56–88. Cambridge: Cambridge University Press.

Balzer, Marjorie Mandelstam. 1999. *The Tenacity of Ethnicity: A Siberian Saga in Global Perspective.* Princeton, NJ: Princeton University Press.

Balzer, Marjorie Mandelstam. 2012. *Shamans, Spirituality, and Cultural Revitalization: Explorations in Siberia and Beyond.* New York: Palgrave MacMillan.

Balzer, Marjorie Mandelstam. 2013. "Shamans Emerging from Repression in Siberia: Lightning Rods of Fear and Hope." In *Shamanism and Violence: Power, Repression, and Suffering in Indigenous Religious Contexts,* edited by Diana Riboli and Davide Torre, 37–50. Farnham, NH: Ashgate.

Balzer, Marjorie Mandelstam. 2014. "Cycles of Violence: Dangers of Islamophobia in the Russian Federation." *Georgetown Journal of International Affairs.* January 7. http://journal.georgetown.edu/cycles-of-violence-dangers-of-islamophobia-in-the-russian-federation-by-marjorie-mandelstam-balzer/ (accessed 5/20/2020).

Balzer, Marjorie Mandelstam. 2015. "Local Legacies of the GULag in Siberia: Anthropological Reflections." *Focaal* 73: 99–113.

Balzer, Marjorie Mandelstam. 2017. "Indigeneity, Land, and Activism in Siberia" In *Land, Indigenous People, and Conflict,* edited by Alan Tidwell and Barry Zellen, 9–27. New York: Routledge.

Balzer, Marjorie Mandelstam. 2020. "Review of Svetlana Stasenko's 2017 film *Shamanic Lessons for Beginners.*" *Slavic Review* 79(4): 839–40.

Balzer, Marjorie Mandelstam, Nicholas Petro, and Lawrence Robertson. 2001. "Culture and Identity." In *Fragmented Space in the Russian Federation,* edited by Blair Ruble, 219–72. Washington, DC: Woodrow Wilson Center Press.

Balzer, Marjorie Mandelstam, and Uliana A. Vinokurova. 1996. "Nationalism, Interethnic Relations, and Federalism: The Case of the Sakha Republic (Yakutia)." *Europe-Asia Studies* 48(1): 101–20.

Baraev, V. 1994. "Aura i karma uchitelia." In *Buddiskii mir*. Moscow: Respublika.

Barth, Fredrik, ed. 1969. *Ethnic Groups and Boundaries*. Boston: Little, Brown.

Basilov, Vladimir, ed. 1989. *Nomads of Eurasia*. Los Angeles: Natural History Museum.

Basilov, Vladimir. 1997. "Chosen by the Spirits." In *Shamanic Worlds: Rituals and Lore of Siberia and Central Asia*, edited by Marjorie Mandelstam Balzer, 3–48. Armonk, NY: M. E. Sharpe.

Bassin, Mark. 2016. *The Gumilev Mystique: Biopolitics, Eurasianism, and the Construction of Community in Modern Russia*. Ithaca, NY: Cornell University Press.

Bazarov, B. V., ed. 2010. *Etnicheskaia istoriia i kul'turno-bytovye traditsii narodov Baikal'skogo regiona*. Irkutsk: Ottisk.

Bazarov, Boris V. 2000. *Tainstva i praktika shamanizma*. Ulan-Ude: Buriaad ünén.

Bazarov, Boris V. 2006. *Zhdanovskii diskurs v natsional'nykh regionakh Rossii poslevoennykh let*. Ulan-Ude: Buryatskii nauchnyi tsentr.

Beahrs, Robert Oliver. 2019. "Post-Soviet Tuvan Throat-Singing (Xöömei) and the Circulation of Nomadic Sensibility." PhD diss., University of California, Berkeley.

Beck, Julie. 2013. "When Nostalgia Was a Disease." *The Atlantic*. August 14. https://www.theatlantic.com/health/archive/2013/08/when-nostalgia-was-a-disease/278648/ (accessed 3/2/2020).

Beissinger, Mark. 2002. *Nationalist Mobilization and the Collapse of the Soviet State*. Cambridge: Cambridge University Press.

Benjamin, Walter. 1969. "Paris, Capital of the Nineteenth Century." *Perspecta* 12: 163–72.

Bernstein, Anya. 2012. "More Alive Than All the Living: Sovereign Bodies and Cosmic Politics in Buddhist Siberia." *Cultural Anthropology* 27(2): 261–85.

Bernstein, Anya. 2013. *Religious Bodies Politic: Rituals of Sovereignty in Buryat Buddhism*. Chicago: University of Chicago Press.

Bicheldei, Kaadyr-ool A., ed. 2010. *Tuvinskaia pis'mennost' i voprosy issledovaniia pis'mennostei i pis'mennykh pamiatnikov Rossii i Tsentral'no-Aziatskogo regiona: Materialy Mezhdunarodnoi nauchnoi konferentsii*. 2 vols. Abakan: Khakasskoe knizhnoe izdatel'stvo.

Bicheldei, Kaadyr-ool A. 2014. "Osobennosti istoricheskogo momenta v Uriankhaiskom krae mezhdu nachertaniiami Nikolaia II 'Soglasen' i 'Uspeshno' v 1914 godu." *Novye issledovaniia Tyvy*, no. 3 (2014). http://www.tuva.asia/journal/tuva/issue_23/7317-bicheldey.html (accessed 2/17/2015).

Biehl, João, and Peter Locke, eds. 2017. *Unfinished: The Anthropology of Becoming*. Durham, NC: Duke University Press.

Bloch, Sidney, and Peter Reddaway. 1984. *Soviet Psychiatric Abuse*. London: Victor Gollancz.

Boiko, Vladimir I., ed. 1983. *Ocherki sotsial'nogo razvitiia Tuvinskoi ASSR*. Novosibirsk: Nauka.

Boronoev, Pavel G. 2018. "Sotsial'noe neblagopoluchie kak faktor suitsidal'nogo povedeniia nesovershennoletnikh v Respublike Buryatiia." *Sotsiodinamika*, no. 12: 10–16.

Boyer, Dominic, and George Marcus, eds. 2020. *Collaborative Anthropology Today: A Collection of Exceptions*. Ithaca, NY: Cornell University Press.

Boym, Svetlana. 2001. *The Future of Nostalgia*. New York: Basic Books.

Brass, Paul. 1991. *Ethnicity and Nationalism: Theory and Comparison*. Newbury Park: Sage.

Bromlei, Yulian, and Victor Kozlov. 1989. "The Theory of Ethnos and Ethnic Processes in Soviet Social Sciences." *Comparative Studies in Society and History* 31(3): 425–38.

Brown, Michael. 2003. *Who Owns Native Culture?* Cambridge, MA: Harvard University Press.

Brubaker, Rogers. 2004. *Ethnicity without Groups.* Cambridge, MA: Harvard University Press.

Buraeva, O. V. 2005. *Etnokul'turnoe vzaimodeistvie narodov Baikal'skogo regiona v XVII–nachale XX veka.* Ulan-Ude: Buri'ia'd ünén.

Burnasheva, Daria. 2019. "Arctic Identity: Global, National and Local Processes of Construction and Transformation." PhD diss., University of Warsaw.

Burrell, Teal. 2016. "Wistful Thinking: Why We Are Wired to Dwell on the Past." *New Scientist* September 21, 2016. https://www.newscientist.com/ (accessed 9/27/2016).

Calazans, José C., Jan Van Alphen, and Steffen Wunderlich. 1997. *Spellbound by the Shaman: Shamanism in Tuva.* Antwerp: Ethnographic Museum.

Canty, Jeanine M., ed. 2019. *Globalism and Localization: Emergent Approaches to Ecological and Social Crises.* New York: Routledge.

Cameron, Ross, ed. 2012. *Russian Regional Politics under Putin and Medvedev.* New York: Routledge.

Chagin, Vladimir V. 2014. *Uriankhai Tuva: V oznemenovanie 100-letiia edineniia Rossii i Tuvy.* Krasnoyarsk: Platina.

Chakars, Melissa. 2014. *The Socialist Way of Life in Siberia.* Budapest: Central European University Press.

Chakars, Melissa. 2019. "Free Time Is Not Meant to be Wasted: Educational, Political, and Taboo Leisure Activities among the Soviet Buryats of Eastern Siberia." *Nationalities Papers* 47(4): 1–14.

Chebankova, Elena. 2008. "Adaptive Federalism and Federation in Putin's Russia." *Europe-Asia Studies* 60(6): 989–1009.

Chevalier, Joan. 2017. "School-based Linguistic and Cultural Revitalization as a Local Practice: Sakha Language Education in the City of Yakutsk, Russian Federation." *Nationalities Papers* 45(4): 613–31.

Chimitdorzhiev, Sh. B. 2004. *Kak ischezla edinaia Buryat-Mongoliia (1937–1958 g.).* Ulan-Ude: Buri'ia'd ünén.

Chirkova, Aleksandra Konstantinovna. 2002. *Shaman: Zhizn' i bessmertie.* Yakutsk: Sakhapoligrafizdat.

Chubarova, Tatiana, and Natalia Grigorieva. 2016. "The Russian Federation." In *Comparative Health Care Federalism*, edited by Katherine Fierlbeck and Howard A. Palley, 195–212. London: Routledge.

Clover, Charles. 2016. *Black Wind, White Snow: The Rise of Russia's New Nationalism.* New Haven: Yale University Press.

Comaroff, John, and Jean Comaroff. 2009. *Ethnicity Inc.* Chicago: University of Chicago Press.

Conner, Walker. 1994. *Ethnonationalism: The Quest for Understanding.* Princeton, NJ: Princeton University Press.

Crate, Susan. 2006. *Cows, Kin, and Globalization: An Ethnography of Sustainability.* Lanham, MD: Alta Mira Press.

Cruikshank, Julie, and Tatiana Argounova. 2000. "Reinscribing Meaning: Memory and Indigenous Identity in Sakha Republic (Yakutia)." *Arctic Anthropology* 37(1): 96–119.

Dabiev, D. F., ed. 2012. *Ekonomicheskaia otsenka effektivnosti osvoeniia mineral'nykh resursov Tuvy.* Kyzyl: TuvIKOPR SO RAN.

Dampilon, Zhargal. 2011. "Environmental Movements in Russia (an Example from the Baikal Region)." MA diss., University of Arizona.

Dandaron, B. D. 1995. *99 pisem o buddizme i liubvi (1956–1959)*. St. Petersburg: Datsan Gunzechoinei.

Dandaron, B. D. 1997. *Mysli Buddista: "Chernaia tetrad'"*. St. Petersburg: Aleteiia.

Daschke, Derek, and W. Michael Ashcraft, eds. (2005) 2017. *New Religious Movements: A Documentary Reader*. New York: New York University Press.

Datsyshen, Vladimir. 2015. "Potentsial' konfliktnosti v zone rossiisko-mongol'skoi granitsy v Tyve." *Mezhdunarodnye protsessy* 13(1): 1–5. http://www.intertrends. ru/seventh/008.htm (accessed 1/2/16).

Dawisha, Karen. 2014. *Putin's Kleptocracy: Who Owns Russia?* New York: Simon and Schuster.

Dawson, Jane. 1996. *Eco-Nationalism: Anti-Nuclear Activism and National Identity in Russia, Lithuania, and Ukraine*. Durham, NC: Duke University Press.

De la Cadena, Marisol. 2010. "Indigenous Cosmopolitics in the Andes: Conceptual Reflections Beyond 'Politics.'" *Cultural Anthropology* 25(2): 334–70.

De la Cadena, Marisol, and Orin Starn, eds. 2007. *Indigenous Experience Today*. Oxford: Berg.

Dean, Bartholomew, and Jerome Levi, eds. 2003. *At the Risk of Being Heard: Identity, Indigenous Rights, and Postcolonial States*. Ann Arbor: University of Michigan Press.

Derluguian, Georgi. 2006. *Bourdieu's Secret Admirer in the Caucasus: A World-System Biography*. Chicago: University of Chicago Press.

Descola, Phillippe. 1994. *In the Society of Nature: A Native Ecology in Amazonia*. Cambridge: Cambridge University Press.

Donohoe, Brian. 2009. "The Law as a Source of Environmental Justice in the Russian Federation." In *Environmental Justice and Sustainability in the Former Soviet Union*, edited by Julian Agyeman and Yelena Ogneva-Himmelberger, 21–46. Cambridge, MA: MIT Press.

Donohoe, Brian. 2012. "Naming, Claiming, Proving? The Burden of Proof Issue for Russia's Indigenous Peoples." In *Law against the State: Ethnographic Forays into Law's Transformations*, edited by Julia Eckert, Brian Donohoe, Christian Strompell, and Zerin Ozlem Biner, 44–69. New York: Cambridge University Press.

Donohoe, Brian, Joachim Otto Habeck, Agnieszka Halemba, and István Sántha. 2008. "Size and Place in the Construction of Indigeneity in the Russian Federation." *Current Anthropology* 49(6): 993–1020.

Dorzhigushaeva, Oiuna. 2002. *Ekologicheskaia etika buddizma, uchebye posobie*. St. Petersburg: Karma Ieshe Paldron. http://dharma.ru/product/22 (accessed 5/20/2020).

Drobizheva, Leokadiia. 2005. "Zavoevaniia demokratii i etnonatsional'nye problemy Rossii (chto mozhet i chego ne mozhet dat' demokratizatsiia)." *Obshchestvennye nauki i sovremmenost'*, no. 2: 16–28.

Drobizheva, Leokadiia. 2011. "Mify i real'nost' sovremennogo polietnicheskogo obshchestva." In *Fenomen identichnosti v sovremennom gumanitarnom znanii*, edited by M. N. Guboglo and N. A. Dubova, 224–32. Moscow: Nauka.

Duara, Prasenjit. 1996. "Historicizing National Identity, or Who Imagines What and When." In *Becoming National*, edited by Geoff Eley and Ronald Suny, 150–77. London: Oxford University Press.

Duara, Prasenjit. 2004. *Sovereignty and Authenticity: Manchukuo and the East Asian Modern*. Lanham, MD: Rowman and Littlefield.

Dugarov, D. S. 1991. *Istoricheskie korni belogo shamanstva: Na materiale obriadovogo fol'klora buryat*. Moscow: Nauka.

Dugarova, Tuiana Ts. 2014. "Arkhetipicheskie obrazy buryatskoi mental'nosti." In *Obrazy, traditsii i kul'tura mnogonatsional'nogo mira i soglasiia*, edited by A. D. Karnyshev, 139–57. Irkutsk: Irkutskskii gosudarstvennyi universitet.

Dugin, Alexander. 1999. *Absoliutnaia Rodina*. Moscow: Arktogeia.

Dulam, Bumochir. 2010. "Degrees of Ritualization: Language Use in Mongolian Shamanic Ritual." *Shaman* 18(1–2): 11–42.

Dulov, Vsevolod I. (1956) 2013. *Sotsial'no-ekonomicheskaia istoriia Tyvy: XIX–nachala XX v.* Kyzyl: Tuvinskii gosudarstvennyi universitet.

Dunn, Elizabeth Cullen, and Michael S. Bobick. 2014. "The Empire Strikes Back: War without War and Occupation without Occupation in the Russian Sphere of Influence." *American Ethnologist* 41(3): 405–13.

Eggan, Fred. 1954. "Social Anthropology and the Method of Controlled Comparison." *American Anthropologist* 56(5): 743–63.

Eley, Geoff, and Ronald Grigor Suny. 1996. *Becoming National*. London: Oxford University Press.

Emelianenko, Vladimir. 2017. "Sobstvennaia gordost': Russkii, tatarin, bashkir, chechenets—a vse vmeste kakoi my natsional'nosti" [Leokadia Drobizheva interview], *Rossiiskaia gazeta*, March 28, 2017. https://rg.ru/2017/03/28/sociolog-o-tom-nuzhen-li-v-rossii-zakon-o-rossijskoj-nacii.html (accessed 12/20/2019).

Erdrich, Louise. 1994. *Love Medicine*. New York: Holt, Rhinehart, Winston.

Erdrich, Louise. 2016. *LaRose*. New York: Harper Collins.

Erdrich, Louise. 2020. *The Night Watchman*. New York: Harper Collins.

Eriksen, Thomas H., and Marek Jacoubek, eds. 2019. *Ethnic Groups and Boundaries Today: A Legacy of Fifty Years*. New York: Routledge.

Etkind, Alexander. 2011. *Internal Colonization: Russia's Imperial Experience*. Cambridge: Polity Press.

Etkind, Alexander. 2013. *Warped Mourning: Stories of the Undead in the Land of the Unburied*. Stanford, CA: Stanford University Press.

Fabian, Johannes. 1983. *Time and the Other: How Anthropology Makes Its Object*. New York: Columbia University Press.

Fedorov, Afanasy S. 2011. *Öbüge siere-tuoma* [Sacred Lands Ritual]. Yakutsk: Bichik (in Sakha).

Fedorova, Lena. 2012. *Dukhovnye osnovy evraziistva: Kul'turno-tsivilizatsionnye aspekty*. Saarbrucken: Lambert.

Ferguson, Jenanne. 2019. *Words Like Birds: Sakha Language Discourses and Practices in the City*. Lincoln: University of Nebraska Press.

Ferguson, Jenanne, ed. 2021. "Checking in on Sakha Studies." *Sibirica* 20(2).

Feshbach, Murray, and Alfred Friendly Jr. 1992. *Ecocide in the USSR: Health and Nature under Siege*. New York: Basic Books.

Filatov, S. B. 2014. "Respublika Buryatiia." In *Religiozno-obshchestvennaia zhizn' rossiiskikh regionov*, edited by S. B. Filatov, 1:328–75. Moscow: Letnii sad.

Fischer, Michael M. J. 2003. *Emergent Forms of Life and the Anthropological Voice*. Durham, NC: Duke University Press.

Fischer, Michael M. J. 2009. *Anthropological Futures*. Durham, NC: Duke University Press.

Fischer, Michael M. J. 2015. "Ethnography for Aging Societies: Dignity, Cultural Genres, and Singapore's Imagined Futures." *American Ethnologist* 42(2): 207–29.

Fish, M. Steven. 2005. *Democracy Derailed in Russia*. Cambridge: Cambridge University Press.

Fondahl, Gail. 2003. "Nature Preserves Threaten Land Rights." *Cultural Survival* 27(1). http://www.culturalsurvival.org/publications/cultural-survival-quarterly/russia/nature-preserves-threaten-land-rights (accessed 9/20/2015).

Fondahl, Gail, Susie Crate, and Victoria Filippova. 2014. "Arctic Social Indicators Application: Sakha Republic (Yakutia), Russian Federation." In *Arctic Social Indicators: ASI II. Implementation*, edited by J. N. Larsen, P. Schweitzer, A. Petrov, 57–92. Copenhagen: Nordic Council of Ministers.

Fondahl, Gail, and Olga Lazebnik. 2001. "Native 'Land Claims,' Russian Style." *Canadian Geographer* 45(4): 545–61.

Forte, Maximilian C., ed. 2010. *Indigenous Cosmopolitans: Transnational and Transcultural Indigeneity in the Twenty-first Century*. New York: Peter Lang.

Fortun, Kim, Mike Fortun, and Steven Rubenstein, eds. 2010. "Emergent Indigeneities." *Cultural Anthropology* 25(2): 222–370.

Garmaeva, T. I., and N. V. Abaev, eds. 2017. "Gumanitarnye issledovaniia Vnutrennei Azii." *Vestnik Buryatskogo gosudarstvennogo universiteta*, no. 1. Ulan-Ude: Buryatskii gosudarstvennyi universitet.

Garri, Irina P., ed. 2014. *Buddism v kul'ture i istorii buryat*. Ulan-Ude: Buriaad-Mongol Nom.

Gelman, Vladimir. 2017. "Raspad Rossii? Eto tochno, ne to, chto stoit boiatsia." *Republic*. https://republic.ru/posts/85462, August 1 (accessed 9/12/2017).

Generalov, A. G. ed. 1982. *Material'naia kul'tura drevnego naseleniia Vostochnoi Sibiri: Sbornik nauchnykh trudov*. Irkutsk: Izdatel'stvo Irkutskogo gosudarstvennogo universiteta.

Germano, David. 1998. "Re-membering the Dismembered Body of Tibet: Contemporary Tibetan Visionary Movements in the People's Republic of China." In *Buddhism in Contemporary Tibet: Religious Revival and Cultural Identity*, edited by Melvyn C. Goldstein and Matthew T. Kapstein, 53–94. Berkeley: University of California Press.

Giuliano, Elise. 2011. *Constructing Grievance: Ethnic Nationalism in Russia's Republics*. Ithaca, NY: Cornell Unversity Press.

Gogolev, Anatoly I. 1986. *Istoricheskaia etnografiia yakutov: Voprosy proiskhozhdeniia yakutov*. Yakutsk: Yakutskii gosudarstvennyi universitet.

Gogolev, Anatoly I. 1992. "The Cultural History of the Yakut (Sakha) People." *Anthropology and Archeology of Eurasia* 31(2): 10–84.

Gogolev, Anatoly I. 1993. *Yakuty: Problemy etnogenez i formirovaniia kul'tury*. Yakutsk: Ministerstvo kul'tury.

Gogolev, Anatoly I. 1994. "Model' mira i mifologicheskikh predstaveleniiakh yakutov." In *Iazyki, kul'tura i budushchee narodov Arktiki*. Yakutsk: Yakutskii nauchnyi tsentr Akademii nauk.

Gogolev, Anatoly I. 2002. *Istoki mifologii i traditsionnyi kalendar' yakutov*. Yakutsk: Ministerstvo obrazovaniia.

Gorenburg, Dmitry. 2003. *Minority Ethnic Mobilization in the Russian Federation*. Cambridge: Cambridge University Press.

Guchinova, Elza-Bair. 2021. "Awaiting the *Chakravarti*-Tsar: Buddhists and Politics in Contemporary Kalmykia." *Anthropology and Archeology of Eurasia* 59(1).

Government statistics. 2004. *Sotsial'no-ekonomicheskoe razvitie Respubliki Tyva*. Kyzyl: Gosudarstvennyi komitet Respubliki Tyva po statistike.

Government statistics. 2010. *Statisticheskii ezhegodnik Respubliki Tyva*. Kyzyl: Territorial'nyi organ Federal'noi sluzhby gosudarstvennoi statistiki po Respublike Tyva.

Graber, Kathryn. 2020. *Mixed Messages: Mediating Native Belonging in Asian Russia*. Ithaca, NY: Cornell University Press.

Graber, Kathryn, and Joseph Long. 2009. "The Dissolution of the Buryat Autonomous Okrugs in Siberia: Notes from the Field." *Inner Asia* 11(1): 147–55.

Graney, Katherine. 2009. *Of Khans and Kremlins: Tatarstan and the Future of Ethno-Federalism in Russia*. Lanham, MD: Rowman and Littlefield.

Grant, Bruce, ed. 1999. *Neotraditionalism in the Russian North: Indigenous Peoples and the Legacy of Perestroika*. Seattle: University of Washington Press.

Grant, Bruce. 2005. "The Good Russian Prisoner: Naturalizing Violence in the Caucasus Mountains." *Cultural Anthropology* 20(1): 39–67.

Grant, Bruce. 2009. *The Captive and the Gift: Cultural Histories of Sovereignty in Russia and the Caucasus*. Ithaca, NY: Cornell University Press.

Grant, Bruce, and Nancy Ries. 2002. "Foreword: The Shifting Fields of Culture and Society after Socialism." In Caroline Humphrey, *The Unmaking of Soviet Life*, ix–xii. Ithaca, NY: Cornell University Press.

Gumilev, Lev N. 2009. *Istoriia Evrazii*. Moscow: Algoritm, EKSMO.

Gusev, Boris, and Tatiana Grekova. 1995. *Doktor Badmaev: Tibetskaia meditsina, tsarskii dvor, sovetskaia vlast'*. Moscow: Russkaia kniga.

Gusewelle, C.W. 1994. *A Great Current Running: The US-Russian Lena River Expedition*. Kansas City: Lowell Press.

Hagendoorn, Louk, Edwin Poppe, and Anca Minescu. 2008. "Support for Separatism in Ethnic Republics of the Russian Federation." *Europe-Asia Studies* 60(3): 353–73.

Hale, Henry. 2014. *Patronal Politics: Eurasian Regime Dynamics in Comparative Perspective*. Cambridge: Cambridge University Press.

Handler, Richard. 1988. *Nationalism and the Politics of Culture in Quebec*. Madison: University of Wisconsin Press.

Heinrich, Hans-Georg, Liudmilla Lobova, and Alexey Malashenko, eds. 2011. *Will Russia Become a Muslim Society?* New York: Peter Lang.

Hendley, Kathryn. 2017. *Everyday Law in Russia*. Ithaca, NY: Cornell University Press.

Hengesback, Alice, and Sergei Shapkhaev. 2003. "Lake Baikal—More Valuable than Oil." *Give and Take* (Autumn): 18–20.

Henry, Laura. 2010. *Red to Green: Environmental Activism in Post-Soviet Russia*. Ithaca, NY: Cornell University Press.

Henry, Laura. 2018. "Russia's Environment and Environmental Movement." In *Understanding Contemporary Russia*, edited by Michael L. Bressler, 275–301. Boulder: Lynne Rienner.

Herd, Graeme, and Anne Aldis. 2002. *Russian Regions and Regionalism*. London: Curzon.

Hobsbawm, Eric, and Terence Ranger, eds. 1983. *The Invention of Tradition*. Cambridge: Cambridge University Press.

Hodgkinson, Tim. 2005–2006. "Musicians, Carvers, Shamans." *Cambridge Anthropology* 25(3): 1–8.

Holland, Edward. 2014. "Religious Practice and Belief in the Republic of Buryatia." *Nationalities Papers* 42(1): 165–80.

Horowitz, Donald. 2000. *Ethnic Groups in Conflict*. Berkeley: University of California Press.

Humphrey, Caroline. 1996. "Buryatiya and the Buryats." In *The Nationalities Question in the Post-Soviet States*, edited by Graham Smith, 113–26. London: Longman.

Humphrey, Caroline. 1998. *Marx Went Away but Karl Stayed Behind*. Ann Arbor: University of Michigan Press. [Originally published as *Karl Marx Collective: Economy, Society, and Religion in a Siberian Collective Farm*. Cambridge: Cambridge University Press, 1983.]

Humphrey, Caroline. 2002. *The Unmaking of Soviet Life*. Ithaca, NY: Cornell University Press.

Humphrey, Caroline. 2008. "Reassembling Individual Subjects: Events and Decisions in Troubled Times." *Anthropological Theory* 8(4): 357–80.

Humphrey, Caroline, and David Sneath.1999. *The End of Nomadism: Society, State, and the Environment in Inner Asia.* Durham, NC: Duke University Press.

Huntington, Samuel. 1996. *The Clash of Civilizations.* New York: Simon and Schuster.

Imetkhenov, A. B., and D. G. Chimitov. 2016. *Osobo okhraniaemye prirodnye territorii Buryatii.* Ulan-Ude: VSGUTU.

Ivanova-Unarova, Zinaida. 2000. *Liki shamana.* Yakutsk: Bichik.

Ivanova-Unarova, Zinaida. 2008. *Fantazii ot Avgustiny Filippovoi.* Yakutsk: Bichik.

Ivanova-Unarova, Zinaida, and L. N. Solov'yeva. 2016. *Eduard Pakhomov: Skul'ptor.* Yakutsk: Salama.

Juvaini, Ata-Malik. 1997. *Genghis Khan: The History of the World-Conqueror.* Seattle: University of Washington Press.

Kabo, Rafail M. 1934. *Ocherki istorii i ekonomiki Tuvy.* Moscow: Gosudarstvennoe sotsial'no-ekonomicheskoe izdatel'stvo.

Kapferer, Bruce, and Dimitrios Theodossopoulos, eds. 2016. *Against Exoticism: Toward the Transcendence of Relativism and Universalism in Anthropology.* New York: Berghahn Books.

Karnyshev, Alexander D., and Elena A. Ivanova. 2014. "Sakral'nye obrazy i traditsionnye verovaniia kak potentsialy mezhnatsional'nogo soglasiia." In *Obrazy, traditsii i kul'tura mnogonatsional'nogo mira i soglasiia,* edited by A. D. Karnyshev, 158–86. Irkutsk: Irkutskii gosudarstvennyi universitet.

Keenan, Edward L. 1991. "Rethinking the USSR, Now That It's Over." *New York Times,* September 8, E3. https://www.nytimes.com/1991/09/08/archives/the-world-rethinking-the-ussr-now-that-its-over.html (accessed 5/30/2020).

Kendall, Laurel. 2021. *Mediums and Magical Things.* Oakland: University of California Press.

Kenin-Lopsan, M. B. 1995. "Algysh." In *Culture Incarnate: Native Ethnography in Russia,* edited by M. M. Balzer, 215–54. Armonk, NY: M. E. Sharpe.

Kenin-Lopsan, M. B. 2006. *Traditsionnaia kul'tura tuvintsev,* translated by Aleksei Artaevich Dugerzhaa and Aleksandr Sotpaevich Dembirel'. Kyzyl: Tuvinskoe knizhnoe izdatel'stvo.

Kenin-Lopsan, M. B. 2010. *Calling the Bear Spirit: Ancient Shamanic Invocations and Working Songs from Tuva,* edited and translated by Anna Kjellin and Aldynai Seden-Khuurak. Borlänge: Kjellin.

Kenin-Lopsan, M. B. 2017. *Sud'ba shamanki.* Kyzyl: Tuvinskoe knizhnoe izdatel'stvo.

Kenin-Lopsan, Mongush Borakovich, and Tat'iana Likhanova. 2006. "Zagovor protiv shamanov raskryt? Pozhiznennyi verkhovnyi shaman Tuvy otvechaev ministru oborony RF." *Novaia gazeta,* March 20. http://2006.novayagazeta.ru/nomer/2006/20n/n20n-s25.shtml (accessed 1/5/2016).

Khakimov, Rafael, ed. 2002. *Federalism in Russia.* Kazan: Institute of History, Tatarstan Academy of Sciences.

Khamutaev, Vladimir A. 2008. *Natsional'nyi vopros v Buryatii.* Ulan-Ude: Buryatskii nauchnyi tsentr.

Khamutaev, Vladimir A. 2012. *Prisoedinenie Buryatii k Rossii.* Ulan-Ude: Domino.

Khangalov, Matvei N. 1889. *Buryatskie skazki i pover'ia.* Irkutsk: Geograficheskoe obshchestvo.

Khazanov, Anatoly M. 1995. *After the USSR: Ethnicity, Nationalism, and Politics in the Commonwealth of Independent States.* Madison: University of Wisconsin Press.

Khilkhanova, Erjen, and Dorji Khilkhanov. 2004. "Language and Ethnic Identity of Minorities in Post-Soviet Russia: The Buryat Case Study." *Journal of Language, Identity, and Education* 3(2): 85–100.

Kilunovskaya, Marina, and Vladimir Semenov. 1995. *Land in the Heart of Asia*, translated by Yuri Pamfilov. St. Petersburg: EGO.

Kimmerer, Robin Wall. 2013. *Braiding Sweetgrass*. Minneapolis, MN: Milkweed Editions.

Kisel', Vladimir Antonevich. 2009. *Poezdka za krasnoi sol'iu: Pogrebal'nye obriady Tuvy, XVIII–nachalo XXI v.* St. Petersburg: Nauka.

Kniazkov, Sergei. 1992. "Priamyi sviaz." *Krasnaia zvezda*, July 29, 3.

Kolstø, Pål, and Helge Blakkisrud, eds. 2004. *Nation-building and Common Values in Russia*. Lanham, MD: Rowman and Littlefield.

Kolstø, Pål, and Helge Blakkisrud, eds. 2016. *The New Russian Nationalism: Imperialism, Ethnicity and Authoritarianism 2000–2015*. Edinburgh: Edinburgh University Press.

Konev, G.M., and S. N. Lomachenko.1998. *Statisticheskii sbornik: Zhenshchina, sem'ia, deti. Uroven' zhizni naseleniia Respubliki Tyva*. Kyzyl: Gosudarstvennyi komitet Respubliki Tyva po statistike.

Kochtcheeva, Lada V. 2009. *Comparative Environmental Regulation in the United States and Russia: Institutions, Flexible Instruments, and Governance*. Albany, NY: SUNY Press.

Kochtcheeva, Lada V. 2020. *Russian Politics and Response to Globalization*. London: Palgrave Macmillan.

Kotkin, Stephen, and David Wolff, eds. 1995. *Rediscovering Russia in Asia: Siberia and the Russian Far East*. Armonk, NY: M. E. Sharpe.

Krivoshapkin-Aiynga, Andrei. 1998. *Evraziiskii soiuz*. Yakutsk: Bichik.

Krupnik, Igor, and Aron Crowell, eds. 2020. *Arctic Crashes: People and Animals in the Changing North*. Washington, DC: Smithsonian Institution Scholarly Press.

Ksenofontov, Gavriil. 1937. *Uraangkhai Sakhalar: Ocherki po drevnei istorii yakutov*. Irkutsk: Vostochno-sibirskoe oblastnoe knizhnoe izdatel'stvo.

Ksenofontov, M. Yu., and D. A. Polzikov. 2020. "On the Issue of the Impact of Climate Change on the Development of Russian Agriculture in the Long Term." *Studies on Russian Economic Development* 31(3): 304–11.

Kucher, Aksana N., ed. 2003. *Tuvintsy: Geny, demografiia, zdorov'e*. Tomsk: Pechatnaia manufaktura.

Kurbatskii, G. N. 2001. *Tuvintsy v svoem fol'klore: Istoriko-etnograficheskie aspekty tuvinskogo fol'klora*. Kyzyl: Tuvinskoe knizhnoe izdatel'stvo.

Kuzhuget, A. K. 2006. *Dukhovnaia kul'tura tuvintsev: Struktura i transformatsiia*. Kemerovo: Kemerovskii gosudarstvennyi universitet kul'tury i iskusstv.

Kuz'min, Iu. V. 2014. *Doktor P. A. Badmaev: Uchenyi, diplomat, predprinimatel'*. Moscow: KMK.

Kyrgyz, Zoia. 1992. *Pesennaia kul'tura tuvinskogo naroda*. Kyzyl: Tuvinskoe knizhnoe izdatel'stvo.

LaDuke, Winona. 2015. *Recovering the Sacred: The Power of Naming and Claiming*. Chicago: Haymarket Books, 2nd edition.

Lamazhaa, Chimiza. 2010. *Klanovost' v politike regionov Rossii: Tuvinskie praviteli*. St. Petersburg: Aleteiia.

Lamazhaa, Chimiza. 2011. *Tuva mezhdy proshlym i budushchim*. 2nd ed. St. Petersburg: Aleteiia.

Lamazhaa, Chimiza. 2012. *Arkhaizatsiia obshchestva: Tuvinskii fenomen*. Moscow: Librokom.

Lamochenko, S. N., and M. N. Tiuliush. 2011. *Respublika Tyva: Istoriia v tsifrakh*. Kyzyl: Territorial'nyi organ Federal'noi sluzhby gosudarstvennoi statistiki po Respublike Tyva.

Landau, Jacob. 1995. *Pan-Turkism: From Irridentism to Cooperation*. Bloomington: Indiana University Press.

Lankina, Tomila. 2004. *Governing the Locals: Local Self Government and Ethnic Mobilization in Russia*. Oxford: Oxford University Press.

Laruelle, Marlène. 2008. *Russian Eurasianism*. Washington, DC: Woodrow Wilson Center Press.

Laruelle, Marlène. 2018. *Russian Nationalism: Imaginaries, Doctrines and Political Battlefields*. London: Routledge.

Laruelle, Marlène. 2021. *Is Russia Fascist? Unraveling Propaganda East and West*. Ithaca, NY: Cornell University Press.

Larsen, Joan Nymand, Peter Schweitzer, and Andrey Petrov, eds. 2014. *Arctic Social Indicators: ASI II. Implementation*. Copenhagen: Nordic Council of Ministers.

Latour, Bruno, ed. 2002. *Iconoclash: Beyond the Image Wars in Science, Religion, and Art*. Cambridge, MA: MIT Press.

Ledeneva, Alena. 1998. *Russia's Economy of Favours: Blat, Networking, and Informal Exchange*. Cambridge: Cambridge University Press.

Leisse, Olaf, and Utta-Kristin Leisse. 2007. "A Siberian Challenge: Dealing with Multiethnicity in the Republic of Buryatia." *Nationality Papers* 35(4): 773–88.

Levin, Gerasim. 2013. *Istoricheskie sviazy yakutskogo iazyka s drevnetiurkskimi iazykami 7–9 vv*. Novosibirsk: Akademiia nauk.

Levin, M. G., and L. P. Potapov, eds. (1956) 1964. *Peoples of Siberia*. Chicago: University of Chicago Press.

Levin, Theodore, with Valentina Süzükei. 2004. *Where Rivers and Mountains Sing: Sound, Music, and Nomadism in Tuva and Beyond*. Bloomington: Indiana University Press.

Lindquist, Galina. 2005. "Healers, Leaders, and Entrepreneurs: Shamanic Revival in Southern Siberia." *Culture and Religion* 6(2): 263–85.

Lindquist, Galina. 2006. *The Quest for the Authentic Shaman: Multiple Meanings of Shamanism on a Siberian Journey*. Stockholm: Almquist and Wiksell.

Lindquist, Galina. 2012. "Ethnic Identity and Religious Competition: Buddhism and Shamanism in Southern Siberia." In *Religion, Politics, and Globalization: Anthropological Approaches*, edited by Galina Lindquist and Don Handelman, 69–90. New York: Berghahn Books.

Magomedov, Arbakhan. 2020. "How Native Peoples of Russia's Arctic Defend Their Interests." *Anthropology and Archeology of Eurasia* 58(4): 215–45.

Malanova, Mara, and Olga Vasil'va, eds. 2007. *Zorikto Dorzhiev*. Moscow: Khankhalaev Gallery.

Man, John. 2013. *Genghis Khan: Life, Death, and Resurrection*. New York: Macmillan.

Markus, Sergei. 2006. *Tuva: Slovar' kul'tury*. Moscow: Akademicheskii proekt, Triksta.

Marks, Steven G. 1991. *Road to Power: The Trans-Siberian Railroad and the Colonization of Asian Russia, 1850–1917*. London: I. B. Tauris.

Martin, Terry. 2001. *The Affirmative Action Empire*. Ithaca, NY: Cornell University Press.

Matunga, Hirimi. 1994. "Waahi Tapu: Maori Sacred Sites." In *Sacred Sites, Sacred Places*, edited by David L. Carmichael et al., 217–26. London: Routledge.

Mekhanik, Aleksandr and Nikolai Ponomarev. 2020. "Chem opasny neprodumannye ob"edineniia regionov." *Ekspert*, no. 24: 59–60.

Mestnikova, Akulina E. 2010a. "Sotsial'nye osnovaniia realizatsii iazykovykh prav korennykh malochislennykh narodov Severa v sisteme obrazovaniia (na primer Respubliki Sakha [Yakutiia])." Kandidat diss. in sociology, Vostochno-Sibirskii gosudarstvennyi tekhnologicheskii universitet, Ulan-Ude.

Mestnikova, Akulina E. 2010b. "Iazyki korennykh malochislennykh narodov Severa v zerkale perepisei naseleniia." *Izvestiia Ural'skogo gosudarstvennogo universiteta*, Seriia 1: *Problemy obrazovaniia, nauki i kul'tury*, no. 5(84): 226–30.

Metzo, Katherine. 2009a. "The Formation of Tunka National Park: Revitalization and Autonomy in Late Socialism." *Slavic Review* 68(1): 50–69.

Metzo, Katherine. 2009b. "Civil Society and the Debate over Pipelines in Tunka National Park, Russia." In *Environmental Justice and Sustainability in the Former Soviet Union*, edited by Julian Agyeman and Yelena Ogneva-Himmelberger, 119–40. Cambridge, MA: MIT Press.

Mihesuah, Devon A., and Elizabeth Hoover, eds. 2019. *Indigenous Food Sovereignty in the US*. Norman: University of Oklahoma Press.

Mikailov, Konstantin E. 2001. *Eco-tourism in Russia: Altai-Sayan Region*. Moscow: Ecotourism Development Fund Dersu Uzala.

Minenko, Nina Adamovna. 1975. *Severo-zapadnaia Sibir'*. Novosibirsk: Nauka.

Mollerov, Nikolai M. 2005. *Istoriia sovetsko-tuvinskikh otnoshenii: 1917–1944*. Moscow: Nauka.

Mongush, Marina. 2001. *Istoriia buddizma v Tuve*. Novosibirsk: Nauka.

Mongush, Mergen. 1993. "The Annexation of Tannu-Tuva and the Formation of the Tuvinskaya ASSR." *Nationalities Papers* 21(2): 47–52.

Montgomery, Robert. 2005. *Late Tsarist and Early Soviet Nationality and Cultural Policy: The Buryats and Their Language*. Lewiston, NY: Edwin Mellen.

Montlevich, V. M. 1992. "Dandaron, Bidiia Dandarovich." *Buddizm: Slovar'*. Moscow: Respublika.

Montlevich, V. M. 1993. "Dela Dandarona." *Buddizm: Kul'turno-istoricheskii zhurnal* 1(2): 42–45.

Mooney, James. (1896) 1965. *The Ghost-Dance Religion and the Sioux Outbreak of 1890*. Chicago: University of Chicago Press.

Morokhoeva, Zoja. 1995. "Cultural Norms in the Baikal Region." In *Culture Incarnate: Native Anthropology from Russia*, edited by Marjorie M. Balzer, 123–39. Armonk, NY: M. E. Sharpe.

Morokhoeva, Zoja. 1998. "The Problem of the National Renaissance of the Buryat and Civil Society." *Anthropology and Archeology of Eurasia* 37(2): 79–100.

Moskalenko, Nelli. 2004. *Etnopoliticheskaia istoriia Tuvy v XX veke*. Moscow: Nauka.

Mote, Victor L. 1998. *Siberia: Worlds Apart*. Boulder, CO: Westview.

Murray, J. 2013. "Building Empire among the Buryats: Conversion Encounters in Russia's Baikal Region, 1860s–1917." PhD diss., University of Illinois.

Nadasdy, Paul. 2007. "The Gift in the Animal: The Ontology of Hunting and Human-Animal Sociality." *American Ethnologist* 34(1): 25–43.

Nadasdy, Paul. 2013. *Hunters and Bureaucrats: Power, Knowledge, and Aboriginal-State Relations in the Southwest Yukon*. Vancouver: University of British Columbia Press.

Nadasdy, Paul. 2017. *Sovereignty's Entailments: First Nation State Formation in the Yukon*. Toronto: University of Toronto Press.

Nader, Laura. 1972. "Up the Anthropologist—Perspectives Gained from Studying Up." In *Reinventing Anthropology*, edited by Dell H. Hymes, 284–311. New York: Pantheon.

Nathans, Benjamin. 2016. "The Real Power of Putin." *New York Review of Books*, September 29.

Nava, Saida S. 2013. *Kochevaia kul'tura tuvintsev skvoz' prizmu kul'turnykh kontaktov: Kul'turologicheskoe issledovanie*. Irkutsk: Ottisk.

Neizen, Ronald. 2003. *The Origin of Indigenism: Human Rights and the Politics of Identity*. Berkeley: University of California Press.

Newell, Josh. 2004. *The Russian Far East: A Reference Guide for Conservation and Development*. McKinleyville, CA: Daniel and Daniel.

Nikanorova, Liudmilla. 2019. "Religion and Indigeneity at Yhyakh." PhD diss., Arctic University of Norway, Tromsø.

Novikova, Natal'ia. 2014. *Okhotniki i neftianiki: Issledovanie po iuridicheskoi antropolo-gii*. Moscow: Nauka.

Nowiska, Ewa, and Ayur Zhanaev. 2016. "Life on the Borderland: Buryats in Russia, Mongolia and China." *Etnologia Polona* 37: 121–32.

Obydenkova, Anastassia, and Alexander Libman. 2015. *Causes and Consequences of Democratization: The Regions of Russia*. New York: Routledge.

Okladnikov, Alexei P. 1970. *Yakutia: Before Its Incorporation in the Russian State*. Montreal: McGill-Queen's University Press.

Ondar, Bichen K. 2011. *Russkaia toponimiia Tuvy*. Kyzyl: Tuvinskii gosudarstvennyi universitet.

Oorzhak, Valerii O. 2002. *Formirovanie i realizatsiia strategii promyshlennogo razvitiia regiona*. Moscow: RAGS.

Orttung, Robert W., Danielle N. Lussier, and Anna Paretskaya, eds. 2000. *The Republics and Regions of the Russian Federation: A Guide to Politics*. Armonk, NY: M. E. Sharpe.

Osipov, Alexander. 2015. "Autonomy as Symbolic Production: The Case of Contemporary Russia." In *Minority Accommodation through Territorial and Non-Territorial Autonomy*, edited by Tove H. Malloy and Francesco Palermo, 179–96. Oxford: Oxford University Press.

Ostrovskikh, P. E. 1899. *Znachenie uriankhaiskoi zemli dlia iuzhnoi Sibir'*. St. Petersburg: Knizhnoe izdatel'stvo.

Otto, Ton, and Poul Pedersen, eds. 2005. *Tradition and Agency: Tracing Cultural Continuity and Invention*. Aarhus, Denmark: Aarhus University Press.

Oushakine, Serguei Alex. 2009. *The Patriotism of Despair: Nation, War, and Loss in Russia*. Ithaca, NY: Cornell University Press.

Pachenkov, Oleg. 2006. "The Issues of 'Ethnicity,' 'Identity,' 'Multiculturalism' and Contemporary Social Sciences." In *Defining Region: Socio-cultural Anthropology and Interdisciplinary Perspectives*, 141–49. Stockholm: Acta Historica Universitatis Klaipedensis XIII, Studia Antropologica II.

Pain, Emil. 2013. "The Ethno-political Pendulum: Dynamics of the Relationship between the Ethnic Minorities and Majorities." In *Managing Ethnic Diversity in Russia*, edited by Oleh Protsyk and Benedikt Harzl, 153–72. New York: Routledge.

Pavlinskaia, Larissa R., and Elena G. Fedorova, eds. 2005. *Sibir' na rubezhe tysia-cheletii: Traditsionnaia kul'tura v kontekste sovremennykh ekonomicheskikh, sotsial'nykh i etnicheskikh protsessov*. St. Petersburg: Evropeiskii dom.

Petrov, Nikolay. 2012. "Putin and the Regions." *Moscow Times*, December 17. http://carnegie.ru/2012/12/17/putin-and-regions/ewet (accessed 12/20/2019).

Petrov, Nikolay. 2013. "Governance and the Types of Political Regimes in the Ethnic Regions of Russia." In *Managing Ethnic Diversity in Russia*, edited by Oleh Protsyk and Benedikt Harzl, 111–29. New York: Routledge.

Petrov, Nikolay. 2017. "Depopulation in Russia's Asian North and Local Political Development." In *New Mobilities and Social Changes in Russia's Arctic Regions*, edited by Marlène Laruelle, 15–29. New York: Routledge.

Piatigorskii, Aleksandr. 1975. "Ukhod Dandarona." *Kontinent*, no. 3: 151–59.

Pika, Alexander, and Boris Prokhorov. 1994. *Neotraditsionalizm na rossiiskom Severe*. Moscow: Institut Narodnokhoziastvennogo prognozirovaniia.

Pimenova, Ksenia. 2007. *Vozrozhdenie i transformatsii traditsionykh verovanykh i praktiki Tyvy v post-Sovetskom periode*. Kandidat diss., Maklukho-Maclay Institute of Ethnology and Anthropology.

Pimenova, Ksenia. 2013. "The 'Vertical of Shamanic Power': The Use of Political Discourse in Post-Soviet Tuvan Shamanism." *Laboratorium* 5(1): 118–40.

Plantan, Elizabeth. 2022. "Not All NGOs Are Treated Equally: Selectivity in Civil Society Management in China and Russia." *Comparative Politics* (April).

Plumley, Dan. 2020. "Requiem, Repression, or Recovery for the South Siberian Border Peoples?" *Cultural Survival Magazine* (March). https://www.culturalsurvival. org/publications/cultural-survival-quarterly/requiem-repression-or-recovery-south-siberian-border (accessed 4/21/2021).

Pod″iapol′skii [Podyapolskiy], Sergei, and Anastasiia Pod″iapol′skaia [Anastasya Podyapolskaya]. 2016. "Etnokul′turnaia situatsiia sovremennoi Yakutii: Demograficheskie tendentsii, istoricheskie mifologemy i gumanitarnye tekhnologii." *Sotsiodinamika*, no. 4: 19–27. https://nbpublish.com/library_read_article. php?id=18195 (accessed 5/15/2020).

Pomerantsev, Peter. 2015. *Nothing Is True and Everything Is Possible: The Surreal Heart of the New Russia*. New York: Perseus.

Pomeranz, William E., and Regina Smyth, eds. 2021. "Russia's 2020 Constitutional Reform: The Politics of Institutionalizing the Status-Quo," *Russian Politics* 6(1).

Popkov, Iurii V., ed. 2015. *Etnosotsial′nye protsessy i etnonatsional′naia politika v regionakh Sibiri*. Novosibirsk: Sibirskoe otdelenie Rossiiskoi akademii nauk.

Popkov, Iurii V., and Evgenii A. Tiugashev. 2014. "Etnosotsial′nye protsessy v Sibiri." *Novye issledovaniia Tuvy*, no. 3. https://www.tuva.asia/journal/issue_23/7330-popkov-tyugashev.html (accessed 5/20/2020).

Poppe, Nicholas N. 1958. "The Buddhists." In *Genocide in the USSR: Studies in Group Destruction*, edited by Nikolai K. Deker and Andrei Lebed, 181–92. New York: Scarecrow Press.

Potapov, Leonid P., ed. 1964. *Istoriia Tuvy*. Moscow: Nauka.

Prina, Frederica. 2016. *National Minorities in Putin's Russia: Diversity and Assimilation*. New York: Routledge.

Protopopova, Nina. 1999. "Ed′ii Dora." *Aiyy Dalbar Khotuna* [Women Masters of Pure Spirits], 146–88. Yakutsk: Republic Press (in Sakha).

Protsyk, Oleh, and Benedikt Harzl, eds. 2013. *Managing Ethnic Diversity in Russia*. New York: Routledge.

Quijada, Justine Buck. 2008. "What If We Don't Know Our Clan? The City *Tailgan* as New Ritual Form in Buryatiia." *Sibirica* 7(1): 1–22.

Quijada, Justine Buck. 2012. "Soviet Science and Post-Soviet Faith: Etigelov's Imperishable Body." *American Ethnologist* 39(1): 138–55.

Quijada, Justine Buck. 2019. *Buddhists, Shamans, and Soviets: Rituals of History in Post-Soviet Buryatia*. New York: Oxford University Press.

Quijada, Justine Buck, Kathryn Graber, and Eric Stephen. 2015. "Finding 'Their Own': Revitalizing Buryat Culture through Shamanic Practices in Ulan-Ude." *Problems of Post-Communism* 62(5): 258–72.

Radkau, Joachim. 2008. *Nature and Power: A Global History of the Environment*. Cambridge: Cambridge University Press.

Radloff, V. V. (1892–1899) 1995. *Atlas drevnostei Mongolii*. Ankara: Tika.

Rappaport, Joanne. 2005. *Intercultural Utopias: Public Intellectuals, Cultural Experimentation, and Ethnic Pluralism in Colombia*. Durham, NC: Duke University Press.

Rasputin, Valentin. 1989. "The Fire." In *Siberia on Fire*, translated and selected by Gerald Mikkelson and Margaret Winchell, 102–61. DeKalb: Northern Illinois University Press.

Ratcliffe, Jonathan. 2019. "Becoming Geser, Becoming Buryat: Oral Epic and the Politics of Navigating Four Identity Crises." PhD diss., Australian National University.

Raygorodetsky, Gleb. 2017. *The Archipelago of Hope: Wisdom and Resilience from the Edge of Climate Change.* New York: Pegasus.

Reddaway, Peter. 2020. *The Dissidents.* Washington, DC: Brookings Institution Press.

Reeves, Madeleine. 2013. "Clean Fake: Authenticating Documents and Persons in Migrant Moscow." *American Ethnologist* 40(3): 508–24.

Reznikov, Evgenii N., and Nataliia O. Tovuu. 2002. *Etnopsikhologicheskie kharakteristiki naroda Tyva: Teoriia i praktika.* Moscow: Per Se.

Ricoeur, Paul. 2004. *Memory, History, Forgetting* [La mémoire, l'histoire, l'oubli], translated by Kathleen Blamey and David Pellauer. Chicago: University of Chicago Press.

Rieber, Alfred J. 2014. *The Struggle for the Eurasian Borderlands: From the Rise of Early Modern Empires to the End of the First World War.* Cambridge: Cambridge University Press.

Ries, Nancy. 1997. *Russian Talk: Culture and Conversation during Perestroika.* Ithaca, NY: Cornell University Press.

Roeder, Philip. 2018. *National Secession: Persuasion and Violence in Independence Campaigns.* Ithaca, NY: Cornell University Press.

Rogers, Doug. 2015. *The Depths of Russia: Oil, Power, and Culture after Socialism.* Ithaca, NY: Cornell University Press.

Romanova, Ekaterina N. 1994. *Yakutskii prazdnik ysyakh: Istoki i predstavleniia.* Novosibirsk: Nauka.

Romanova, Ekaterina N. 1997. *"Liudi sol'nechnykh luchei s povod'iami za spinoi" (Sud'ba v kontekste miforitual'noi traditsii yakutov).* Moscow: Russian Academy of Sciences.

Romanova, Ekaterina N. 2008. "Mifologiia sovremennogo shamanstva: K interpretatsii fenomena 'pomniashaia kul'tura.'" In *Mif, simbol, ritual: Narody Sibiri,* edited by S. Iu. Nekliudov, 309–26. Moscow: Gumanitarnyi universitet.

Romanova, Ekaterina N., and V. B. Ignat'eva. 2012. "The Yakut [Sakha] National Festival Ysyakh in Transition: Historical Myth, Ethnocultural Image, and Contemporary Festival Narrative." *Anthropology and Archeology of Eurasia* 50(4): 42–55.

Romanova, Ekaterina N., U. Vinokurova, V. Iakovlev, S. Petrova, and A. Fedorov, eds. 2017. *Yhyakh: V blagoslovennoi doline Tuimaada.* Yakutsk: Bichik.

Roshwald, Aviel. 2006. *The Endurance of Nationalism: Ancient Roots and Modern Dilemmas.* Cambridge: Cambridge University Press.

Ross, Cameron, ed. 2012. *Russian Regional Politics under Putin and Medvedev.* New York: Routledge.

Rouhier-Willouby, Jean-Marie. 2015. "The Gulag Reclaimed as Sacred Space: Negotiation of Memory at the Holy Spring of Iskitim." *Laboratorium,* no. 1: 51–70.

Rubin, Amalia H. 2015. "Revival of Indigenous Practices and Identity in 21st Century Inner Asia." MA diss., University of Washington.

Rzhevskii, Aleksandr. 2005. *Zhivaia voda Eniseia: Sergei Shoigu.* Moscow: Geroi Otechestva.

Sablin, Ivan. 2018. *The Rise and Fall of Russia's Far Eastern Republic, 1905–1922: Nationalisms, Imperialisms, and Regionalisms in and after the Russian Empire.* London: Routledge.

Saidukova-Romanova, Marina S. 2007. "Krizis natsional'noi identichnosti i fenomen molodezhnogo natsional'no-demokraticheskogo dvizheniia Buryatii v nachale XXI veka." *Politeks* 3(4): 284–92. https://cyberleninka.ru/article/n/

krizis-natsionalnoy-identichnosti-i-fenomen-molodezhnogo-natsionalno-demokraticheskogo-dvizheniya-buryatii-v-nachale-xxi-veka (accessed 6/21/2020).

Sal'nikova, E. 2008. "Dashi Namdakov: Dukh kochevnika." *Kul'tpokhod* (March): 32–37.

Sambu, I. U., ed. 1994. *Svod arkheologicheskikh pamiatnikov Respubliki Tyva*. Kyzyl: Ministerstvo kul'tury.

Samushkina, Ekaterina V. 2009. *Simvolicheskie i sotsio-normativnye aspekty sovremennogo etnopoliticheskogo dvizheniia respublik Altai, Tyva, Khakasiia (konets XX–nachalo XXI v.)*. Novosibirsk: Izdatel'stvo Instituta arkheologii i etnografii SO RAN.

Saxer, Martin, and Reuben Andersson. 2019. "The Return of Remoteness: Insecurity, Isolation and Connectivity in the New World Disorder." *Social Anthropology* 27(2): 140–55. https://onlinelibrary.wiley.com/doi/full/10.1111/1469-8676.12652.

Scott, James C. 1987. *Weapons of the Weak: Everyday Forms of Peasant Resistance*. New Haven: Yale University Press.

Seden-Khuurak, Aldynai. 2003. *English-Tuvan Phrasebook*. Kyzyl: Tyvanyng nom undurer cheri.

Semeka, Elena S., ed. 1974. *Delo Dandarona*. Florence: Edizioni Aurora.

Semeka, Elena S. 1991. "Delo Dandarona." *Soel*, no. 1: 6.

Senchin, Roman. 2012. *Tuva*. Moscow: Ad Marginem.

Serdobov, Nikolai A. 1971. *Istoriia formirovaniia tuvinskoi natsii*. Kyzyl: Tuvknigizdat.

Sevek, Viacheslav K. 2011. *Turisticheskii potentsial Chedi-Khol'skogo kozhuuna Respubliki Tyva*. Kyzyl: Izdatel'stvo RIO TuvGU.

Shaglakhaev, V. A. 2014. *U podnozh'ia Altan Mondarga*. Ulan-Ude: Buryatskii gosudarstvennyi universitet.

Shagzhiev, K. Sh. 2015. *Ekologicheskaia pasportizatsiia pamiatnikov prirody Respubliki Buryatiia*. Ulan-Ude: Buryatskii gosudarstvennyi universitet.

Sharafutdinova, Gulnaz, and Rostislav Turovsky. 2016. "The Politics of Federal Transfers in Putin's Russia: Regional Competition, Lobbying, and Federal Priorities." *Post-Soviet Affairs* 32 (March): 161–75.

Sharafutdinova, Gulnaz. 2020. *The Red Mirror: Putin's Leadership and Russia's Insecure Identity*. Oxford: Oxford University Press.

Sherstova, Liudmila I. 2010. *Burkhanism: Istoki etnosa i religii*. Tomsk: Tomskoe gosudarstvennoe izdatel'stvo.

Shimamura, Ippei. 2014. *The Roots Seekers: Shamanism and Ethnicity among the Mongol Buryats*. Kanagawa, Japan: Shumpusha Publishing.

Shinkareva, A. P. 2006. "Rol' sibirskogo knigoizdaniia v pechati i razvitii gramotnosti buryat v XIX–XX veka." In *Mir fol'klora v kontekste istorii i kul'tury mongol'skikh narodov*. Irkutsk: Izdatel'stvo Irkutskogo gosudarstvennogo universiteta.

Sidortsov, Roman, Aitalina Ivanova, and Florian Stammler. 2016. "Localizing Governance of Systemic Risks: A Case Study of the Power of Siberia Pipeline in Siberia." *Energy Research and Social Science* 16: 54–68.

Sieroszewski, Wacław. 1896. *Yakuty: Opyt etnograficheskogo issledovaniia*. St. Petersburg.

Shoigu, Kuzhuget. 2000. *Pero chernogo grifa: Nevydumannye rasskazy starozhila Tuvy o svoei maloi rodine*. Kyzyl: Novosti Tuvy.

Shoigu, Kuzhuget. 2004. *Tannu-Tyva: Strana ozer i golubykh rek*. Kyzyl: Novosti Tuvy.

Shoigu, Sergei K., et al., eds. 2005. *Chrezvychainaia sluzhba Rossii: 1990–2005*. Moscow: Moskovskaia tipografiia.

Shoigu, Sergei K., et al., eds. 2006–2007. *Grazhdanskaia zashchita*. Moscow: Moskovskaia tipografiia.

Shoigu, Sergei K., et al., eds. 2007–2008. *Uriankhai: Tyva depter. antologiia*. 7 vols. Moscow: Slova.

Shoigu, Sergei K., Iu. L. Vorob'ev, and V. A. Vladmirov, eds. 1997. *Katastrofy i gosudarstvo*. Moscow: Energoatomizdat.

Sidorov, Oleg. 2017. *Mikhail Nikolaev*. Moscow: Molodaia gvardiia.

Simpson, Audra. 2014. *Mohawk Interruptus: Political Life across the Borders of Settler States*. Durham, NC: Duke University Press.

Simpson, Audra. 2016. "Consent's Revenge." *Cultural Anthropology* 31(3): 326–33.

Simpson, Audra, and Andrea Smith, eds. 2014. *Theorizing Native Studies*. Durham, NC: Duke University Press.

Smyth, Regina. 2006. *Candidate Strategies and Electoral Competition in the Russian Federation: Democracy without Foundation*. Cambridge: Cambridge University Press.

Solomon, Peter, ed. 2005. *Recrafting Federalism in Russia and Canada*. Toronto: University of Toronto Press.

Solomonov, N. G. 2000. "Regional Features of the System of Specially Protected Areas in the Sakha Republic (Yakutia)." *USDA Forest Service RMRS-P-4*. http://www.fs.fed.us/rm/.../rmrs_p004_006_010.pdf (accessed 9/3/2015).

Solovyeva, Vera. 2018. "Ecology Activism in the Sakha Republic: Russia's 'Large numbered' Indigenous Peoples and the United Nations Declaration of the Rights of Indigenous Peoples." In *Walking and Learning with Indigenous Peoples*, edited by Pamela Cala and Elsa Stamatopoulou, 119–39. New York: Columbia University Press.

Solovyeva, Vera. 2019. "Are People Really More Expensive than Diamonds?" American Association of Geographers presentation on panel "Post-Socialist Political Ecologies."

Solovyeva, Vera. 2021. "Climate Change in Oymyakon: Perceptions, Responses and How Local Knowledge May Inform Policy." PhD diss., George Mason University.

Solovyeva, Vera, and Vera Kuklina. 2020. "Resilience in a Changing World: Indigenous Sharing Networks in the Republic of Sakha (Yakutia)." *Polar Record* 56 (E39): 1–9.

Sponsel, Leslie. 2012. *Spiritual Ecology: A Quiet Revolution*. Santa Barbara, CA: Praeger.

Ssorin-Chaikov, Nikolai. 2017. *Two Lenins: A Brief Anthropology of Time*. Chicago: University of Chicago Press.

Stammler, Florian, and Aitalina Ivanova. 2016. "Resources, Rights and Communities: Extractive Mega-Projects and Local People in the Russian Arctic." *Europe-Asia Studies* 68(7): 1220–44.

Starinova, Iuliia. 2019. "'Strana ustroena po printsipu pylesosa.' Kto na samom dele 'kormit Moskvu'?" [Interview with N. Zubarevich]. https://www.sibreal.org/a/30244000.html (accessed 12/20/2019).

Starovoitova, Galina. 1997. *Sovereignty after Empire*. Washington, DC: US Institute of Peace.

State Committee of the Russian Federation for Environmental Protection. 1997. *First National Report of the Russian Federation: Biodiversity Conservation in the Russian Federation*. Moscow: State Committee of Russian Federation Press.

Stoeker, Sally, and Ramziya Shakirova, eds. 2013. *Environmental Crime and Corruption in Russia: Federal and Regional Perspectives*. New York: Routledge.

Stoliarov, Mikhail. 2001. *Federalism and the Dictatorship of Power in Russia*. London: Curzon.

Stoner-Weiss, Kathryn. 1997. *Local Heroes: The Political Economy of Russian Regional Governance*. Princeton, NJ: Princeton University Press.

Sugorakova, A. M., ed. 2012. *GeoEkologicheskoe sostoianie prirodnoi sredy v raione Kyzyl-Tashtygskogo kolchedanno-polimetallicheskogo mestorozhdeniia (Tuva)*. Kyzyl: TuvIKOPR.

Suny, Ronald Grigor. 1994. *The Making of the Georgian Nation*. Bloomington: Indiana University Press.

Süzükei, Valentina Iu. 2007. *Muzykal'naia kul'tura Tuvy v XX stoletii*. Moscow: Kompozitor.

Süzükei, Valentina Iu. 2014. *Singing My Life: The Story of Kongar-ool Ondar, Legendary Throat-singer from Tuva*. Translated by Aksai Bapa. San Francisco: Bapalar.

Tagangaeva, Maria. 2015. "Visualizing (Post-)Soviet Ethnicity: Fine Art of Buryatia." *Anthropology and Archeology of Eurasia* 54(3): 24–57.

Takasaeva, Kyunney. 2017. "Yakutian Works by Wacław Sieroszewski in the Context of the Transformation of Sacha (Yakuts) National Consciousness." PhD diss., University of Warsaw.

Tal'taeva, Viktoriia D. 2001. *Tuva za 80 let*. Kyzyl: Gosudarstvennyi komitet Respubliki Tyva po statistike.

TallBear, Kim. 2013. *Native American DNA: Tribal Belonging and the False Promise of Genetic Science*. Minneapolis: University of Minnesota Press.

TallBear, Kim. 2016. "The US-Dakota War and Failed Settler Kinship." *Anthropology News* 24–25. https://www.anthropology-news.org.

Tamir, Yael. 1993. *Liberal Nationalism*. Princeton, NJ: Princeton University Press.

Tanova, Elizaveta. 2006. *Istoriia vozniknoveniia i razvitiia pechati Tuvy*. Kyzyl: Tuvinskoe knizhnoe izdatel'stvo.

Tarbastaeva, Inna S. 2018a. "Buddiiskie tsennosti kak vozmozhnaia ekonomicheskaia determinanta razvitiia Tuvinskogo obshchestva." *Novye issledovaniia Tuvy*, no. 2. https://nit.tuva.asia/nit/article/view/772 (accessed 2/28/2020).

Tarbastaeva, Inna S. 2018b. "Tuva prevrashchaetsia v monoethnichnyi region: Riski i perspektivy." *EKO: Vserossiiskii ekonomicheskii zhurnal*, no. 5(527): 65–80.

Tatarinsteva, Margarita, and Nikolai Mollerov. 2017. *Russkie v Tuve: Istoriia, etno-grafiia, kul'tura*. Kyzyl: Tuvinskii institut gumanitarnykh i prikladnykh sotsial'no-ekonomicheskikh issledovanii.

Tichotsky, John. 2000. *Russia's Diamond Colony: The Republic of Sakha*. Amsterdam: Harwood Academic Publishers.

Tidwell, Alan, and Barry Zellen, eds. 2017. *Land, Indigenous People, and Conflict*. New York: Routledge.

Tishkov, Valerii. 2020. "Otkrytoe pis'mo Akademika Tishkova." http://www.materik.ru/rubric/detail.php?ID=103216, March 16, 2020 (accessed 3/17/2020).

Tishkov, Valerii, and Iurii Shabaev. 2019. *Etnopolitologiia*. Moscow: Moskovskii gosu-darstvennyi universitet.

Todorova, Maria, and Zsuzsa Gille, eds. 2012. *Post-Communist Nostalgia*. New York: Berghahn Books.

Treuer, David. 2019. *The Heartbeat of Wounded Knee: Native America from 1890 to the Present*. New York: Riverhead Penguin.

Triesman, Daniel. 1999. *After the Deluge: Regional Crises and Political Consolidation in Russia*. Ann Arbor: University of Michigan Press.

Trubetzkoy, Nikolai. 1991. "Europe and Mankind." In *The Legacy of Genghis Khan and Other Essays on Russia's Identity*, edited by Anatoly Liberman. Ann Arbor: Michigan Slavic Publications.

Tsyrempilov, Nikolai V. 2009. "Za sviatuiu dkharmu i belogo tsaria: Rossiiskaia impe-riia glazami buryatskikh buddistov XVIII–nachala XX vekov." *Ab Imperio*, no. 2: 105–30.

Tsyrempilov, Nikolai V. 2013. "Buddizm v Rossii: Proshloe i nastoiashchee." *Vlast'*, no. 4.

Tsyrempilov, Nikolai V. 2016. "The Constitutional Theocracy of Lubsan Samdan Tsydenov: An Attempt to Establish a Buddhist State in Transbaikalia (1918–22)." *State, Religion, and Church* 3(2): 26–52.

Urbanaeva, Irina. 1994. "The Fate of Baikal within Russia." *Anthropology and Archeol-ogy of Eurasia* 32(4): 62–78.

Vainshtein, Sev'ian I. 1980. *Nomads of South Siberia: The Pastoral Economies of Tuva.* Introduced by Caroline Humphrey, translated by Michael Colenso. Cambridge: Cambridge University Press.

Varfolomeeva, Anna. 2019. "Articulations of Indigeneity in Two Mining Regions of Russia: A Comparative Case Study of Karelia and Buryatia." PhD diss., Central European University.

Ventsel, Aimar. 2015. "Reluctant Entrepreneurs of the Russian Far East." Paper pre-pared for "Promoting Arctic Urban Sustainability in Russia," George Washing-ton University.

Verdery, Katherine. 1999. *The Political Lives of Dead Bodies.* New York: Columbia Uni-versity Press.

Vinogradov, Andrei. 2010. "The Phenomenon of 'White Faith' in Southern Siberia." In *Religion and Politics in Russia*, edited by M. M. Balzer, 245–57. Armonk, NY: M. E. Sharpe.

Vinokurova, Uliana A. 1992. "Yakutiia velika i bogata." *Yakutiia* (January): 1, 4.

Vinokurova, Uliana A. 2011. *Tsirkumpoliarnaia tsivilizatsiia: Idei i proekty.* Yakutsk: AGIIK.

Vinokurova, Uliana A. 2017. "Yakutskie tsennosti v nachale XXI veka." *Novye issledo-vaniia Tuvy*, no. 3: 84–99. https://nit.tuva.asia/nit/article/view/727 (accessed 5/30/2020).

Vinokurova, Uliana A. 2018. "Indigenous Peoples of Siberia and the Challenges of the Twenty-First Century." *Sibirica* 17(3): 3–15.

Vinokurova, Uliana A., V. F. Iakovlev, V. I. Bochnina, L. A. Leont'eva, and L. G. Popova, eds. 2009. *Sviashchennye mesta Yakutii: Izuchenie, okhrana and ispol'zovanie.* Yakutsk: AGIIK.

Vitebsky, Piers. 1995. *The Shaman.* London: Macmillan.

Viveiros de Castro, Eduardo. 2014. *Cannibal Metaphysics.* Minneapolis: University of Minnesota.

Vostrikov, A. I., and N. N. Poppe. 2007. *Letopis' barguzinskikh buryat: Teksty i issledo-vaniia.* Ulan-Ude: BNTs SO RAN.

Wallace, Anthony F. C. 1956. "Acculturation: Revitalization Movements." *American Anthropologist* 58(2): 264–81.

Wallace, Anthony F. C. 1969. *The Death and Rebirth of the Seneca.* New York: Vintage.

Walters, Philip. 2001. "Religion in Tuva: Restoration or Innovation?" *Religion, State, and Society* 29(1): 23–38.

Weatherford, Jack. 2005. *Genghis Khan and the Making of the Modern World.* New York: Broadway.

Weir, Fred. 2018. "Buddhism Flourishes in Siberia, Opening Window on Its Pre-Soviet Past." *Christian Science Monitor.* https://www.csmonitor.com/World/Europe/2018/0810/Buddhism-flourishes-in-Siberia-opening-window-on-its-pre-Soviet-past, August 10 (accessed 8/15/2018).

Whyte, Kyle Powys. 2017. "Food Sovereignty, Justice, and Indigenous Peoples: An Essay on Settler Colonialism and Collective Continuance." *Oxford Handbook on Food Ethics*. Edited by A. Barnhill, T. Doggett, and A. Egan. Oxford: Oxford University Press.

Whyte, Kyle Powys. 2018. "Settler Colonialism, Ecology, and Environmental Injustice," *Environment and Society: Advances in Research* 9 (2018): 125–44.

Willerslev, Rane. 2007. *Soul Hunters: Hunting, Animism, and Personhood among the Siberian Yukaghir*. Berkeley: University of California Press.

Wixman, Ronald. 1984. *The Peoples of the USSR (an Ethnographic Handbook)*. Armonk, NY: M. E. Sharpe.

Wolfson, Zev [penname Boris Komarov]. 1980. *Destruction of Nature in the Soviet Union*. Armonk, NY: M. E. Sharpe.

Wolfson, Zev. 1992. *The Geography of Survival: Ecology in the Post-Soviet Era*. New York: Routledge.

Yakovlev, Villiam. 2009. "Ytyk sirdérgé suruyiyy—Bylyr, biligin, kélér kémngé." In *Sviashchennye mesta Yakutii: Izuchenie, okhrana and ispol'zovanie*, edited by U. A. Vinokurova et al., 107–12. Yakutsk: AGIIK (in Sakha).

Yurchak, Alexei. 2006. *Everything Was Forever until It Was No More*. Princeton, NJ: Princeton University Press.

Zenkovsky, Sergei. (1960) 2011. *Pan-Turkism and Islam in Russia*. Cambridge, MA: Harvard University Press.

Zhegusov, Yuri. 2015. "Index-based Assessment of Arctic Urban Sustainability: Social Indexes." Paper prepared for "Promoting Arctic Urban Sustainability in Russia," George Washington University.

Zhukovskaia, Natal'ia L. 2004. "Neoshamanstvo v Buryatii." In *Buryaty*, edited by L. Abaeva and N. Zhukovskaia, 390–96. Moscow: Nauka.

Zhukovskaia, Natal'ia L. 2010. "The Revival of Buddhism in Buryatia: Problems and Prospects." In *Religion and Politics in Russia*, edited by M. M. Balzer, 197–219. Armonk, NY: M. E. Sharpe.

Zubarevich, Nataliia. 2015. "Privykanie k khudchemu—natsional'naia cherta rossiian." http://7x7-journal.ru/item/63758 4/7/2015 (accessed 12/20/2019).

Zubarevich, Nataliia. 2017. "Na karte Rossii net tochek, gde situatsiia 'osobenno kriticheskaia'—ona takaia vezde." https://snob.ru/selected/entry/122402 (accessed 9/7/2017).

Index